EXECUTIVE SUMMARY

The current law on limitation periods suffers from a number of problems. The Limitation Act 1980 makes different provision in respect of different causes of action. It is not always clear which category a cause of action falls into, and thus how it should be treated for limitation purposes. The date on which the limitation period starts to run does not always take account of the claimant's knowledge of the relevant facts, leading in some cases to unfairness. In some cases the Act provides no protection to the claimant under a disability; in others, the protection given is too extensive, giving the claimant unlimited protection at the expense of the defendant even when the claimant has a representative who is fully aware of the relevant facts. Cases such as *Brocklesbury v Armitage & Guest*[1] have shown that the provisions of the Act on deliberate concealment do not work well with the limitation regime applying to claims for latent damage other than personal injuries, and that they can penalise defendants who had no intention of concealing information from the claimant. In addition, the Act cannot readily be applied to new causes of action, such as claims for restitution.

In this Report we recommend that these problems should be resolved by the introduction of a single, core limitation regime, which will apply, as far as possible, to all claims for a remedy for a wrong, claims for the enforcement of a right and claims for restitution. This regime will consist of:

1. A primary limitation period of three years starting from the date on which the claimant knows, or ought reasonably to know (a) the facts which give rise to the cause of action; (b) the identity of the defendant; and (c) if the claimant has suffered injury, loss or damage or the defendant has received a benefit, that the injury, loss, damage or benefit was significant.

2. A long-stop limitation period of 10 years, starting from the date of the accrual of the cause of action or (for those claims in tort where loss is an essential element of the cause of action, or claims for breach of statutory duty) from the date of the act or omission which gives rise to the cause of action (but for personal injuries claims see below).

We recommend that the above core regime should apply without any qualification to the following actions: the majority of tort claims, contract claims, restitutionary claims, claims for breach of trust and related claims, claims on a judgment or arbitration award, and claims on a statute.

The core regime will be modified in its application to claims in respect of personal injuries. The court should have a discretion to disapply the primary limitation period, and no long-stop limitation period will apply. All personal injury claims will be subject to this modified regime, whether the claim concerned is made in negligence or trespass to the person.

We recommend that claims to recover land and related claims, though not subject to the core regime, should be subject to a limitation period of the same length as the long-stop limitation period, running from the date on which the cause of action accrues.

We also recommend that the core regime should extend, but with some qualifications, to the following claims: claims under the Law Reform (Miscellaneous Provisions) Act

---

[1] [2001] 1 All ER 172.

1934, the Fatal Accidents Act 1976 and the Consumer Protection Act 1987; claims for conversion; claims by a subsequent owner of damaged property; claims in relation to mortgages and charges; and claims under the Companies Act 1985 and in insolvency proceedings. Subject to a few exceptions, we do not propose to alter other specific limitation periods laid down in enactments other than the Limitation Act 1980.

We further recommend that where the core regime applies to common law remedies for a cause of action, it should also apply to equitable remedies for that cause of action; but that delay may still bar a remedy before the limitation period under the core regime has expired. We recommend that the core regime should apply to all claims unless excluded by another provision of the proposed Bill (or any other enactment).

During the claimant's minority the initial limitation period should not run. The long-stop limitation period should run during minority, but not so as to bar an action before the claimant reaches the age of 21. Adult disability (including supervening disability) should suspend the initial limitation period, but will not affect the long-stop limitation period.

However, the protection given to the adult claimant suffering from a disability will not be unlimited. Where the claimant under a disability has suffered personal injury (to which no long stop period will apply) and is in the care of a responsible adult ten years after the later of (a) the act or omission giving rise to the claim and (b) the onset of disability, the primary limitation period should run from the date the responsible adult knew or ought to have known the relevant facts unless the responsible adult is a defendant to the claim.

The long-stop limitation period should not run where the defendant has concealed relevant facts, but only if the concealment was dishonest. Acknowledgments and part payments should start time running again, but not once the initial or long-stop limitation period has expired.

The parties may agree that the limitation regime we recommend should not apply to disputes between them, or should only apply in modified form. They will not however be able to reduce the protection afforded by our provisions on concealment, minority or other disability nor to modify the application of the long-stop limitation period to claims under the Consumer Protection Act 1987.

THE LAW COMMISSION

LIMITATION OF ACTIONS

CONTENTS

PART IV: REFORM II: APPLICATION OF THE CORE REGIME   96

THE LAW COMMISSION

Item 2 of the Seventh Programme of Law Reform: Limitation of Actions

LIMITATION OF ACTIONS

To the Right Honourable the Lord Irvine of Lairg, Lord High Chancellor of Great Britain

PART I
INTRODUCTION

1.   THE SCOPE OF THIS REVIEW

1.1   In our Sixth Programme of Law Reform we recommended that "there should be a comprehensive review of the law on limitation periods with a view to its simplification and rationalisation." The first stage of this review was completed with the publication of our Consultation Paper, *Limitation of Actions*, in January 1998. We received a very large number of responses (182) to the Consultation Paper, and we have derived enormous assistance from them. We are most grateful to consultees for the time which has been spent in considering, and responding to, our provisional proposals. A list of those who responded is included in Appendix B to this Report.

1.2   In this Report we now make our final recommendations for the reform of the law on limitation periods for civil claims. The prosecution of criminal offences is therefore by its nature excluded. We are also of the view that our recommendations should not apply to applications related to matrimonial and family proceedings. It would be inappropriate, for example, for an application in relation to the care of children following a divorce to be subject to a limitation period. We therefore propose to exclude any claim relating to 'family proceedings'.[1] Similarly, our recommendations will not extend to purely administrative claims, such as an application for directions by a trustee.

1.3   In a number of cases, claims which would otherwise come within our recommended limitations regime are subject to a limitation period which is prescribed in an enactment other than the Limitation Act 1980. With a few exceptions,[2] we do not propose to include these claims within our regime. This will, for example, exclude applications for judicial review, and claims under the Human Rights Act 1998, from the scope of the new Act. The other major exclusion from our review is what we described, in our Consultation Paper, as "purely procedural" aspects of the law. With one exception, relating to the rules

---

[1]   'Family proceedings', for this purposes, will be defined by reference to s 32 of the Matrimonial and Family Proceedings Act 1984, including claims relating to matrimonial causes, legitimacy, adoptions, applications for consent to the marriage of a minor or a declaration under s 27B(5) of the Marriage Act 1949, and under Part III of the Family Law Act 1986.

[2]   Which are discussed at paras 4.279 - 4.288 below.

governing the addition of new claims to existing actions,[3] we do not make recommendations in respect of any areas that are dealt with by Rules of Court or under the courts' inherent jurisdiction to determine matters of practice and procedure.[4] Our recommendations will be limited to claims for substantive relief - that is, claims for a remedy for a wrong, the enforcement of a right, or for restitution.

2. PROBLEMS WITH THE CURRENT LAW

1.4 In the Consultation Paper we identified the major problems of the current law:[5] it is unfair, complex, uncertain and outdated.

1.5 Traditionally, the limitation period has started from the date the cause of action accrued, whether or not the claimant knows of the potential claim. This caused injustice where the injury suffered by the claimant did not become apparent for several years. Provision has been made for such cases of latent damage in actions for personal injuries,[6] under the Consumer Protection Act 1987[7] and in some other cases.[8] However, the provision for latent damage does not extend to most causes of action. Outside the areas of personal injuries and consumer protection, the limitation period will only run from the date the claimant knows the relevant facts if the claim is brought in negligence. Even where the claim is for personal injuries, provision for latent damage does not extend to deliberately caused injuries. Here the limitation period remains six years, running from the date of accrual of the cause of action. This has led to the anomalous result that a claimant who has been sexually abused by her father may have longer to bring a claim for damages against her mother for negligently failing to prevent the abuse than to bring a claim against her father for actually committing the abuse.[9]

1.6 It is necessary to balance the interests of the claimant (who wishes to have as long as possible to bring a claim) and the defendant (who must be protected from stale claims) in setting a limitation period. It will never be possible to achieve complete fairness between the parties (indeed the imposition of any limitation period could be regarded as doing 'rough justice' to the claimant). However the balance struck under the present law does not give sufficient recognition to the interests of the

---

[3] We consider that it is necessary to deal with this for two reasons. First, this area is governed by section 35 of the Limitation Act 1980, and cannot be reformed without primary legislation. Secondly, as discussed in our Consultation Paper (at paras 9.28 - 9.33) the rules under the current law have proved difficult to apply.

[4] Examples of these "procedural matters" include applications to extend the period for which a claim form is valid (Civil Procedure Rules 1998 ("CPR"), r 7.6), matters which must be specifically included in the particulars of claim or the claim form (CPR, Parts 8 and 16), the rules governing the amendment of statements of case (CPR, Part 17) and applications to strike out an action for abuse of process (CPR, r 3.4).

[5] Limitation of Actions, Consultation Paper No 151 (1998), paras 1.1 - 1.5 and 11.1 - 11.15.

[6] Limitation of Actions, Consultation Paper No 151 (1998), paras 1.13 - 1.14 and 3.29 - 3.76.

[7] Limitation of Actions, Consultation Paper No 151 (1998), paras 1.19 and 3.101 - 3.104.

[8] Limitation of Actions, Consultation Paper No 151 (1998), para 1.18 and 3.87 - 3.3.100.

[9] *S v W* [1995] 1 FLR 862; *Stubbings v Webb* [1993] AC 498.

claimant. And even though the changes referred to have resulted in some improvement, in each case a different regime has been adopted, introducing needless complexity into the law.

1.7 The law lacks certainty in some areas. For example, it is unclear precisely what "actions to recover sums recoverable by virtue of an enactment" are under section 9 of the Limitation Act 1980.[10] The correct interpretation of the provisions in the Limitation Act 1980 on breach of trust,[11] on conversion[12] and on actual and constructive knowledge[13] is also unclear.

1.8 The law is outdated in some respects. The traditional limitation period of six years which applies to some actions founded on tort and actions founded on breach of (simple) contract originated in the Limitation Act 1623 when communication and gathering information was far more difficult than it is today. The law has also preserved some traditional distinctions which no longer have any relevance, such as the restriction of the concept of acknowledgments to claims for specified amounts[14] and the distinction between actions on a simple contract (subject to the six year limitation period) and actions on a specialty (subject to a twelve year limitation period).

1.9 More importantly, the Limitation Act 1980 cannot be applied straightforwardly to causes of action such as the newly recognised law of restitution founded on unjust enrichment. This has been recently illustrated by *Kleinwort Benson Ltd v Lincoln City Council.*[15] The House of Lords recognised that money paid under a mistake of law should be recoverable, and held that section 32(1) of the Limitation Act 1980 applied, so that the period of limitation does not begin to run until the claimant could with reasonable diligence have discovered the mistake. Where the 'mistake' results from a 'change' in the common law after the relevant payment has been made, the limitation period under the current law will only begin to run when the claimant should have discovered the 'change', no matter how long before the 'change' the payment has been made. This led Lord Goff of Chieveley to remark:

> I realise that this consequence may not have been fully appreciated at the time when this provision was enacted, and further that the recognition of the right at common law to recover money on the ground that it was paid under a mistake of law may call for legislative reform to provide for some time limit to the right of recovery in such cases.[16]

---

[10] Limitation of Actions, Consultation Paper No 151 (1998), paras 7.10 - 7.16.

[11] Limitation of Actions, Consultation Paper No 151 (1998), paras 4.6 - 4.13.

[12] Limitation of Actions, Consultation Paper No 151 (1998), paras 3.108 - 3.115.

[13] Limitation of Actions, Consultation Paper No 151 (1998), paras 3.52 - 3.65.

[14] Previously known as "liquidated damages".

[15] [1999] 2 AC 349.

[16] [1998] 2 AC 349, 389.

3. THE PROVISIONAL PROPOSALS IN OUR CONSULTATION PAPER

1.10 In our Consultation Paper on limitation periods we proposed to resolve the problems identified above by applying a single, unified, limitations regime as far as possible to all causes of action. The main elements of this "core regime" were provisionally recommended to be as follows:

(1) There would be an initial limitation period of three years that would run from when the claimant knows, or ought reasonably to know, that he or she has a cause of action.

(2) There would be a long-stop limitation period of ten years, or in personal injury claims of thirty years, that would run from the date of the act or omission which gives rise to the claim.

(3) The claimant's disability (including supervening disability) would extend the initial limitation period (unless, possibly, there is a representative adult other than the defendant). Adult disability would not extend the long-stop limitation period (and we sought views as to whether minority should do so). Deliberate concealment (initial and subsequent) would extend the long-stop. Acknowledgments and part payments should start time running again but not once the initial or long-stop limitation period has expired.

(4) The courts would *not* have a discretion to disapply a limitation period.

1.11 With two exceptions, the main elements of the core regime, and in particular the move to a limitation period starting from the date on which the facts establishing the claimant's cause of action are discoverable by the claimant, were welcomed by the majority of consultees. The two exceptions were, first, our proposal that there should be a long-stop of thirty years applying to actions for personal injury; and, secondly, our proposal to remove the courts' discretion to disapply the limitation period in relation to personal injury claims. With some hesitation, we have been persuaded by consultees' responses that these two provisional proposals should not form part of our final recommendations.

4. OUTLINE OF OUR MAIN RECOMMENDATIONS

1.12 We recommend that there should be a core limitation regime[17] which will apply to claims for a remedy for a wrong, claims for the enforcement of a right and claims for restitution, as follows:

(1) There should be a primary limitation period of three years starting from the date that the claimant knows, or ought reasonably to know:

(a) the facts which give rise to the cause of action;

(b) the identity of the defendant; and

---

[17] Which will be enacted in Parts I and III of the Bill: the "standard limitations provisions" and "general modifications of the standard limitations provisions".

(c)   if the claimant has suffered injury, loss or damage or the defendant has received a benefit, that the injury, loss, damage or benefit was significant.

(2)   For the purposes of the definition of the date of knowledge, the injury, loss, damage or benefit will be considered to be significant if

(a)   the claimant knows the full extent of the injury, loss, or damage suffered by the claimant or benefit obtained by the defendant or

(b)   if a reasonable person would think that, on the assumption that the defendant does not dispute liability and is able to satisfy a judgment, it is worth making a civil claim.

(3)   The courts will not have a discretion to disapply the primary limitation period, except in relation to claims in respect of personal injuries.

(4)   There should be a long-stop limitation period of ten years, starting from the date of the accrual of the cause of action or (for those claims in tort where loss is an essential element of the cause of action, or claims for breach of statutory duty) from the date of the act or omission which gives rise to the cause of action (but for personal injuries claims see below).

(5)   During the claimant's minority the primary limitation period should not run. The long-stop limitation period should run during minority, but not so as to bar an action before the claimant reaches the age of twenty-one.

(6)   Adult disability (including supervening disability) should suspend the primary limitation period. Adult disability should not affect the long-stop limitation period.

(7)   The long-stop limitation period should not run where the defendant has dishonestly concealed relevant facts.

(8)   Acknowledgments and part payments should start time running again, but not once the primary or long-stop limitation period has expired.

(9)   The parties may agree that the limitation regime we recommend should not apply to disputes between them, or should only apply in modified form. They will not however be able to modify our provisions on concealment, minority or other disability or the application of the long-stop limitation period to claims under the Consumer Protection Act 1987.

1.13   We recommend that the above core regime should apply without any qualification to the following actions:

(1)   tort claims (except for personal injury claims, and conversion claims);

(2)   contract claims (on both simple contracts and specialties);

(3)   restitutionary claims;

(4) claims for breach of trust and related claims, including claims in respect of the personal estate of a deceased person;[18]

(5) claims on a judgment or arbitration award; and

(6) claims on a statute.

1.14 The core regime will be modified in its application to claims in respect of personal injuries. The court should have a discretion to disapply the primary limitation period, and no long-stop limitation period will apply. However, the protection given to the adult claimant suffering from a disability will not be unlimited. Where the claimant under a disability is in the care of a responsible adult ten years after the later of (a) the act or omission giving rise to the claim and (b) the onset of disability, the primary limitation period should run from the date the responsible adult knew or ought to have known the relevant facts unless the responsible adult is a defendant to the claim. All personal injury claims will be subject to this regime, whether the claim concerned is made in negligence or trespass to the person (including claims in respect of personal injury).

1.15 We also recommend that the core regime should extend, but with some qualifications, to the following claims:

(1) claims under the Law Reform (Miscellaneous Provisions) Act 1934 and the Fatal Accidents Act 1976;

(2) claims under the Consumer Protection Act 1987;

(3) conversion;

(4) claims by a subsequent owner of damaged property;

(5) claims for a contribution or an indemnity;

(6) claims in relation to mortgages and charges; and

(7) claims under the Companies Act 1985 and insolvency proceedings.

1.16 We recommend that claims to recover land and related claims, though not subject to the core regime, should be subject to a limitation period of the same length as the long-stop limitation period, running from the date on which the cause of action accrues.

1.17 We further recommend that actions against public authorities should not be subject to special (shorter) limitation periods; that where the core regime applies to common law remedies for a cause of action, it should also apply to equitable remedies for that cause of action; but that delay may still bar a remedy before the limitation period under the core regime has expired. Subject to a few exceptions,

---

[18] Though we do make special provision in respect of bare trusts and future interests, and we except claims made by the Attorney General or the Charity Commissioners. See paras 4.105 - 4.106, 4.110 - 4.112 and 4.116 - 4.119 below.

we do not propose to alter specific limitation periods laid down in enactments other than the Limitation Act 1980. We recommend that the core regime would apply to all actions unless excluded by another provision of the proposed Bill (or any other enactment).

1.18 We have considered our recommendations in the light of the European Convention of Human Rights. Any law which imposes a limitation period on the time within which a claimant may bring a civil claim limits the claimant's right of access to the court. This is not an absolute right under the Convention, but any limitations imposed on it must not restrict or reduce the claimant's right of access to the court to such an extent that the essence of the right is impaired. In addition, such limitations must pursue a legitimate aim and be proportionate to that aim in order to comply with Article 6 of the Convention.

1.19 The European Court of Human Rights has considered the extent to which statutory limitation periods are compatible with Article 6 of the Convention in *Stubbings v United Kingdom* in the context of a claim for damages for sexual abuse. It noted the margin of appreciation afforded to states to regulate the right of access to the courts, and recognised that limitation periods serve a legitimate aim and in the case in question were proportionate. The Court suggested however that the law on limitation periods as applied to claims in relation to sexual abuse might have to be reconsidered in the light of developing awareness of the problems of such claimants. In the course of our review we have therefore given this issue particular attention,[19] as well as considering generally whether our recommendations comply with the European Convention on Human Rights.

1.20 We are satisfied that the recommendations we make in this report are compatible with the Convention rights implemented in the Human Rights Act 1998.

5.   THE STRUCTURE OF THIS REPORT

1.21 The rest of this Report is set out as follows. In part II we describe the present law on limitations in outline, and the developments in the law which have taken place since the publication of the Consultation Paper in some detail. In part III we discuss the core regime in the light of the comments we have received from consultees, and in part IV we discuss the application of the core regime to a number of causes of action which are regarded as in some way problematic under the current law, and which are therefore accorded special treatment. In part V we set out our final recommendations in relation to a number of additional issues connected with the law on limitation periods. We summarise our recommendations in part VI.

---

[19]   See paras 3.125, 3.162 and 4.23 - 4.33 below.

PART II
AN OUTLINE OF THE PRESENT LAW

1. INTRODUCTION

2.1 In the Consultation Paper it required 159 pages to set out the then current law on limitation periods.[1] We do not intend to repeat that statement in this Report, so readers who are seeking a detailed analysis of the current law are referred back to that paper.[2] Rather in this Part we set out, in bare outline only, the present law applying under the Limitation Act 1980, with detail being confined to recent developments.

2. CLAIMS FOR BREACH OF CONTRACT[3]

2.2 The time limit for a claim for breach of contract is six years from the date on which the breach occurs.[4] However, if the contract is made by deed the limitation period is twelve years.[5]

2.3 In the Consultation Paper we noted the difficulties pertaining to contracts of loan.[6] At common law, unless provision is made for the date of repayment or repayment is made conditional upon an event, the borrower is instantly liable to repay the debt. Thus the creditor's cause of action accrues immediately the loan is made.[7] The rigour of this common law rule is mitigated by section 6 of the 1980 Act which provides that in such a situation the six year limitation period runs not from the date of the accrual of the cause of action but rather from the date on which the creditor makes a written demand for repayment.[8]

3. CLAIMS FOUNDED ON TORT[9]

(1) General

2.4 The limitation period applicable to a claim in tort (other than a claim for damages in respect of personal injuries) is six years from the date on which the cause of

---

[1] Limitation of Actions, Consultation Paper No 151 (1998), Section A. The law was stated as at 22 October 1997.

[2] Which is available on our website www.lawcom.gov.uk.

[3] See Limitation of Actions, Consultation Paper No 151 (1998), paras 3.1 - 3.11.

[4] Limitation Act 1980, s 5; *Gibbs v Guild* (1881) 8 QBD 296, 302, *per* Field J; *Gulf Oil (Great Britain) Ltd v Phillis* [1998] PNLR 166, 168, *per* Harman J.

[5] Limitation Act 1980, s 8. See also paras 2.71 - 2.75, below.

[6] Limitation of Actions, Consultation Paper No 151 (1998), para 3.8.

[7] *Re Brown's Estate* [1893] 2 Ch 300, 304, *per* Chitty J.

[8] For recent examples of the application of this section see *Von Goetz v Rogers*, CA, unreported, 29 July 1998 and *Bank of Baroda v Mahomed* [1999] CLC 463, CA.

[9] Limitation of Actions, Consultation Paper No 151 (1998), paras 3.12 - 3.119.

action accrues.[10] In respect of torts actionable per se, the cause of action accrues immediately the tort is committed. In respect of torts actionable only on proof of damage, the cause of action accrues upon the damage occurring.[11]

2.5 In the Consultation Paper we referred to *Pirelli General Cable Works v Oscar Faber & Partners*,[12] where the House of Lords held that the cause of action arising from the defective design of a chimney arose when damage first occurred and not when that damage was discoverable. Already subject to much criticism,[13] *Pirelli* has recently come under renewed attack in *New Islington & Hackney Housing Association Ltd v Pollard Thomas & Edwards Ltd*.[14] Dyson J said that in *Murphy v Brentwood District Council*[15] the House of Lords had "re-interpreted" the loss in *Pirelli* as economic loss rather than property damage. The result was that:

> if it is now to be understood as a case on economic loss, then *Pirelli* cannot stand. That is because it makes no sense to say that the plaintiffs in that case first suffered economic loss when, unknown to them, cracks first occurred in the chimney.[16]

Instead, said Dyson J, economic loss would occur either when the property was acquired, because a higher price was paid than was warranted, or when the defect was discoverable, because it was only then that the actual value of the property diminished.[17] Despite this being his preferred reasoning, Dyson J felt that, because in *Murphy* the House of Lords had not explicitly said that *Pirelli* was wrong, he was still bound by the rule in *Pirelli* that a cause of action in such a case accrues when damage occurs and not when the defect is discoverable.

2.6 In the Consultation Paper we also noted the difficulties in determining when economic loss caused by negligent advice occurs.[18] This issue was reconsidered by the House of Lords in *Nykredit Mortgage Bank plc v Edward Erdman Group Ltd*

---

[10] Limitation Act 1980, s 2. Recently, in *R v Secretary of State for Transport, ex p Factortame (No 6)*, QBD, *The Times*, 10 January 2001, Judge Toulmin QC held that s 2 of the 1980 Act also applies to a claim for damages for breach of European Community law.

[11] Where a solicitor negligently fails to draft a will, the beneficiary's cause of action accrues when the would-be testator dies: *Bacon v Kennedy* [1999] PNLR 1. See also *Macaulay & Farley v Premium Life Assurance Company*, Ch D, unreported, 29 April 1999. In malicious prosecution the cause of action accrues when the criminal proceedings against the claimant end: *Dunlop v Commissioners of Customs & Excise*, CA, *The Times*, 17 March 1998.

[12] [1983] 2 AC 1, see paras 3.15 - 3.19 of the Consultation Paper.

[13] Following *Pirelli*, ss 14A and 14B were inserted into the Limitations Act 1980 to prevent time running against a claimant who is not aware of any damage. Also, see *Invercargill City Council v Hamlin* [1996] AC 624 where the Privy Council declined to follow *Pirelli*.

[14] QBD, unreported, 8 December 2000.

[15] [1991] 1 AC 398.

[16] Smith Bernal transcript, Case No 1998/ORB/200, at para 43.

[17] Dyson J preferred the former option since adopting the discoverability test would undermine the 15 year long-stop period in s 14B of the 1980 Act.

[18] Limitation of Actions, Consultation Paper No 151 (1998), paras 3.20 - 3.23.

(No 2).[19] The claimants had advanced £2,450,000 on the security of a property negligently valued by the defendants at £3,500,000. The borrower immediately defaulted and the property, although initially worth £2,100,000, was eventually sold for £345,000. The question that fell for determination was when the claimants' cause of action had arisen within the meaning of section 35A(1) of the Supreme Court Act 1981.[20] Lord Nicholls and Lord Hoffmann held that the cause of action accrues when the comparison between (a) what the claimant's position would have been if the defendant had fulfilled his or her duty of care and (b) the claimant's actual position, reveals a loss. In the present case that comparison revealed a loss immediately the loan transaction was executed.[21] The claimant's cause of action therefore accrued on the date of the loan transaction.[22]

2.7 Although *Nykredit* does provide useful guidance in determining when a claimant suffers loss, in practice its application is not always easy. For example, in *Lloyd's Bank plc v Burd Pearse*[23] the claimant bank sought damages against a firm of solicitors who had failed to advise it that land, taken as security for a loan, was subject to restrictive covenants. Evans-Lombe J held that, although the claimant's security was worth less than it had believed, it did not suffer loss immediately upon the loan transaction being executed. The reason was that the claimant might still have eventually been able to recover its advance either through the realisation of the security or through the covenants of the debtor and guarantor to repay it. As there was no evidence that in July 1990 the claimant would not be able to recover the advance through these means, the claimant had not at that stage suffered any loss. Therefore the writ, issued in July 1996, was issued in time.[24]

2.8 More recently, in *Gordon v JB Wheatley & Co*,[25] the claimant alleged that the defendant solicitors had negligently failed to advise him that to enter into a collective investment scheme in 1991 he required authorisation from the Securities Investment Board (SIB). As a result, having been investigated by the SIB, he was required to underwrite his investors' losses in 1992. The Court of Appeal held that it was wrong to suggest that the claimant was only potentially worse off in 1991 when the investments were made, and not actually worse off

---

[19] [1997] 1 WLR 1627.

[20] S 35A of the 1981 Act allows a court to award simple interest on "damages in respect of which judgment is given ... for all or any part of the period between the date when the cause of action arose and ... the date of judgment." For the purposes of this act and the Limitation Act 1980, "arose" and "accrue" have the same meaning: *Nykredit Mortgage Bank plc v Edward Erdman Group Ltd (No 2)* [1997] 1 WLR 1627, 1638, *per* Lord Hoffmann.

[21] Since in return for making its advance of £2,450,000, which it would not have done had the defendant not breached its duty of care, the claimant received a security of a value of £2,100,000 and covenants from the debtor which were worthless.

[22] Where purchasers rely on a negligent under-valuation to buy property which is worth less than they are led to believe, the cause of action accrues upon the exchange of contracts, since that is when the claimants, being irrevocably committed to acquiring the property, first suffer loss: *Byrne v Pain & Foster* [1999] 1 WLR 1849, CA.

[23] [2000] PNLR 71, Ch D.

[24] See also *White v Woodroffe Vaughan*, CA, unreported, 24 January 2000.

[25] [2000] Lloyd's Rep PN 605.

until 1992. Rather, in 1991 the claimant was exposed to the risk of being liable to his investors and since that was a liability, albeit a contingent liability, he suffered loss on that date.

(2) Claims for damages consisting of or including damages for personal injuries and related claims

(a) General

2.9 The limitation period applicable to any claim in negligence, nuisance or breach of duty which consists of, or includes, a claim for damages for personal injuries is three years from the date on which the cause of action accrues, or if later, three years from the date of knowledge of the person injured.[26]

2.10 Claims in respect of intentional trespass to the person do not fall within the terms of this provision.[27] However the phrase "breach of duty" does cover any action based on a breach of contract, even where the contractual duty imposed is strict, as opposed to being a duty to exercise reasonable care.[28]

2.11 Section 14(1) of the 1980 Act provides that a person's date of knowledge is the date on which he first had knowledge of the following facts:

(1) that the injury in question was significant;[29]

(2) that the injury was attributable in whole or in part to the act or omission which is alleged to constitute negligence, nuisance or breach of duty;

(3) the identity of the defendant; and

(4) if it is alleged that the act or omission was that of a person other than the defendant, the identity of that person and the additional facts supporting the bringing of an action against the defendant.

This subsection also provides that knowledge that any act or omission did or did not, as a matter of law, involve negligence, nuisance or breach of duty is irrelevant.

2.12 Section 14(3) provides that a person's knowledge includes knowledge which he might reasonably have been expected to acquire:

---

[26] Limitation Act 1980, s 11(1), (2) - (4). "Personal injuries" are defined in s 38(1).

[27] *Stubbings v Webb* [1993] AC 498.

[28] *Foster v Zott GmbH & Co*, CA, unreported, 24 May 2000. The Court of Appeal went as far as to say that, subject to the exception in respect of deliberate assault, the three year limitation period applies to all personal injury cases whether founded on contract or on tort.

[29] An injury is significant if the claimant would reasonably have considered it sufficiently serious to justify instituting proceedings against a defendant who did not dispute liability and could satisfy the judgment: Limitation Act 1980, s 14(2). See recently *Berry v Calderdale Health Authority* [1998] Lloyd's Rep Med 179, CA; *Briggs v Pitt-Payne* (1999) 46 BMLR 132, CA, and *James v East Dorset Health Authority*, CA, unreported, 24 November 1999.

(1)   from facts observable or ascertainable by him; or,

(2)   from facts ascertainable by him with the help of medical or other appropriate expert advice which it is reasonable for him to seek;

but also provides that a person is not to be fixed with knowledge of a fact ascertainable only with the help of expert advice so long as he has taken all reasonable steps to obtain and act on that advice.[30]

2.13   The court may disapply the limitation period described above if it is equitable to do so in all the circumstances of the case.[31] Recently, the courts have emphasised that the onus is on the claimant to satisfy the court that it would be equitable to disapply the limitation period, and that the onus is a heavy one.[32]

(i)   Damages in respect of personal injuries to the claimant or any other person

2.14   As a number of recent cases have shown, determining whether an action is one which includes a claim for damages in respect of personal injuries is a matter of some difficulty.

2.15   In *Bennett v Greenland Houchen & Co*,[33] solicitors representing the claimant compromised a claim on very unfavourable terms. The claimant instituted an action against the solicitors, alleging that their negligence had caused him "distress, loss, damage and expense", his particulars of claim stating that he "came into debt ... and he became and is clinically depressed".[34] If this action included a claim for damages in respect of personal injuries it would have been statute-barred because the claimant had not made the claim within three years of the date on which he had acquired knowledge of the facts listed in section 14(1). The claimant argued that his action was essentially a claim for damages for economic loss, and that the claim in respect of depression was merely peripheral. The Court of Appeal rejected this, Peter Gibson LJ saying that section 11 of the 1980 Act:

expressly contemplates that the action might be one where the damages claimed by the plaintiff for the negligence, nuisance or

---

[30]   In *Henderson v Temple Pier Co Ltd* [1998] 1 WLR 1540 the Court of Appeal held that advice given by a solicitor could only ever be called "expert advice" if it related to matters of fact upon which expert advice was required, and that the identity of the shipowner was not a matter of fact ascertainable only with the help of expert advice.

[31]   Limitation Act 1980, s 33. Since the publication of the Consultation Paper, s 33 has been considered in a number of Court of Appeal cases, including: *Farthing v North East Essex Health Authority* [1998] Lloyd's Rep Med 37; *Hammond v West Lancashire Health Authority* [1998] Lloyd's Rep Med 146; *Hayward v Sharrard* (2000) 56 BMLR 155; *Roberts v Winbow* [1999] PIQR P77; *Das v Ganju* [1999] PIQR P260; and *Lennon v Alvis Industries plc*, CA, unreported, 27 July 2000.

[32]   *Price v United Engineering Steels Ltd* [1998] PIQR P407, P414, *per* Brooke LJ. In *Mold v Hayton & Newson*, unreported, 17 April 2000 the Court of Appeal held that if a judge gives a large extension of time, he is under a duty to explain his reasons with meticulous care.

[33]   [1998] PNLR 458.

[34]   [1998] PNLR 458, 463-464.

breach of duty do not consist of, but only include, damages in respect of personal injuries. It is wrong, in my view, to ... look for some other limitation to which section 11 must be subject.[35]

Hence the court held that the proceedings brought by the claimant did include a claim for damages in respect of personal injuries.[36]

2.16   In *Burns v Shuttlehurst Ltd,*[37] the Court of Appeal held that a claim under the Third Party (Rights Against Insurers) Act 1930 is not a claim for damages in respect of personal injuries, because it is a claim for an indemnity once a claim for damages has been quantified.[38] However, in *Norman v Ali,*[39] the Court of Appeal held that a claim against a car owner for allowing an uninsured driver to use his vehicle may be a claim in respect of personal injuries.

2.17   Most recently, in *Phelps v Mayor and Burgesses of London Borough of Hillingdon,*[40] the House of Lords held that a failure to ameliorate or mitigate the effects of dyslexia could amount to a personal injury.

2.18   In the Consultation Paper we noted that claims for wrongful birth have created difficulties of classification.[41] Those difficulties were revisited in *Das v Ganju*[42] where the claimant sought damages for the continuation of her pregnancy following the defendant's failure to detect that her foetus was at risk from rubella. Garland J applied the decision of the Court of Appeal in *Walkin v South Manchester Health Authority,*[43] and held that the continuation of the claimant's pregnancy and the subsequent birth of her child amounted to a personal injury to her.[44] He went on to hold that, because the claimant's daughter had been born with a personal injury, congenital rubella syndrome, the claim to recover expenses for her care was also a claim in respect of a personal injury. The fact that the

---

[35]   [1998] PNLR 458, 466, *per* Peter Gibson LJ. In so formulating, Peter Gibson LJ had particular regard to *Ackbar v Green* [1975] QB 582; see para 3.30 of the Consultation Paper.

[36]   *Bennett v Greenland Houchen* has since been followed and applied twice: *Oates v Harte Reade & Co* [1999] 1 FLR 1221, QBD and *Shade v Compton Partnerships* [2000] PNLR 218, CA.

[37]   [1999] 1 WLR 1449.

[38]   In *Gaud v Leeds Health Authority* [1999] BMLR 105, CA, the claimant, who had contracted hepatitis B and tuberculosis, sought damages from his employer for failing to advise him of his rights to benefits to which he was entitled because of his illness. Lord Woolf MR held that this was not a personal injuries case.

[39]   [2000] PIQR P73.

[40]   [2000] 3 WLR 776.

[41]   Limitation of Actions, Consultation Paper No 151 (1998), para 3.37.

[42]   (1998) 42 BMLR 28, QBD. The case has now been decided by the Court of Appeal ([1999] PIQR P260) but this point was not argued.

[43]   [1995] 1 WLR 1543.

[44]   This has now been affirmed by the House of Lords in *McFarlane v Tayside Health Board* [2000] 2 AC 59 where it was held, in considering the duty of care in negligence, that the pain, discomfort and inconvenience of an unwanted pregnancy is a personal injury, whereas the cost of bringing up a healthy child is pure economic loss.

injury had not been caused by the defendant, since her injuries pre-dated the defendant's negligence, was irrelevant.[45]

(ii) Actual and constructive knowledge[46]

2.19 In several recent cases the Court of Appeal has re-examined the issue of how to determine whether a claimant should reasonably have ascertained the relevant facts and so be fixed with constructive knowledge.

2.20 In *Smith v Leicester Health Authority*,[47] the court referred to the conflicting statements in *Nash v Eli Lilly & Co*[48] and *Forbes v Wandsworth Health Authority*,[49] and continued:

> We are prepared to accept for the purposes of this appeal that the proper approach to this question is "what would the reasonable person have done placed in the situation of the plaintiff" and that the answer in each case must depend on its own facts ... We accept that the plaintiff's individual characteristics which might distinguish her from the reasonable woman should be disregarded.[50]

Thus the court disregarded characteristics such as the claimant's fortitude, her lack of bitterness at becoming a tetraplegic, and the determination and devotion she had demonstrated in making herself an independent and useful member of her family and society. However, the claimant's 'situation', the fact that she was wheelchair-bound and had no means of her own, were relevant in determining whether she had acted reasonably in not investigating the cause of her condition.

2.21 The Court of Appeal took a rather different approach in *Ali v Courtaulds Textiles Ltd*,[51] where it held that it was "essential to that enquiry into the claimant's actual and constructive knowledge that regard is had to the man he is".[52] The claimant suffered from industrial deafness, but had very limited English, and could neither read nor write in any language. The court held that the claimant was not to be fixed with constructive knowledge that his deafness was noise-induced because his was a case where he could only be satisfied of that after receiving medical advice.

---

[45] *Rand v East Dorset Health Authority* (2000) 56 BMLR 39 casts some doubt on this aspect of the decision because Newman J held, again in the context of duty of care, that a claim for the cost of maintenance of a disabled child is a claim for pure economic loss.

[46] See paras 3.52 - 3.65 of the Consultation Paper. Also, in addition to the cases considered in the following paragraphs, see the latent damage cases discussed at paras 2.29 - 2.34 below.

[47] [1998] Lloyd's Rep Med 77.

[48] [1993] 1 WLR 782.

[49] [1997] QB 402.

[50] [1998] Lloyd's Rep Med 77, 86.

[51] (2000) 52 BMLR 129.

[52] (2000) 52 BMLR 129, 132, *per* Henry LJ.

2.22 The apparently conflicting reasoning in *Smith* and *Ali* has caused some difficulty in cases which have followed. In *Fenech v East London & City Health Authority*,[53] the Court of Appeal avoided any reconciliation of the cases, stating that it was sufficient to recognise that "some degree of objectivity at least must be required in determining when it is reasonable for someone to seek advice".[54] Thus the court held that the claimant did have constructive knowledge because it made no sense for her to remain silent about her pain, however stoical or shy she was.[55]

2.23 In *Sniezek v Bundy*[56] the Court of Appeal did at least clarify that objective criteria are irrelevant in determining whether the claimant has actual knowledge. The claimant had suffered a gradually deteriorating throat injury and, as he believed that it was attributable to his work, he went to see his GP in April 1989. His doctor did not detect any abnormality, and it was not until 1992 that the claimant was finally referred to a specialist where he was told his suspicions had been correct. The court held that because the claimant had firmly attributed his condition to his work before visiting his GP he had actual knowledge of that fact. That was enough to start the limitation period. The incorrect expert advice he then received did not stop time running, but would be a good reason to disapply the limitation period under section 33. Judge LJ added that the question of knowledge is essentially one of fact in each case and doubted whether "any considerable legal refinement is normally necessary or appropriate".[57]

(b) Claims in respect of personal injuries surviving under the Law Reform (Miscellaneous Provisions) Act 1934

2.24 The limitation period for a claim in respect of personal injuries under the Law Reform (Miscellaneous Provisions) Act 1934 is three years from (a) the date of the deceased's death, or (b) the date of the personal representative's knowledge, whichever is later.[58] The facts of which the personal representative must have knowledge are set out in section 14 of the 1980 Act,[59] and the court may disapply the limitation period if it is equitable to do so.[60]

(3) Claims under the Fatal Accidents Act 1976

2.25 The limitation period for a claim under the Fatal Accidents Act 1976 is three years from (a) the date of the deceased's death, or (b) the date of knowledge of the dependant for whose benefit the action is brought, whichever is later.[61] The facts

---

[53] [2000] Lloyd's Rep Med 35.

[54] [2000] Lloyd's Rep Med 35, 38, *per* Simon Brown LJ.

[55] See also *Mold v Hayton & Newson*, CA, unreported, 17 April 2000, where the Court of Appeal applied a similarly objective test.

[56] [2000] PIQR P213.

[57] [2000] PIQR P213, P232.

[58] Limitation Act 1980, s 11(5).

[59] See paras 2.11 - 2.12 above.

[60] Limitation Act 1980, s 33.

[61] Limitation Act 1980, s 12.

of which the dependant must have knowledge are set out in section 14 of the 1980 Act,[62] and the court may disapply the limitation period if it is equitable to do so.[63]

(4)   Latent damage (other than personal injury) caused by negligence

2.26   The limitation period applicable to any claim in negligence, other than one which includes a claim for personal injuries, is either (a) six years from the date on which the cause of action accrues, or (b) three years from the 'starting date', whichever is later.[64]

2.27   The 'starting date' is the earliest date on which the claimant first had both the right to bring the action and either actual or constructive knowledge of:

(1)   such facts about the damage as would lead a reasonable person to consider it sufficiently serious to institute proceedings against a defendant who did not dispute liability and who was able to satisfy a judgment;

(2)   that the damage was attributable in whole or in part to the act or omission which is alleged to constitute negligence;

(3)   the identity of the defendant; and

(4)   if it is alleged that the act or omission was that of a person other than the defendant, the identity of that person and the additional facts supporting the bringing of an action against the defendant.[65]

Section 14A(9) of the 1980 Act provides that knowledge that any acts or omissions did or did not, as a matter of law, involve negligence is irrelevant.

2.28   These provisions are subject to an overriding limitation period of fifteen years from the date on which the negligent act or omission occurred.[66]

2.29   In the Consultation Paper we noted the difficulty in differentiating, especially in cases of omissions, between knowledge of attributability, which is relevant, and knowledge of negligence, which is not.[67] This difficulty has been further demonstrated in the case of *Oakes v Hopcroft*.[68] The claimant was suing a medical

---

[62]   See paras 2.11 - 2.12 above.

[63]   Limitation Act 1980, s 33.

[64]   Limitation Act 1980, s 14A(1) and (4).

[65]   Limitation Act 1980, s 14A(5) - (8). Section 14A(10) deals with constructive knowledge using exactly the same wording as in s 14(3): see para 2.12 above.

[66]   Limitation Act 1980, s 14B.

[67]   See Limitation of Actions, Consultation Paper No 151 (1998), paras 3.47 - 3.49. We noted that the strict rule in *Broadley v Guy Clapham & Co* [1994] 4 All ER 439 and *Dobbie v Medway Health Authority* [1994] 1 WLR 1234, that knowledge of fault is irrelevant, has not been applied rigorously in all cases, eg, *Smith v West Lancashire Health Authority* [1995] PIQR P514 and *Forbes v Wandsworth Health Authority* [1997] QB 402. Now see also *Smith v National Health Litigation Authority*, QBD, unreported, 14 November 2000.

[68]   (2000) 56 BMLR 136.

expert who had caused her to settle a personal injuries claim for less than its true worth by failing to correctly diagnose the severity of her injuries. Lord Woolf CJ held that, although the claimant had known for more than three years before commencing the action that her injuries were worse than reported, there had been no reason for her to know her settlement was too low *because of* that misdiagnosis. Waller LJ and Clarke LJ reasoned differently saying that although the claimant was aware that her condition was worse than had been reported, she could not have known that there had been a misdiagnosis. This would seem to suggest that the claimant had to be aware, not only that the defendant had been wrong, but also that he had also been at fault. However Waller LJ added that:

> the question is whether she was aware of the essence of the omission which had caused the original settlement to be too low, i.e. that there had been a misdiagnosis; not, it should be noted, whether that misdiagnosis had been negligent but simply whether there had been a misdiagnosis.[69]

2.30   In contrast to this case the Court of Appeal took a strict approach in both *Fennon v Hodari*,[70] and *Sage v Ministry of Defence*.[71] In *Fennon* the claimant claimed that the defendant had failed to advise her about a charge on her house. In *Sage* the claimant alleged that the defendant had failed to inform him of his hearing loss. In each case the Court of Appeal held that because the claimant knew that the defendant had not given him or her any advice on the relevant matter, and because it was irrelevant that the claimant did not know that the defendant should, as a matter of law, have done so, the limitation period began running.

2.31   Two recent cases also show that it is not easy to differentiate between knowledge of facts and knowledge of law. In *Perry v Moysey*,[72] the claimant had been advised that he did not need to pay income tax under section 311 of the Companies Act 1985. This advice was incorrect. Hence, when the claimant was later faced with a substantial tax demand to recover the arrears which had been due, he sued his accountant. His Honour Judge Jack QC held that whether the claimant owed the money to the Inland Revenue was a question of fact, and that therefore time did not start running against him until he was aware of that debt.

2.32   However *Perry v Moysey* was distinguished in *HF Pension Trustees Ltd v Ellison*.[73] In that case the defendant solicitors advised the claimant trustee that it could transfer the surplus trust funds of an occupational pension scheme to a different scheme. That advice was incorrect and the transfer was in fact invalid. The claimant sought to recover from the defendant payments made to the Inland Revenue as a result of the transfer. Jonathan Parker J held that the damage incurred by the claimant was the making of the payments, and therefore that time started as soon

---

[69]   (2000) 56 BMLR 136, 145.

[70]   CA, unreported, 21 November 2000.

[71]   [2001] EWCA Civ 190 (CA, unreported, 9 February 2001).

[72]   [1998] PNLR 657.

[73]   [1999] PNLR 894.

as those payments were made. He held that it was irrelevant that the claimant did not know that it was suffering damage since that was a matter of law. He said:

> What [the claimant] did not know and could not have known was that at some time in the future a court would hold that the transfer was unlawful; but although the making of the decision is undoubtedly a fact, the unlawfulness of the transfer is a matter of law. What the plaintiff's argument boils down to is that although it knew all the material facts, it did not know until later that those facts gave rise to a claim in negligence. In my judgment, however, in cases under section 14A as in personal injury cases, mere ignorance that the known facts give rise to a claim in law cannot postpone the running of time ...[74]

Perry v Moysey was distinguished on the grounds that 'in that case the plaintiff did not know until some time after he had entered into the transaction in question that it had caused him any damage at all'.[75]

2.33 Finally, the question of what amounts to constructive knowledge within section 14A(10) of the 1980 Act where the claimant is a corporation was considered in *Abbey National plc v Sayer Moore*.[76] The claimant bank sued the defendant solicitors for negligently failing to report matters relating to a fraudulent land valuation in 1989. During 1991 and 1992, the Abbey National learned of fraud by the surveyors in other transactions and pursued matters through the police. It was held that this knowledge was enough to give the Abbey National constructive knowledge of the over-valuation in this particular transaction, and hence constructive knowledge of their loss. As Jacob J held:

> I do not think it was reasonable for no one to look at the papers in a realistic way until they were looked at ... in 1997. This is a case in which the left hand of the Abbey National did not know what the right hand was doing.[77]

2.34 Jacob J quoted from the unreported judgment of His Honour Judge McGonical in *Abbey National v Wilkin & Chapman*,[78] that:

> In any large organisation like Abbey National there are lines of responsibility and reporting and layers of management ... A large organisation can reasonably be expected to have in place procedures whereby facts and matters are reported to the relevant level of management, where appropriate and/or the relevant managers are required as part of their supervisory function to take steps to ensure that facts and matters which should be reported to them are reported to them or that they obtain the information in some other way, such as by reading all incoming correspondence. Such an organisation can

---

[74] [1999] PNLR 894, 904.

[75] [1999] PNLR 894, 904, *per* Jonathan Parker J.

[76] Ch D, *The Times*, 30 August 1999.

[77] Smith Bernal transcript, Case No CH 1998/A/32, 23 July 1999.

[78] QBD, unreported, 7 October 1997.

also reasonably be expected to have procedures whereby facts and matters are reported upwards within the management to the appropriate level of management responsible for evaluating them and deciding what action, if any, to take or to recommend to be taken.[79]

(5)   Claims under the Consumer Protection Act 1987

2.35   The limitation period applicable to a claim for damages in respect of personal injuries or loss of, or damage to, property under Part I of the Consumer Protection Act 1987 is three years from (a) the date on which the cause of action accrues, or (b) the date of knowledge of the claimant, whichever is later.[80] The facts of which the claimant must have actual or constructive knowledge are:

(1)   such facts about the damage as would lead a reasonable person to consider it sufficiently serious to institute proceedings against a defendant who did not dispute liability and who was able to satisfy a judgment;

(2)   that the damage was wholly or partly attributable to the facts and circumstances alleged to constitute the defect; and

(3)   the identity of the defendant.[81]

2.36   This is subject to an overriding limitation period of ten years from the date on which the defective product is supplied by either its manufacturer or by the person who imported it into the European Union, and the expiry of the overriding limitation period operates to extinguish the right of action.[82] The court may disapply the primary limitation period if it is equitable to do so, but cannot disapply the overriding limitation period.[83]

(6)   Claims for defamation and malicious falsehood

2.37   The limitation period applicable to a claim for libel, slander, slander of title, slander of goods, or other malicious falsehood, is one year from the date on which the cause of action accrues. The court may disapply this limitation period if it is equitable to do so in all the circumstances of the case.[84]

(7)   Conversion

2.38   The limitation period applicable to a claim in respect of the conversion of a chattel, and any subsequent conversion of that chattel, is six years from the date of

---

[79]   The knowledge of corporations has also been considered in fraud cases, within the context of s 32(1)(a) of the 1980 Act. See paras 2.80 - 2.83 below.

[80]   Limitation Act 1980, s 11A(4).

[81]   Limitation Act 1980, s 14(1A). Section 14(3) applies in relation to constructive knowledge: see para 2.12, above.

[82]   Limitation Act 1980, s 11A(3); Consumer Protection Act 1987, ss 4(2) and 2(2).

[83]   Limitation Act 1980, s 33(1) and (1A).

[84]   Limitation Act 1980, ss 4A and 32A.

the original conversion.[85] However where the original conversion constitutes theft, time does not begin to run until the chattel is purchased in good faith.[86]

4. CLAIMS IN RESPECT OF TRUST PROPERTY[87]

(1) Claims for breach of trust

2.39 Section 21(3) of the 1980 Act provides that the limitation period for a claim by a beneficiary in respect of trust property is six years from the date on which the right of action accrues. However, section 21(1) states that no limitation period applies to:

(a) actions in respect of any fraud or fraudulent breach of trust to which the trustee was a party or privy; or

(b) actions to recover from the trustee trust property, or the proceeds of trust property, either in the trustee's possession or converted to his use.

2.40 In the Consultation Paper we cited *Nelson v Rye*[88] as a case examining the circumstances in which a fiduciary becomes a constructive trustee so that a claim against him is also a claim for breach of trust to which section 21 applies. The reasoning in that case must now be seen as incorrect following the Court of Appeal case of *Paragon Finance plc v DB Thakerar & Co*[89] in which Millett LJ re-examined the question of which claims do in fact fall within section 21.

2.41 Millett LJ distinguished two categories of constructive trusteeship. First, cases where the trustee, though not expressly appointed as such, assumes the duties of a trustee by a lawful transaction that is independent of and precedes the breach of trust impugned by the claimant. The constructive trustee really is a trustee, as his or her possession of the trust property is affected from the outset by the trust and confidence through which it was obtained. The court held that this category of constructive trusteeship falls within section 21 of the 1980 Act.

2.42 The second category of constructive trusteeship encompasses cases where the trust obligation arises as a direct consequence of the unlawful transaction that is impeached by the claimant. The court held that this category of constructive trusteeship falls outside section 21 of the 1980 Act.[90] The court observed that the words of section 21(1) of the 1980 Act are only applicable to those whose trusteeship precedes the occurrence which is the subject of the claim, and not

---

[85] Limitation Act 1980, ss 2 and 3(1). The expiry of the limitation period operates to extinguish the owner's title to the converted property: Limitation Act 1980, s 3(2).

[86] Limitation Act 1980, s 4. *City of Gotha v Sotheby's (No 2)*, QBD, *The Times*, 8 October 1998.

[87] Limitation of Actions, Consultation Paper No 151 (1998), paras 4.1 - 4.36.

[88] [1996] 1 WLR 1378, see para 4.7 of the Consultation Paper.

[89] [1999] 1 All ER 400.

[90] Contrast the decision of Harman J in *Gwembe Valley Development Co Ltd v Koshy* [1998] 2 BCLC 613, 623, decided 6 months before *Paragon*, that an action for knowing receipt of trust property falls within the terms of s 21(1)(b) of the 1980 Act.

those whose trusteeship arises only by reason of that occurrence. Moreover, the "constructive trustee" is not in fact a trustee at all, as he or she never assumes the position of a trustee, and the "constructive trust" is no more than a remedial mechanism by which equity gives relief for fraud. Millett LJ, observed that:

> There is a case for treating fraudulent breach of trust differently from other frauds, but only if what is involved really is a breach of trust. There is no case for distinguishing between an action for damages for fraud at common law and its counterpart in equity based on the same facts merely because equity employs the formula of constructive trust to justify the exercise of the equitable jurisdiction.[91]

2.43   Although the comments of Millet LJ in *Paragon* are strictly *obiter dicta*, they have since been followed. In *Coulthard v Disco Mix Club Ltd*,[92] Jules Sher QC held that section 21(1) of the 1980 Act did not apply where the claimant sought damages for breach of both management and agency contracts and of fiduciary duty. There was no trust property before the defendants' breaches as they were not required to keep the claimant's money separate from theirs. Therefore the constructive trust which arose was merely a creation of the court to remedy the wrongdoing by the defendants and so section 21 did not apply.

2.44   Cases which fall into Millett LJ's first category are those in which the claimant can prove that there was pre-existing trust property. For example, in *Bank of Credit & Commerce International (Overseas) Ltd v Jan*,[93] the claimant bank alleged that one of the defendants, who was also its employee, had fraudulently misappropriated and misapplied its funds. Jonathan Parker J held that this was a case falling into the first category of constructive trust because the defendant:

> was at all material times a constructive trustee of the funds under his control in that he was under a subsisting fiduciary duty to apply those funds for the benefit of the BCCI. His misapplication of those funds was a breach of that pre-existing duty.[94]

Hence, section 21(1) of the 1980 Act applied and the defendant's limitation defence failed.[95]

2.45   Finally, in *James v Williams*,[96] the Court of Appeal held that a defendant who had taken it upon himself to take possession of inherited property as an executor with full knowledge of the claimant's part interest in that property, held it for the

---

[91] [1999] 1 All ER 400, 414. Millett LJ also said that *Nelson v Rye* was wrong insofar as it was held that a simple claim for breach of fiduciary duty falls outside the 1980 Act so that no time limit applies. Instead, the correct rule (preserved by s 36 of the 1980 Act) is that equity imposes time limits on equitable actions by analogy with the statutory limitation periods for common law claims. For a fuller discussion see paras 2.100 - 2.102 below.

[92] [2000] 1 WLR 707.

[93] Ch D, unreported, 17 November 1999.

[94] Smith Bernal transcript, Case No CH 1998/B/1572.

[95] See also *UCB Home Loans Corporation Ltd v Carr* [2000] Lloyds Rep PN 754, QBD.

[96] [2000] Ch 1.

claimant as a constructive trustee. Therefore the claimant's action to recover her share fell within section 21(1)(b) of the 1980 Act and was not subject to a limitation period.

(2) Claims in respect of the personal estate of a deceased person

2.46 The limitation period for any claim to the personal estate of a deceased person is twelve years from when the right to receive the share or interest accrues.[97] However if the action falls within section 21(1) of the 1980 Act, no period of limitation applies.

2.47 The limitation period applicable to a claim to recover arrears of interest in respect of a legacy, or damages in respect of such arrears, is six years from the date on which the interest becomes due.[98]

5. CLAIMS FOR RESTITUTION[99]

2.48 Unjust enrichment was only recognised by the House of Lords as an independent cause of action in 1991.[100] Hence the Limitation Act 1980 does not contain a limitation period which explicitly applies to restitutionary claims.[101]

2.49 The 1980 Act does, however, contain provisions applicable to many restitutionary claims. For example, section 9 sets a six year limitation period for claims under the Law Reform (Frustrated Contracts) Act 1943; section 10(1) sets a two year limitation period for claims under the Civil Liability (Contribution) Act 1978; section 21(3) lays down a six year limitation period for claims to recover trust property; section 22 applies a twelve year limitation period to claims to recover the personal estate of a deceased person; and section 23 applies a six year limitation period to actions for an account. Also, section 32(1)(c) of the 1980 Act postpones the limitation period for a claim for relief from the consequences of a mistake until the mistake is, or could with reasonable diligence be, discovered.[102]

2.50 In addition to these specific provisions, the courts have held that other, more general, provisions of the 1980 Act are applicable to restitutionary claims. For instance, claims which were previously characterised as quasi-contractual, such as an action for money had and received and a quantum meruit, fall within section 5

---

[97] Limitation Act 1980, s 22(a).

[98] Limitation Act 1980, s 22(b).

[99] Limitation of Actions, Consultation Paper No 151 (1998), paras 5.1 - 5.19.

[100] *Lipkin Gorman v Karpnale Ltd* [1991] 2 AC 548.

[101] See *Portman Building Society v Hamlyn Taylor Neck* [1998] 4 All ER 202, 209, where Brooke LJ called for statutory reform to bring restitutionary remedies within a coherent and principled limitation regime.

[102] See the detailed discussion of the House of Lords' seminal decision in *Kleinwort Benson Ltd v Lincoln City Council* [1999] 2 AC 349, at para 2.90 below.

of the 1980 Act.[103] Thus the limitation period applicable to such actions is six years from the date on which the defendant is unjustly enriched.[104]

2.51 Where the claimant seeks to rescind an executed contract for misrepresentation, mistake, duress or undue influence, or recover damages for breach of confidence, the equitable doctrine of laches may apply in addition to any limitation defence.[105]

6. CLAIMS TO RECOVER LAND AND RELATED CLAIMS[106]

(1) Claims to recover land

2.52 The limitation period applicable to a claim to recover land is twelve years from the date on which the right of action accrues.[107]

2.53 The circumstances in which a right to recover land accrues are set out in section 15 of, and the first schedule to, the 1980 Act. The overriding requirement for the right to recover the land to be treated as having accrued, so the limitation period begins to run, is that the land is in adverse possession. If the land ceases to be held in this way, the right of action will cease to be treated as having accrued.[108]

2.54 To be in adverse possession both factual possession of the land in question, and an intention to possess it (*animus possidendi*) must be demonstrated.[109] Factual possession signifies an appropriate degree of exclusive physical control according to all the circumstances of the case, particularly the nature of the land and the manner in which land of that nature is commonly used or enjoyed.[110] The *animus possidendi* involves an intention to possess the land to the exclusion of all other persons, including the owner with the paper title, so far as is reasonably

---

[103] *Kleinwort Benson Ltd v Sandwell Borough Council* [1994] 4 All ER 890, 942-943, *per* Hobhouse J.

[104] *BP Exploration Co (Libya) Ltd v Hunt (No 2)* [1983] 2 AC 352, 373-374, *per* Lord Brandon. Where the claimant pays money to the defendant pursuant to a mistake, the cause of action accrues on the date of payment (or, if later, the date of receipt): *Kleinwort Benson Ltd v Lincoln City Council* [1999] 2 AC 349, 359, *per* Lord Browne-Wilkinson, 386, *per* Lord Goff, 409, *per* Lord Hope. A Burrows, *The Law of Restitution* (1993) p 442 - 443.

[105] See, eg, *West Sussex Properties Ltd v Chichester District Council* [2000] NPC 74, CA, where neither defence was successful. See also paras 2.97 - 2.99 below.

[106] Limitation of Actions, Consultation Paper No 151 (1998), paras 6.1 - 6.50.

[107] Limitation Act 1980, s 15(1). Section 15(2) contains the exception that where the interest claimed was a future interest, the claimant has either 12 years from when the person entitled to the previous interest was dispossessed or 6 years from when his own interest fell into possession, whichever is the later.

[108] Limitation Act 1980, Sch 1, para 8(1) and (2).

[109] *Buckinghamshire County Council v Moran* [1990] 1 Ch 623, 635 - 636 *per* Slade LJ, 645 *per* Nourse LJ.

[110] *Powell v McFarlane* (1979) 38 P & CR, 452, 470 - 471. See recently eg *Green v Wheatley* [1999] 96/22 LSG 36, CA.

23

practicable and so far as the process of law permits.[111] Possession pursuant to a lawful title is never adverse.[112]

2.55 Section 17 of the 1980 Act states that the expiry of the limitation period extinguishes the title of the person entitled to maintain the action to recover land. The effect of this, and the nature of the title thereby passed to the squatter, varies according to whether the land is freehold or leasehold, registered or unregistered.

2.56 Where the freehold estate is unregistered, the person in adverse possession does not succeed to the old title, but is entitled to a separate possessory title in the land. Where the freehold estate is registered, the paper owner holds that estate on trust for the person in adverse possession until he is, as he is entitled to be, registered as proprietor.[113]

2.57 Where the leasehold estate is unregistered, the squatter obtains a possessory title as against the lessee but not as against the lessor. Hence if the former lessee surrenders his interest to the lessor, the lessor can lawfully eject the squatter.[114] The position is significantly different where the leasehold estate is registered because the squatter is entitled to be registered as proprietor of the lease and, once registered, cannot be disturbed by a purported surrender of it.[115] In *Central London Commercial Estates Ltd v Kato Kagaku Ltd*,[116] Sedley J confirmed that a squatter is protected even before he or she is registered as proprietor.[117]

2.58 In *JA Pye Ltd v Graham*,[118] Neuberger J, having decided that a squatter had obtained title to land by adverse possession, went on to criticise the present law as follows:

> I believe that the result is disproportionate, because, particularly in a climate of increasing awareness of human rights including the right to enjoy one's own property, it does seem Draconian to the owner and a windfall for the squatter that, just because the owner has taken no

---

[111] *Buckinghamshire County Council v Moran* [1990] 1 Ch 623, 643, *per* Slade LJ, 645, *per* Nourse LJ; see also *Prudential Assurance Co Ltd v Waterloo Real Estate Inc* [1999] 2 EGLR 85, CA and *JA Pye Ltd v Graham* [2001] EWCA Civ 117, CA, *The Times,* 13 February 2001.

[112] *Hyde v Pearce* [1982] 1 WLR 560; see also *Black Country Housing Association Ltd v Shand* [1998] NPC 92, CA, and *Bromley London Borough Council v Morritt* [2000] EHLR 24, CA.

[113] Land Registration Act 1925, s 75.

[114] *Fairweather v St Marylebone Property Co Ltd* [1963] AC 510. The lessor's cause of action against the squatter only accrues once the lease is ended: Limitation Act 1980, Sch 1, para 4.

[115] *Spectrum Investment Co v Holmes* [1981] 1 WLR 221: Limitation of Actions, Consultation Paper No 151 (1998), para 6.39.

[116] [1998] 4 All ER 948. See C Harpum, "Estates in the Clouds - The Squatter, The Lease and The Car Park" (1999) 115 LQR 187.

[117] Immediately the limitation period expires, s 75 of the Land Registration Act 1925 creates a trust of the leasehold estate in favour of the person in adverse possession. This trust is an overriding interest under s 70 of the 1925 Act. Accordingly, if the lessee surrenders the lease to the lessor, the statutory trusteeship passes to the lessor, thereby preserving the right of the person in adverse possession to be registered as proprietor of the leasehold estate.

[118] [2000] Ch 676.

steps to evict a squatter for 12 years, the owner should lose 25 hectares of land to the squatter with no compensation whatsoever.[119]

2.59 In the Court of Appeal the owner took up this passage and argued that his right to peaceably enjoy property, under the Human Rights Act 1988 and Article 1 of the First Protocol to the European Convention on Human Rights, had been breached.[120] The court rejected this, noting that limitation periods are not inherently incompatible with the Convention,[121] nor is the limitation period in section 15 of the 1980 Act disproportionate, discriminatory, impossible or so excessively difficult to comply with as to render the owner's right to his property ineffective to exercise.

(2)   Claims to recover proceeds of the sale of land

2.60 The limitation period for a claim to recover the proceeds of the sale of land is twelve years from the date on which the right to receive the money accrues.[122] The limitation period for an action to recover arrears of interest payable in respect of such proceeds, or to recover damages in respect of such arrears, is six years from the date on which the interest becomes due.[123]

(3)   Claims to recover rent

2.61 The time limit for a claim to recover arrears of rent, or damages in respect of such arrears, is six years from the date on which the arrears become due.[124]

7.   CLAIMS IN RELATION TO MORTGAGES AND CHARGES[125]

2.62 The limitation period for a mortgagor's claim to redeem a mortgage is twelve years from the date on which the mortgagee takes possession of the property.[126]

2.63 The limitation period applicable to a claim to recover any principal sum of money secured by a mortgage or other charge on real or personal property is twelve years from the date on which the right to receive the money accrues.[127]

---

[119] [2000] Ch 676, 710. *Ellis v Lambeth London Borough Council* [1999] EGCS 101, CA, another case of adverse possession, attracted widespread media comment. See, eg, *The Times,* 21 July 1999, where adverse possession was said to be "a loophole in the 1980 Limitations Act": A Sherwin, "A Free Home is my Right, says Happy Squatter".

[120] *JA Pye Ltd v Graham* [2001] EWCA Civ 117, CA, *The Times,* 13 February 2001.

[121] *Stubbings v United Kingdom* [1996] 23 EHRR 213, ECHR.

[122] Limitation Act 1980, s 20(1)(b).

[123] Limitation Act 1980, s 20(5).

[124] Limitation Act 1980, s 19.

[125] Limitation of Actions, Consultation Paper No 151 (1998), paras 6.46 - 6.50.

[126] Limitation Act 1980, s 16.

[127] Limitation Act 1980, s 20(1)(a). The date on which the right to receive money accrues where the mortgaged property is a future interest is provided for in s 20(3) and (7).

2.64 In a claim to recover arrears of interest payable on any sum of money secured by a mortgage or other charge, or to recover damages in respect of such arrears, the time limit is six years from the date on which the interest becomes due.[128]

2.65 Finally, the limitation period for a foreclosure action in respect of mortgaged personal property is twelve years from the date on which the right to foreclose accrues. If the mortgagee is in possession of the mortgaged property after that date, the right to foreclose is treated as accruing when the mortgagee discontinues possession.[129]

2.66 The recent case of *Re Maxwell Fleet & Facilities Management Ltd (in Administration)*,[130] demonstrates a situation in which the twelve year time limit in section 20 of the 1980 Act applies. The issue was whether a claim for wages and holiday pay by twelve former employees of a liquidated company would be time-barred. By virtue of section 19(5) of the Insolvency Act 1986 the employees had priority claims for the sums due, and any such sums were to be charged on and paid out of any property of the company at the end of the administration.[131] Jules Sher QC held that, as the administration had not yet ended, the statutory duty to pay had not yet arisen and therefore the limitation period had not yet begun. However he also held that the claims were not simple contractual claims which, under section 5 of the 1980 Act, would have become timed-barred six years after the end of the administration. Rather, they were actions to enforce the statutory charge created by the 1986 Act. Hence section 20 of the 1980 Act applied, and the employees' claims would only become barred after twelve years.

8. MISCELLANEOUS CLAIMS[132]

(1) Claims on a judgment

2.67 Section 24(1) of the Limitation Act 1980 provides that the limitation period for an action to enforce a judgment is six years from the date on which the judgment becomes enforceable. In *Lowsley v Forbes*,[133] the House of Lords affirmed that section 24(1) does not apply to prevent the execution of a judgment after six years, but applies only to bar fresh claims to enforce that judgment.[134]

---

[128] Limitation Act 1980, s 20(5). However s 20(6) provides that, where the property was previously in the possession of a prior mortgagee and an action is brought within one year of the end of that possession, all arrears due from the previous possession are recoverable.

[129] Limitation Act 1980, s 20(2). This section does not apply to foreclosure actions in respect of mortgaged land - s 15 applies: Limitation Act 1980, s 20(4).

[130] [2001] 1 WLR 323.

[131] *Powdrill v Watson* [1995] 2 AC 394.

[132] Limitation of Actions, Consultation Paper No 151 (1998), paras 7.1 - 7.39.

[133] [1999] 1 AC 329.

[134] An example of a fresh claim to enforce a judgment is a petition for bankruptcy: *Chohan v Times Newspapers Ltd* [2001] 1 WLR 184. This is to be contrasted with court proceedings aimed simply at executing a judgment to which no limitation period applies. However, when seeking execution after more than six years, the applicant must first obtain the leave of the court: RSC, O 46, r 2: see *Duer v Frazer* [2001] 1 All ER 249.

2.68   Section 24(2) of the 1980 Act provides that no arrears of interest in respect of any judgment are recoverable after six years from the date on which the interest becomes due. In *Lowsley v Forbes*, the House of Lords held that section 24(2) applies to both the interest recoverable in an action on a judgment and the interest recoverable in proceedings to execute a judgment.[135]

(2)   Arbitration

2.69   The limitation period applicable to a claim to enforce an arbitration award is six years from the date of the defendant's failure to honour the award when called upon to do so.[136]

2.70   Furthermore, the provisions of the Limitation Act 1980 apply to arbitral proceedings as they apply to legal proceedings.[137] The parties are free to agree when arbitral proceedings are to be regarded as commencing for the purposes of the 1980 Act.[138] In the absence of such an agreement, the arbitral proceedings will be deemed to have started when one party serves a notice in writing on the other party making it clear that the sender is invoking the arbitration agreement and requiring the receiver to take steps accordingly.[139]

(3)   Claims on a statute (including claims for contribution)

(a)   Claims on a statute

2.71   Section 8(1) of the 1980 Act provides that the limitation period for an action on a specialty, of which a statute is an example,[140] is twelve years from the date on which the cause of action accrues. However, section 9(1) of the 1980 Act provides that the limitation period for a claim to recover a 'sum recoverable by virtue of any enactment' is six years from the date on which the cause of action accrues.[141]

2.72   As we noted in the Consultation Paper, it is the nature of the relief sought that determines whether a statutory action is governed by section 8(1) or by section 9(1).[142] Where the claimant seeks non-monetary relief the limitation period is twelve years under section 8(1), but where the claimant seeks a sum of money the limitation period is six years under section 9(1).

---

[135]   Reversing the decision of the Court of Appeal, noted at para 7.2 of the Consultation Paper, that the limitation period in s 24(2) applies only to actions on a judgment.

[136]   Limitation Act 1980, s 7; *Agromet Motoimport v Maulden Engineering Co (Beds) Ltd* [1985] 1 WLR 762.

[137]   Arbitration Act 1996, s 13.

[138]   Arbitration Act 1996, s 14.

[139]   By either selecting an arbitrator or by submitting to a previously designated one: Arbitration Act 1996, s 14(3) - (4). In addition to the cases cited in para 7.6 of the Consultation Paper, see *Cathiship SA v Allanasons Ltd, The Catherine Helen* [1998] 3 All ER 714, QBD and *Allianz Versicherungs AG v Fortuna Co Inc, The Baltic Universal* [1999] 1 WLR 2117, QBD.

[140]   *Collin v Duke of Westminster* [1985] QB 581. A deed is also a specialty, see para 2.75 below.

[141]   By virtue of s 8(2), s 9(1) takes precedence over s 8(1).

[142]   Limitation of Actions, Consultation Paper No 151 (1998), para 7.15.

2.73 Recent cases have confirmed this distinction. In *Re Farmizer (Products) Ltd,*[143] the Court of Appeal held that section 9(1) applied to a claim under section 214 of the Insolvency Act 1986 against a director for a contribution towards a company's assets. 'Contribution' within these provisions meant a contribution of a sum of money. Peter Gibson LJ added that even where the statutory provision relied upon enabled the court to give either monetary or non-monetary relief, the court should look at what is actually being claimed in the proceedings to determine which limitation period applies.[144]

2.74 A recent case in which section 8(1) applied is *Rahman v Sterling Credit Ltd.*[145] The claimants sought to reopen a credit agreement by virtue of the Consumer Credit Act 1974. The Court of Appeal held that the six year time limit for a claim upon a simple contract in section 5 of the 1980 Act did not apply since the cause of action arose out of, and only out of, the provisions of the 1974 Act. Nor did section 9(1) of the 1980 Act apply, because the relief sought was the reopening of the credit bargain, which was non-monetary relief.[146] As a result, it was the twelve year time limit in section 8(1) of the 1980 Act that was applicable.

2.75 Finally, in order for section 9(1) to apply, the sum of money sought must be recoverable 'by virtue of' an enactment. This is demonstrated by *Global Financial Recoveries v Jones.*[147] Under the Insolvency Act 1986 the claimant made a statutory demand in order to establish the defendant's inability to pay an outstanding loan. The court held that such a petition did not itself give rise to a right to recover money, but simply provided a mechanism whereby a claimant hoped to be paid. Therefore the money was not recoverable "by virtue of" an enactment and the six year time limit in section 9(1) of the 1980 Act did not apply. Nor, however, did the six year time limit for simple contract as set down in section 5 apply. This was because the outstanding loan was the shortfall following the repossession of property according to a mortgage executed as a deed. As the mortgage contained a specific term which addressed the situation in which there was a shortfall, the claimant's action was an action on a specialty and hence the twelve year time limit in section 8(1) applied.[148]

---

[143] *Re Farmizer (Products) Ltd* [1997] 1 BCLC 589

[144] In *Rowan Companies Inc v Lambert Eggink Offshore Transport Consultants VOF (No 2)* [1999] 2 Lloyd's Rep 443, David Steel J followed *Re Farmizer* holding that the application of s 9(1) of the 1980 Act was not restricted to liquidated sums, but that it applied to any monetary relief whether in the form of a debt, damages, compensation or otherwise.

[145] [2001] 1 WLR 496.

[146] Mummery LJ added that if the claimant had sought the repayment of money by the creditor, the six year time limit in s 9(1) would have applied to that claim.

[147] [2000] BPIR 1029.

[148] As authority for this last point Robert Englehart QC, sitting as a Deputy High Court Judge, pointed to *Arbuthnot Latham Bank Ltd v Trafalgar Holdings Ltd* [1998] 1 WLR 1426, CA. In doing so he distinguished *Hopkinson v Tupper,* CA, unreported, 30 January 1997, where Auld LJ had said that it was seriously arguable that such a claim was one in simple contract whatever the nature of the instrument under which the debt was initially secured. Cf *Raja v Lloyds TSB Bank plc* [2001] EWCA Civ 210 (CA, unreported, 24 January 2001) where it was held that a mortgagee's duty to obtain a proper price on the sale of property arose in

2.76   Where section 9(1) of the 1980 Act does apply the court may have to consider when the right to recover the sum of money accrues. In *Hillingdon London Borough Council v ARC Ltd (No 1)*,[149] the Court of Appeal affirmed that the right to compensation under the Compulsory Purchase Act 1965 accrues immediately the acquiring body enters the land compulsorily acquired.[150]

(b)   Claims under the Civil Liability (Contribution) Act 1978

2.77   The limitation period applicable to a claim for contribution pursuant to section 1 of the Civil Liability (Contribution) Act 1978 is two years from the date on which the right to recover contribution accrues.[151]

9.   FACTORS POSTPONING THE RUNNING OF TIME[152]

(1)   Claimant under a disability

2.78   Where a right of action accrues to a person under a disability, the general rule is that proceedings may be commenced at any time within six years of the date on which the disability ends or the person dies.[153] However, if the person comes under a disability after the cause of action has accrued, the normal limitation period applies.[154]

2.79   A person is under a disability if he is a child or a person who, by reason of mental disorder, is incapable of managing and administering his property and affairs.[155]

(2)   Claim based on fraud

2.80   Section 32(1)(a) of the 1980 Act provides that where a claim is based upon the fraud of the defendant, the limitation period does not begin to run until the claimant discovers the fraud, or could with reasonable diligence discover it.[156]

2.81   The standard of diligence required in cases where the claimant is a company was considered in *Paragon Finance plc v DB Thakerar & Co.*[157] Millett LJ said that the

---

equity, rather than from the contract or deed. Hence, the limitation period in s 2 of the 1980 Act applied by analogy through s 36: see paras 2.100 - 2.102 below.

[149]   [1999] Ch 139, affirming the decision of Stanley Burnton QC, referred to in para 7.13 of the Consultation Paper. The court also held that the Lands Tribunal is a court of law for the purposes of the 1980 Act.

[150]   Cf *Halstead v Manchester City Council* [1998] 1 All ER 33, where the Court of Appeal held that the right to recover interest on compensation under the Compulsory Purchase Act 1965 does not accrue until the amount on which the interest is payable is awarded or agreed.

[151]   Limitation Act 1980, s 10.

[152]   Limitation of Actions, Consultation Paper No 151 (1998), paras 8.1 - 8.48.

[153]   Limitation Act 1980, s 28. This rule is subject to the important provisos in s 28(2) - (7).

[154]   *Purnell v Roche* [1927] 2 Ch 142, 149, *per* Romer J.

[155]   Limitation Act 1980, s 38(2) and (3).

[156]   An action is based upon the fraud of the defendant if fraud is an essential ingredient of the cause of action: *Beaman v ARTS Ltd* [1949] 1 KB 550.

[157]   [1999] 1 All ER 400, CA.

test to apply was how a person carrying on a business of the relevant kind would act if he had adequate, but not unlimited, staff and resources, and was motivated by a reasonable but not excessive sense of urgency. Millett LJ continued:

> The question is not whether the plaintiffs *should* have discovered the fraud sooner; but whether they *could* with reasonable diligence have done so. The burden of proof is on them. They must establish that they *could not* have discovered the fraud without exceptional measures which they could not reasonably have been expected to take.[158]

2.82 In *UCB Home Loans Corporation v Carr*,[159] Crane J cited this test but, stating that the remarks were made *obiter*, suggested that the word "exceptional" should be omitted since it raises the standard too high. Crane J went on to hold that reasonable diligence on the part of a company required not just that individual employees were diligent in noticing possible claims, but also that those in control of the company had in place proper systems to detect them.[160]

2.83 In *Haque v Bank of Credit & Commerce International SA*,[161] the Court of Appeal considered the situation in which it was an employee of the company that had been fraudulent. The court said that the relevant question was: could the claimant company, for this purpose represented by some non-fraudulent officer, or perhaps its auditor, have discovered the fraud with reasonable diligence? The court held that as all necessary inquiries had been made, and as the only people to have seen incriminating documents were those implicated in the fraud, the claimant company could not with reasonable diligence have discovered it.[162]

(3) Deliberate concealment

2.84 Where the defendant deliberately conceals a fact relevant to the claimant's right of action, the limitation period does not begin to run until the claimant discovers the concealment, or could with reasonable diligence discover it.[163]

2.85 Section 32(2) of the 1980 Act provides that a 'deliberate commission of a breach of duty in circumstances in which it is unlikely to be discovered for some time

---

[158] [1999] 1 All ER 400, 418. This formulation was adopted in *Birmingham Midshires Building Society v Infields* [1999] Lloyd's Rep PN 874, QBD; *Clef Aquitaine SARL v Laporte Materials (Barrow) Ltd* [2000] 3 All ER 493, CA; and *Halifax plc v Ringrose & Co* [2000] PNLR 483, QBD.

[159] [2000] Lloyds Rep PN 754, QBD.

[160] Crane J cited several cases in which corporate knowledge had been considered in the context of s 14A of the 1980 Act including *Abbey National v Wilkin & Chapman*, QBD, unreported, 7 October 1997; and *Abbey National plc v Sayer Moore*, Ch D, *The Times*, 30 August 1999. See paras 2.33 - 2.34 above.

[161] CA, unreported, 24 November 1999.

[162] See also *Bank of Credit and Commerce International (Overseas) Ltd v Jan*, Ch D, unreported, 17 November 1999.

[163] Limitation Act 1980, s 32(1)(b). If concealment is subsequent to the accrual of the cause of action, the limitation period is restarted (i.e. the clock is reset) after the concealment has been discovered: *Sheldon v RHM Outhwaite (Underwriting Agencies) Ltd* [1996] 1 AC 102.

amounts to deliberate concealment of the facts involved in that breach of duty'. There have been important developments in relation to this provision.

2.86   In *Brocklesby v Armitage & Guest*,[164] the defendant solicitors had negligently failed to release the claimant from mortgage obligations. The two-man Court of Appeal held that, despite there being no allegation of impropriety against the solicitors, they had deliberately committed a breach of duty within the meaning of section 32(2). The six year limitation period did not therefore start to run until the breach could be discovered. Morritt LJ said that, since it was trite law that ignorance of the law is no defence, if Parliament had intended that the defendant should know, not simply that he was acting, but also that his act gave rise to a breach of duty, it required clearer words to spell that out. Morritt LJ continued:

> it is not necessary for the purpose of extending the limitation period pursuant to section 32(1)(b) to the 1980 Act to demonstrate that the fact relevant to the claimant's right of action has been deliberately concealed in any sense greater than that the commission of the act was deliberate in the sense of being intentional and that that act or omission, as the case may be, did involved a breach of duty whether or not the actor appreciated that legal consequence.[165]

2.87   This decision was followed in *Liverpool Roman Catholic Archdiocese Trustees Inc v Goldberg*,[166] where Laddie J suggested that claimants could benefit from the extension of the limitation period under section 32 even where they are aware at all times of all the facts giving rise to the cause of action:

> [Section 32(2) treats] intentional commission of a breach of duty which is unlikely to be discovered in the same way as if it were a deliberate concealment of the facts which are necessary to maintain the action for breach of duty. Thus even if all the facts are known to the claimant, the intentional commission of the breach of duty in circumstances where that breach is unlikely to be discovered, results in the creation of a legal fiction, namely that the facts are unknown.[167]

Laddie J added that the limitation period will only then begin to run once the claimant has discovered that there was a breach of duty.[168]

2.88   *Brocklesby* has now been upheld by the full Court of Appeal in *Cave v Robinson Jarvis & Rolf*.[169] The court recognised the force of the arguments against *Brocklesby*: in particular, that the natural meaning of the phrase 'deliberate breach of duty' in section 32(2) of the 1980 Act is ignored, so that the word 'deliberate'

---

[164]   [2001] 1 All ER 172.

[165]   [2001] 1 All ER 172, 181. This reasoning has since been followed in *Halifax v Ringrose* [2000] PNLR 483, QBD and *Tucker v Allen* [2000] NPC 132, QBD.

[166]   [2001] 1 All ER 182.

[167]   [2001] 1 All ER 182, 191, *per* Laddie J.

[168]   [2001] 1 All ER 182, 191. This results in a conflict between s 32(2) of the 1980 Act and the provisions as to knowledge of the law in ss 14(1) and14A(9): see paras 2.11 and 2.27, above.

[169]   [2001] EWCA Civ 245 (CA, unreported, 20 February 2001).

becomes redundant; that dicta from the House of Lords case of *Sheldon v RHM Outhwaite (Underwriting Agencies) Ltd*[170] suggest that an element of impropriety on the defendant's part is required; and that the effect of *Brocklesby* is to override the discoverability provisions, including the long-stop, in sections 14A and 14B of the 1980 Act. However the court felt bound by *Brocklesby* and, although minded to grant permission to appeal, refused to do so given that the House of Lords had itself refused to hear an appeal in *Brocklesby*.

(4)   Relief from the consequences of a mistake

2.89   Where an action is for relief from the consequences of a mistake, the limitation period does not begin to run until the claimant discovers the mistake, or could with reasonable diligence discover it.[171]

2.90   In *Kleinwort Benson Ltd v Lincoln City Council*,[172] a majority of the House of Lords held that there is a general right to recover money paid under a mistake, thus abrogating the rule that money paid under a mistake of law is irrecoverable. The House of Lords also held that an action to recover the money falls within the terms of section 32(1)(c) of the 1980 Act, so that the relevant limitation period is six years from the date on which the mistake is discoverable. Accordingly, if a payment is made pursuant to the law as stated by a decision of the Court of Appeal, and the House of Lords later overrules that decision, the payment may be recovered up to six years after the House of Lords case. This aspect of the decision prompted Lord Browne-Wilkinson and Lord Lloyd to dissent, Lord Browne-Wilkinson expressing his disagreement in the following terms:

> On every occasion in which a higher court changed the law by judicial decision, all those who had made payments on the basis that the old law was correct (however long ago such payments were made) would have six years in which to bring a claim to recover money paid under a mistake of law. All your Lordships accept that this position cannot be cured save by primary legislation altering the relevant limitation period. In the circumstances, I believe that it would be quite wrong for your Lordships to change the law so as to make money paid under a mistake of law recoverable since to do so would leave this gaping omission in the law.[173]

The majority of their Lordships recognised this difficulty but thought that it could be adequately dealt with by statutory reform of the applicable limitation period and called for consideration of this by the Law Commission.[174]

---

[170]   [1996] 1 AC 102.

[171]   Limitation Act 1980, s 32(1)(c). An action is one for relief from the consequences of a mistake where the mistake is an essential ingredient of the cause of action: see recently *Malkin v Birmingham City Council*, CA, unreported, 12 January 2000.

[172]   [1999] 2 AC 349.

[173]   [1999] 2 AC 349, 364.

[174]   [1999] 2 AC 349, 389, *per* Lord Goff, 401, *per* Lord Hoffmann, 417 - 418, *per* Lord Hope. It appears that their Lordships' attention was not drawn to our provisional recommendation

(5)   Acknowledgment and part payment

2.91   Section 29 of the 1980 Act provides for the fresh accrual of the cause of action where the defendant either acknowledges the title or claim of the claimant, or makes a payment in respect of it. However this section only applies to claims for the recovery of land, claims in relation to mortgages, claims to recover a debt or other liquidated sum, and claims to recover a share or interest in the personal estate of a deceased person.[175]

2.92   The limitation period may be repeatedly extended by further acknowledgments or payments. However an acknowledgment or payment cannot revive a right of action already time-barred.[176]

10.   ADDITIONAL ISSUES[177]

(1)   What happens when time expires?

2.93   Generally the expiry of the limitation period bars the claimant's remedy, but does not extinguish his or her right.[178] It follows that if the defendant does not include details of the expiry of the limitation period in the defence, the claimant may obtain a remedy notwithstanding the fact that the limitation period has expired.[179]

(2)   What the claimant has to do to prevent the expiry of the limitation period

2.94   Time ceases to run against a claimant when he or she commences proceedings, that is, when a claim form is issued by the court at the claimant's request.[180]

2.95   In *Riniker v University College London*,[181] the claimant's writ was received by the court within the relevant limitation period. However, due to an administrative error, the writ was not issued until after the limitation period had expired. The Court of Appeal held that, pursuant to its inherent jurisdiction, it had a discretionary power to direct that a writ should be treated as if it had been issued on a date earlier than that on which it was actually issued. Hence, the court, which

---

that there should be a uniform long-stop limitation period of ten years from the date of the relevant act or omission applicable to all actions (other than actions in respect of personal injuries): Limitation of Actions, Consultation Paper No 151 (1998), para 12.113.

[175]   Limitation Act 1980, s 29(1) - (6). See recently *Bank of Baroda v Mahomed* [1999] CLC 463, CA, for an example of the conduct amounting to acknowledgment and part-payment.

[176]   Limitation Act 1980, s 29(7).

[177]   Limitation of Actions, Consultation Paper No 151 (1998), paras 9.1 - 9.39.

[178]   *Royal Norwegian Government v Constant & Constant* [1960] 2 Lloyds List Law Rep 431, 442, *per* Diplock J. For exceptions to this rule, see paras 2.36, 2.38 and 2.55 above.

[179]   Civil Procedure Rules 1998, Rule 16.5; *Ronex Properties Ltd v John Laing Construction Ltd* [1983] 1 QB 398, CA.

[180]   *Thompson v Brown* [1981] 1 WLR 744; *Dresser UK Ltd v Falcongate Freight Management Ltd* [1992] 1 QB 502, 517-518; Civil Procedure Rules, Rule 7.2.

[181]   CA, *The Times*, 17 April 1999.

was unable to identify any fault on the claimant's part, ordered that her writ should be deemed to have been issued on the date on which it was received.[182]

(3)   Contracting out of, or waiving, the statutory limitation period

2.96   The limitation period may be excluded by agreement, express or implied.[183] Similarly a party may be estopped by his own conduct from asserting a limitation defence.[184]

(4)   Laches and acquiescence

2.97   Section 36(2) of the 1980 Act expressly preserves the equitable jurisdiction to refuse relief on the ground of acquiescence or laches.

2.98   Laches is available as a defence where a claimant, who knows of his entitlement to relief, delays in instituting legal proceedings with the result that it would be unjust to award the remedy sought against the defendant.[185] In each case the test is whether the balance of justice or injustice is in favour of granting a remedy or withholding it.[186] In *Frawley v Neill*,[187] the Court of Appeal recently emphasised that the modern approach to laches does not require an investigation as to whether the circumstances of a particular case can be fitted within the confines of a preconceived formula derived from earlier cases. Rather, the court should adopt a broad approach to ascertain whether it would, in all the circumstances, be unconscionable for a party to be permitted to assert his beneficial right.

2.99   Acquiescence is available as a defence where a claimant, who knows of his or her rights, acquiesces in a breach of those rights by the defendant so that, in all the circumstances, it is unconscionable for the claimant to rely on them.[188] In *Jones v Stones*,[189] the Court of Appeal reaffirmed that it is not sufficient to show delay by the claimant. Rather, the defendant must establish that he or she relied, to his or her detriment, upon the action or inaction of the claimant.

---

[182]   Practice Direction 5.1 to Part 7 of the CPR now provides that where the claim form was received in the court office on a date earlier than the date on which it was issued by the court, the claim is 'brought' for the purposes of the Limitation Act 1980 on that earlier date.

[183]   *Lade v Trill* (1842) 11 LJ Ch 102.

[184]   See recently *Co-operative Wholesale Society Ltd v Chester le Street District Council* [1998] RVR 202; *Ellis v Lambeth London Borough Council* [2000] 32 HLR 596, CA; *Cotterrell v Leeds Day*, CA, unreported, 13 June 2000; *London Borough of Hillingdon v ARC Ltd (No 2)* [2000] RVR 283, CA.

[185]   In addition to the cases cited at paras 9.14 - 9.17 of the Consultation Paper, see *Gwembe Valley Development Co Ltd v Koshy* [1998] 2 BCLC 613, 623, *per* Harman J; and *West Sussex Properties Ltd v Chichester District Council* [2000] NPC 74, CA.

[186]   *Lindsay Petroleum Company v Hurd* (1874) LR 5 PC 221, 239-240, *per* Sir Barnes Peacock; *Nelson v Rye* [1996] 1 WLR 1378, 1392, *per* Laddie J.

[187]   CA, *The Times*, 5 April 1999.

[188]   *Shaw v Applegate* [1977] 1 WLR 970, 978, *per* Buckley LJ, 980, *per* Goff LJ.

[189]   [1999] 1 WLR 1739.

(5)   Application of the 1980 Act to equitable remedies by analogy

2.100   Section 36(1) of the 1980 Act provides that the court may apply time limits to claims for equitable relief by analogy with the provisions of the 1980 Act. In *Paragon Finance plc v DB Thakerar & Co*,[190] Millett LJ stated that this provision preserved the rule in *Knox v Gye*[191] that, even where there is no contractual relationship between parties so that liability is exclusively equitable, the court may still impose a time limit by analogy.[192]

2.101   Further explanation was provided in *Coulthard v Disco Mix Club Ltd*,[193] where Jules Sher QC, sitting as a deputy judge of the High Court, said that the court would apply the Act by analogy in two situations:

   (1)   where a court is simply exercising a concurrent equitable jurisdiction to give the same relief as is available at law; and,

   (2)   where there is a "correspondence" between the remedies available at law or in equity, even if the equitable relief is wider than the relief available at law.[194]

Jules Sher QC held that the alleged breaches of fiduciary duty were based on the same factual allegations as, and were the equitable counterparts of, a common law claim for fraud. Therefore, he held that section 5 of the 1980 Act applied by analogy.

2.102   *Coulthard* was approved by the Court of Appeal in *Cia De Seguros Imperio v Heath (REBX) Ltd*.[195] The court held that, where the facts of a case give rise to both a common law action for fraudulent breach of contract and an equitable claim for breach of fiduciary duty, the six year limitation period in section 5 of the 1980 Act applies to both. Clarke LJ said:

> If the claims for damages for breach of contract and duty are time barred ... no rational system should permit the plaintiff to proceed with a claim for damages which is essentially based on the same facts, merely because it is strictly a claim for compensation in equity.[196]

---

[190]   [1999] 1 All ER 400, 415 - 416.

[191]   (1872) LR 5 HL.

[192]   Hence, although there is no provision in the Limitation Act 1980 which explicitly applies to claim against a fiduciary for breach of fiduciary duty, that does not prevent a time limit applying to such a claim. For this reason Millett LJ said that *Nelson v Rye* [1996] 1 WLR 1378, had been wrongly decided.

[193]   [2000] 1 WLR 707.

[194]   [2000] 1 WLR 707, 730

[195]   [2001] 1 WLR 112.

[196]   [2001] 1 WLR 112, 126. Other cases in which a limitation period has been applied to an equitable claim by analogy include: *Mortgage Company v Johnson*, Ch D, *The Times*, 22 September 1999; and *Raja v Lloyds TSB Bank plc* [2001] EWCA Civ 210 (CA, unreported, 24 January 2001).

(6) Burden of proof

2.103 Where the defendant raises a limitation defence, the legal burden of proof rests throughout on the claimant, although the evidential burden may rest on the defendant according to the particular matter in issue.[197]

(7) The 'Sevcon' problem: restrictions on the claimant's right to sue

2.104 Generally time begins to run under the 1980 Act as soon as a cause of action accrues, irrespective of any procedural bars precluding legal proceedings. Thus a right of action may be time-barred before it can be enforced.[198]

(8) Adding new claims in existing proceedings

2.105 A new claim made in the course of proceedings is deemed to be a separate claim and, unless made in or by way of third party proceedings, to have been commenced on the same date as the original proceedings.[199]

2.106 However, the court may only allow a new claim to be made after the expiry of a relevant time limit if: (a) it is an original set-off or counterclaim;[200] or (b) the conditions in section 35 of the 1980 Act, and rules 17 and 19 of the Civil Procedure Rules 1998,[201] are satisfied.

2.107 According to these provisions the new claim may be allowed in the following circumstances:

(1) if the new claim is one which adds a new cause of action, that new cause of action must arise out of the same facts or substantially the same facts as are already in issue;[202] or,

(2) if the new claim is one which adds or substitutes a new party, either:

---

[197] *Crocker v British Coal Corporation* (1996) 29 BMLR 159. Cf *Lloyd's Bank plc v Burd Pearse* [2000] PNLR 71, Ch D. Limitation of Actions, Consultation Paper No 151 (1998), paras 9.23 - 9.25.

[198] *Sevcon Ltd v Lucas CAV Ltd* [1986] 1 WLR 462, HL. Limitation of Actions, Consultation Paper No 151 (1998), paras 9.26 - 9.27.

[199] Limitation Act 1980, s 35(1). A new claim means any claim by way of set-off or counterclaim, any claim involving the addition or substitution of a new cause of action, or any claim involving the addition or substitution of a new party: Limitation Act 1980, s 35(2). In *Filross Securities Ltd v Midgeley* (1999) 31 HLR 465, CA, the court held that an equitable set-off is not a new claim within s 35 because it is an equitable defence. However s 36(2) applies, so the set-off may be refused on the grounds of delay.

[200] A claim is an original set-off or counterclaim if the party making it has not previously made any claim in the action: Limitation Act 1980, s 35(3). A mere positive averment in a defence is not a 'claim in the action': *JFS (UK) Ltd v DWR Cyrmu Cyf (No 1)* [1999] 1 WLR 231.

[201] These have replaced the Rules of the Supreme Court (RSC, O 15, r 6 and O 20, r 5) set out at para 9.30 of the Consultation Paper.

[202] Limitation Act 1980, s 35(5)(a); Civil Procedure Rules, Rule 17.4(2).

(a) the introduction of the new party must be necessary for the determination of the original action. 'Necessary' for this purpose means that either:

    (i) the new party is substituted for a party who was named in the claim form in mistake for the new party; or,

    (ii) a claim made in the original action cannot properly be maintained unless the new party is joined or substituted; or,

    (iii) the original party has died or been subject to a bankruptcy order, so that their interest or liability has passed to the new party;[203] or

(b) the court must direct that, by virtue of section 33 of the 1980 Act, the three year limitation period does not apply to the new claim.[204]

2.108 The question of whether an amendment adds a new cause of action, and if so, whether that new cause of action arises out of the same or substantially the same facts as a previous cause of action, fell for consideration in *Paragon Finance plc v DB Thakerar & Co.*[205] The Court of Appeal held that an amendment to make an allegation of intentional wrongdoing, where previously no intentional wrongdoing had been alleged, did constitute the introduction of a new cause of action. Millett LJ relied upon the following definition by Diplock LJ in *Letang v Cooper*:[206]

> A cause of action is simply a factual situation the existence of which entitles one person to obtain from the court a remedy against another person.

2.109 In *Lloyds Bank plc v Rogers*,[207] Auld LJ followed this by holding that a building society which had originally only sought possession of a property, but now sought to amend its pleadings to include a claim for a money judgment, would not be adding a new cause of action to its claim. Auld LJ held that, although seeking a new remedy, the claimant was relying on facts already pleaded (the same factual situation) so that there was no new cause of action. Evans LJ disagreed, saying that, even if no new facts were to be pleaded, the claim for possession under a legal charge and guarantee was a different cause of action to the claim for sums due as principal and interest under the guarantee.[208]

---

[203] Limitation Act 1980, s 35(5)(b) and (6); Civil Procedure Rules, Rule 19.5(2) and (3).

[204] Civil Procedure Rules, Rule 19.5(4).

[205] [1999] 1 All ER 400.

[206] [1965] 1 QB 232, 242 - 243.

[207] [1999] 3 EGLR 83.

[208] Both judges in the two-man Court of Appeal did however agree that even if there was a new cause of action the facts relied upon were the same, or substantially the same, and hence the building society was permitted to amend its particulars of claim.

2.110 In *Stewart v Engel*,[209] the claimant sought rectification of a contract and damages for conversion in addition to a previously pleaded claim in negligence. The Court of Appeal held that, in the light of Diplock LJ's definition of a cause of action, amending the pleadings to include a conversion claim would not add a new cause of action if all the facts relied upon had already been pleaded. However, as the original pleadings had not included one fact essential to the claim for conversion the effect of the new claim would be to add a new cause of action. Despite this, the court did allow the amendment since the evidence for the negligence claim would have covered substantially, albeit not all, the same ground as would have been covered in presenting the new claim.[210]

2.111 Another issue which the courts have considered recently is whether a claimant, who has sought damages for both personal injury and economic loss, but whose claim is time-barred by virtue of the three year limitation period in section 11 of the 1980 Act, may be permitted to delete the personal injury claim and take advantage of the six year limitation period for non-personal injury claims.[211]

2.112 In *Oates v Harte Reade & Co*,[212] Singer J held that the deletion of one type of damage claimed could not amount to adding or substituting a new cause of action. Section 35(5) of the 1980 Act therefore did not apply. However he still refused to allow the claimant to amend the pleadings[213] because it would have deprived the defendant of a good limitation defence which had arisen out of the way in which the claimant had chosen to plead her case.

2.113 In *Shade v Compton Partnership*,[214] the Court of Appeal said that the reasoning in *Oates* was less than fully satisfactory. The court disagreed that section 35 of the 1980 Act and part 17.4 of the Civil Procedure Rules could be irrelevant when the issue of limitation arose in connection with a proposed amendment. Also it said that the fact that an amendment would deprive the defendant of an accrued limitation defence was only relevant when the claimant could not usefully start new proceedings. In this case, if the claimant wished to bring a new action without seeking damages for personal injuries he would not be time-barred and so he should have been allowed to amend his pleadings.

(9) Commencement and retrospectivity

2.114 Statutes are not interpreted retrospectively so as to impair existing rights or obligations unless that interpretation is unavoidable from the language used. An

---

[209] [2000] 1 WLR 2268.

[210] See also *Pledger v Martin* [2000] PIQR P31, QBD, *Darlington Building Society v O'Rourke James Scourfield & McCarthy* [1999] Lloyd's Rep PN 33, CA, and *R v Secretary of State for Transport, ex p Factortame (No 6)*, QBD, *The Times*, 10 January 2001.

[211] See the discussion of *Bennett v Greenland Houchen & Co* [1998] PNLR 458, at para 2.15 above.

[212] [1999] 1 FLR 1221.

[213] Under RSC, O 20, r 5(1), now replaced by CPR Rule 17.1(2).

[214] [2000] PNLR 218.

accrued right to a limitation defence is in every sense a legal right. Accordingly statutes of limitation are not applied retrospectively where such an application would abrogate an accrued right to plead a time bar.[215]

2.115   These propositions were confirmed in *Marsal v Apong*,[216] where the Privy Council, considering Brunei law, had to determine whether section 2 of the Emergency (Limitation) Order 1991 applied retrospectively to an action that was otherwise already statute-barred. That section provided:

> (1) This Order shall apply to any action commenced after the date of coming into force of this Order, whether the cause of action accrued before or after that date. (2) Any action commenced before the date of coming into force of this Order, shall continue in accordance with, and be bound by, the provisions of the Act repealed by section 52 of this Order.

2.116   The Privy Council held that section 2(2) of this Order preserved the defendant's acquired limitation defence. Lord Slynn expressed himself in the following terms:

> it is quite impossible to say that it is "unavoidable" to construe the Order as removing rights acquired under the Limitation Act itself. On the contrary, in the absence of an express provision in section 2(2) of the Order that existing acquired rights to a limitation defence were removed, the clear presumption must be the other way.[217]

[215]   *Yew Bon Tew v Kenderaan Bas Mara* [1983] 1 AC 553, 558 - 563, *per* Lord Brightman.

[216]   [1998] 1 WLR 674.

[217]   [1998] 1 WLR 674, 679.

PART III
REFORM I: THE CORE REGIME

1. INTRODUCTION

3.1   In this Part we consider the main components of the recommended core regime, namely:-

(1)   When should time start to run in relation to a claim?

(2)   How long should the primary limitation period be?

(3)   The long-stop limitation period.

(4)   The factors extending or excluding the limitation periods.

(5)   Should the court have a discretion to disapply a limitation period?

(6)   Agreements to change the limitation period.

3.2   It may prove helpful, first, to explain what we mean by "claim". We are concerned with the case where the claimant is bringing legal proceedings to seek a form of relief from the defendant. Relief for these purposes may fall into one of the following three categories:

(1)   a remedy for a wrong;

(2)   restitution; or

(3)   the enforcement of a right.

3.3   Claims for a remedy for a wrong will include any claims for damages for a breach of duty by the defendant (such as a claim for damages for negligence or for breach of contract). Restitutionary claims will include any claim for unjust enrichment (such as for the recovery of money paid under mistake). Claims for the enforcement of a right will include any claim by the claimant to enforce rights under a contract (such as a claim for specific performance or to recover the price), or to receive any money or other benefit conferred by statute (such as a claim for compensation for compulsory purchase).

3.4   Our recommendations do not extend to those cases where the claimant is bringing an administrative application - such as an application for the appointment of a new trustee, or where a trustee seeks directions from the court as to the exercise of his functions under the Settled Land Act 1925 in relation to a trust or trust property.

2. WHEN SHOULD TIME START TO RUN?
(1) The Date of Knowledge

3.5   In our Consultation Paper, we set out five options to be considered as the general starting point for the limitation period, ranging from the date of accrual of the cause of action to the date of 'discoverability', whereby the starting point for the limitation period would be decided by reference to the date the claimant has or ought to have knowledge of the cause of action.[1] We provisionally proposed that the date of discoverability should be used as the general starting point for limitation periods. This has been supported by over seventy per cent of consultees.

3.6 The great merit of the date of discoverability, or 'date of knowledge' (the label used in the Limitation Act 1980)[2] is that it is fair to claimants in that time will not run against them until they know, or could reasonably be expected to know, the facts necessary to bring a claim. Moreover, the benefits of a uniform limitations regime mean that the same starting point should be applied 'across the board', unless there are very strong arguments to the contrary. We recognise that adopting the 'date of knowledge' as the starting point for the limitation period has certain disadvantages, in that it is inherently less certain than, for example, the date that the cause of action accrues. There is therefore a risk that it will produce some satellite litigation. However, a number of those consultees choosing the 'date of knowledge' for the starting point argued that this danger could be exaggerated, and that the advantages of a uniform starting date outweigh the disadvantages. Another important factor in favour of the 'date of knowledge' as the starting point is that, as the Council of Her Majesty's Circuit Judges noted, it is the most likely option "to be regarded by most people (whether lawyers or not) as the fairest, simplest and most sensible of the five".

3.7 **We recommend that the primary limitation period should start to run from the 'date of knowledge' rather than, for example, the date the cause of action accrues (Draft Bill, Cl 1(1)).[3]**

(2) Definition of the Date of Knowledge: The Relevant Facts

3.8 In the Consultation Paper,[4] we proposed that the definition of the date of knowledge should focus on three main *factual* elements:

(1) knowledge of the facts establishing the cause of action;

(2) knowledge of the identity of the defendant; and

---

[1] See Limitation of Actions, Consultation Paper No 151 (1998), paras 12.9 - 12.21. The five options suggested as starting dates for the primary limitation period were:

    i)   the date of discoverability;

    ii)   the date of discoverability or accrual of the cause of action;

    iii)   the date of accrual of the cause of action;

    iv)   the date of the act or omission giving rise to the cause of action;

    v)   the date of accrual of the cause of action for contract claims; date of discoverability for tort claims.

[2] Which has the advantage of familiarity.

[3] In addition to the primary limitation period, we propose that claims should also be subject to a long-stop limitation period. This is discussed at paras 3.99 - 3.101 below.

[4] See Limitation of Actions, Consultation Paper No 151 (1998), paras 12.29 and 12.44.

(3)   knowledge that the cause of action is significant.

(a)   The facts establishing the cause of action

3.9   Over seventy per cent of consultees who commented on this provisional proposal agreed that at least the first two factual elements proposed for the date of knowledge, namely knowledge of the facts establishing the cause of action and knowledge of the identity of the defendant, should be included in the definition. A small minority expressed concern that the phrase 'cause of action' is ambiguous in this context, leaving it unclear precisely what facts the claimant needs to know before the limitation period starts to run. We have considered whether it is possible to express this concept more precisely by providing exactly what facts a claimant must know in relation to a particular cause of action. However it has proved impracticable to identify exactly which facts would be relevant in relation to every single cause of action which will be covered by the regime we propose. We remain of the view that "the facts giving rise to the cause of action" is a sufficiently clear concept to indicate in any one case what the claimant needs to know to start time running.

3.10   Our recommendations, therefore, differ from the position under the current law, where the constituent elements which the claimant needs to know before time starts running against him or her are set out in detail in sections 14 and 14A of the Limitation Act 1980. The problems to which this has given rise are illustrated in *Dobbie v Medway Health Authority*.[5] Here, the claimant was admitted to hospital for the excision of a lump from her breast. The defendant considered that the lump appeared to be cancerous and, without further examination, removed the claimant's breast. Very shortly after the operation the claimant learned that the lump had not been cancerous, but she was led to believe that the practice followed was usual and proper. Only fifteen years later she learned that the lump could (and indeed should) have been excised first and subjected to a pathological examination which would have shown that the removal of her breast was unnecessary.

3.11   The Court of Appeal upheld the trial judge's decision that within three years of the operation the claimant had knowledge of all the relevant facts and that her claim was therefore time-barred. The claimant was aware of the facts required by section 14 of the Limitation Act 1980 as soon as she knew that her breast had been removed by the doctor and that it was not cancerous. She knew, that is, that the injury (the loss of a breast) was significant, that it was attributable to the act alleged to be negligent (the operation performed on her) and the identity of the defendant (the health authority concerned). Whether or not she knew that it would have been possible to pre-test for cancer, and that the act in question could therefore be considered negligent, was seemingly irrelevant. In contrast, under the definition of the date of knowledge which we recommend the claimant would not have actual knowledge of all the relevant facts giving rise to the cause of action

---

[5]   [1994] 1 WLR 1234.

42

until she knew that the lump could have been removed and tested for cancer before her breast was removed.[6]

3.12 Similarly, in *Saxby v Morgan*[7] the claimant was seeking damages for an unwanted pregnancy after her doctor had wrongly advised her that her pregnancy was too advanced for her to have an abortion. She did not discover that the doctor's advice was incorrect until she obtained copies of her medical records. However, the court held that under section 14 of the Limitation Act 1980 she knew all the relevant facts on the date that she visited her doctor. That is, she knew of her injury (the continuation of an unwanted pregnancy); the act of the defendant (the advice that she could not have an abortion); and that this act caused the injury (since by relying on it, she did not have an abortion). Under our recommended definition of the date of knowledge, this would change because Mrs Saxby would not have actual knowledge of one of the facts giving rise to the cause of action until the date when she learnt that the doctor's advice was incorrect.[8]

3.13 In general this element of the definition will require the claimant to know matters of fact, as opposed to matters of law. There will however be an exception to this rule where the claimant's knowledge of his cause of action would be incomplete unless he knows, for example that legal advice on which he has acted is wrong. This is discussed further at paragraphs 3.35 to 3.39 below.

(b)   The identity of the defendant

3.14 Knowledge of the identity of the defendant is, in general, a straightforward and uncontroversial concept. But under sections 14(1)(d) and 14A(8)(c) of the Limitation Act 1980, special provision is made for cases where the defendant is vicariously liable for the acts or omissions of another person. The claimant must know not only the identity of the (vicariously liable) defendant, but the identity of the person responsible for the act or omission, and the additional facts which support the bringing of proceedings against the defendant. We provisionally proposed that there should be no similar provision in the new Act.[9] If the claimant knows the identity of the defendant (for example, the employer) against whom the claim is being brought, we see no need to delay the running of time because the

---

[6]   We do not mean to suggest that Mrs Dobbie might not have had constructive knowledge of the fact that the lump could, and should have been tested for cancer before the removal of her breast at an earlier date. The Court of Appeal's decision in relation to actual knowledge made it unnecessary for them to consider this question, and the facts are not entirely clear.

[7]   [1997] PIQR P531.

[8]   The adoption of our definition would have the additional advantage of resolving the conflict between those cases relying on *Dobbie v Medway Health Authority* and those relying on *Hallam-Eames v Merrett Syndicates Ltd* [1996] 7 Med LR 122, a case where the Court of Appeal held that the claimant needed to know the facts which "can fairly be described as constituting the negligence of which he complains" in addition to the loss - a far broader approach than *Dobbie v Medway Health Authority* and *Saxby v Morgan*.

[9]   See Limitation of Actions, Consultation Paper No 151 (1998), para 12.32.

claimant is unable to identify precisely which individual (for example, which employee) was responsible.[10] This approach has been approved by consultees.

(c) The significance of the claim

3.15 We provisionally proposed that the definition of the date of knowledge should incorporate the claimant's knowledge that the cause of action is significant.[11]

3.16 Two main issues arise. First, should the test include a requirement that the claimant knows that the claim is significant? Secondly, if so, what is meant by 'significance'?

(i) Should the test for the date of knowledge incorporate knowledge of the 'significance' of the claim?

3.17 The majority of consultees recognised that knowledge of the 'significance' of the claim should be included in the definition of the date of knowledge (over eighty per cent agreed with our provisional proposals).

3.18 The purpose of including knowledge of the significance of the claim in the definition of the date of knowledge is twofold. First, it delays the start of the limitation period to protect the claimant who has received an injury, or suffered damage or loss, which at first seems trivial when it later becomes clear that the injury, loss or damage is far more serious. Secondly, it reduces the pressure on a claimant who has received a trivial injury or loss to bring proceedings immediately, without waiting to see if the injury or loss gets worse, for fear of being time-barred. Without this assurance the amount of premature litigation could significantly increase.

3.19 However, where the extent of the damage suffered by the claimant is apparent either immediately, or by the time when the claimant has knowledge of the other relevant facts, and does not change over time, the claimant should be treated as knowing that the damage is 'significant'. Otherwise the primary limitation period will never be triggered if the claimant had an entirely trivial claim, which would enable the claimant to bring proceedings in respect of that claim at any time before the expiry of the long-stop limitation period, whereas a claimant with a more serious claim would be time-barred after the expiry of the three year primary limitation period.

(ii) The definition of 'significance': subjective or objective?

3.20 There is less agreement as to how 'significance' should be defined. We provisionally proposed the following definition of 'significance':

---

[10] This may in some cases mean that the claimant is able to bring a claim directly against the person responsible for the act or omission after the limitation period in respect of a claim against that person's (vicariously liable) employer has expired. However, we do not consider that this is sufficiently undesirable to justify adding to the complexity of the definition of the date of knowledge unnecessarily by providing for vicarious liability.

[11] See Limitation of Actions, Consultation Paper No 151 (1998), para 12.44.

> A cause of action should be regarded as significant if a person with the plaintiff's abilities would have reasonably considered the cause of action sufficiently serious to justify instituting proceedings against the defendant, on the assumption that the defendant does not dispute liability and has the resources to meet the claim.[12]

This definition was primarily objective, but with a small subjective element, allowing the claimant's abilities to be taken into account. It is not as subjective as the test under the current law in relation to personal injury claims (in section 14(3)), or as objective as the test for significance in relation to Consumer Protection Act claims or claims for latent damage not involving personal injury (in sections 14(1A)(a) and 14A(7) respectively).

3.21 This objective / subjective mix was accepted by fifty per cent of consultees. However, a minority of consultees objected that the proposed definition was too subjective.[13] It has been argued that it would be unclear what should be regarded as the claimant's abilities:

> It is acknowledged (p266 fn 68) that no view has been taken as to whether this is confined to intellectual abilities or includes financial abilities. What about psychological 'ability' (e.g. the depressive who can't face litigation) and emotional 'abilities', such as the laudable reaction that one could not bring oneself to sue the old lady next door for subsidence until it was quite unavoidable. What about the employee who reasonably [took] into account his employment position before bringing proceedings (as in *McCaffrey*, referred to in the paper at p 263, fn 54)? (Andrew Smith J).

3.22 One factor which would clearly affect whether a claimant viewed a claim as significant would be the claimant's resources. A claim which to a poor person would be very significant may be trivial to a rich person. However, to take account of this factor would allow rich claimants a longer limitation period than poor claimants, which seems inherently unjust.

3.23 It has also been argued strongly that to take any account of the individual circumstances of a particular claimant only serves to increase the uncertainty inherent in the 'date of knowledge' starting point. A defendant would never be able to know when the limitation period had started in respect of any cause of action without also knowing everything about the claimant's character, and circumstances. In addition, it could be argued that a wholly subjective definition of what is 'significant' would allow a claimant who has an injury which gradually worsens to choose when the limitation period should start.

3.24 For these reasons, we have concluded that the element of subjectivity that we provisionally proposed should be abandoned and that to protect the defendant from the 'unreasonable' claimant, and to produce greater certainty, the test for significance should be objective: that is, only claims in respect of which a

---

[12] See Limitation of Actions, Consultation Paper No 151 (1998), para 12.44.

[13] Though an equal minority argued that it was too objective.

reasonable person would have thought it worthwhile issuing proceedings will qualify as 'significant'. We propose, in other words, to follow the approach of the current law in sections 14(1A)(a) and 14A(7) (that is, in relation to Consumer Protection Act claims and claims for latent damage not involving personal injury).

(iii) The definition of significance: are the present (or any) assumptions necessary?

3.25 The test proposed in the Consultation Paper adopted the definition of 'significance' used in the current law for personal injury claims (and for 'materiality' for facts relating to other latent damage negligence claims). This defines 'significance' in terms of whether it is worth bringing proceedings against the defendant. This is the ultimate test for any claim - if it is never thought to be worth asserting a claim in court, that claim cannot have any value. The benefits to the claimant of bringing the claim must outweigh the costs and inconvenience of pursuing it.

3.26 Some consultees have suggested that the assumptions that the defendant admits liability and is solvent, which we provisionally proposed in the Consultation Paper should form part of the definition, are unfair to claimants because they set far too low a threshold for 'significance'. It could be said that it is unreasonable for the claimant to decide not to bring proceedings for almost any injury if the claimant can be sure that he or she will recover damages for that injury. While the present test does give the courts some flexibility, we accept that it sets a low threshold.[14]

3.27 However it is not possible for the definition of 'significance' to reflect accurately all the factors which would be taken into account in deciding whether or not to bring proceedings. The factors would differ for every claimant. The most important factor, in many cases, would be the chances of success of the claim. To ask the court to decide when the claimant should have known that the claim was more likely to succeed than otherwise would require a trial of the merits of the claimant's case every time the defendant raised a limitation defence. It is also hard to justify giving the claimant a longer limitation period when the defendant is in financial difficulties. Unrealistic though the assumptions undoubtedly are, they provide a measure of protection necessary for defendants.

3.28 We have also carefully considered, albeit to reject, some different tests. For example, the definition could provide that a claim is significant if the recoverable damages are (1) more than nominal; (2) more than a fixed sum; or (3) less than a set proportion of the total award. In the first case, we consider that reliance on 'nominal damages' might set too low a threshold. In any event, 'nominal damages' is a legal term of art which, strictly speaking, refers to damages being awarded where there is no loss at all.

3.29 The other two possibilities attempt to set a tariff. However it would be extremely difficult to quantify a 'significant' amount which would be considered to be fair. If a sum was identified, it would need to be constantly reviewed (or perhaps index linked). Further it would require the court to ascertain precisely the probable

---

[14] Limitation of Actions, Consultation Paper No 151 (1998), paras 3.40 - 3.44.

quantum of damages and costs which the claimant might recover at a particular date. This would not necessarily increase the certainty of the definition.

3.30   The same objection applies to any attempt to define the significance of the claim by reference to a proportion of the damages recoverable (so that the claim would be insignificant until the claimant knew of at least, for example, loss giving rise to ten per cent of the damages ultimately recoverable). Any percentage chosen would be arbitrary. The court would again be required to calculate the damages which would have been awarded at two different points in time. A more fundamental objection is the fact that, where the claimant has a very large claim, even a small proportion of that claim (such as five per cent) may be a large amount.

3.31   We have concluded that there is no alternative to defining 'significance' by reference to the point when the facts establish that it is worth making a claim in civil proceedings. We are, therefore, following the approach of the current law on this issue.[15]

3.32   **We recommend that the date of knowledge (which is when the primary limitation period should start to run) should be the date when the claimant has (actual or constructive)[16] knowledge of the following facts:-**

   (1)   the facts which give rise to the cause of action;

   (2)   the identity of the defendant; and

   (3)   where injury, loss or damage has occurred or a benefit has been received, that the injury, loss, damage or benefit are significant. (Draft Bill, Cl 2(1)).

3.33   **For the purposes of the definition of the date of knowledge, a claimant will be deemed to know that the injury, loss, damage or benefit is significant if**

   (1)   the claimant knows the full extent of the injury, loss, damage suffered by the claimant (or any other relevant person), or (in relation to a claim for restitution) of any benefit obtained by the defendant (or any other relevant person); or

   (2)   a reasonable person would think that, on the assumption that the defendant does not dispute liability and is able to satisfy a judgment, a civil claim was worth making in respect of the injury, loss, damage or benefit concerned. (Draft Bill, Cl 2(5)).

3.34   It should be emphasised that the test for the date of knowledge will not be satisfied until the claimant knows (or should know) each of the matters set out above. In some cases the necessary facts may be discoverable by the claimant at different times. The primary limitation period will not start running against the

---

[15]   See para 2.11 above, and particularly n 29 to that paragraph.

[16]   We discuss below, at paras 3.40 - 3.50, the meaning of actual and constructive knowledge.

claimant until the date on which he or she knows (or should know) the last piece of information needed for the "date of knowledge" test.

(3) Definition of the Date of Knowledge: Fact and Law

3.35 In the Consultation Paper we discussed, without reaching a provisional view, the part which knowledge of the law should play in the definition of the date of knowledge.[17] Two alternatives were suggested to consultees:

(1) that knowledge for the purposes of the date of knowledge should always include knowledge of the law, including knowledge of one's entitlement to a legal remedy for what has occurred; or

(2) that knowledge should include knowledge of the law only in so far as such knowledge is necessary for the claimant to know all the elements of his or her cause of action (for example, where the claim is for restitution of payments made by a mistake of law, one has to know the true legal position to know that one has made a mistake).

3.36 Those consultees who responded on this point were divided on the issue. Approximately thirty per cent agreed with the first alternative proposed, suggesting that this was necessary to do justice to the claimant. As Judge Altman commented, "A plaintiff who has all the elements of knowledge except that of entitlement to a legal remedy may not take proceedings in time." It was suggested that the existence of a long-stop limitation period would provide sufficient protection for the defendant. However, over thirty-five per cent felt that legal knowledge should play no part in deciding when time should start to run against the claimant. A major concern expressed by consultees was that incorporating knowledge of the law in the definition would significantly increase uncertainty as to when the primary limitation period would start running.

3.37 We agree that, in general, knowledge of the law should not be relevant. Our view on this has further been influenced by our recommendation, discussed below, that a long-stop limitation period should not apply to personal injury claims, and that the courts should have a discretion to disapply the limitation period for such claims, thereby reducing the risk of injustice to the personal injury claimant.[18] We have therefore concluded that the general rule should be that the claimant is assumed to have all the legal knowledge relevant to his or her cause of action. Thus, the date when the claimant discovers that the relevant facts give rise, as a matter of law, to a claim will be irrelevant.

3.38 However, we think that an exception must be made to this rule on the lines suggested in the second alternative: namely where the claimant necessarily has to establish that he or she did not know the law in order to establish that he or she has a claim. It seems to us that there are two such cases: first, claims in respect of

---

[17] See Limitation of Actions, Consultation Paper No 151 (1998), paras 12.59 - 12.69, and paras 2.31 - 2.32 above.

[18] See paras 3.160 - 3.169 below.

incorrect legal advice,[19] and secondly, claims to recover money paid by (or other restitutionary claims for) mistake of law.[20] It would be unjust for the date of knowledge to run from the date the advice was given, before the claimant had sufficient information to suggest that the defendant has not give the correct advice on the law, or that the understanding of the law on which the payment was made was mistaken.[21] The claimant cannot be said to know all the 'facts which give rise to the cause of action' until he or she has this information. However, this necessarily requires the claimant's knowledge of the law to be considered. Put another way, the essence of the cause of action contradicts the presumption that, as a reasonable person, the claimant knows the law because the claimant necessarily has to establish that he or she did not know the law in order to succeed.

3.39 **We recommend that, for the purposes of the test for the 'date of knowledge', the claimant is presumed to know the law, so that the claimant's lack of knowledge that the facts would or would not, as a matter of law, give rise to a cause of action shall be irrelevant. (Draft Bill, Cl 2(2)). This will not apply to:**

(1) **a cause of action in respect of breach of duty where the breach of duty concerned is a failure to give correct advice as to the law, and the fact that correct advice had not (or may not) have been given shall be treated as one of the facts giving rise to the cause of action (Draft Bill, Cl 2(3)); or**

(2) **a cause of action in respect of restitution based on a mistake of law, and the fact that a mistake of law has been, or may have been, made, shall be treated as one of the facts giving rise to the cause of action. (Draft Bill, Cl 2(4)).**

(4) What is meant by 'actual knowledge'?

3.40 Should a claimant be treated as 'knowing' a fact if he or she merely believes it to be true but it is not possible to establish it without expert evidence?[22] It may

---

[19] See Limitation of Actions, Consultation Paper No 151 (1998), para 12.67.

[20] As allowed by the House of Lords in *Kleinwort Benson v Lincoln City Council* [1999] 2 AC 349.

[21] Under the current law the claimant has an automatic extension of the limitation period under section 32 of the Limitation Act 1980 where the claimant's claim is for relief from the consequences of a mistake, whether of fact or law. In such a case, time only starts running from the date the claimant discovers, or could with reasonable diligence have discovered, the mistake. As the primary limitation period we propose will only start from the date on which the claimant knows or ought to know the relevant facts, this additional provision will not be necessary.

[22] Some cases brought under section 14 of the Limitation Act 1980 have been concerned to distinguish between the claimant who has actual knowledge of the facts required by that section, and the claimant who believes but does not know a particular fact. See *Davis v Ministry of Defence, The Times,* 7 August 1985 (CA); *Stephen v Riverside Health Authority* [1990] 1 Med LR 261 (Auld J). See further para 2.23 above.

appear unreasonable to equate 'belief' that, for example, the injuries suffered by the claimant are attributable to a particular cause with actual knowledge, particularly where the claimant is initially assured by any experts consulted that, contrary to the belief held, there is no cause of action. However, if only detailed knowledge of all the facts, following thorough investigations and verification by all the experts consulted by the claimant were accepted as 'actual knowledge', the start of the primary limitation period would be unreasonably postponed.

3.41 We suggested in the Consultation Paper[23] that the actual knowledge of the claimant should be treated as a straightforward concept, which will need to be decided according to the circumstances of any particular case, but that some guidance could be obtained from the test proposed by Brooke LJ in *Spargo v North Essex District Health Authority*.[24] We therefore proposed that:

> the courts should treat actual knowledge as a subjective concept; and a plaintiff, who so firmly believes that he or she has a significant cause of action against the defendant that he or she goes to a solicitor to seek advice about making a claim, should be regarded as having actual knowledge.[25]

3.42 This approach was supported by around sixty-five per cent of the consultees who commented on this provisional proposal. However, a difficulty with the approach, as some consultees have noted,[26] is that it suggests that the claimant who has consulted a solicitor in respect of a potential cause of action should always be held to have actual knowledge of the facts establishing that cause of action. This is too strict a test. It would require a claimant who seeks legal advice, only to be told that he does not have a claim, to be treated as having actual knowledge. However, in some cases, the fact that the claimant has started to act on his or her firm belief by seeking legal advice or commissioning an expert report is a strong indicator that the claimant should be considered to have actual knowledge of the relevant facts. All the facts of the case must be referred to, including the results of any preliminary enquiries made by the claimant. The issue remains one of fact in each case, and no general test may be prescribed. To attempt to do so confuses actual and constructive knowledge. Whether the claimant ought, in certain circumstances, to know of the facts giving rise to the cause of action is a completely separate question, relating to the claimant's constructive knowledge, which is irrelevant in terms of actual knowledge.

3.43 We also provisionally proposed in the Consultation Paper that once the claimant has actual knowledge of the relevant facts, that knowledge cannot be lost.[27] It will not be open to a claimant to argue that, although he or she had actual knowledge

---

[23] See Limitation of Actions, Consultation Paper No 151 (1998), paras 12.45 - 12.49.

[24] [1997] PIQR P235.

[25] Limitation of Actions, Consultation Paper No 151 (1998), para 12.49.

[26] And in particular the Treasury Solicitor's Department, the General Council of the Bar, and the Law Society.

[27] Limitation of Actions, Consultation Paper No 151 (1998), para 12.48.

of, for example, the cause of an injury, sufficient to start the limitation period running, the limitation period is subsequently suspended because expert investigations have later suggested that the claimant is wrong. This is the position under the current law in relation to personal injury claims.[28]

3.44 **We therefore recommend that 'actual knowledge' should not be defined in the proposed legislation and should be treated as a straightforward issue of fact which does not require elaboration.**

(5) What is meant by 'constructive knowledge'?

3.45 We provisionally proposed that the primary limitation period should start, in the absence of actual knowledge, on the date the claimant *ought* to have known the relevant facts; that is, when the claimant could be said to have constructive knowledge. This reflects the position under the current law where the claimant's date of knowledge is relevant to the start of the limitation period.[29] It increases the complexity of the definition of the date of knowledge, but provides some protection for the defendant from claimants who, for whatever reason, decide that they would rather not investigate a potential problem. To rely entirely on 'actual knowledge' as the starting point for the primary limitation period would risk allowing the claimant to choose when the limitation period starts running, by delaying any investigations necessary. It was generally accepted by consultees that the definition of the date of knowledge should make provision for the claimant's constructive knowledge.[30]

3.46 The tests adopted for the 'date of knowledge' in the Limitation Act 1963, and the Limitation Act 1975 (later the Limitation Act 1980) have always provided for a subjective element in the objective test, in the sense that the question has been what knowledge might the claimant "reasonably have been expected to acquire from facts observable or ascertainable by him; or from facts ascertainable by him with the help of medical or other appropriate expert advice which it is reasonable for him to seek".[31] The reasonable person has been treated as having the information available to the claimant, and any injuries suffered by the claimant, but the objective nature of the test has been held to require the characteristics of the claimant to be disregarded. This has led the courts, in some cases, to draw artificial distinctions between matters which should be considered to be an aspect of the claimant's situation - which may be taken into account - and characteristics of the claimant, which should be disregarded.[32]

---

[28] See *Nash v Eli Lilly & Co* [1993] 1 WLR 782, 796, *per* Purchas LJ, and Limitation of Actions, Consultation Paper No 151 (1998), para 3.57.

[29] See Limitation Act 1980, s 14(3) and 14A(10).

[30] Only two consultees disagreed, arguing that the primary limitation period should only start when the claimant has actual knowledge of the relevant facts.

[31] Limitation Act 1980, s 14(3).

[32] See the discussion in paras 2.20 - 2.22 and, for example, *O'Driscoll v Dudley Health Authority* [1998] Lloyd's Rep Med 210, where the court held that it was permissible to have regard not only to the claimant's profound physical disability, but also to the fact the claimant was

3.47 The test for constructive knowledge, as provisionally proposed in the Consultation Paper, combined both objective and subjective elements by defining constructive knowledge as "what the claimant in his or her circumstances and with his or her abilities ought to have known had he or she acted reasonably." This proposal was accepted by over fifty-five per cent of consultees. A minority of consultees (around twenty per cent) argued that taking any account of the subjective characteristics of the claimant makes the starting point of the limitation period too uncertain.

3.48 An entirely objective test for constructive knowledge, which took no account of either the claimant's characteristics or the situation in which the claimant is placed, could be devised but it is unclear how it would work. Preventing the courts from giving any consideration at all to any characteristic of the claimant (which is what would be required by a wholly objective test) runs counter to the justification for a discoverability test; that the limitation period should only start when the claimant has had a reasonable opportunity to discover the facts which give rise to the cause of action. Although all tests for the date of knowledge provide for the constructive knowledge of the claimant, the purpose of this is to fix the claimant with the knowledge he or she would have had if he or she had acted reasonably, not to fix the claimant with knowledge which he or she could not possibly have. It also creates difficulties for the courts: what resources is the reasonable person supposed to have available to carry out expert investigations? When should the reasonable person be regarded as having the knowledge available to his or her doctors? A test which is completely objective could cause considerable injustice to the claimant, without providing sufficient certainty to compensate for this. We therefore adhere to our provisional view that the test for constructive knowledge should take account of the circumstances and abilities of the claimant in order to do justice to the particular claimant.[33] In this it is different from the test for 'significance' which is less central to the starting date in a discoverability based limitation system, and, as we have discussed,[34] must make artificial assumptions if it is to be workable.

3.49 The circumstances of the claimant will be relevant to his or her constructive knowledge. The circumstances of the claimant will include the claimant's financial resources, if information could not reasonably be available to the claimant unless expensive expert or other investigations have been carried out. The abilities of the claimant will also be relevant. 'Abilities' for this purpose encompasses any capacity of the claimant which might affect the date on which he or she could be expected to know the relevant facts. Most obviously, the claimant's intellectual abilities will be relevant.[35]

heavily dependent on her parents. Similarly, in *Skitt v Khan* [1997] 8 Med LR 105, the court held that regard could be had to the deceased's financial circumstances, the gravity of the deceased's injury, and the effect that injury had on the deceased and his family.

[33] See Limitation of Actions, Consultation Paper No 151 (1998), para 12.54.

[34] See paras 3.15 - 3.33 above.

[35] It has been suggested by Andrew Smith J, that 'abilities' could be considered to include 'psychological abilities' or 'emotional abilities'. But however relevant these 'abilities' might be to a decision that it is worth starting litigation to resolve a dispute, in most cases they will not

3.50   **We recommend that the claimant should be considered to have constructive knowledge of the relevant facts when the claimant in his or her circumstances and with his or her abilities ought reasonably to have known of the relevant facts.** (Draft Bill, Cl 4(1)(a), 4(2))

(6)   Knowledge and Experts

3.51   A separate issue is the extent to which the claimant should be considered to have knowledge of information which has been - or should have been - discovered by any expert whom he or she has consulted. We noted in the Consultation Paper[36] that the present provisions on this issue, in personal injury and latent damage cases, contained in sections 14(3) and 14A(10) of the Limitation Act 1980, are extremely complex and do not always achieve fair results. We suggested that a simpler approach should be adopted. This would rely first on the rules of agency (which impute an agent's actual knowledge to the principal when the agent receives information within his or her authority to act for the principal); and, secondly, on the general test for constructive knowledge set out above (what ought the claimant, in his or her circumstances and with his or her abilities, reasonably have known).

3.52   Some consultees however did not agree that an agent's constructive knowledge would not be imputed to the principal under the law on agency, and suggested that, to avoid uncertainty, statutory guidelines are essential.[37] We also now think that it is problematic to talk of normal rules of agency in this context. The rules of agency have been developed for other reasons and it is largely a new question how they should apply to knowledge for the purposes of limitation. We discuss this further below.[38]

3.53   Two situations should be considered in relation to expert knowledge: the first is where the expert consulted has failed to discover information which is relevant and which a competent expert would have discovered or where the expert has discovered the relevant facts but has failed to pass that information to the claimant. The second is where the claimant has unreasonably failed to consult an appropriate expert.

3.54   The purpose of a starting date for the primary limitation period which is founded on 'discoverability' is to ensure that the limitation period does not start running until the claimant knows, or has a reasonable opportunity of knowing, the facts necessary to bring a claim. The interests of the claimant are paramount. The reason that the claimant's constructive knowledge is taken into account is to oblige the claimant to act with reasonable diligence, and to protect the defendant from a claimant who unreasonably fails to investigate his or her claim. It should

---

affect the claimant's capacity to appreciate information. If they do, they should be taken into account.

[36]   Limitation of Actions, Consultation Paper No 151 (1998), paras 12.50 - 12.51, 12.55 - 12.56.

[37]   In particular, Michael Lerego QC and Longmore LJ.

[38]   See paras 3.61 - 3.62.

not result in the limitation period starting at a date when a claimant, who acted entirely reasonably, did not know the facts necessary to bring a claim in respect of a cause of action.

3.55 This would suggest that where the claimant has consulted an expert, knowledge of information which the expert should have found out, but did not discover, should not be imputed to the claimant. The claimant has fulfilled his or her obligation to act reasonably to investigate the relevant facts. Unless it becomes apparent to the claimant that there is something wrong with the expert's opinion, the claimant should not be held to have knowledge of information which the expert should have discovered.

3.56 Are there any factors to displace this view? The argument for imputing the expert's knowledge to the claimant is that to fail to do so is unjust to the defendant. However, the defendant should not expect to escape his or her liability because of the negligence of a third party. The defendant will, in any event, be protected (at least for claims other than personal injury claims) by the long-stop limitation period ten years after the date of the accrual of the cause of action (or the act or omission giving rise to the cause of action where this is different).[39]

3.57 The extent to which the claimant will have a cause of action against an expert for failure either to find out the relevant information, or to inform the claimant of that information is a factor to be taken into account. Where the expert gives advice to the claimant acting as adviser rather than as an expert witness there may be a claim in negligence against that adviser. However, this will not always apply.[40] And even if the claimant has a viable claim against his or her expert, this is likely to be a less than satisfactory alternative to a claim against the defendant.

3.58 This suggests that the simplest, and certainly the most cost-effective, solution[41] is to recommend that the claimant is not regarded as having knowledge of what the expert should have discovered, or did discover, but failed to inform the claimant. This adopts the policy followed under the current law in the proviso to section 14(3) of the 1980 Act, and accords with the view suggested by the need to do

---

[39] See paras 3.99 - 3.101.

[40] Where the advice is given as part of a report destined to form part of the expert's evidence in proceedings against the defendant, the expert will benefit from the immunity accorded to such witnesses: see *Hughes v Lloyds Bank plc* [1998] PIQR P98. And there may well be cases where an expert deliberately withholds knowledge relevant to the claimant's cause of action to spare the claimant unnecessary worry. This is particularly likely to occur where the claimant consults a doctor, who diagnoses the claimant's actual condition, but does not disclose the diagnosis to protect the claimant. Evidence of this problem has been given by some of our consultees. If a doctor chooses to withhold information from the claimant for 'sound medical reasons' it is unlikely that the claimant will have a cause of action against the doctor, even if his or her cause of action against the defendant becomes time-barred.

[41] Placing reliance on the existence of a claim against the expert raises the prospect of the expert's negligence being tried twice - once by the court trying the claim against the defendant, and once by a court trying the claim against the expert. These decisions could conflict - and the costs generated by the issue of what the expert ought to have known or discovered would have increased exponentially.

justice to the claimant. It is also consistent with the subjective definition of constructive knowledge.

3.59 The position changes where the claimant has unreasonably decided not to seek expert advice. Here it is not unfair to the claimant to treat him or her as knowing the facts which an expert would have discovered if the claimant had sought expert advice. Indeed, this knowledge must be attributed to the claimant to protect the interests of the defendant in order to avoid the limitation period being artificially extended by the claimant's inaction.

3.60 **We therefore recommend that unless the claimant has acted unreasonably in not seeking advice from an expert, the claimant should not be treated as having constructive knowledge of any fact which an expert might have acquired. Where an expert has been consulted, the claimant will not be deemed to have constructive knowledge of any information which the expert either acquired, but failed to communicate to the claimant, or failed to acquire.** (Draft Bill, Cl 4(1)(b))

(7)   Agency

3.61 We suggested in the Consultation Paper that any new legislation should clarify that normal rules of agency would apply, so that an agent's knowledge of facts would be imputed to the claimant where the agent's actual knowledge of information was acquired within the agent's authority to act for the claimant.[42] Most consultees responding on this issue agreed. It was however noted that it is not necessarily clear what the normal rules are. To avoid any doubt, we propose to make express provision in the new Limitation Act that a claimant is to be taken to have knowledge of any fact of which his agent has actual knowledge, where the agent concerned is under a duty (whether express or implied) to communicate that fact to the claimant or the agent has authority to act in relation to the claim (by, for example, issuing proceedings in respect of the claim) him or herself. Unless one of these two cases apply, the knowledge of an agent will not be imputed to the claimant. In no case will the 'constructive' knowledge of agent (that is, facts which it could be argued that the agent should have known if he had acted reasonably) be imputed to the claimant.

3.62 **We therefore recommend that a claimant is to be treated as knowing any fact of which his or her agent has actual knowledge if, the agent in question**

   (1)   is under a duty to communicate that fact to the principal, or

   (2)   has authority to act in relation to the cause of action

   but if this does not apply, no person shall be treated as having knowledge of a fact merely because an agent of his has knowledge of a fact (Draft Bill, Cl 4(3)).

---

[42]   See Limitation of Actions, Consultation Paper No 151 (1998), paras 12.50 - 12.51.

(8)   Knowledge and Organisations

(a)   *The application of the 'date of knowledge' to organisations*

3.63   In the Consultation Paper we provisionally recommended that there should be specific statutory provisions setting out how the date of knowledge would apply to corporate claimants. Where the limitation period starts from the date of knowledge of the claimant, it must be clear whose knowledge is relevant for the purposes of calculating that date. Knowledge may be imputed to the organisation under the rules we recommend in relation to agents, but relying solely on this rule will not accurately reflect the information which is in practice available to the organisation. The principle that any new Act should contain specific rules setting out the circumstances in which a corporation should be considered to satisfy the test for the date of knowledge was accepted by over eighty-five per cent of consultees. Though the courts have recently become more accustomed to determining the date on which a corporate body can be considered to have knowledge for the purpose of the Limitation Act 1980,[43] we consider that the provision of specific rules will increase certainty.

3.64   This difficulty arises in the case of all corporations aggregate, and we consider therefore, that our provisions on 'corporate knowledge' should apply to all such corporations. It might at first appear that the same difficulty does not apply in the case of corporations sole, where the holder of a particular office is accorded corporate personality.[44] However, a corporation sole can in practice be the head of a large and complex organisation.[45] If the primary limitation period is only to start when the holder of the office in question has, or ought to have, the requisite knowledge, the organisation would benefit from an extended limitation period by comparison to companies and individual claimants. It is difficult to justify this.

3.65   There are also a number of bodies which have in practice been given a form of legal personality by statute for limited purposes, though they have not been incorporated (and do not therefore have full legal personality independent of their membership). In particular, and most relevantly for our purposes, a number of organisations have been given the right to bring proceedings in their own names by statute.[46] Such bodies present a similar problem to corporate bodies for a discoverability based limitation regime: a single entity will be bringing the claim, and it is necessary to identify an individual whose knowledge will be attributed to the entity for the purposes of deciding when the primary limitation period should start. The same applies to partnerships. They do not have legal personality, but

---

[43]   See paras 2.33 - 2.34 and 2.81 - 2.83 above.

[44]   *Halsbury's Laws of England* (4th ed 1998 reissue) vol 9(2) paras 1007 - 1008.

[45]   Such as some (but not all) Ministers of the Crown, the Metropolitan Police Commissioner and some, though not all, spiritual corporations sole, which include archbishops, bishops, vicars and certain other holders of office in the Church of England.

[46]   These organisations include, for example, trade unions and unincorporated employers' associations (Trade Union and Labour Relations (Consolidation) Act 1992, s 10 and s 127), and a number of Government departments (Crown Proceedings Act 1947, s 17).

they can sue and be sued in the firm name in the same way as the organisations discussed above.[47]

3.66 **We therefore recommend that our provisions in respect of 'corporate knowledge' should apply to the following 'relevant bodies': all corporations (whether bodies corporate or corporations sole), and all other bodies which have a right to sue or be sued in their own names, including Government departments which are 'authorised departments' in accordance with section 17 of the Crown Proceedings Act 1947 and partnerships.** (Draft Bill, Cl 5(2)).

(b) The test for an organisation's knowledge

3.67 We provisionally proposed a two stage test for corporate knowledge.[48] Prima facie a company or other corporation should be assumed to have the knowledge of any officer or employee. However, this assumption would be displaced if the corporation could show that the person in question had no authority to act on the information, had not communicated the information and (in the case of constructive knowledge) could not be expected to communicate the information to someone with that authority.[49] Consultees were not in agreement on the form which those rules should take, whether for actual or constructive corporate knowledge.

(i) Actual knowledge

3.68 Under the formulation set out in the Consultation Paper, the limitation period would start to run against the company (or any other relevant body) as soon as the relevant information reached an employee or officer who, if not able to take action him or herself, would be expected to pass the information on to someone with the relevant authority. This provisional proposal was supported in principle by around fifty per cent of consultees responding on this issue (subject in some cases to concerns over the drafting of the provision). However concerns were expressed that the concepts of 'expectation' and 'act on the information' are too vague to provide sufficient guidance to the courts or litigants, and that in consequence the provisions would generate substantial satellite litigation. It was suggested[50] that the definition of what counts as the corporation for the purposes of the provisions on the 'date of knowledge' is too wide; that it is unreasonable to attribute the knowledge of a junior employee to the corporation. At the same time it was suggested[51] that problems could arise in a large multi-national company, where for example, the person with authority to act on the information may be on the board

---

[47] Though this right is granted by the Rules of Court (CPR Sch 1, RSC O 81, r 1), rather than by statute, the principle is the same.

[48] See Limitation of Actions, Consultation Paper No 151 (1998), paras 12.70 - 12.87.

[49] See further Limitation of Actions, Consultation Paper No 151 (1998), paras 12.77 - 12.87.

[50] By Kim Lewison QC.

[51] By Munich Reinsurance Company and Ernst & Young.

of management at head office, so that information has to pass through several layers, giving the company an extended time limit.

3.69   Two alternatives were put forward by consultees. One proposal was that, instead of asking whether a particular employee would be 'expected' to communicate information, the question should be whether the duties of that employee would require communication of the relevant information.[52]

3.70   An alternative proposal was that only the knowledge of a company's 'directing mind' should be attributed to the company (or other corporation).[53] The difficulty with this is that it is unclear how the courts would apply the concept of a company's 'directing mind' when limitation issues are raised. The authorities were reconsidered by the Privy Council in *Meridian Global Funds Management v Securities Commission*.[54] Lord Hoffmann stated that "the rule of attribution is a matter of interpretation or construction of the relevant substantive rule", and "It is a question of construction in each case as to whether the particular rule requires that the knowledge that an act has been done, or the state of mind with which it was done, should be attributed to the company."[55]

3.71   As we noted in the Consultation Paper, this does not provide any certainty as to who in a corporate hierarchy should be regarded as the person whose knowledge is to be attributed to the company.[56]

3.72   In addition, it would be unreasonable to prevent the primary limitation period starting to run against a corporation or similar organisation until information reaches its controllers. Such a body would have a longer limitation period than an individual, particularly in the case of a large company, or a multi-national grouping with a complicated corporate structure. It is also seems artificial to say that a corporation (or any similar organisation) does not yet know the relevant facts where information has been received by an employee of the corporation who is under a duty to report that information to the management, or who would be expected to pass that information on.

3.73   We consider, therefore, that, largely in line with what we provisionally proposed in the Consultation Paper, a relevant body should be deemed to have the actual knowledge of the people who meet the following descriptions:

(1)   First, an officer of the relevant body or a person with authority to take decisions in relation to the claim on behalf of the organisation. For these purposes, "the decisions in relation to the claim" would mean (a) a

---

[52]   By Michael Lerego QC.

[53]   Favoured by the Treasury Solicitor's Department.

[54]   [1995] 2 AC 500.

[55]   [1995] 2 AC 500, 507, 511.

[56]   Limitation of Actions, Consultation Paper No 151 (1998), para 12.75, citing PL Davies, *Gower's Principles of Modern Company Law* (6th ed 1997), p 231.

decision to seek legal advice in relation to the cause of action and (b) a decision whether or not to issue proceedings in relation to the claim.

(2)   Secondly, any employee of the organisation who is under a duty to communicate the relevant information either to someone having the relevant authority or any other employee of the organisation.

(ii)   Constructive knowledge

3.74   The issues arising in the case of constructive knowledge for organisations are very similar,[57] and our recommended approach is analogous. That is, the basic approach would be to ask when either

(1)   any officer of the relevant body or a person with authority to take the relevant decisions, or

(2)   an employee of the relevant body who is under a duty to disclose that information to someone with that authority or to any other employee

ought reasonably to have known of the relevant facts.

3.75   However, the application of this is less straightforward than with regard to actual knowledge. As noted in the Consultation Paper,[58] there are two possible situations where it could be said that someone in the relevant class ought reasonably to have the information. In the first situation, it may be possible to identify someone who has failed to make the reasonable enquiries. In the second situation, it is not possible to identify any one person as being at fault: the organisation does not have the information because its procedures are deficient.

3.76   The first situation is less complicated. In relation to any relevant information, the court will need to consider whether one or more identified people, who fall within the two classes described above, should be regarded as having constructive knowledge of that information. The test is the same as for any individual claimant, and simply requires an examination of the sources of information available to the relevant person.

3.77   The second situation is more complex. No one within the organisation can be identified as being at fault - the information was not collected because the organisation did not have the relevant structures in place to ensure that this was done. We suggested in the Consultation Paper that taking account of what can be termed 'structural constructive knowledge' for a company, for example, would require the court to assess the management structures of the company concerned by reference to the structures of a 'reasonable' company of the same type. The same would apply to other relevant bodies. This would necessarily involve costs wholly disproportionate to any benefit which might be gained from including that 'knowledge' within the definition of the date of knowledge. Over eighty per cent of

---

[57]   Fifty-six per cent of consultees responding on this issue approved the provisional proposal.

[58]   See Limitation of Actions, Consultation Paper No 151 (1998), paras 12.84 - 12.87.

consultees agreed that no provision should be made for structural constructive knowledge. The corollary is that it may in some cases be true that a poorly managed, inefficient organisation is at an advantage as regards limitation by comparison with a organisation with better management structures. This drew criticism from Andrew Smith J, the City of London Law Society Litigation Sub-Committee[59] and the SPTL Contract and Commercial Law Panel. However, we adhere to the view, supported by a majority of consultees, that, as Stuart Brown QC noted:

> The incorporation of 'structural constructive knowledge' would inevitably lead to massive costs in investigating peripheral issues in a limited number of cases.

3.78 **We recommend that a relevant body should be considered to have actual or constructive knowledge when that knowledge is imputed to the body under our recommendations in relation to agency, or when**

>   (1) **an officer of the body (including a partner in the case of a partnership), or a person with authority to take the relevant decisions on its behalf; or**

>   (2) **an employee of the relevant body who is under a duty to disclose that information to someone with that authority or to any other employee**

has that knowledge. For these purposes, decisions in relation to the claim are (a) a decision to seek legal advice in relation to the claim and (b) a decision whether or not to issue proceedings in relation to the claim. (Draft Bill, Cl 5(1), 5(3) and 5(5)).

(c) Concealment of information by a person whose knowledge would be attributable to the organisation

3.79 We provisionally proposed in the Consultation Paper[60] that there should be an exception to the general rule where the company (which we would now extend to cover any relevant body) is suing one of its employees or officers and the defendant has concealed information from the organisation, or in other words, has concealed it from a person in the organisation whose knowledge would be attributed to the organisation under our recommendations in paragraph 3.78 above. In that case, we proposed that the knowledge of the defendant in question should not count as the knowledge of the organisation. This proposal was supported by over ninety per cent of consultees responding on this issue. However, it was pointed out[61] that it does not go far enough. There may be cases in which an organisation has decided not to sue one of its own employees, perhaps

---

[59] Though Lindsay Marr, a member of the sub-committee, expressed a different view on this issue.

[60] Limitation of Actions, Consultation Paper No 151 (1998), para 12.83.

[61] By, in particular, Kim Lewison QC, Lovells and the Law Society.

because the employee does not have the resources to satisfy any judgment. However, that employee may have information which is relevant to the cause of action, which he or she has concealed from the organisation. We are of the view that it would be equally unreasonable to attribute the knowledge of such an employee to the organisation. The exception should extend to all cases where the employee in question is a defendant to a claim by the organisation, or is guilty of dishonest concealment of facts relevant to the cause of action.

3.80 **We recommend that where an officer of the body, or a person with authority to act on the information on behalf of the relevant body, or any employee of the relevant body who is under a duty to communicate that information to a person with that authority or another employee**

> (1) **is a defendant to the claim of the relevant body; or**

> (2) **has dishonestly concealed information relevant to that claim from someone whose knowledge would be attributed to the relevant body under the rule set out in paragraph 3.78 above**

that person's knowledge shall not be regarded as the knowledge of the relevant body. (Draft Bill, Cl 5(4), (5)).

(9) Joint claimants

3.81 In a number of cases, more than one claimant may be joined in the same proceedings against the defendant. This does not present a difficulty where, though all the causes of action arise out of the same events, each claimant is pursuing a claim against the defendant on his or her own behalf. For example, several claimants may have been injured in the same accident as a consequence of the defendant's negligent driving. The cause of action accruing to each claimant will be subject to a separate limitation period whether that claimant joins in proceedings against the defendant or pursues separate proceedings against the defendant. The only knowledge relevant for the purpose of calculating the start of the primary limitation period is the knowledge of the claimant in question.

3.82 There are two other possibilities. The claimants may be jointly and severally entitled to the remedy sought (as where two or more creditors seek to recover a debt to which they are jointly and severally entitled). Alternatively, they may simply be jointly entitled to the remedy sought.

3.83 Where a claimant is suing on a joint and several obligation owed to him, he is entitled to bring the claim without joining the other claimants who are jointly entitled.[62] In addition, if the claimant dies, the benefit of the several promise will pass to his estate (and not to the other joint claimants). The position is therefore in many respects similar to the case where there is more than one claimant with a wholly separate interest in the claim. It therefore seems appropriate that only the

---

[62] *Catlin v Cyprus Finance Corporation (London) Ltd* [1983] QB 759.

knowledge of the particular claimant should be relevant in deciding when the primary limitation period for his claim starts.

3.84   Where there is only a joint entitlement to the remedy, it could be argued that the position is different. Under the Civil Procedure Rules where a claim is brought by two or more claimants who are jointly entitled to the same remedy, all persons jointly entitled to a remedy claimed by the claimant must be parties to the claim unless the court orders otherwise.[63] When a joint claimant dies, the rules on survivorship ensure that the right of action vests in the surviving joint claimants, not in the estate of the deceased.[64]

3.85   However, under the current law, joint claimants are for a number of purposes treated individually by the law on limitation periods. It has in the past been held that the fact that one of a number of joint claimants is under a disability does not serve to extend the limitation period for the claim in question as far as the other claimants are concerned, on the grounds that they are in a position to protect their interests by bringing proceedings.[65] Equally, an acknowledgment made to one of a number of joint claimants will only benefit that claimant and his successors, rather than anyone else entitled to claim on the debt.[66]

3.86   Following (and extending) the current approach holds a number of advantages. If joint claimants are treated separately, so that the primary limitation period only starts to run against a claimant when that claimant has the necessary knowledge, irrespective of the knowledge of the other claimants, there will be no risk that one claimant could prejudice the position of the others by discovering the necessary information and deciding to take no action. In practice, it is likely that each of the joint claimants will have knowledge of the relevant facts at the same time - and it should be said that, in those cases where this is not the case, the approach we recommend will not benefit the defendant, as he or she will remain liable on the claim until each of the joint claimants has been become time-barred.

3.87   **We therefore recommend that where a claim is brought by two or more claimants who are jointly entitled to the remedy sought, the start of the primary limitation period shall be calculated separately for each claimant, by reference to the knowledge of that claimant. A defence may only be raised against those claimants against whom the primary limitation period has expired.** (Draft Bill, Cl 6(1), (2)).

3.88   A similar issue may arise where it is necessary for more than one claimant to be joined in the proceedings as representatives for the entity entitled to the benefit of the cause of action. In most representative claims, proceedings may be brought on

---

[63]   CPR, r 19.3(1), which re-enacts RSC, r 15.4(2).

[64]   *Attwood v Rattenbury* (1822) CP 6 Moore 579; 23 RR 633.

[65]   *Perry v Jackson* (1792) 4 TR 516.

[66]   See Limitation Act 1980, s 31(6). A different rule is followed in relation to part payments under s 31(7).

behalf of the interested third party by a single claimant. For example, a derivative claim may be brought by a single shareholder on behalf of a company.[67]

3.89 Where, in contrast, a claim can only be brought by two or more claimants on behalf of the relevant entity, the same question arises as with joint claimants: whose knowledge is to trigger the primary limitation period? The classic example is where there are two or more personal representatives for a deceased's estate. All must join in bringing any claim on behalf of the estate (such as a claim under the Law Reform (Miscellaneous) Provisions Act 1934).[68] Similarly, where there are two or more trustees, all must join in bringing proceedings on behalf of the beneficiaries of a trust (unless the trust is of a public or charitable nature).[69] It does not appear to be appropriate to follow the rule we suggest above: the personal representatives acting on behalf of the deceased's estate are bringing a claim in respect of a single cause of action which is vested in another person (and because of the nature of their duties it can be expected that any information relevant to a potential claim will soon become known to each one). The same applies to the trustees. It should therefore be governed by a single limitation period.

3.90 Where the cause of action in question is a claim under the 1934 Act in relation to the personal injuries of the deceased, section 11(7) (and 11A(7)) of the Limitation Act 1980) provides that the limitation period should start from the earliest 'date of knowledge' of the personal representatives. We propose to adopt the same solution. This will only apply where proceedings must be brought by more than one representative for those entitled to the remedy sought.

3.91 **We therefore recommend that where a claim must be brought by two or more claimants acting as trustees or personal representatives, the primary limitation period in respect of that claim should start from the earliest date on which one of the trustees or personal representatives has actual or constructive knowledge of the relevant facts. (Draft Bill, Cl 6(3), (4)).**

(10) Assignments

3.92 In some cases the cause of action may have accrued to someone other than the claimant, and then have been assigned to the claimant. Where the primary limitation period did not start before the date of the assignment because the assignor had no knowledge of the relevant facts few difficulties will arise. In some cases the claimant may have acquired knowledge of the relevant facts before the date of the assignment. However, it would seem unreasonable for that knowledge to trigger the primary limitation period before the claimant also has the right to bring a claim in respect of the cause of action. This problem has arisen under the

---

[67] The issues arising in connection with derivative actions are discussed at paras 4.205 - 4.210 below.

[68] *Latch v Latch* (1875) LR 10 Ch 464.

[69] *Luke v South Kensington Hotel Co* (1879) 11 ChD 121, Supreme Court Practice 1999, 15/14/3.

current law in relation to claims for latent damage not involving personal injuries: section 14A(5) of the 1980 Act provides that the limitation period should start from the date on which the claimant had both the knowledge required for bringing a claim and a right to bring such a claim. We consider that the same rule should apply under the regime we propose.

3.93 The primary limitation period may have started before the date of the assignment. In this case, if the only knowledge taken into account is to be that of the claimant, he or she would in practice receive an extension of the limitation period. If the primary limitation period had ended before the date of the assignment, a defence would have accrued to the defendant. It is hard to justify either allowing the claimant an extended limitation period or removing the defendant's accrued defence simply because there has been an assignment (which could lead to assignments motivated purely to avoid the expiry of a limitation period). It will therefore be necessary to consider both the knowledge of the claimant and the knowledge of any person in whom the right to make a claim was previously vested in order to determine whether the primary limitation period has started to run.

3.94 **We recommend that where a cause of action has been assigned to the claimant:**

(1) **the expiry of the primary limitation period in relation to a claim by any person in whom the cause of action was vested before the claimant will give rise to a defence (Draft Bill, Cl 7(2));**

(2) **where the primary limitation period had started to run in relation to a claim by any person in whom the cause of action was vested before it was assigned to the claimant because that person acquired the relevant knowledge at the time when he or she had the right to bring a claim, it will continue to run against the claimant (Draft Bill, Cl 7(3),(6));**

(3) **where the primary limitation period has not started to run before the date of the assignment it will run from the later of**

(a) **the date of the assignment and**

(b) **the date of knowledge of the claimant (Draft Bill, Cl 7(4)).**

3. HOW LONG SHOULD THE PRIMARY LIMITATION PERIOD BE?

3.95 The majority of consultees (over seventy per cent) agreed that there should be a uniform primary limitation period which applies, as far as possible, to all causes of action, to ensure greater certainty and simplification of the present law.[70] The Munich Reinsurance Company noted:

> This can only lead to greater certainty and simplification of the current law. In addition it will remove the incentive which plaintiffs

---

[70] See Limitation of Actions, Consultation Paper No 151 (1998), paras 12.88 - 12.89.

currently have to try to bring their right of action within one category rather than another. The current law, especially in relation to the different limitation periods for actions in contract and, for example, unintentional personal injury in tort, cannot be rationally defended.

3.96 We proposed in the Consultation Paper that this period should be three years.[71] This has the benefit of familiarity, as it is the period used in personal injury claims and claims under the Consumer Protection Act 1987, and is the period (calculated from the date of knowledge) which in latent damage cases serves as an alternative to the limitation period of six years from the accrual of the cause of action.[72] The limitation period chosen needs to provide sufficient time for claimants to consider their position once the facts are known, take legal advice, investigate the claim and negotiate a settlement with the defendant, where this is possible. At the same time it should not be so long that the claimant is able to delay unreasonably in issuing proceedings. Experience in this jurisdiction in relation to these claims suggests that the three year period provides sufficient time for the claimant to bring a claim in the vast majority of cases. A majority of consultees (around sixty per cent) supported a primary limitation period of three years.

3.97 It has been suggested that a three year limitation period would create unacceptable problems for patent claims in relation to patents granted in the European Patent Office, as opposition proceedings before that office are notoriously slow, and for liquidators. Although we recognise that there may be difficulties in bringing a claim in respect of a European patent, one solution may be for anyone with such a cause of action to bring proceedings, and apply to have them stayed pending resolution of any opposition proceedings before the European Patent Office. This alone would not therefore appear to be sufficient reason to choose a longer limitation period. The application of the core regime in cases where the nominal claimant has gone into liquidation, and there is a liquidator acting on its behalf, is discussed below.[73]

3.98 **We recommend that the primary limitation period applying under the core regime should be three years.** (Draft Bill, Cl 1(1)).

4. THE LONG-STOP LIMITATION PERIOD

(1) Should there be a long-stop limitation period?

3.99 We provisionally proposed in the Consultation Paper that the core regime should include a long-stop limitation period of ten years applicable to all claims other than for personal injury, and that personal injury claims should be subject to a long-stop limitation period of thirty years.[74] The expiry of the long-stop period will bar a claim even where the primary limitation period has not expired because

---

[71] See Limitation of Actions, Consultation Paper No 151 (1998), paras 12.90 - 12.95.

[72] See the Limitation Act 1980, ss 11, 11A and 14A.

[73] See Part IV, paras 4.242 - 4.248 below.

[74] See Limitation of Actions, Consultation Paper No 151 (1998), paras 12.97 - 12.113.

the claimant does not have knowledge of the relevant facts. Under the current law, a long-stop limitation period applies to negligence claims for latent damage not relating to personal injuries, and to claims under the Consumer Protection Act 1987.[75] In contrast, no long-stop limitation period applies to negligence claims in respect of personal injuries (though where the cause of action is for trespass to the person, the knowledge based limitation period applicable under section 11 of the Limitation Act 1980 does not apply, and such claims are in effect therefore subject to a long-stop limitation period of six years).[76]

(a) Claims other than for personal injuries

3.100 Our proposal that there should be a long-stop limitation period of ten years applying to claims unrelated to personal injuries attracted significant support. Excluding those consultees who only expressed a view in relation to personal injury claims (over forty per cent of the total), over eighty-five per cent of consultees responding on this question supported the proposal that there should be a long-stop in relation to claims unrelated to personal injury. A key concern is the need to protect defendants from claims being brought at a date so long after the events to which the claim relates that defendants are no longer properly able to defend themselves. We noted in the Consultation Paper that where a claim is brought after many years there may be a risk of serious injustice to the defendant, as witnesses may no longer be available, and any documentary evidence may have been lost or destroyed.[77] Moreover, defendants are entitled to some limit on their need to insure themselves against liability. The imposition of a long-stop also compensates for the loss of certainty which is inherent in the adoption of a limitation regime dependent on the date of knowledge of the relevant facts by the claimant. This is particularly important in the case of those causes of action which have previously been subject to a limitation period starting from a fixed point, namely the accrual of the cause of action (the most notable example being claims for breach of contract).

3.101 **We recommend that a claim, other than in respect of a personal injury, should be subject to a long-stop limitation period of ten years.** (Draft Bill, Cl 1(2)).

(b) Personal injury claims

3.102 Different considerations apply in relation to personal injury claims, and, despite the arguments cited above, we are minded to exempt such claims from the long-stop limitation period we recommend. Our provisional proposal that there should be a long-stop limitation period in personal injury claims was rejected by around fifty-five per cent of consultees. The major concern at the suggestion that a long-stop should apply to personal injury claims was that this would be unjust to claimants suffering from latent diseases, where the disease in question does not manifest itself within the long-stop period. Claims for asbestos-related disease

---

[75] See Limitation Act 1980, ss 11A(3) and 14B.

[76] See *Stubbings v Webb* [1993] AC 498.

[77] See Limitation of Actions, Consultation Paper No 151 (1998), paras 12.98 - 12.101.

present particular problems. The latency period for mesothelioma, a cancer of the lining of the lung caused by exposure to asbestos, can be anything between fifteen and sixty years, and we have been informed by consultees who are consultant physicians practising in asbestosis-related disease that the median latency period is over thirty years.[78] Thus, a long-stop limitation period of thirty years would prevent most claimants suffering from mesothelioma from recovering damages for that disease. We have also been informed that the incidence of asbestos-related disease is increasing, and is expected to continue to do so for at least the next twenty-five years.

3.103   Some consultees also expressed concern that imposing a long-stop in personal injury cases could unjustifiably bar claims being made by victims of sexual abuse. There are a growing number of cases in which victims are now coming forward to testify about abuse which took place in the 1970's and early 1980's (as the evidence presented to the enquiry chaired by Sir Ronald Waterhouse into child abuse in local authority homes in North Wales demonstrates very clearly),[79] who have not reported the abuse before because of the traumatic memories this would revive. Victims of such abuse frequently need time to recover sufficiently from the trauma consequent upon the abuse to be able to contemplate bringing a claim against their abusers. It could also be argued that the public interest in protecting the defendant from stale claims, and in ensuring that there is an end to litigation, does not apply where the defendant has been guilty of sexual abuse (which could be considered to make the case for exempting such claims from the long-stop limitation period even stronger than is the case for other personal injury claims such as for asbestosis).[80]

3.104   In the light of this evidence, it is clear that the period of thirty years which we provisionally proposed is too short. Increasing the length of the long-stop would not guarantee that all claimants with latent disease claims are covered, while making the long-stop too long to serve any useful purpose. We have considered

---

[78]   We have been referred to BP Lanphear and CR Buncher "Latent Period for Malignant Mesothelioma of Occupational Origin" (1992) 34 JOM 718 - 721, which, on the basis of a study of literature documenting 1105 cases of mesothelioma, found a median latency period of thirty-two years.

[79]   See Lost in Care: Report of the Tribunal of Inquiry into the abuse of children in care in the former county council areas of Gwynedd and Clwyd since 1974 (1999 - 2000) HC 201.

[80]   See the arguments of La Forest J in the Canadian case of *KM v HM* (1992) 96 DLR (4th) 289, 302. It has also been suggested that there is more need for a limitation period to protect defendants in sexual abuse cases, because of the possibility that the claim may stem from "recovered memory syndrome" where claimants do not suspect that they may have suffered child abuse until memories of that abuse emerge on prompting, often during therapy. It is been alleged with some force that such memories are wholly unreliable (see S Brandon, J Boakes, D Glaser and R Green "Recovered Memories of Childhood Sexual Abuse" (1998) 172 Br J Psychiatry 296 - 307). The prospects of such claims causes organisations such as the British False Memory Society considerable concern. However, the task of distinguishing between genuine and mistaken claimants in cases of sexual abuse must be one for the courts, not the limitations regime, and, given that there are well documented cases where the victims of such abuse have been unable to bring actions against their abusers for several years, the risk that some claims might be false cannot be used as the sole justification for having a long-stop limitation period for personal injury claims.

whether it would be possible to modify the application of the long-stop limitation period, by providing that it should be disapplied in cases where the claimant's claim relates to personal injury, and the claimant was not diagnosed as suffering from that injury until a date less than three years before proceedings were issued. This proposal would protect personal injury claimants where they do not know of their injury at the end of the long-stop limitation period (but not where the primary limitation period has not expired because they do not know one of the other relevant facts). The claim would in such a case be governed only by the primary limitation period. This proposal attracted the support of several of those consultees who objected to a personal injury long-stop because of the potential injustice in respect of asbestos-related claims. However, we have concluded that it would increase the complexity of the core regime without necessarily providing any compensating advantages, particularly in the light of our revised proposals (discussed below) in relation to a judicial discretion to disapply the limitation period in personal injury claims.[81]

3.105 We noted in the Consultation Paper that the lack of any long-stop limitation period has caused significant difficulties, particularly where the claimant is of unsound mind, and thus potentially indefinitely under a disability. Without the long-stop, no limitation period would apply to such claimants, so that claims could still be brought years, if not decades, after the events giving rise to the cause of action.[82] However these problems only affect a small number of personal injury claims. In the light of the concerns which have been expressed by consultees at the suggestion that any long-stop limitation period should apply to personal injury claims, we discuss below how the unlimited protection which is available to the claimant under a disability under the current law may be reduced if a long-stop is not imposed on all personal injury claims.[83] We therefore consider that the long-stop limitation period should not apply in the case of personal injury claims.

3.106 For the purposes of our limitations regime, we propose to adopt the definition of personal injuries which is given in section 38(1) of the Limitation Act 1980: "'personal injuries' includes any disease and any impairment or a person's physical or mental condition."[84] In contrast to section 11 of the Limitation Act 1980 we refer to "personal injury claims" and not to claims which "include damages in respect of personal injuries to the plaintiff or any other person". The disapplication of the long-stop is, in our view, appropriate only in respect of personal injury claims (which can be regarded as claims for the most serious type of harm).[85] One should focus separately on, for example, claims in respect of

---

[81] See paras 3.156 - 3.169 below.

[82] This problems is illustrated by cases such as *Headford v Bristol & District Health Authority*, [1995] PIQR P180 and *Turner v WH Malcolm Ltd* (1992) 15 BMLR 40 which we highlighted in the Consultation Paper (at para 12.142, n 212). See further paras 3.127 - 3.128 below.

[83] See paras 3.127 - 3.133 below.

[84] See paras 2.14 - 2.18 above, for a discussion of cases on what amounts to 'personal injury' under the current definition.

[85] The same applies to other modifications to the core regime which we recommend for personal injury claims. See para 3.160 below.

personal injury and claims in respect of property damage and should not apply this (or any other similar) modification of the core regime to property damage claims merely because they are claimed in the same proceedings as a personal injury claim. Nor do we believe that it is necessary to refer to "any other person". This has been interpreted to allow an employer the advantage of the limitation regime for personal injury claims for a claim against a supplier of equipment (which has injured an employee) for an indemnity in respect of damages paid by the employer to the employee.[86]

3.107 **We recommend that no long-stop limitation period should be applied to claims in respect of personal injuries to the claimant (or, in the case of an action brought under the Law Reform (Miscellaneous Provisions) Act 1934 or the Fatal Accidents Act 1976, to the deceased).** (Draft Bill, Cl 9).

(2)   When should the long-stop limitation period start?

3.108 Under the current law, the long-stop limitation period provided for in relation to latent damage claims start from the date of the act or omission which is alleged to constitute negligence. Similarly, the long-stop limitation period for Consumer Protection Act claims starts from the date of the act giving rise to the claim under the Act.[87] In the Consultation Paper we provisionally proposed that the long-stop limitation period under the core regime should run from the date of the act or omission (or statement) of the defendant which gives rise to the cause of action. A substantial majority of consultees responding on this issue supported our proposal. The date of the act or omission giving rise to the cause of action has the advantage that it is easier to ascertain than the date on which the claimant suffers loss. The disadvantage is that in some cases loss is an essential element of the cause of action and there is therefore no cause of action until the claimant has suffered loss, which may be some time after the date of the act or omission giving rise to the cause of action.

3.109 It has been suggested that where there have been a number of acts or omissions by the defendant, it may be difficult to identify which act or omission "gives rise to the cause of action". To minimise this difficulty we consider that our provisional proposal should be changed so that, as a general rule, the long-stop limitation period will start on the date of the accrual of the cause of action. When loss is not an essential element of the cause of action, the date on which the cause of action accrues will in most cases be the date of the act or omission which gives rise to the cause of action. The courts will, however, be able to draw on the guidance of the current law as to when a cause of action accrues to identify this date. To avoid the need to ascertain precisely when the claimant has suffered injury loss or other damage, there will be an exception to the general rule for those causes of action in tort and breach of statutory duty where loss is an essential element of the cause of action. Here, in line with our provisional proposal, the starting date for the long-stop limitation period will be the date of the act or omission giving rise to the cause of action.

---

[86]   See *Howe v David Brown Tractors (Retail) Ltd* [1991] 4 All ER 30.

[87]   See para 2.36 above.

3.110   It has also been suggested by the Association of Personal Injury Lawyers that it could be difficult to determine the date of the act or omission giving rise to the cause of action, particularly where the cause of action depends on an omission by the defendant, rather than a positive act. This type of problem can also occur under the current law where the limitation period starts from the date of the accrual of the cause of action. The courts have held that where the claimant relies on an omission by the defendant, the cause of action accrues on the latest date on which the defendant was under a duty to the claimant to act.[88] The same principle would apply where the starting point for the long-stop limitation period is calculated from the date of the act or omission. Where the defendant is under a continuing duty to perform, but fails to do so, there would be a fresh omission on each day on which he or she failed to perform. For limitation purposes the long-stop limitation period would start on the latest day on which the defendant should have performed the relevant act. The position is the same where the claimant's cause of action is founded on a continuing act by the defendant. In practice, a fresh cause of action will accrue on each day the act continues, and a new long-stop limitation period will start in respect of that cause of action. When, in contrast, the cause of action is only complete when there has been a series of acts or omissions, the long-stop limitation period will start from the date of the last act (or omission) necessary to complete the cause of action.

3.111   We asked consultees whether there should be a special starting point for the long-stop limitation period in the case of construction-related claims. We suggested that, in such cases, the date of the act or omission could be defined as the 'date of completion' of the construction works. The arguments are finely balanced. It is in this area where the claimant is particularly likely to have concurrent claims in both contract and tort. The starting date for the long-stop limitation period under our proposals in relation to contract claims will be the date on which the cause of action accrues. In relation to tort, it will be the date of the act or omission giving rise to the cause of action. Depending on the nature of the breach of duty alleged, the starting date may be different for each type of claim, and there may be some uncertainty as to the relevant date. Providing for a separate starting point for all construction related claims would avoid this problem and increase certainty. In addition, it has been argued that in the absence of such a provision, it would be impossible to sue sub-contractors involved early on in a long project, as any negligence in their work may well only come to light when the building was finished. Most construction liability claims relate, by their nature, to latent damage.

3.112   Against a separate starting point for construction-related claims it has been argued that it would be wrong to ring-fence a particular industry: it is not a principled approach, and would risk creating anomalies. Further the legal problems faced by the construction industry are said to be common to the whole law. Some consultees also pointed out that it would be difficult to identify when the completion of the works took place, that sub-contractors involved early on in a

---

[88]   See *Midland Bank v Hett, Stubbs & Kemp* [1979] Ch 384; *Bell v Peter Browne & Co* [1990] 3 All ER 124.

project would be subject to a considerably extended limitation period, and that considerable hardship would be caused to the professionals involved, in terms of increased insurance costs. In addition, it will be possible for the parties concerned to reach an express agreement extending the limitation period applying to claims in relation to a particular project if necessary. We are not convinced that the additional complexity which would be caused by a separate regime for construction-related claims would be justified by the benefits it would bring.

3.113 **We recommend that the long-stop limitation period should, as a general rule, start to run from the date on which the cause of action accrues, but that there should be an exception for those claims in tort where injury, loss or damage is an essential element of the cause of action and for claims for breach of statutory duty. In these cases, the long-stop limitation period will start to run from the date of the act or omission that gives rise to the cause of action.** (Draft Bill, Cl 3).

5. FACTORS EXTENDING OR EXCLUDING THE LIMITATION PERIODS

(1) Disability

3.114 Under the current law, 'disability' extends the limitation period in two situations: where the claimant is a minor, and where the claimant is of unsound mind, in the sense of being incapable of managing property and affairs by reason of mental disorder.[89] We shall deal with each in turn.

(a) Minority

(i) Minority and the primary limitation period

3.115 Two questions arise here: first, should the primary limitation period be extended for minors who have no-one to act on their behalf, and secondly, should the existence of an adult able to act for the minor make any difference? In relation to the first question, we provisionally proposed that disability, including minority, should extend a primary limitation period so that the period starts to run only when the claimant's disability has ceased.[90] So, where the claimant is a minor, the primary limitation period would only start to run when the claimant reached the age of eighteen. In some cases, the justification for this flows naturally from the adoption of a date of knowledge test: a minor below a certain age may be incapable of having actual or constructive knowledge. Although this will not be true in all cases, preserving the general rule protects all minors while they are unable to bring proceedings on their own behalf, and prevents further disputes between the parties as to the age at which the minor could properly 'know' the relevant facts. Over eighty-five per cent of consultees supported this proposal,

[89] See paras 2.78 - 2.79 above. 'Mental disorder' is defined according to the Mental Health Act 1983, s 1(2) as "mental illness, arrested or incomplete development of mind, psychopathic disorder and any other disorder or disability of mind". "Psychopathic disorder" is defined as "a persistent disorder or disability of mind (whether or not including significant impairment of intelligence) which results in abnormally aggressive or seriously irresponsible conduct on the part of the person concerned".

[90] See Limitation of Actions, Consultation Paper No 151 (1998), para 12.115.

which we now confirm as a final recommendation. It means (coupled with our recommendation on the operation of the long-stop limitation period where the claimant is a minor)[91] that a minor with a cause of action will have at least until the age of twenty-one to bring proceedings in respect of that cause of action.

3.116　We did not express a provisional view on the second question, but asked consultees whether a limitation period should run against a person under a disability who has a representative adult capable of bringing proceedings on his or her behalf (except where the claim is against the representative).[92] Such a provision was included in the Limitation Act 1939, but, as we noted in the Consultation Paper, that rule was found to have a number of defects. The Law Reform Committee which examined the rule in its report on limitation periods in claims for personal injury suggested that the basic assumption underlying the rule, namely that where the minor is "in the charge of a competent adult, that adult can be trusted to seek legal advice and, if appropriate, to institute legal proceedings on his behalf" can be questioned.[93] On the recommendation of the Law Reform Committee the rule was repealed by section 2 of the Limitation Act 1975.

3.117　A majority of consultees responding on this issue were of the opinion that time should not run against a minor even though there is a representative adult, so that the interests of the minor are fully protected. There was concern that if time was to run, the minor would inevitably suffer, as appears to have been the case when a 'representative adult' provision was included in the Limitation Act 1939.[94] Wherever the minor has a representative adult who is conscious of his or her responsibilities, and willing and able to take action, it is likely that proceedings will be issued on behalf of the child promptly even under the current law. The only practical effect of providing that time runs where there is a representative adult would be to penalise those minors where the representative adult is negligent. **We therefore do not recommend any rule to the effect that time should run against a minor where there is a representative adult.**[95]

(ii)　Minority and the long-stop limitation period

3.118　Although we have recommended that no long-stop limitation period should apply to personal injury claims,[96] we have recommended a ten year long-stop limitation period for all other claims. This would apply if, for example, a minor suffers damage to property or, perhaps more relevantly, where there was a breach of trust in relation to assets held on trust for the minor. The question which we must now

---

[91]　See para 3.121 below.

[92]　See Limitation of Actions, Consultation Paper No 151 (1998), paras 12.129 - 12.136.

[93]　Law Reform Committee, *Twentieth Report (Interim Report on Limitation of Actions: in Personal Injury Claims)* (1974) Cmnd 5630, para 108.

[94]　See the Law Reform Committee, *Twentieth Report (Interim Report on Limitation of Actions: in Personal Injury Claims)* (1974) Cmnd 5630, para 107 - 109.

[95]　Although, as we shall see below, we do make use of the 'representative adult' in relation to adult disability where there is no necessary end to the disability.

[96]　See paras 3.102 - 3.107 above.

address, therefore, is whether minority should override a long-stop. There are two opposing arguments. It could be said that it is unduly harsh for the minor to lose his or her cause of action before he or she is regarded as having the capacity fully to understand it, and to bring proceedings on his or her own behalf. The opposing argument is that there is an interest in preventing claims in respect of stale claims, regardless of the identity of the claimant.

3.119 We provisionally proposed[97] three alternative options to consultees on this issue:

(1) Option 1: Minority should override a long-stop (so that for any act or omission committed during the claimant's minority the ten year long-stop limitation period would not commence until the claimant was eighteen).

(2) Option 2: Minority should not override a long-stop (so that a ten year long-stop would potentially bar a non-personal injury claim even though the claimant is a minor).

(3) Option 3: There should be a special long-stop for minors which would end on the later of two dates:

(a) the date the claimant reached the age of twenty-one, or

(b) the date the long-stop would have ended in the absence of disability.

3.120 Over sixty per cent of consultees favoured option three. We agree. It is best expressed by saying that any long-stop limitation period shall run but not so as to bar a claim before the claimant has reached the age of twenty-one. This allows the minor a reasonable chance to bring proceedings on reaching majority. It avoids over-protecting the claimant (as the first option would do, by allowing the minor a further ten years on reaching majority). It also avoids under-protecting the claimant, which would be the result of adopting the second option, which could time-bar a claimant who had not reached majority.

3.121 **We therefore recommend that:**

During the period when the claimant lacks capacity because he or she is under the age of eighteen

(a)   the primary limitation period shall not run;

(b)   any long-stop limitation period shall run but will end on the later of the following dates:

(i)   the date on which the claimant reaches the age of twenty-one; or

---

[97] See Limitation of Actions, Consultation Paper No 151 (1998), para 12.143 - 12.144.

(ii) **the date ten years after the starting date for the long-stop limitation period.** (Draft Bill, Cl 28).

(b) *Adult disability*

(i) *The effect of adult disability*

3.122 We provisionally proposed that disability should extend a primary limitation period so that the period starts to run only when the claimant's disability has ceased.[98] As we have seen in relation to minority,[99] over eighty-five per cent of consultees agreed with this; and its justification can be regarded as flowing naturally from the adoption of a 'date of knowledge' test. We further provisionally recommended that adult disability (where in contrast to minority there is no necessary end to the disability) should not override a long-stop.[100] Over seventy per cent of consultees responding on this issue agreed. As regards claims other than personal injury claims, we now confirm these provisional proposals as final recommendations.[101]

(ii) *The definition of adult disability*

3.123 In the Consultation Paper we provisionally proposed that the definition of adult disability should focus on lack of capacity, rather than only mental disability;[102] and that this 'lack of capacity' should be defined (as we had defined it in our Report on Mental Incapacity)[103] as follows:

> A person is without capacity if at the material time:
>
> (a) he or she is unable by reason of mental disability to make a decision for himself on the matter in question or
>
> (b) he or she is unable to communicate his [or her] decision on that matter because he or she is unconscious or for any other reason.
>
> 'Mental disability' for the purposes of this definition is "a disability or disorder of the mind or brain, whether permanent or temporary, which results in an impairment or disturbance of mental functioning."

3.124 This definition ensures that claimants will be protected both in the case where they are unable to appreciate or to remember the facts relevant to the claim because of their disability, and where the nature of the disability is such that,

---

[98] Limitation of Actions, Consultation Paper No 151 (1998), para 12.115.

[99] See para 3.115 above.

[100] Limitation of Actions, Consultation Paper No 151 (1998), para 12.142.

[101] Different issues arise in relation to personal injury claims, where we have proposed that there should not be any long-stop limitation period, and we discuss these below. See paras 3.126 - 3.132 below.

[102] Limitation of Actions, Consultation Paper No 151 (1998), paras 12.123 - 12.125.

[103] Mental Incapacity (1995) Law Com No 231, clause 2 of the Draft Bill annexed to that Report.

although aware of the facts, they are unable to reach any decision in relation to the claim. This proposal was accepted by a large majority of our consultees, and we now confirm it as a final recommendation, subject to a clarification to ensure that "inability to communicate" only extends to inability which is due to mental disability or physical impairment (such as unconsciousness).[104]

3.125 Consultees were also asked in the Consultation Paper whether the definition of 'disability' should make specific provision for the psychological incapacity suffered by victims of sexual abuse.[105] The majority (over seventy-five per cent) of those consultees who expressed an opinion on this point were against such a provision. It was noted that it would be very difficult to define this incapacity. There is also considerable controversy as to whether there exists a single 'sexual abuse syndrome' with identified symptoms.[106] **We therefore recommend that there should be no specific provision for the psychological incapacity suffered by victims of sexual abuse.[107]**

(iii) Supervening disability

3.126 Under the current law, the claimant does not receive the benefit of an extension of the limitation period where he or she suffers from a disability which commences after the cause of action accrues.[108] Over eighty-five per cent of consultees agreed with the provisional proposal made in the Consultation Paper that the claimant under a disability should be protected by an extension of the limitation period both where the lack of capacity exists when the cause of action arose, and when it develops some time later.[109] We now confirm this as a final recommendation. The primary limitation period will be suspended from the date of the onset of the claimant's lack of capacity (subject to the proposals discussed in paragraphs 3.130 to 3.133 below). Should the claimant recover capacity the primary limitation period will continue to run from the point at which it was suspended, so that the claimant has the benefit of the unexpired part of the limitation period.

(iv) Should there be a limit to the protection given to adults under a disability in personal injury cases?

3.127 The position in relation to personal injury claims is complicated by our abandonment of a long-stop limitation period. To recommend that time does not run where the claimant lacks capacity would mean that in contrast to minority (where the incapacity has a definite end, namely when the claimant reaches the

---

[104] It was pointed out by Professor Andrew Tettenborn that without this clarification a claimant who had chosen to put himself physically beyond communication would benefit from an extension to the limitation period applying to his claim.

[105] Limitation of Actions, Consultation Paper No 151 (1998), para 12.125.

[106] See J Mosher, "Challenging Limitation Periods: Civil Claims by Adult Survivors of Incest" (1994) 44 U of Toronto LJ 169, 214.

[107] We discuss the problems posed for the limitations regime by claims in relation to sexual abuse in paras 3.162 and 4.23 - 4.33 below.

[108] See *Purnell v Roche* [1927] 2 Ch 142.

[109] See Limitation of Actions, Consultation Paper No 151 (1998), paras 12.126 - 12.128.

age of eighteen) there could be an indefinite suspension of the primary limitation period, so that the claimant is in practice not subject to a limitation period.

3.128   This problem already arises under the present law and is one of the current problems in limitation law that we were hoping to solve in this project.[110] For example, in *Headford v Bristol and District Health Authority*[111] proceedings were started on behalf of a claimant (who had suffered brain damage at birth) twenty-eight years after the birth, despite the fact that the parents, who brought the proceedings, were aware that there were grounds for a claim within a few months of the birth. No reasons were given for this delay.[112]

3.129   This has given rise to significant criticism of the unlimited protection the present law allows claimants who remain under a permanent disability. Ralph Gibson LJ commented in *Headford v Bristol and District Health Authority*[113] that the present state of the law in which there is no long-stop limitation in the case of persons under a disability, "seems to call for consideration in the light of cases such as this".[114] Professor Michael Jones suggests in his article "Limitation Periods and Plaintiffs under a Disability - a Zealous Protection?"[115] that the protection given to disabled claimants is haphazard, and some disabled claimants receive too much protection under the present law.[116]

3.130   For personal injury claims, we now therefore recommend a new solution which draws first on an analogy with the ten year long-stop in non-personal injury claims; and secondly, on the fact that in most cases a person without capacity over more than a short period of time will be in the care of an adult who is able to act on his or her behalf. Although we recommend that in personal injury cases the primary limitation period should not run against a claimant who lacks capacity, that protection will only last for a period of ten years from the date on which the cause of action accrues or, if later, the onset of the lack of capacity. After ten years have passed, provided that there is a representative adult able to act for the

---

[110]   See Limitation of Actions, Consultation Paper No 151 (1998), para 12.142, and nn 212 and 213.

[111]   [1995] PIQR P180.

[112]   The extended protection given to claimants under a disability has also caused difficulties where the proceedings have been issued, but the claimant's representatives have been dilatory in bringing them to trial. In *Tolley v Morris* [1979] 1 WLR 205 the claimant was injured in a road traffic accident as a child. The case was eventually tried over fifteen years after the accident. The House of Lords noted that as the claimant would be able to issue a fresh writ until the limitation period expired, no useful purpose would be served by dismissing the action for want of prosecution. See also *Turner v WH Malcolm Ltd* (1992) 15 BMLR 40.

[113]   [1995] PIQR P180.

[114]   [1995] PIQR P180, P185.

[115]   (1995) 14 CJQ 258.

[116]   It should also noted that the present law does impose a long-stop (of ten years) on personal injuries where the injury is caused by a defective product (Limitation Act 1980, s 11A(3)), applicable even where the claimant is under a disability - see s 28(7)). Further, though perhaps less relevant, s 28(4) imposes a long-stop of thirty years for claimants under a disability in the case of an action to recover land or money charged on land.

claimant, the primary limitation period will run against the claimant when the representative adult has the required knowledge. Any time that has already elapsed in the limitation period (where for example the claimant knew or ought to have known the facts relevant to the cause of action before the onset of the lack of capacity, so triggering the primary limitation period at an earlier date) will be disregarded.

3.131 The representative adult for these purposes will be the member of the claimant's family who is responsible for the day to day care of the claimant, or a person who is authorised under Part VII of the Mental Health Act 1983 to conduct proceedings in the name of the claimant. If there is no-one who falls into either of these categories at the end of the ten year period, the claimant will continue to be protected. It is unlikely that a claimant who lacks capacity, and does not recover, could ever have either actual or constructive knowledge sufficient to start the primary limitation period. Further, if the cause of action is against the representative adult him or herself, that person's knowledge will not be considered in deciding whether the primary limitation period has started. There may therefore still be some cases in which a claimant who lacks capacity is able to bring a claim in respect of his or her cause of action many years after the events which gave rise to the cause of action, but this should be exceptional.[117] An example may help to illustrate the effect of our proposals. Q, aged twenty-six, was involved in a car accident, caused by the negligence of R, as a result of which he suffers brain damage. He is treated in hospital for five years, and then is cared for at his mother's home. Because of his disability, he is unable to appreciate the facts giving rise to his claim, and thus (being unable to take any decision regarding the claim as a result of mental disability) is under a disability. The primary limitation period for his personal injury will not run for at least ten years after the accident while he is under a disability. As his mother is responsible for his day-to-day care at that date she is the "responsible adult", and her knowledge is relevant to the test for the 'date of knowledge'. She learnt all the relevant facts within a year of the accident. The primary limitation period in respect of Q's claim will therefore start running immediately on the date ten years after Q suffered brain damage (in this case, the date of the accident).

3.132 Though with this proposal we are departing from the approach we have adopted in relation to minority, where we have recommended that the existence of a representative adult is not sufficient reason to allow the limitation period to run against the claimant, we believe this to be justified. The problems caused by the unlimited protection given to claimants under a disability do not arise in relation to minority, where there is a natural term to the potential extension of the limitation period which the minor can claim. And our proposal ensures that the claimant under a disability will benefit from absolute protection for at least ten years from the starting date (considerably longer than would be the case if no protection was given to a child in the custody of an adult).

---

[117] In some cases, the claimant may both be a minor and otherwise lack capacity. In such cases, the claimant will remain protected under our recommendations in respect of minority until majority. Where the claimant reaches majority before the end of the ten year 'protection period', he or she will continue to be protected by that period.

3.133 We therefore recommend that:

(1) During the period when a claimant over eighteen lacks capacity because he or she is unable by reason of mental disability to make a decision for him or herself on the matters in question, or he or she is unable to communicate his or her decision on that matter because of mental disability or physical impairment (Draft Bill, Cl 29(6)):

  (a) subject to sub-paragraph (c) below, the primary limitation period should not run. (Draft Bill, Cl 29(2))

    This will apply whether the lack of capacity exists on the date when the cause of action accrues (so that the primary limitation period does not start running), or develops after that date (suspending the primary limitation period after it has begun to run). When the claimant regains capacity, the primary limitation period will continue to run from the point at which it was suspended, so that the claimant has the benefit of the unexpired part of the limitation period;

  (b) in claims which are not related to personal injuries, a long-stop limitation period should run;

  (c) in personal injury cases, after a period of ten years from the accrual of the cause of action or, if later, from the onset of the lack of capacity, the primary limitation period should run but with the knowledge of the claimant's Representative Adult regarded as the knowledge of the claimant, except where the cause of action is against the Representative Adult. Where the claimant was a minor at the end of the ten year period, the primary limitation period shall not run by reference to the knowledge of the Representative Adult until the claimant's majority. (Draft Bill, Cl 29(3), (4) and (5)).

(2) 'Mental disability' for the purposes of this definition is defined as 'a disability or disorder of the mind or brain, whether permanent or temporary, which results in an impairment or disturbance of mental functioning'. (Draft Bill, Cl 29(7)).

(3) A person is a Representative Adult if he or she is the member of the claimant's family who is responsible for the day to day care of the claimant, or a person who is authorised under Part VII of the Mental Health Act 1983 to conduct proceedings in the name of the claimant. (Draft Bill, Cl 29(8)).

(2) Concealment

(a) The meaning of 'concealment'

3.134 We provisionally proposed in the Consultation Paper that for there to be 'concealment' for limitation purposes, the defendant must conceal the relevant facts intending the claimant not to discover the truth or reckless as to whether the claimant discovers the truth or not.[118] We did not regard this test as differing from the position with regard to 'deliberate concealment' under the current law. Though it was accepted by the majority of consultees (over seventy per cent of consultees agreed with our provisional proposals on concealment), two consultees[119] have expressed concern that it could penalise defendants where the nature of the work done by the defendant is such that any negligence would inevitably be covered up in the ordinary course of that work even where no concealment was intended. This is a particular difficulty in the construction industry: as a house is being built, work done on the foundations of the house must inevitably be covered up to enable the rest of the building to be completed. Inevitably this will conceal any negligent work on the foundations (for example, the builder may have given the house foundations which are too shallow to support it). However, far from intending to conceal the facts from the claimant, the builder may not appreciate that he or she has been negligent. In this instance, it has been suggested to us that it would be unfair to the defendant to allow the claimant the benefit of a longer limitation period on the grounds of 'concealment'.

3.135 In addition, since the publication of the Consultation Paper, the concept of 'deliberate concealment' seems to have been extended by *Brocklesby v Armitage & Guest*[120] and *Liverpool Roman Catholic Archdiocese Trustees Inc v Goldberg.*[121] It was suggested in the latter case that the claimants could benefit from the extension of the limitation period under section 32 even where the claimants are aware at all times of all the facts giving rise to the cause of action.[122] This gives the claimant far more protection than was ever intended by the concept of "deliberate concealment", and penalises the defendant even though he cannot be said to be in any way culpable for the 'concealment'.

3.136 In removing the need for any 'unconscionable conduct' by the defendant, *Brocklesby v Armitage & Guest* and *Cave v Robinson Jarvis and Rolf* ignore the rationale of section 32, which is that the defendant should not be able to profit from his own behaviour in concealing facts relevant to the claimant's claim.[123] In addition, the courts have failed to consider the fact that section 32 is only intended to protect the claimant until the date when he or she could with reasonable diligence have discovered the concealed facts, when time starts running

---

[118] Paras 12.151 - 12.153, Limitation of Actions, Consultation Paper No 151 (1998).

[119] IN Duncan Wallace QC and the Construction Industry Council.

[120] [2001] 1 All ER 172. See the discussion in paras 2.84 - 2.88 above.

[121] [2001] 1 All ER 182. See also *Cave v Robinson Jarvis & Rolf* [2001] EWCA Civ 245, (unreported) 20 February 2001, discussed in para 2.88 above.

[122] See para 2.87 above.

[123] See *Sheldon v Outhwaite* [1996] 1 AC 102, 145 *per* Lord Browne-Wilkinson.

again. In *Liverpool Archdiocese Trustees v Goldberg* Laddie J found that the claimants were aware of the facts relevant to their right of action. Section 32 should not therefore have had any affect on the limitation period, even assuming that there had been any 'concealment' within the meaning of section 32(2). It has been suggested that the courts have been guilty of "a travesty of statutory interpretation".[124]

3.137 We are of the view that our proposals in relation to 'concealment' should only apply where the defendant has been guilty of 'unconscionable conduct' - or in other words, if the concealment can be said to be 'dishonest'. The claimant will have to demonstrate two things before being able to claim the benefit of our provisions. First the claimant must show that the defendant has concealed one of the facts the claimant must know to trigger the primary limitation period. The defendant will, under our proposals, be taken to have 'concealed' information from the claimant where he has taken any action which has the result that the claimant has failed to discover that information for some time, or if he has failed to disclose information to the claimant in breach of a duty to do so. Secondly, the claimant must show that the defendant was being dishonest in doing so. We do not consider that the concealment could be described as 'dishonest' unless the person concealing it is aware of what is being concealed and does not wish the claimant to discover it. This requirement is intended to restore the need for the claimant to demonstrate some unconscionable behaviour or impropriety on the part of the defendant before the claimant may benefit from an extension of the limitation period. Thus, by covering up shallow foundations the builder has 'concealed' them for the purposes of our test. However, the builder cannot be said to have been guilty of 'dishonest concealment' unless he was aware that his work was defective or negligent, and does not want the claimant to discover this. Equally, a lawyer who has given negligent advice, but is not aware of having done so, cannot be said solely on this ground to have been guilty of 'dishonest concealment', even if the circumstances are such that the claimant does not discover the negligence for some time.

(b)   Concealment and the primary limitation period

3.138 We suggested in the Consultation Paper that the adoption of a 'date of knowledge' starting point for the core regime would make deliberate (or dishonest) concealment irrelevant to the primary limitation period.[125] We adhere to that position. However, we have thought carefully about the following argument: where the defendant has concealed any of the relevant facts from the claimant, no account should be taken of the constructive knowledge of the claimant in

---

[124] C Nasir, "Deliberate Concealment and the Limitation Act", (2000) New LJ 1526 - 1528. See also J O'Sullivan, "Intentional Acts, Breaches of Duty and the Limitation Act - A Warning for Negligent Professionals" (2000) 16 PN 241 - 251.

[125] Limitation of Actions, Consultation Paper No 151 (1998), paras 12.146 - 12.147. Our recommendation that the primary limitation period should start from the date of knowledge makes the distinction between initial and subsequent concealment largely irrelevant; and in consequence the unsatisfactory decision in *Sheldon v Outhwaite (Underwriting Agencies) Ltd* [1996] AC 102 (discussed in Limitation of Actions, Consultation Paper No 151 (1998), paras 8.17 - 8.20, and 12.146 - 12.147) is nullified.

determining the date of knowledge, because concealment on the part of the defendant can be said to outweigh any 'fault' of the claimant in not investigating the potential cause of action. According to this argument, therefore, such concealment should mean that the primary limitation period runs from the date on which the claimant has actual knowledge of the relevant facts, and constructive knowledge is irrelevant.

3.139 However, the purpose of including the claimant's constructive knowledge in the definition of the date of knowledge is not only to protect the defendant but also to ensure that the claimant has an incentive not to delay unreasonably in bringing proceedings. We are not convinced that the fact that the defendant has concealed information from the claimant should allow the claimant a longer limitation period where the relevant information is available to the claimant either because the defendant's efforts at concealment were not wholly effective or because there is some other source from which the claimant should reasonably have obtained the relevant information. The fact that information has been concealed from the claimant will be taken into account in deciding when the claimant should have known of the relevant facts. Our conclusion is that no further protection is needed for the claimant, and that the date of knowledge should not exclude constructive knowledge where the defendant has been guilty of concealment.

(c)   Concealment and the long-stop limitation period

3.140 We provisionally proposed in the Consultation Paper that the long-stop limitation period would not apply where the defendant has concealed any of the facts relevant to the test for the 'date of knowledge' from the claimant:[126] but in the absence of such concealment the long-stop limitation period should apply where the cause of action rests on the mistake of the claimant or the fraud of the defendant. A majority of consultees responding on this point agreed that the long-stop limitation period should not apply where there has been any concealment by the defendant. We are therefore confirmed in our original view that the long-stop limitation period should not run where the defendant has been guilty of dishonest concealment. Time should only start running from the date on which the claimant knows, or ought to know the relevant facts, both where the primary limitation period applies to the claim and where it does not (because the claim in question is subject to a modified version of the core regime under our provisions, or because the parties have themselves agreed to disapply the primary limitation period). We therefore propose to suspend the long-stop limitation period (or agreed limitation period) applicable to the claim where the facts have been dishonestly concealed.

3.141 We propose to extend the category of people who are able to rely on the dishonest concealment of the defendant (or his or her agent) to extend the long-stop limitation period. Section 32 of the Limitation Act 1980, does not extend the limitation period for any claimant who claims through the person from whom the facts were originally concealed. In contrast, section 32(1) does provide that concealment by any person through whom the defendant claims is sufficient to extend time as against the defendant. We propose to retain this provision, and in

---

[126] See Limitation of Actions, Consultation Paper No 151 (1998), para 12.154.

addition to ensure that the claimant claiming through a person from whom the facts were originally concealed is protected. Similarly, where the defendant conceals the facts relevant to a claim in respect of defective property, and that property is then sold, we consider that the purchaser (who has the benefit of a new cause of action accruing on the date of his purchase under section 3 of the Latent Damage Act 1986) should also be able to rely on that concealment to extend the long-stop limitation period applying to his claim against the defendant. This is subject to the same starting date as the claim which originally accrued to the seller.

3.142   We propose to retain the protection given to innocent third parties by section 32(3) of the 1980 Act. Under this provision the limitation period applying to a claim to recover property (or its value), or to set aside a charge against the property (or any other transaction affecting it), against a bona fide purchaser for value is not extended where there has been deliberate concealment provided that the purchaser was not party to the concealment and had not reason to believe that it had taken place. If this provision is not re-enacted, an innocent third party would be penalised by the removal of the protection afforded to them by the long-stop limitation period for something he or she had had no part in. This seems unreasonable.

(d) The long-stop limitation period and claims for fraud

3.143   Under the current law, where a claim is "based upon the fraud of the defendant", the limitation period only starts to run when the claimant has discovered the fraud.[127] Our proposal that the long-stop limitation period should apply in claims of fraud has proved controversial. John Grace QC noted

> Fraud should be treated seriously by the law, and it is fundamentally wrong that a Defendant should be able to get away, or think that he can get away, with fraud after any period, and the fact that so many cases of fraud also involve deliberate concealment is not a good reason for the Commission's provisional view in this regard.

3.144   However, we adhere to our provisional view that, absent concealment by the defendant, the long-stop limitation period should apply even where the cause of action is for fraud. Our reasoning is that the limitation regime should only be modified to take account of factors which affect the operation of the regime. Where there has been concealment by the defendant, the actions of the defendant have prevented the primary limitation period operating; and, similarly, the concealment means that, because the claimant has no chance to discover the relevant facts, it would also be unjust to apply the long-stop limitation period to bar the claim. In the unlikely event that a defendant who is guilty of fraud has not concealed information from the claimant, by act or omission, the claimant who is the victim of fraud is not at a disadvantage in discovering the facts relevant to his or her cause of action by comparison with any other claimant.

---

[127]   Limitation Act 1980, s 32(1)(a). See paras 2.80 - 2.83 above.

3.145   We recommend that:

(1)   where:

(a)   the defendant or any person through whom the defendant claims (or any of their agents) has concealed any of the relevant facts from the claimant or any person through whom he claims (or any of their agents) (whether before or after the cause of action has accrued) and

(b)   the concealment was dishonest

the long-stop limitation period or any limitation period agreed between the parties should be suspended from the date on which the fact was concealed until the date on which it was discovered (or should have been discovered) by the claimant (or any person through whom he or she claims) (Draft Bill, Cl 26(1), (2), (4));

(2)   the defendant will be regarded as concealing a fact from the claimant

(a)   if the defendant takes any action, or is a party to any action the effect of which is to prevent the claimant discovering that fact for some time, or

(b)   if the defendant fails to disclose that fact to the claimant in breach of a duty to do so (Draft Bill, Cl 26(6));

(3)   the long-stop limitation period applying to a claim by the purchaser of defective property will be extended where the defendant has dishonestly concealed the relevant facts from the seller of that property (Draft Bill, Cl 26(3));

(4)   the long-stop limitation period applying to a claim against a bona fide purchaser of property to recover that property (or its value) or to enforce a charge (or set aside a transaction) affecting it will not be extended by dishonest concealment if

(a)   the purchase took place after the concealment and

(b)   the purchaser was not party to the concealment and had no reason to suppose that it had taken place. (Draft Bill, Cl 26(5)).

(3)   Acknowledgments and Part Payments

3.146   We provisionally proposed in the Consultation Paper that an acknowledgment or part payment should continue to restart a limitation period in relation to, at least, the same claims for which this is presently the law,[128] and, further, that the law should be extended so that acknowledgments and part payments should start time running again for all claims, whether the amount claimed by the claimant is specified or unspecified.[129] These proposals were accepted by the vast majority of consultees (over ninety per cent of consultees agreed with the first proposition, and around eighty-five per cent agreed with the second proposition).

3.147 However, it has been suggested by some consultees[130] that in some cases there might be practical difficulties in extending the principle to claims for unspecified amounts. Where the amount claimed is not specified, there could be greater difficulties in identifying an acknowledgment, and insurers might be inhibited in making a reasonable assessment of the insured's liability by the thought that their correspondence could be construed as an acknowledgment sufficient to restart the limitation period.

3.148 There does not appear to be any reason in principle to distinguish between claims for specified amounts and claims for unspecified amounts, and the suggested difficulties do not appear to be insuperable. The question "what constitutes an acknowledgment?" has in the past given rise to a number of problems of interpretation, which the courts have been able to resolve.[131] Extending the principle to claims for unspecified amounts should not give rise to significantly greater problems of interpretation.

3.149 We provisionally proposed that the requirement that an acknowledgment must be in writing if it is to restart a limitation period should remain. It may be the case that some insurers are likely to choose their words more carefully in correspondence with claimants' representatives. However this in itself is insufficient reason to maintain the present anomalous distinction between claims for specified amounts and claims for unspecified amounts. We do not propose to retain the requirement that the acknowledgment should be signed by the defendant, as this would unnecessarily limit the documents which could serve as 'acknowledgments'. This change will enable bank statements, for example, to serve as acknowledgments. Requiring a signature is also unnecessary to protect the interests of the defendant as the claimant must still demonstrate that the acknowledgment has been made by the defendant. The requirement that the acknowledgment must be in writing (accepted by over eighty-five per cent of consultees) considerably reduces the scope for uncertainty.

3.150 We noted in the Consultation Paper[132] that the New Zealand Law Commission had recommended that the principle that a part payment or acknowledgment

---

[128] That is, in respect of claims for a specified amount (previously known as a liquidated pecuniary claim); a claim to the personal estate of a deceased; claims to recover land and claims in respect of mortgages (see paras 2.91 - 2.92 above).

[129] Limitation of Actions, Consultation Paper No 151 (1998), paras 12.155 - 12.167.

[130] A member of the Council of Her Majesty's Circuit Judges and Henriques J (responding on behalf of the Northern Circuit).

[131] See the cases cited in paras 8.33 to 8.35 of the Consultation Paper.

[132] See para 12.157, Limitation of Actions, Consultation Paper No 151 (1998).

should restart the limitation period should be extended to claims for unspecified amounts. However, the Commission suggested that an additional requirement should apply: the claimant must show that he or she had relied on the acknowledgment or part payment. Our provisional view was that this requirement is inappropriate.[133] This was supported by all those consultees who expressed an opinion on this point, on the grounds that this would introduce an undesirable element of uncertainty and inconsistency.

3.151   Under the current law, where a number of people are liable in respect of the same debt or liability for any other specified amount, an acknowledgment made by one of them will bind only the acknowledgor, so that the others may continue to benefit from the running of the limitation period.[134] However, where one of those liable makes a part payment in respect of the debt or other claim, all those liable are bound by that payment, and in consequence subject to a new limitation period, running from the time of the part payment.[135] We noted in the Consultation Paper that this distinction introduces additional complexity into this area of the law.[136] The change[137] from the uniform treatment which had previously been given to acknowledgments and part payments was justified on the basis that as all the co-debtors would receive the benefit of the part payment, it was right that they should also suffer the burden. We took the view that it would be more beneficial to increase the level of uniformity in this area of the law, and we provisionally proposed that, subject to the special rules applying to mortgages and for possession of land, only the acknowledgor or the person making the part payment should be bound by the acknowledgment or part payment. This proposal was accepted by over ninety-five per cent of consultees responding on this issue, and we propose to adopt this as a final recommendation though we will extend the exception to cover acknowledgments made by trustees and personal representatives.[138] Similarly, where there are two or more joint (or joint and several) claimants and an acknowledgment is made to one or more of them (but not to all), we consider that the limitation period should only be extended for the benefit of the person to whom the acknowledgment is given and not for the benefit of the other joint claimants, except in the case of trustees and personal representatives. We also propose to clarify the position of the purchaser of defective property who has a cause of action dating from his or her purchase of the property under the provisions of section 3 of the Latent Damage Act 1986. Under the current law it is not clear whether the purchaser is able to rely on an acknowledgment which has been made by the defendant to the previous owner of

---

[133]   Limitation of Actions, Consultation Paper No 151 (1998), para 12.157.

[134]   Limitation Act 1980, s 31(6). See Limitation of Actions, Consultation Paper No 151 (1998), paras 8.44 - 8.48.

[135]   Limitation Act, s 31(7).

[136]   Limitation of Actions, Consultation Paper No 151 (1998), paras 12.168 - 169.

[137]   Introduced by the Limitation Act 1939 on the recommendation of the Law Revision Committee, *Fifth Interim Report (Statutes of Limitation)* (1936) Cmd 5334, para 21.

[138]   In line with the approach we recommend in paras 3.89 - 3.91 in the context of joint claims made by trustees and personal representatives.

the property. We consider that the purchaser should be able to rely on any such acknowledgment.

3.152   We will retain the provisions of section 30(2) of the Limitation Act 1980, whereby an acknowledgment or part payment made by an agent will bind the principal (and equally that a principal can rely on an acknowledgment or part payment made to his or her agent). Equally, an acknowledgment will continue to bind the successors of the person making it, and it may also be relied on by the successors of the person to whom it was made.

3.153   We provisionally proposed that there should be no reform of the law to enable an acknowledgment or part payment to revive a cause of action once a limitation period had expired.[139] Over eighty-five per cent of consultees responding on this issue agreed. We left open the question whether a contract could be effective to revive a party's rights even when those rights would otherwise have been extinguished by the operation of the law of limitation.[140] There was a consensus (reflected in the views of over ninety per cent of the consultees who responded on this point) that a contract, and in particular a contractual compromise of litigation, should be effective to revive a party's rights when those rights would otherwise have been extinguished by the expiry of the relevant limitation period.

3.154   An agreement containing an acknowledgment can be distinguished from an acknowledgment per se. The agreement is likely to be a compromise of litigation and there is a clear public interest in recognising and giving effect to compromises of litigation, which arguably outweighs the conflicting public interest in enforcing the original limitation period. It was noted that the party entering into such an arrangement and making the acknowledgment would be likely to have the benefit of legal advice, which would minimise the risk of prejudice to that party.[141]

3.155   **We recommend that:**

(1)   **a written acknowledgment or a part payment, by the defendant (or someone previously liable to the claim), and irrespective of the nature of the claim, should restart the running of time for both the primary and long-stop limitation periods applying to the claim. This applies whether the acknowledgment or payment was made before or after the cause of action accrued (Draft Bill, Cl 27(1),(7)(8);**

(2)   **a written acknowledgment or a part payment should not be effective to revive a cause of action once the primary or long-stop limitation period has expired (Draft Bill, Cl 27(1)(c));**

---

[139]   Limitation of Actions, Consultation Paper No 151 (1998), para 12.177.

[140]   Limitation of Actions, Consultation Paper No 151 (1998), paras 12.178 - 12.181.

[141]   And, as Professor Andrew Tettenborn noted, the acknowledgor may be able to sue his or her advisor in any case where prejudice had been suffered.

(3) subject to special rules applying to mortgages and for the possession of land (and in the case of trustees and personal representatives), only the acknowledgor, the person making the part payment or the principal of the agent giving the acknowledgment or making the part payment, and his or her successors, should be bound by the acknowledgment or part payment (Draft Bill, Cl 27(2), (4), (5), (9));

(4) similarly, where an acknowledgment or part payment is made to one or more of a number of joint (or joint and several) claimants (who are not trustees or personal representatives), only the person (or persons) to whom it is made may rely on it to extend the limitation period (Draft Bill, Cl 27(3), (4));

(5) where the purchaser of defective property has a cause of action under section 3 of the Latent Damage Act 1986, an acknowledgment made by the defendant to the previous owner of that property in relation to the original cause of action will also extend the limitation period apply to a claim brought by the purchaser against the defendant (Draft Bill, Cl 27(6));

(6) as under the present law, the acknowledgment shall be valid only if made to the person, or to the agent of the person, whose title or claim is being acknowledged or in respect of whose claim the payment is being made. (Draft Bill, Cl 27(1), (9)).

6. A JUDICIAL DISCRETION?

(1) A General Discretion?

3.156 Under the current law, the court has a discretion to disapply the limitation period in claims in respect of personal injuries and claims for defamation.[142] The question whether there should be a judicial discretion to disapply the limitation period under our regime (whether the primary limitation period, the long-stop limitation period or both) proved to be one of the most controversial areas of our proposals. In the Consultation Paper, we took the provisional view that the disadvantages of allowing the courts a discretion to disapply a limitation period (whether the primary limitation period or the long-stop limitation period) outweighed the advantages.[143] Those consultees responding on this issue have been divided equally between those in favour of a discretion, and those who agreed with our provisional view that the discretion available under the current law has caused significant uncertainty, and costs, and that it should be abolished. The majority of those consultees who disagreed with our proposals were particularly concerned at the possible consequences for personal injuries claims.

---

[142] See paras 2.13 and 2.37 above.

[143] See Limitation of Actions, Consultation Paper No 151 (1998), paras 12.187 - 12.196.

3.157   The chief merit of a judicial discretion is that it allows the judge to take account of the individual circumstances of a particular case: the judge is not restricted to the application of a general rule. The judge can therefore prevent injustice to an individual claimant where that claimant has failed to issue proceedings within the limitation period applicable to his or her cause of action for excusable reasons.

3.158   However, this must be balanced against the risk of injustice to the defendant, in allowing a claim outside the limitation period. And the disadvantage of any discretion is that it produces uncertainty, on two counts. First, defendants can never have the certainty that, after the expiry of a fixed period of time, no claim can be brought in respect of a past event. They must face potential liability for an indefinite period, with all the associated costs (such as the cost of maintaining indemnity insurance for a prolonged period and retaining records). Secondly, additional uncertainty will result from the exercise of the discretion. It is impossible to ensure consistency in the application of a discretion. The decision taken by the judge will depend more on the judge's perception of the facts of the case than on the interpretation of the applicable rule of law. Different judges may well reach a different decision on cases with similar facts.[144] This produces inconsistency and may give rise to unfairness: the decision in a particular case may depend on which judge hears the case. The only way in which this can be controlled is through the appellate courts. However the exercise of a discretion is an area where the higher courts are rarely willing to intervene. Further, the Court of Appeal has refused to lay down general guidelines for the application of the section 33 discretion.[145] We have received conflicting evidence from consultees on the issue whether it is possible to predict the outcome of an application to the court to disapply the limitation period under the discretion given in cases of personal injury under section 33. Some practitioners suggest that it is possible to give reasonably accurate advice to litigants on this issue. Others maintain that claimants are encouraged to make applications to the court where the prospects of success, if not completely hopeless, fall well below fifty per cent.

3.159   This level of uncertainty would not be acceptable as part of the core regime applying to all claims (as the process of consultation has made clear: only fifteen per cent of consultees responding on this issue favoured a general discretion). Justice for the individual claimant may come at the cost of increased uncertainty for claimants in general, their advisers, and other parties who need to be able to rely on the certainty which could be provided by a limitation period. For this reason we do not propose to extend the discretion available under the current law to claims which do not involve personal injuries.

---

[144] This has been recognised by the Court of Appeal in a number of cases where members of the court have noted that, though they themselves might well have decided the case differently, it is not appropriate to overturn the exercise of the discretion by the first instance judge. See, for example *Farthing v North Essex HA* [1998] Lloyd's Rep Med 37, *Hammond v West Lancashire HA* [1998] Lloyd's Rep Med 146, *Coad v Cornwall & Isles of Scilly HA* [1997] 1 WLR 189.

[145] *Harrison v Allerdale DC* (unreported, 19 April 1989); *Hartley v Birmingham City District Council* [1992] 2 All ER 213.

(2)   A Discretion in Personal Injury Claims?

3.160   This leaves the question whether the court should have a discretion to disapply the limitation period in personal injury claims. Those consultees favouring a discretion have expressed most concern in relation to personal injury claims. Of those who favoured a judicial discretion to disapply the limitation periods (around forty-five per cent of consultees responding on this issue), approximately two-thirds argued for the retention of the judicial discretion to disapply the limitation period only for claims relating to personal injuries, as opposed to around fifteen per cent who suggested that there should be a more general discretion. It was argued that the ability to take account of the circumstances of a particular case is more important in personal injuries cases than other claims. The claimant who has suffered a personal injury can justifiably be said to have suffered a more extreme form of harm than the claimant with a claim relating to property damage or economic loss. The loss of the opportunity to bring proceedings against the defendant because of the expiry of a limitation period is therefore, in general terms, more serious for a claimant with a personal injury claim than any other claimant. There is therefore an argument for giving the court, in personal injury claims, but not in other cases, the power to disapply the limitation period in exceptional circumstances, depending on the merits of a particular claim.

3.161   An additional factor to be considered is the fact that, on the recommendation of the Law Reform Committee,[146] a discretion was introduced for personal injury claims in the Limitation Act 1975. That discretion, now contained in section 33 of the Limitation Act 1980 has therefore been available to the courts for over twenty years, and is well established. It is difficult to turn the clock back.

3.162   We are also concerned that our proposals would not operate fairly for all sexual abuse claims unless there is a discretion. We discuss below whether any limitation period should apply to claims in respect of child sexual abuse. Our conclusion is that the standard limitation period for personal injury claims should apply. In any case where the claimant has been physically injured by the abuse the facts giving rise to the cause of action, the identity of the perpetrator and the fact that it is worth bringing proceedings in respect of the claim will be clear to the victim as soon as the abuse has been committed - or very soon after it. But on that basis, the core regime is likely in many cases to reduce the time available to child sexual abuse claimants from six years from majority (the limitation period applying to claims for trespass to the person under the current law) to three years from majority. The six year period which the claimant has to bring a claim for trespass to the person under the current law has been criticised as inadequate. It is argued that sexual abuse claimants require far longer periods to accept what has been done to them, and to recover sufficiently from the trauma to be able to consider bringing proceedings. Under our proposals, however, the claimant will, in many cases, only have three years from majority to bring a claim. We are therefore of the

---

[146]   The Law Reform Committee assumed that it would only apply in "a residual class of cases": *Twentieth Report (Interim Report on Limitation of Actions: in Personal Injury Claims)* (1974) Cmnd 5630, para 56.

view that, in these cases, the court should have a discretion to disapply the limitation period where the court finds that it is unjust not to do so.

3.163 We noted above that the central argument against the discretion is that it produces uncertainty, and in particular makes it impossible for the defendant to know that after a set period no claim may be brought against him or her. However, this argument is less compelling in the case of personal injury claims in the light of our recommendation that no long-stop limitation period should apply to such claims. In the light of consultees' views, we therefore recommend, with some hesitation, that the courts should retain a discretion to disapply the limitation period in personal injury cases.

3.164 We have considered whether any restriction should be placed on the use of such a discretion. When the Law Reform Committee first recommended that a discretion to disapply the limitation period be introduced in personal injury cases, they intended the discretion to apply only to exceptional cases.[147] However, it has in practice become generally available. It is arguable that under the regime we recommend this will be unnecessary. The core regime will relax the definition of the date of knowledge in favour of the claimant, by incorporating a more subjective definition of constructive knowledge. In addition, the primary limitation period running from the date of knowledge will be the only limitation period applying to personal injury claims. The claimant will therefore have had three years from the date on which he or she should have discovered the relevant facts, whenever that was, to bring proceedings against the defendant. Once this time limit has expired, it should only be in the most exceptional cases that the court will be justified in allowing a claimant a more generous time period within which to bring a claim.

3.165 We do not consider that it is practical to provide for a restricted discretion. It is simply too difficult to identify all those circumstances which should qualify as 'exceptional cases'. In consequence we propose that the discretion currently contained in section 33 of the Limitation Act 1980 should be re-enacted with minimal changes. The court will be able to exercise its discretion where, in the opinion of the court, it would be unjust not to allow a claim to proceed. Section 33 of the Limitation Act 1980 contains a list of factors to which the court must have regard in deciding whether to exercise its discretion. This guidance has proved helpful, and we propose that it should be retained.

3.166 However, we consider that some amendments should be made to the current form of the discretion. An artificial distinction exists under the current law between the claimant who has not issued any proceedings within the limitation period (in which case the discretion applies), and the claimant who has issued proceedings, but failed to serve them within the limitation period (in which case the discretion

---

[147] *Twentieth Report (Interim Report on Limitation of Actions: in Personal Injury Claims)* (1974) Cmnd 5630, para 57.

does not apply).[148] We recommend that the court must have regard to 'any hardship' which would be caused to the claimant if the direction were not given.

3.167 Under the current law, the 'delay' to be taken into account by the court in exercising its discretion under section 33 is only that occurring after the primary limitation period has expired.[149] Several years may have elapsed between the events giving rise to the claim and the date on which the claimant has actual or constructive knowledge of the relevant facts. Where, for example, the claim relates to a disease with a long latency period, the primary limitation period may only start thirty years or more after the original events. In this time, the evidence available to the defendant will have deteriorated significantly (the original factory where the claimant worked may have been closed, the workers dispersed and any records destroyed). It would be unreasonable for a claimant to be able to argue that because so much time had already elapsed by the end of the limitation period, the defendant has suffered no further disadvantage because of an additional two years delay.[150] We recommend that the court should be obliged to consider the effect of the passage of time since the events giving rise to the claim on defendants' ability to defend the claim.

3.168 We also propose to include two additional factors in the list of matters which must be considered by the court in deciding whether or not to exercise its discretion to disapply the limitation period, namely whether the claimant has any alternative remedy or compensation available, and the strength of the claimant's case. There has in the past been some doubt as to whether the fact that the claimant has a good claim in negligence against his solicitor for failing to issue proceedings in time should be considered.[151] We also wish to highlight the fact that the strength of the claimant's case must be considered in every case. Where the claimant does not have a strong claim, we would not expect the court to be ready to disapply the limitation period.

3.169 **We recommend that:**

(1) **in respect of a personal injury claim, the court may direct that the limitation period which would otherwise bar the claimant's claim shall be disapplied if, but only if, it is satisfied that it would be unjust not to give such a direction having regard to**

---

[148] See *Walkley v Precision Forgings Ltd* [1979] 1 WLR 606.

[149] See *Thompson v Brown* [1981] 1 WLR 744, 751 *per* Lord Diplock.

[150] As the Court of Appeal noted in *Guidera v NEI Projects (India) Ltd* (CA, unreported, 30 January 1990): "So far as the effect of the delay upon the cogency of the evidence was concerned, the judge pointed out, with justice, that even if the plaintiff were presumed to have 'knowledge' by April 1976, it was still 23 ½ years after his initial exposure to asbestos. By then, both sides would have been in considerable difficulty in calling evidence of conditions at Poplar Power Station at the material time, particularly as during the construction of this Power Station conditions were obviously changing all the time." (Transcript, p 20).

[151] See *Firman v Ellis* [1978] QB 886.

(a) any hardship which would be caused to the defendant if the direction were given; and

(b) any hardship which would be caused to the claimant if the direction were not given (Draft Bill, Cl 12(1), (2)).

(2) The court shall take into account the following factors in the exercise of its discretion:

(a) the length of, and the reasons for, the delay on the part of the claimant;

(b) the effect of the passage of time on the ability of the defendant to defend the claim;

(c) the effect of the passage of time on the cogency of any evidence which might be called by the claimant or the defendant;

(d) the conduct of the defendant after the cause of action arose, including the extent (if any) to which he or she responded to requests reasonably made by the claimant for information or inspection for the purpose of ascertaining facts which were or might be relevant to the claim;

(e) the extent to which the claimant acted promptly and reasonably once he or she knew that the facts gave rise to a claim;

(f) the steps, if any, taken by the claimant to obtain medical, legal or other expert advice and the nature of any such advice he or she may have received;

(g) any alternative remedy or compensation available to the claimant; and

(h) the strength of the claimant's case.

In addition the court should be empowered to consider any other relevant circumstances. (Draft Bill, Cl 12(3)).

7. AGREEMENTS TO CHANGE THE LIMITATION PERIOD

3.170 The 1980 Act makes no provision in relation to whether it is possible for parties to agree to change the relevant limitation period. There is however case law to suggest that such agreements will be upheld by the courts.[152] In the Consultation Paper we expressed the provisional view that (providing that the agreement is otherwise valid) it should be possible for parties to agree: (i) to reduce the primary

---

[152] See Limitation of Actions, Consultation Paper No 151 (1998), paras 9.7 - 9.11.

limitation period or the long-stop limitation period; (ii) to extend the primary limitation period; and (iii) to change the starting date of the primary limitation period.[153] We explained that any such agreement would need to comply with the Unfair Contract Terms Act 1977[154] and the Unfair Terms in Consumer Contracts Regulations 1994 (now the Unfair Terms in Consumer Contracts Regulations 1999),[155] both of which provide some protection in relation to the imposition of short limitation periods where there is an imbalance of bargaining power between the parties.

3.171   Our provisional proposals received a large degree of support from consultees. Over seventy-five per cent of those who responded on this issue agreed with our provisional views. Several noted that they could see no reason in principle to restrict the parties' freedom of contract, and two pointed out that it is, after all, always a defendant's option not to rely on limitation as a defence to a claim. However, some consultees were concerned that further protection should be given to persons in a position of weak bargaining power, over and above that which is already provided by the Unfair Contract Terms Act 1977 and the Unfair Terms in Consumer Contracts Regulations 1999. We agree that some further protection should be provided. A clause which provides that a reduced limitation period shall apply to one or each party's liability will normally be subject to the various controls imposed by the Unfair Contract Terms Act 1977, as the clause will in effect be a restriction of liability,[156] but a clause which extends the period in which one or each may bring an action will not.[157] If such a clause is used in a consumer contract in favour of the business and was not individually negotiated, it will fall within the Unfair Terms in Consumer Contracts Regulations 1999.[158] We recommend that any clause affecting the limitation period should be valid only if

---

[153]   Limitation of Actions, Consultation Paper No 151 (1998), para 14.6.

[154]   The Unfair Contract Terms Act 1977 applies to agreements to shorten the statutory limitation period for "business liability" in relation to claims for negligence and to claims for breach of contract where one party deals as a consumer or on the other party's standard terms. It would appear that an agreement to extend the statutory limitation period would not be caught by the Act.

[155]   SI 1999 No 2083. If contained in a consumer contract, a clause altering the statutory limitation period might be struck down as "an unfair term": Reg 5(1).

[156]   As a result it may be of no effect if it falls within the Unfair Contract Terms Act 1977, s 2(1) (business liability for death or personal injury caused by negligence), s 5 (liability in tort for loss or injury caused by goods proving defective while in consumer use), s 6(1) (implied term as to title in sales), s 6(2) (implied terms as to quality, description etc in sales and hire purchase) or s 7(2) (the equivalent in other contracts under which the ownership of goods passes); or it may be subjected to a reasonableness test under s 2(2) (business liability for other loss or damage), ss 6(3) or 7(3) (the equivalent of ss 6(2) and 7(2) but in business to business contracts) or s 3(2)(a) (when in a consumer contract on the defendant's standard written terms of business).

[157]   It neither restricts one party's liability within the definition given by Unfair Contract Terms Act 1977, s 13, nor allows him to perform in a way which is different to what the other party reasonably expected within s 3(2)(b).

[158]   See especially SI 1999 No 2083, reg 5(1).

it is shown by the party seeking to rely on it to be fair and reasonable within the meaning of section 11 of the Unfair Contract Terms Act 1979.[159]

3.172   In the Consultation Paper we made no provisional recommendation in relation to agreements to extend the long-stop limitation period or to change the long-stop starting date, but asked consultees for their views.[160] We pointed out that the strength of the case for refusing to recognise parties' agreements is possibly strongest here, since it is not in the interests of the public or the legal system for disputes to be brought to trial years after the events giving rise to the cause of action, when the available evidence may have deteriorated to the extent that it is no longer possible to give a fair trial. Over sixty-five per cent of consultees who responded on this issue were of the view that it should be possible both to extend the long-stop limitation period and to change the long-stop starting date by agreement. On the whole consultees said that the principles of freedom of contract overrode any other limitation considerations. We agree, subject to one point. We do not believe that it would be appropriate to allow the parties to contract out of those provisions of the new Act which relate to disability (whether as a result of minority or adult disability) or dishonest concealment. It is also necessary to provide that parties should not be permitted to contract out of the ten year limitation period which applies to claims under the Consumer Protection Act 1987, as, under the Product Liability Directive[161] this period is absolute and leads to the extinction of the claimant's claim.

3.173   In the Consultation Paper we did not suggest that any distinction should be drawn between agreements to vary limitation periods which are made (i) before the limitation period starts running; (ii) while the limitation period is running; or (iii) after the limitation period would otherwise have expired. Nor did consultees suggest that any such distinction should be drawn. We remain of the view that this is generally the correct approach. In each case one party is simply agreeing not to plead a particular defence if a claim is brought against him or her.

3.174   An agreement made while the limitation period is running or after its expiry will almost invariably be part of a compromise between the parties. Such agreements are not subject to the operation of the Unfair Contract Terms Act 1977.[162] We think they should equally be exempted from the operation of the general control

---

[159]   Section 11(1) provides that

> In relation to a contract term, the requirement of reasonableness for the purposes of this Part of this Act, s 3 of the Misrepresentation Act 1967 and s 3 of the Misrepresentation Act (Northern Ireland) 1967 is that the term shall have been a fair and reasonable one to be included having regard to the circumstances which were, or ought reasonably to have been, known to or in the contemplation of the parties when the contract was made.

> Section 11(5) states that it is "for those claiming that a contract term or notice satisfies the requirement of reasonableness to show that it does".

[160]   Limitation of Actions, Consultation Paper No 151 (1998), para 14.6.

[161]   Council Directive 85/374/EC.

[162]   Section 10 (evasion by secondary contract), as interpreted in *Tudor Grange Holdings Ltd v Citibank NA* [1992] Ch 53, does not apply.

proposed earlier for agreements to alter the period. They will remain subject to the Unfair Terms in Consumer Contracts Regulations 1999.[163]

3.175 **We therefore recommend that:**

(1) **subject to (2) and (3) below, nothing in the new Act shall prevent the making of an agreement which modifies or disapplies any of its provisions or makes alternative provision** (Draft Bill, Cl 31(1));

(2) **any clause in such an agreement which affects the limitation period will be valid only if it is shown by the party seeking to rely on it to be fair and reasonable within the meaning of section 11 of the Unfair Contract Terms Act 1977** (Draft Bill, Cl 31(3));

(3) **an agreement will be unenforceable to the extent that its terms modify or disapply, or make provision in place of the Act's provision in relation to disability, dishonest concealment or the ten year limitation period applying to claims under the Consumer Protection Act 1987.** (Draft Bill, Cl 31(2)).

---

[163] Though the operation of these Regulations in this context is not wholly clear since the waiver of the limitation period may be exempt from control as part of the definition of the main subject matter of the contract: SI 1999, No 2083, reg 6(2).

PART IV
REFORM II: APPLICATION OF THE CORE REGIME

1. INTRODUCTION

4.1 As we have explained above, we envisage the core regime applying to the vast majority of claims in contract and tort, including claims for breach of a simple contract, claims for negligence resulting in personal injury, property damage or economic loss; or claims for other torts such as nuisance, breach of statutory duty or trespass to the person. We discuss in this part whether the core regime should be applied to claims in respect of other causes of action which fall under the Limitation Act 1980 (most of which have been accorded some form of special treatment under the current law and/or are regarded as problematic in some way). These claims are:

(1) claims to recover loans repayable on demand;

(2) claims on a specialty;

(3) claims under the Law Reform (Miscellaneous Provisions) Act 1934;

(4) claims under the Fatal Accidents Act 1976;

(5) claims by victims of child sexual abuse;

(6) claims under the Consumer Protection Act 1987;

(7) claims for defamation or malicious falsehood;

(8) claims for conversion;

(9) claims by a subsequent owner of damaged property;

(10) claims for restitution;

(11) claims for a contribution or an indemnity;

(12) claims for breach of trust and related claims;

(13) claims to recover land and related claims;

(14) claims in relation to mortgages and charges;

(15) claims on a judgment or on an arbitration award;

(16) claims on a statute; and

(17) claims against public authorities.

4.2   We also discuss in this Part:

(1)   how the core regime should apply to claims under the Companies Act 1985;

(2)   how the core regime should apply where one of the parties is subject to insolvency proceedings;

(3)   whether the core regime should apply to equitable, as well as common law, remedies;

(4)   the interrelationship between the core regime and the numerous specific limitation periods laid down in various statutes outside the Limitation Act 1980; and

(5)   whether there should be a 'sweeping-up' or 'default' provision.

4.3   We should stress at the outset that nearly all our provisional proposals regarding the application of the core regime received strong support from consultees.[1]

2.   CLAIMS TO RECOVER LOANS REPAYABLE ON DEMAND

4.4   Under the common law, if there is no provision in a contract of loan specifying a date for repayment, the debt accrues due and is payable immediately the money is lent, whether or not the parties intended the loan to be repayable immediately.[2] To mitigate this rule, section 6 of the Limitation Act 1980 lays down that, for contracts of loan to which it applies, the limitation period should apply as though the cause of action accrued on the date of a written demand for repayment. The section applies to a contract of loan which

(1)   does not provide for repayment of the debt on a fixed or determinable date and

(2)   does not effectively make the obligation to repay conditional on a demand for repayment made by or on behalf of the creditor (or conditional on any other matter).

But section 6 does not apply where the debtor enters into a collateral obligation to pay the amount of the debt or any part of it on a fixed or determinable date or conditional on a demand for repayment (or other condition).

4.5   We noted in the Consultation Paper that we do not wish to undermine the policy behind section 6.[3] We therefore propose to provide that the cause of action in

---

[1]   The one major exception was our provisional proposal that there should be a <u>single</u> long-stop limitation period applicable to claims for an indemnity or contribution running from the date of the judgment or settlement in the original proceedings to which the claim relates. See paras 4.80 - 4.93 below.

[2]   *Reeves v Butcher* [1891] 2 QB 509.

[3]   Limitation of Actions, Consultation Paper No 151 (1998), para 12.24.

relation to the repayment of a loan which satisfies the conditions laid down by section 6 will not accrue until a written demand for repayment is made. In consequence, the fact that a written demand has been made will be one of the relevant facts which the claimant needs to know before the primary limitation period is triggered, and the long-stop limitation period will not start until the date of the demand.

4.6 **We therefore recommend that the cause of action in relation to a claim for repayment of a 'qualifying loan' should not accrue until a written demand for repayment has been made. "Qualifying loan" for the purposes of this recommendation will have the same meaning as in section 6 of the Limitation Act 1980.** (Draft Bill, Cl 32).

3. CLAIMS ON A SPECIALTY

4.7 Under section 8 of the 1980 Act, claims on a specialty have a limitation period of twelve years. This applies to a contract executed as a deed. It also applies to claims on a statute (though its importance here has been considerably diminished by section 9 of the 1980 Act, which provides that the limitation period applicable to a claim to recover a sum recoverable by virtue of any enactment is six years).

4.8 We provisionally proposed in the Consultation Paper that specialties should be subject to the core regime.[4] All consultees who responded to this question agreed with the proposal. Under the current law, specialties perform a useful function, allowing a choice of a longer limitation period for breach of contract than the normal six years, but this will not be necessary when parties have an express power to choose an extended limitation period.[5] The existence of separate limitation periods for claims for breach of a contract that has been executed as a deed, as opposed to a simple contract, creates needless complexity. In addition, statutes are considered to be 'specialties'. This means that a claim to enforce a right given by statute may under the current law fall within the definition of an "action upon a specialty" within the meaning of section 8 of the 1980 Act or it may be a claim to recover money recoverable by virtue of an enactment under section 9 of the 1980 Act or a claim for breach of statutory duty which is governed by the limitation period in section 2 of the Act. Assimilating specialties to the core regime will have the advantage of avoiding the problems which currently arise in interpreting the relationship between these sections of the Limitation Act 1980.[6]

4.9 **We recommend that specialties should be subject to the core regime.**

---

[4] Limitation of Actions, Consultation Paper No 151 (1998), paras 13.4 - 13.6.

[5] We discuss the parties' power to change the applicable limitation period by contract at paras 3.170 - 3.175 above. We propose that agreements in the form of specialties which have been entered into before the new Act comes into force should be subject to special transitional provisions. See further para 5.36 below.

[6] Limitation of Actions, Consultation Paper No 151 (1998), paras 7.10 - 7.20.

4. CLAIMS UNDER THE LAW REFORM (MISCELLANEOUS PROVISIONS) ACT 1934

4.10 In the Consultation Paper we provisionally proposed that claims under the Law Reform (Miscellaneous Provisions) Act 1934 should be subject to the core regime, with a minor modification: namely that the limitation period should start on the later of either the date on which the cause of action is discoverable by the personal representative (who will be the claimant) or the date of death of the deceased.[7] This replicates the position under the current law for personal injury claims (where the date of knowledge is the starting point for the limitation period).[8] The current law also ensures that the estate is not put in a better position than the deceased (though as a matter of general principle, rather than limitations law): the estate is not, therefore, able to bring a claim which was time-barred at the date of death of the deceased. We envisage the same general principle applying under our new limitations regime.

4.11 These proposals attracted the support of a majority of consultees (over eighty per cent of those responding on this issue expressed complete agreement with our provisional views). It was however suggested by two consultees[9] that the personal representative should succeed to the same rights as the deceased. In other words, the primary limitation period should run from the date on which the deceased knew or ought to have known of the cause of action. It was suggested that if the deceased had known of the cause of action for two years and done nothing, the personal representative should not benefit from an extension to the limitation period; and that in many cases measuring the date by reference to the knowledge of the personal representative would mean that the only applicable limitation period would be the long-stop, as the personal representative might never have either actual or constructive knowledge sufficient to start the limitation period.

4.12 Starting the primary limitation period from the date of knowledge of the personal representative does allow the personal representative a longer limitation period than would have been available to the deceased. However, this seems justified, given the disruption which inevitably follows a death; and it would also reduce the risk that the limitation period may run against the estate when no one has the authority to bring proceedings on its behalf.[10] Where there is more than one personal representative, the primary limitation period will start from the date of knowledge of the first personal representative who can be said to have actual or constructive knowledge of the relevant facts.[11]

---

[7] Limitation of Actions, Consultation Paper No 151 (1998), paras 13.7 - 13.10.

[8] Limitation of Actions, Consultation Paper No 151 (1998), paras 3.77 - 3.80. See para 2.24 above.

[9] Professor Andrew Tettenborn and Nicholas Underhill QC.

[10] A problem noted by Pinsent Curtis, John Galt of T G Baynes and Nicholas Underhill QC.

[11] As Limitation Act 1980, s 11(7) provides under the present law for personal injury claims brought under the Law Reform (Miscellaneous Provisions) Act 1934.

4.13 In addition, we have recommended that the court should have a discretion to disapply the limitation period in personal injury claims.[12] This discretion will also be available (where the pre-condition for its exercise is satisfied) where a claim is brought under the Law Reform (Miscellaneous Provisions) Act 1934 on behalf of the estate of the deceased. The claimant, for the purposes of the discretion, will be the personal representative, except that, in considering any delay, the court will take into account any delay by the deceased in addition to delay by the personal representative.

4.14 Under the core regime, the long-stop limitation period will run from the date of the act or omission of the defendant giving rise to the cause of action. As we noted in the Consultation Paper,[13] this may mean that the personal representative has comparatively little time within which to bring proceedings (this does not, of course apply to the survival of a claim in respect of personal injuries because of our recommendation that such claims should not be subject to any long-stop limitation period).[14] The only way to compensate for this would be to adopt the date of death as an alternative starting point for the long-stop limitation period. This would subvert the principle applicable under the current law: that the estate of the deceased should not be able to bring a claim where the deceased would have been time-barred. It would also unreasonably extend the amount of time within which a claim could be brought. Our provisional proposal not to modify the long-stop limitation period under the core regime for claims under the 1934 Act has proved acceptable to consultees.[15]

4.15 **We recommend that claims under the Law Reform (Miscellaneous Provisions) Act 1934 should be subject to the core regime, save that (as under the present law in relation to the survival of personal injury claims) the primary limitation period should start from the later of the date the cause of action was discoverable by the claimant (that is, the personal representative) or the date of death of the deceased. (Draft Bill, Cl 10). As regards the survival of personal injury claims, where, as we have seen, we recommend no long-stop limitation period and a judicial discretion to disapply the primary limitation period, the court in exercising that discretion shall take into account the deceased's delay as well as that of the personal representative. (Draft Bill, Cl 12(4), (8)(b)).**

5. CLAIMS UNDER THE FATAL ACCIDENTS ACT 1976

4.16 Under the Fatal Accidents Act 1976 a cause of action accrues for the benefit of the dependants of the deceased where the death was caused by conduct which would have given the deceased a right of action had he or she survived. The cause

---

[12] Discussed in more detail at paras 3.156 - 3.169 above.

[13] Limitation of Actions, Consultation Paper No 151 (1998), para 13.9.

[14] See paras 3.102 - 3.107 above.

[15] Only two consultees expressed reservations on the application of the long-stop limitation period to claims under the Law Reform (Miscellaneous) Provisions Act 1934, and those reservations concerned the possible consequences for personal injury claims which, under the core regime we now recommend, are not subject to a long-stop limitation period.

of action accrues only on the date of death, and is separate from any cause of action in respect of which the deceased might have brought a claim (and which survives for the benefit of the estate under the Law Reform (Miscellaneous Provisions) Act 1934). However, a claim under the 1976 Act may not be brought if a claim by the deceased would have been time-barred at the date of death. For limitation purposes the current law views a claim under the 1976 Act as being analogous to a personal injuries claim. It is subject to a limitation period of three years running from the later of the date of death or the date of knowledge of the dependants for whose benefit the claim is brought, and the limitation period may be disapplied at the discretion of the court under section 33 of the Limitation Act 1980.

4.17   We provisionally proposed that claims under the Fatal Accidents Act 1976 should be subject to the core regime, save that the date of knowledge should refer to the knowledge of the dependant for whom the claim is brought.[16] As with claims under the Law Reform (Miscellaneous) Provisions Act 1934, this reflects the present law.[17] Similarly, this proposal was strongly supported (over eighty per cent of consultees answering this question agreed with our proposals). However, some concern was expressed[18] that we proposed to continue applying different limitation periods on behalf of different dependants. This is necessary, we believe, to ensure that minor dependants are sufficiently protected, and do not lose the benefit of a claim under the Fatal Accidents Act 1976 because of the inaction of, for example, the widow of the deceased. We apply the same policy in relation to other claims by minors.[19]

4.18   It was suggested that the limitation period for all dependants could be unjustifiably prolonged by the fact that one of the dependants was very young at the time of the death.[20] This suggestion misunderstands the effect of the proposal. Although the starting point for the limitation period for a claim on behalf of one dependant will be decided by reference to the knowledge of that dependant, this will have no effect on claims on behalf of any other dependant. Indeed, we provide that the expiry of the primary limitation period in respect of one of a number of dependants will give rise to a defence against that dependant.

4.19   How our recommendations will operate in practice can be illustrated by reference to the following example: a man dies in January 2000, leaving a widow and three dependent children, aged 3, 6 and 12. A claim may be brought on behalf of the widow until January 2003 (assuming that the widow is aware of the cause of her husband's death when it occurs). Although a claim could be brought on behalf of the youngest child until 29 July 2017 (three years after the child reaches the age of 18 on 30 July 2014), this does not extend the limitation periods for claims on behalf of the older children (which expire in 2014, and 2008 respectively) or the

---

[16]   Limitation of Actions, Consultation Paper No 151 (1998), paras 13.11 - 13.16.

[17]   Limitation of Actions, Consultation Paper No 151 (1998), paras 3.81 - 3.86.

[18]   By Stuart Brown QC.

[19]   See paras 3.115 - 3.121 above.

[20]   By the General Council of the Bar.

widow. Indeed, since only one set of proceedings may be brought under the Fatal Accidents Act 1976,[21] if the widow commences the proceedings within the limitation period applicable to her claim, those proceedings must also include claims on behalf of the children.

4.20 The remaining issue is whether a claim under the Fatal Accidents Act 1976 should continue to be treated analogously to a personal injury claim. If it is so regarded, it will not be subject to a long-stop limitation period,[22] and the courts will have a discretion to disapply the primary limitation period. If the personal injuries limitation regime is not applied to claims under the Fatal Accidents Act 1976, a claim under that Act will be subject to a long-stop limitation period of ten years, and there will be no discretion for the court to disapply the limitation period.

4.21 We have argued above[23] that special treatment for personal injury claims can be justified on the grounds that the claimant who has suffered a personal injury has suffered a more extreme form of harm than the claimant with a claim relating to property damage or economic loss. Losing the opportunity to bring a claim because of the expiry of the limitation period is therefore more serious for the claimant with a personal injury claim than any other claim. A claim under the Fatal Accidents Act 1976 is not directly a personal injury claim: the claimant (and any other dependants) will not have suffered a personal injury. However, it is a claim for compensation for the loss suffered as a consequence of death - which must be regarded as the most extreme form of personal injury. The fact that the person who has suffered the injury is no longer in a position to bring proceedings in respect of the claim does not alter the nature of the event giving rise to the claim. It is also, of course, the case that the present law applies an analogous regime for fatal accident claims as to personal injury claims and it would now be difficult to turn back the clock by removing the courts' well-established discretion. The availability of bereavement damages for some claimants clearly distinguishes a claim under the 1976 Act from a claim for 'pure economic loss'.

4.22 **We recommend that claims under the Fatal Accidents Act 1976 should be treated as analogous to personal injury claims under our core regime (so that proceedings in respect of such claims should not be subject to a long-stop limitation period and there should be a judicial discretion[24] to disapply the primary limitation period) save that the date of knowledge should refer to the knowledge of the dependants for whom the claim is brought.** (Draft Bill, Cl 11, Cl 12(5), (6)).

---

[21] See the Fatal Accidents Act 1976, s 2(3).

[22] See paras 3.102 - 3.107 above.

[23] See para 3.160 above.

[24] Slight modifications to the formulation of the discretion will be needed to deal with the relevant delay being potentially both that of the deceased and the dependants.

6. CLAIMS BY VICTIMS OF CHILD SEXUAL ABUSE

(1) Should any limitation period apply?

4.23 Claims by victims of child sexual abuse pose particular problems for any limitations regime. The acts giving rise to the cause of action will, by their nature, occur when the claimant is a child. Depending on the nature of the abuse, the claimant may suffer immediate physical injury. However the abuse may also cause extensive, and prolonged, psychiatric problems. This later injury may only manifest itself - or at least be recognised as such by the victim - several years after the abuse. This creates problems similar to those of latent disease.

4.24 The problem is compounded under the current law because of the anomalous distinction made between claims in respect of injuries which are deliberately inflicted, which are subject to a six year limitation period running from the date the injury was inflicted, and claims in respect of negligently inflicted injuries, which are subject to a limitation period of three years from the date on which the claimant knows the relevant facts.[25] In *Stubbings v Webb*[26] it was held that a claim in respect of sexual abuse is a claim for intentional trespass, giving the claimant a limitation period of six years from the date of majority. This led to an application to the European Court of Human Rights on the ground that the law in this area contravened the European Convention on Human Rights. The application failed, but the European Court of Human Rights noted that:

> There has been a developing awareness in recent years of the range of problems caused by child abuse and its psychological effects on victims, and it is possible that the rules on limitation of actions applying in Member States of the Council of Europe may have to be amended to make special provision for this group of claimants in the near future.[27]

4.25 We considered in the Consultation Paper whether sexual abuse claims are so unique that they should not be subject to any limitation period.[28] We concluded that they were not. It can be argued forcibly that in the case of sexual abuse (at least where the defendant has been tried and convicted for a criminal offence in respect of the abuse) there may be no justification for protecting the interests of the defendant (an important function of a limitation regime). However, it may not have been established that the defendant committed the assault, and the principle that litigation should be stifled at some point (irrespective of the merits of the case) to prevent claims being brought at a time when it is no longer possible to give a fair trial to the dispute, remains valid. We provisionally proposed, therefore, that such claims should continue to be subject to a limitation period.[29] This was supported by around ninety per cent of consultees answering this question and we

---

[25] See Limitation of Actions, Consultation Paper No 151 (1998), paras 3.32 - 3.36.

[26] [1993] AC 498.

[27] *Stubbings v United Kingdom* (1997) 23 EHRR 213, 234.

[28] See Limitation of Actions, Consultation Paper No 151 (1998), paras 13.19 - 13.25.

[29] See Limitation of Actions, Consultation Paper No 151 (1998), para 13.25.

now therefore confirm as a final recommendation that claims in sexual abuse cases should be subject to at least the primary limitation period.

4.26   Three consultees[30] pointed out, in addition to the arguments we put forward in the Consultation Paper in support of our provisional proposal, that it is difficult to justify giving special treatment to sexual abuse claims alone, without according similar protection to, for example, non-sexual assaults against children. Sexual abuse may, in the current climate, be regarded as uniquely unacceptable but other non-sexual abuse of children may be as damaging. Yet it would be difficult to argue that all attacks against children should be exempted from the limitation regime.

4.27   However, two consultees[31] argued that no limitation period should apply to sexual abuse claims because, among other reasons, sexual abuse victims commonly suffer from 'dissociation' making them unable to bring claims against their abusers. The term 'dissociation' is used in two senses. Lee Moore refers to 'dissociative amnesia', which is a diagnostic category of the Diagnostic and Statistical Manual of Mental Disorders,[32] describing an inability to recall personal information of a stressful and traumatic nature - such as sexual abuse suffered. Pannone & Partners use the term in a more general sense, to describe the position where "the plaintiff is aware of both the trauma and of its consequences for his psychological make-up but the trauma was so awful that memories or reminders of it would be too psychologically damaging for the plaintiff, and thus, the plaintiff dissociates himself or herself from these memory triggers, for example litigation."

4.28   Where 'dissociative amnesia' (or a similar mental condition) is responsible for the claimant's inability to bring a claim within the limitation period, the claimant will be afforded some protection by our recommendations in respect of 'lack of capacity'.[33] Dissociative amnesia would appear to fall within the terms of 'mental disability' as we have defined it above. Where therefore the claimant can show that this was the cause of his or her inability to bring proceedings, the primary limitation period would be suspended for at least ten years from the onset of the disability. This would also apply where the claimant suffered from another recognised mental disorder. We have rejected the suggestion that 'disability' should be defined to include any separate provision for the psychological incapacity suffered by victims of sexual abuse because of the difficulty of defining this incapacity.[34] However, the definition of disability is sufficiently wide to ensure that where a claimant is psychologically incapable of commencing proceedings,

[30]   Professor Andrew Tettenborn, Michael Lerego QC and His Honour Judge John Griffith Williams QC (responding on behalf of the Wales and Chester Circuit).

[31]   Lee Moore and Pannone & Partners.

[32]   American Psychiatric Association (4th ed 1994), 300.12.

[33]   See paras 3.123 - 3.133 above.

[34]   And considerable academic controversy exists as to whether there is a "sexual abuse syndrome" with recognised symptoms which affects most, if not all, victims of sexual abuse. See para 3.125 above.

and this incapacity can be identified as a mental disability, that claimant will be given the same protection as any other claimant under a disability.

(2)   Do any further modifications need to be made to the core regime?

4.29   A majority of consultees (over sixty-five per cent of those replying to this question) agreed with our provisional proposal that the core regime should be applied to claims by sexual abuse victims. However, a number of consultees disagreed, arguing that the long-stop provisionally proposed for personal injury claims should not apply,[35] and that there should be a discretion to disapply the limitation period.[36]

4.30   As we have explained above, we have decided to depart from our provisional proposals to apply a long-stop to personal injury claims, and to remove a discretion for personal injury claims.[37] In consequence the concerns of those consultees who criticised the core regime as being insufficiently favourable to victims of sexual abuse (while nevertheless recognising the need for claims in respect of sexual abuse to be subject to a limitation period) have been satisfied.

4.31   We do have some concerns that claims may be brought many years after the events on which the claimant's cause of action is based, at a time when it is difficult for a fair trial to be given to the claimant's allegations.[38] However, subject to the provision on disability, the victim is likely to have immediate knowledge of the relevant facts, so that the primary limitation period expires three years after majority. Although the court will have a discretion to disapply the primary limitation period, it must consider whether the defendant's ability to defend the claim will be prejudiced due to the lapse of time since the events giving rise to the cause of action. And our concerns are no greater in respect of sexual abuse claims than personal injury cases generally. In other words, these concerns are not a good reason for making a separate modification in respect of sexual abuse claims, but a factor to be considered in deciding whether or not there should be a long-stop for personal injury claims.[39]

4.32   **We recommend that claims by child abuse victims should be subject to the core regime as modified in relation to other personal injury claims.**

4.33   It is worth emphasising that one beneficial effect of this recommendation is that the same limitation regime will apply whether the sexual abuse claim is based on a

---

[35]   Elizabeth Palmer, John Grace QC (responding on behalf of the South Eastern Circuit), The Law Society, and Thompsons. In contrast the Holborn Law Society felt that the long-stop applicable to such claims should be shorter than thirty years.

[36]   The Law Society.

[37]   See paras 3.102 - 3.107 and 3.160 - 3.169 above. The decision to retain the court's discretion to disapply the limitation period in cases of personal injury was influenced by the need to do justice to sexual abuse claimants.

[38]   A concern expressed by Professor Andrew Tettenborn, Michael Lerego QC and Nicholas Underhill QC.

[39]   See paras 3.102 - 3.107 above, where this issue is discussed.

deliberate tort (trespass to the person) or on the tort of negligence. The anomaly created by *Stubbings v Webb*[40] will therefore be removed.

7.   CLAIMS UNDER THE CONSUMER PROTECTION ACT 1987

4.34   Under the current law there is a separate limitations regime for claims under the Consumer Protection Act 1987, encapsulated in sections 11A and 14(1A) of the Limitation Act 1980.[41] Such claims are subject to a limitation period of three years from the date of knowledge, and a long-stop limitation period of ten years from the date the product which caused the damage was put into circulation by the producer. The expiry of this limitation period extinguishes any rights the claimant may have had. In claims in respect of personal injury and death under the 1987 Act the courts have the usual discretion under section 33 of the Limitation Act 1980 to disapply the primary limitation period but the long-stop limitation period cannot be disapplied.[42]

4.35   The Consumer Protection Act 1987 (and the associated provisions on limitation of claims contained in the Limitation Act 1980) implement the provisions of the Product Liability Directive.[43] The limitation provisions of that Directive are as follows:

> Member States shall provide in their legislation that a limitation period of three years shall apply to proceedings for the recovery of damages as provided for in this Directive. The limitation period shall begin to run from the day on which the plaintiff becomes aware, or should reasonably have become aware, of the damage, the defect and the identity of the producer (Article 10(1)).

> The laws of Member States regulating suspension or interruption of the limitation period shall not be affected by this Directive (Article 10(2)).

> Member States shall provide in their legislation that the rights conferred upon the injured person pursuant to this Directive shall be extinguished upon the expiry of a period of ten years from the date on which the producer put into circulation the actual product which caused the damage, unless the injured person has in the meantime instituted proceedings against the producer (Article 11).

4.36   This limitations regime cannot be altered by unilateral legislation by the United Kingdom. Its provisions are very similar to the main elements we propose as part of the core regime. The major difference is that, under the Product Liability Directive, there is a long-stop limitation period which applies to all claims,

---

[40]   [1993] AC 498. This anomaly is discussed in detail in Limitation of Actions, Consultation Paper No 151 (1998), paras 3.32 - 3.36. See also para 1.5 above.

[41]   See Limitation of Actions, Consultation Paper No 151 (1998), paras 3.101 - 3.104, and paras 2.35 - 2.36 above.

[42]   Limitation Act 1980, s 33(1) and (1A).

[43]   Council Directive 85/374/EEC of 25 July 1985.

including claims in respect of personal injury claims, the expiry of which extinguishes the claimant's rights. The core regime will therefore require some modification in its application to claims under the Consumer Protection Act 1987 to ensure that there is no breach of the provisions of the Product Liability Directive. Further, for the avoidance of doubt, we consider that a new limitations statute should also specify the starting point for the long-stop limitation period for a claim under the Consumer Protection Act 1987. With these modifications, we consider that the application of the core regime to claims under the 1987 Act will be compatible with the Product Liability Directive.

4.37 **We recommend that the core regime should apply to claims under the Consumer Protection Act 1987, subject to the following modifications:**

(1) **The starting date for the long-stop limitation period will be the date on which the defective product is supplied by the producer of the product, or by the person who imported the product into a Member State of the European Union.** (Draft Bill, Cl 8(1), (2)).

(2) **The long-stop limitation period will apply to all claims under the Consumer Protection Act 1987, including personal injury claims.** (Draft Bill, Cl 8(2), (4)).

(3) **The expiry of the long-stop limitation period will extinguish the claimant's right of action.** (Draft Bill, Cl 8(3)).

(4) **The court's discretion to disapply the limitation period in respect of personal injury claims will only apply to the primary limitation period.** (Draft Bill, Cl 8(4)).

(5) **The parties may agree to extend the primary limitation period applicable to a claim under the Consumer Protection Act 1987. Otherwise, the starting date of the initial and long-stop limitation period and the length of those periods so far as they apply to a claim under that Act may not be changed by agreement between the parties.** (Draft Bill, Cl 31(2)).

8. DEFAMATION AND MALICIOUS FALSEHOOD

4.38 We provisionally proposed in the Consultation Paper that claims for defamation and malicious falsehood should be subject to the core regime. This would overturn the changes made by the Defamation Act 1996.[44] That Act implemented the recommendations of the Supreme Court Procedure Committee.[45] The Committee, stressing the difficulties faced by media representatives in defending claims brought after some time (due in particular to the loss of supporting

---

[44] Discussed in the Consultation Paper at para 13.38. See para 2.37 above.

[45] Supreme Court Procedure Committee, *Report of Practice and Procedure in Defamation*, July 1991.

evidence),[46] recommended that the limitation period should be further reduced to one year, but that (to avoid injustice to claimants) this should be coupled with a discretion for the court to disapply the limitation period. Our proposals would replace this one year limitation period (and the court's discretion to disapply the limitation period) with a three year limitation period running from the date of knowledge (with no discretion to disapply).

4.39 Consultees have been almost equally divided on the issue, with just over fifty per cent of those responding on this issue expressing the view that the core regime should apply, and around forty-five per cent saying that the limitation regime provided in the Defamation Act 1996 should be retained. In support of our provisional recommendation, it has been suggested to us by claimants' representatives that the one year limitation period applying under the current law does not provide the claimant with sufficient time to prepare his or her case, and in particular to carry out all the factual investigations necessary to serve a fully detailed statement of claim.

4.40 The main sets of arguments put against our provisional recommendations were twofold: first, in relation to evidence, and secondly, in relation to free speech.

4.41 As regards evidence, the defence of justification plays a unique role in claims for defamation. The defendant bears the burden of proof that the publication is justified. The claimant does not have to prove that it is untrue. In consequence, it was argued by some consultees that the prejudice to the defendant when proceedings are commenced after a long period of time is much greater than for other causes of action, when the claimant has to prove his or her case to recover damages against the defendant.

4.42 It was argued that this factor is exacerbated by the fact that records are kept by potential defamation defendants for far shorter periods of time than might be expected in other cases,[47] and by the nature of the evidence likely to be relevant. Associated Newspapers pointed out that defamation claims turn on oral evidence rather than written evidence (particularly where justification is being claimed). The BBC agreed, noting that:

> In defamation actions, much of the evidence depends upon personal impression rather than factual assertion. Inevitably, impressions fade and distort over time. As a practical matter ... the evidence becomes much more difficult to assemble if the action is delayed.

---

[46] "We have canvassed opinion and found a wide measure of agreement (not surprisingly) among media representatives that the same reasoning would justify an even shorter period. Memories fade. Journalists and their sources scatter and become, not infrequently, untraceable. Notes and other records are retained only for short periods, not least because of limitations on storage": Supreme Court Procedure Committee, *Report on Practice and Procedure in Defamation*, July 1991, p 81, para VIII 2.

[47] The possibility that records might have to be kept for ten years post publication was described by Associated Newspapers Ltd as presenting "a near impossible task".

4.43   It was further argued that an additional complication is created by the possibility of claims based on 'fleeting publication upon the internet'.[48] In such cases the defendant concerned may be faced with the task of locating and preserving electronic evidence which may have existed for only a short time.[49]

4.44   Turning to the arguments on free speech, it was suggested by The Newspaper Society and the BBC that claimants often deliberately wait until the last possible moment to bring proceedings, to ensure that the defendant is placed at the maximum possible disadvantage. This is said to be particularly the case where the proceedings are being funded by trade unions and professional associations. It has been suggested that defamation claims are used to discourage coverage of particular issues. In our view, however, any chilling effect of libel claims is a consequence of the general law on defamation rather than specifically due to the limitation period applied to defamation claims.

4.45   We conclude that, though there is some resistance to any amendment of the limitation regime introduced by the Defamation Act 1996, the one year limitation period which is at the heart of that regime would not be acceptable or fair to claimants in the absence of any discretion for the court to disapply the limitation period. We are informed by solicitors with experience of acting for the claimant in defamation claims that the one year period does not give claimants sufficient time to prepare a claim properly. Moreover, there are additional reasons to reverse the one year limitation period adopted under the Defamation Act 1996. As we noted in the Consultation Paper, the limitation period applicable to claims for defamation in Scotland is three years from the date of knowledge.[50] Allowing such a significant difference between the limitation regimes applicable in England and Wales and in Scotland can only encourage forum shopping. Subjecting claims for defamation and for malicious falsehood to the core regime would increase uniformity, reducing the complexity of the law on limitations. It would also avoid the current anomalous differences highlighted in the Consultation Paper,[51] such as that between the limitation period applicable to claims for negligent misstatement and that applicable to claims for defamation and malicious falsehood.

4.46   **Therefore, we recommend that claims for defamation and for malicious falsehood should be subject to the core regime.**

9.   CLAIMS FOR CONVERSION

(1)   Introduction

4.47   The limitation period prescribed generally for claims for conversion is six years from accrual of the cause of action. However, this rule is modified for successive conversions and conversions constituting, or relating to, theft. In the case of successive conversions, the limitation period does not restart on each conversion,

---

[48]   The Newspaper Society.

[49]   A point made by Associated Newspapers Ltd, The Newspaper Society, and Lovells.

[50]   See Limitation of Actions, Consultation Paper No 151 (1998), para 13.41, n 61.

[51]   See Limitation of Actions, Consultation Paper No 151 (1998), para 13.42.

but rather runs from the date of the first conversion only. And in the case of conversions constituting theft or relating to theft (that is following the theft), no limitation period applies until the stolen property passes into the hands of a purchaser acting in good faith.[52] The limitation period then runs from that date even against subsequent conversions.

4.48 In the Consultation Paper we provisionally proposed that the core regime should apply to all claims for conversion, subject to the following modifications:[53]

(1) The definition of the date of knowledge applying to claims to recover converted property (and possibly for all claims for conversion) should require knowledge of the location of the property in addition to the other three elements (knowledge of the facts establishing the cause of action, the identity of the defendant and the significance of the claim) to start time running.

(2) In respect of claims for conversions which are not thefts or related to thefts, the long-stop limitation period should run from the date of the first conversion only.

(3) Where goods have been stolen the long-stop limitation period should not apply to claims for conversion brought against anyone other than bona fide purchasers of the goods and, where there has been more than one such purchase, the long-stop limitation period should commence on the date of the first purchase.

We also made provisional recommendations on the effect of the expiry of the limitation period.[54]

(2) The Core Regime and Conversions unrelated to Theft

(a) The definition of the date of knowledge

4.49 We provisionally proposed that the definition of 'discoverability' should be modified for all claims for conversion to include knowledge of the location of the property in question.[55] This proposal was influenced by the ease with which chattels can be moved from place to place (and not least into another jurisdiction). Another factor was that Council Directive 93/7/EEC and UNIDROIT Convention on Stolen or Illegally Exported Cultural Objects, 1995 each require both knowledge of the possessor of a stolen object and the location of the object to start the limitation period running.

---

[52] Limitation Act 1980, s 4. For detailed discussion of the current law, see Limitation of Actions, Consultation Paper No 151 (1998), paras 3.108 - 3.115.

[53] Limitation of Actions, Consultation Paper No 151 (1998), paras 13.44 - 13.64.

[54] Limitation of Actions, Consultation Paper No 151 (1998), paras 13.65 - 13.69.

[55] Limitation of Actions, Consultation Paper No 151 (1998), paras 13.48 - 13.49.

4.50   Over sixty-five per cent of consultees responding on this issue agreed with our provisional proposal that the date of knowledge should include knowledge of the location of the converted goods. However, several consultees put forward strong arguments against the proposal. First, it was suggested that, provided that the claimant can identify the defendant, knowledge of the location of the converted chattels is unnecessary to enable the claimant to commence proceedings against the defendant. Secondly, as noted in the Consultation Paper,[56] there is no good reason to alter the knowledge required for the date of knowledge in the case of a claim for damages (rather than specific delivery) for conversion. While the Consultation Paper left open the possibility that a different rule could be adopted where the claimant sought recovery of the property as opposed to damages, this approach received limited approval. Thirdly, the property may no longer be locatable in its original form.

4.51   In the light of these objections, we have reconsidered our proposal to modify the definition of the date of knowledge for all claims in conversion. Where the conversion is not related to theft, therefore, the claimant will not have to know of the location of his or her property to start the primary limitation period running.[57]

(b)   The long-stop limitation period

4.52   We also provisionally proposed in the Consultation Paper that, where there had been successive conversions, the ten year long-stop limitation period should run from the date of the first conversion only.[58] This reflects the rule under the current law whereby the claimant may not bring a claim in respect of any further conversion after the expiry of six years from the accrual of the cause of action in respect of the original conversion.[59] We noted that if the long-stop limitation period is to start running from every fresh conversion, it would be deprived of most of its purpose. That is, in any claim by the claimant against a subsequent converter, the circumstances surrounding the original conversion, which could have been many years previously, may need to be considered in order to establish the cause of action. In addition, where there has been an extended chain of conversions, to permit claims against subsequent innocent converters, who would no longer be able to bring a claim against the person from whom they obtained the goods because such a claim would be time-barred by the limitation period, might cause injustice.

4.53   Consultees overwhelmingly supported our provisional proposal that the long-stop limitation period should commence from the date of the first conversion only. Over ninety per cent of those responding on this issue agreed. We therefore confirm it as a final recommendation.

---

[56]   Limitation of Actions, Consultation Paper No 151 (1998), para 13.49, n 75.

[57]   For our proposals for theft-related conversions, see para 4.57 below.

[58]   Limitation of Actions, Consultation Paper No 151 (1998), para 13.50.

[59]   Limitation Act 1980, s 3(1).

(3) The Core Regime and Conversions Constituting or Related to Theft

(a) Should the primary limitation period apply?

4.54 We argued in the Consultation Paper that there is no need to make specific provision for theft-related conversions, on the grounds that the claimant is adequately protected both by the date of knowledge starting point (in the case of the primary limitation period) and by the provisions on dishonest concealment (as far as the long-stop limitation period is concerned).[60] This received the support of a small majority of consultees (over fifty-five per cent). There was however a substantial minority (over forty per cent) who opposed the removal of the theft exception which applies under the current law.

4.55 The minority argued that the law should ensure that the thief could never benefit from his or her crime. The British Museum in particular stressed that while it may be acceptable to bar a claim by the victim of theft where he or she actually knows all the relevant facts, it is unacceptable to bar the claim where the victim merely ought to have known the relevant facts. The Museum suggested that to do so is to favour the thief over the victim, and where the victim's fault may only be indolence - as opposed to the active dishonesty of the thief - the result arguably looks wrong. A number of other consultees also felt that no limitation period should apply in the case of theft.[61]

4.56 Since the publication of the Consultation Paper, Mr Justice Moses has held, in *City of Gotha v Sotheby's (No 2)*,[62] that there is a public policy in England that time does not run either in favour of the thief or in favour of any transferee who is not a purchaser in good faith. He identified that policy from sections 3 and 4 of the Limitation Act 1980, commenting that: "The law favours the true owner of property which has been stolen, however long the period which has elapsed since the original theft."[63] Therefore, although he found that German limitation law (applying a thirty year limitation period to theft) was applicable to the facts of the case, Moses J also held that, had the German limitation period expired, it would have been disapplied as being contrary to English public policy. He said:

> To permit a party which admits it has not acted in good faith to retain the advantage of lapse of time during which the plaintiffs had no knowledge of the whereabouts of the painting and no possibility of recovering it, is, in my judgment, contrary to the public policy which finds statutory expression in section 4.[64]

4.57 We agree with Moses J that it would be wrong to allow a limitation period to extinguish the claimant's right to his or her stolen property in favour of the thief, if the claimant has had no opportunity to bring a claim against the thief. However,

---

[60] See Limitation of Actions, Consultation Paper No 151 (1998), paras 13.51 - 13.64.

[61] John Grace QC (responding on behalf of the South Easter Circuit), Lovells, Holborn Law Society, and London Solicitors' Litigation Association.

[62] QBD, *The Times,* 8 October 1998.

[63] QBD, *The Times,* 8 October 1998, transcript, case no 1997/G/185, 9 September 1998, p 57.

[64] QBD, *The Times,* 8 October 1998, transcript, case no 1997/G/185, 9 September 1998, p 57.

we believe that the interests of the claimant will be sufficiently protected by the operation of the primary limitation period proposed under the core regime. In contrast to the current limitation regime, where the limitation period runs from the date of the accrual of the cause of action, the primary limitation period of the core regime starts from the date of knowledge. This is designed to ensure that the limitation period does not start to run until the claimant has had an opportunity to discover the relevant facts. And we propose to modify the date of knowledge so that the primary limitation period does not start until the claimant knows (or should know) of the location of the property. Where goods have been stolen, we think that the arguments against this modification have less force, and it is necessary to provide the claimant with additional protection.

4.58   It has, however, been suggested by the British Museum that the burden of demonstrating that reasonable steps have been taken to discover the relevant facts will be difficult for the claimant to discharge. Is it sufficient for the victim to have reported the theft to the police, and left them to take any further action? Must the victim also take action on his or her own behalf, by, for example, advertising the loss of valuable property in trade magazines?

4.59   We believe, however, that this puts no greater burden on the claimant than would be the case for any other cause of action for which the claimant is required to show that he or she had no constructive knowledge of the relevant facts. In each case, the claimant will be expected to act reasonably in relation to his or her potential cause of action. What the court regards as reasonable behaviour will be influenced by the fact that there has been a theft, and that there may be very little the claimant can do in practice to obtain the necessary information. The nature of the enquiries the owner can reasonably be expected to make will depend on the nature (and the value) of the property which has been stolen.[65] Given the subjective nature of the recommended test for constructive knowledge,[66] the court will also take into account the circumstances and abilities of the claimant. We consider therefore that the claimant is adequately protected by the operation of a primary limitation period based on the date of knowledge. As *City of Gotha v Sotheby's (No 2)*[67] illustrates, the courts are unlikely to have much sympathy for the thief, or for any purchaser who cannot demonstrate good faith. The claimant may therefore not have to face a very high hurdle. We do not consider that the fact that the thief has committed an act which is morally wrong excuses the claimant from his or her own obligation to pursue litigation within a reasonable time. We

---

[65]   In some cases (particularly where valuable art property is involved), the victim will be able to publicise the loss by entering details of the stolen property in the Arts Loss Register set up by insurance companies, dealer associations and auctioneers. This is a computerised information centre with offices in (inter alia) London and New York. All the main UK insurance companies subscribe to the Arts Loss Register, and when a theft is reported by an owner, the relevant information together with a picture of the stolen object is entered onto the register. The register is available for public searching, and is used by the major British auction houses to check provenance. See Patrick J O'Keefe, "The use of databases to combat theft of cultural heritage material" (1997) 2 AA&L 357, and DL Carey Miller, "Title to Art: Developments in the USA" [1996] SLPQ 115.

[66]   See paras 3.45 - 3.50 above.

[67]   QBD, *The Times*, 8 October 1998.

therefore adhere to our original view that the primary limitation period should apply to all claims for conversion, whether or not the conversion constitutes, or is related to, theft.

(b)   Theft and the long-stop limitation period

4.60   We suggested in the Consultation Paper that the long-stop limitation period should be disapplied in relation to claims for conversion constituting or relating to theft against anyone other than bona fide purchasers of the goods.[68] In claims for conversion the claimant may well, even after ten years, still be unable to identify the defendant, whether he or she be the original thief or a person to whom the stolen property has been passed. Consultees were strongly of the view that no long-stop limitation period should apply to claims for conversions constituting or relating to theft at least as against persons other than a bona fide purchaser. Indeed every consultee who considered this issue was of this view.

4.61   In the Consultation Paper we suggested that there was no need to modify the core regime, since the desired result could be achieved by reliance on our provisions for deliberate (or dishonest) concealment.[69] Under the core regime the long-stop limitation period will be disapplied wherever the defendant has been guilty of dishonest concealment of the relevant facts from the claimant.[70] We are now less confident that our recommendations on concealment will provide sufficient protection to the claimant whose stolen goods have passed out of the hands of the original thief to a donee or a purchaser who is not acting in good faith. Here, the defendant will usually have no connection with the claimant, and may have no idea who the original owner of the goods is, or where the goods originated from. It will therefore be less easy to argue that he or she has concealed information from the claimant. In order to remove any element of doubt, we no longer believe that it is sensible to rely solely on the concealment provisions. We therefore recommend that the core regime should be modified in relation to claims in respect of conversions which constitute theft or are subsequent to the theft, to provide that the long-stop limitation period should not commence until the date of the first bona fide purchase. However, to clarify the provisional proposal made in the Consultation Paper, once the long-stop limitation period has commenced on the date of the first bona fide purchase, it should apply for the benefit not only of the purchaser, but also any subsequent converter of the goods. Where however a conversion has been followed by a theft (from the convertor or from a third party who received the goods in succession to the convertor), the subsequent theft will not stop the long-stop limitation period running. In other words, we intend to retain the position under section 4 of the Limitation Act 1980, which limits the application of the special theft provision to thefts which precede any subsequent conversion.

---

[68]   Limitation of Actions, Consultation Paper No 151 (1998), paras 13.58 - 13.64.

[69]   Limitation of Actions, Consultation Paper No 151 (1998), paras 13.58 - 13.64.

[70]   See paras 3.140 - 3.145 above.

(4)   The Effect of the Expiry of the Limitation Period

4.62   Under the present law, as an exception to the general rule that the expiry of the limitation period merely bars the claimant's remedy, once the limitation period for a claim for conversion has expired, the claimant's title to the property is extinguished.[71] In the Consultation Paper we provisionally proposed that this exception should remain. We explained that we believe that it would be anomalous if a claimant were unable, because of limitation, to bring a claim in conversion against any defendant, yet was still regarded as the owner of the goods, and was thus able to retake the goods (if opportunity arose). However, because the operation of a date of knowledge test will mean that there may be a different limitation period in respect of claims against different defendants, we suggested that some modification was required.[72] We therefore provisionally proposed that where goods have been converted (whether or not there has been a theft) the claimant's title should become extinguished when both of the following conditions are satisfied:

(1)   the limitation period (whether the primary limitation period or the long-stop limitation period) has expired in relation to the claimant's claim in conversion against a defendant; and

(2)   at the time when that limitation period expired the goods remained in the possession of that defendant.

4.63   These provisional proposals were approved by over sixty-five per cent of consultees responding on this issue. Those consultees who disagreed felt that there should be no possibility of the thief or the mala fide purchaser ever benefiting from the expiry of the limitation period. The Council of Her Majesty's Circuit Judges argued that either a claimant whose goods had been stolen should never lose title to the goods (even where they are in the possession of a bona fide purchaser), or that title should only be extinguished after a period of at least thirty years.

4.64   The introduction of an exemption in relation to theft on the terms recommended above (paragraph 4.61) for the long-stop limitation period will go some way to meet the concerns of these consultees. However, we believe that a bona fide purchaser should be able to benefit from the expiry of a limitation period. Notwithstanding the comments of the Council of Her Majesty's Circuit Judges, it seems right to afford the bona fide purchaser some protection. The Council expressed particular concern about the trade in stolen antiquities and works of art. Here it is possible for the owner of stolen goods to seek to protect his or her position by registering the loss. It may well be difficult for a buyer who has not carried out searches in, for example, the Arts Loss Register, to demonstrate bona fides.

---

[71]   Limitation Act 1980, s 3(2).

[72]   Limitation of Actions, Consultation Paper No 151 (1998), para 13.69.

4.65 We remain of our provisional view that where goods have been converted the claimant's title should become extinguished when, because of limitation, he or she can no longer bring a claim against any defendant. However, we have reconsidered whether the modification to the general principle proposed in the Consultation Paper is necessary. We now think that, under the core regime, as under the present law, there should be one date on which all claims by the claimant (present or future) will be time-barred: the expiry of the long-stop limitation period. Our provisional proposals meant that the claimant would have lost the right to sue a second converter before the expiry of the long-stop limitation period (or the primary limitation period relevant to the claim against that defendant), because his or her title to the property would have been extinguished by the expiry of the primary limitation period governing a claim against the first converter. This seems wrong.[73] We therefore recommend that title should only be extinguished on the expiry of the long-stop limitation period.

4.66 The consequence of this recommendation, together with our recommendation that the long-stop limitation period should not apply to claims against a thief, means that a thief, or a male fide purchaser from a thief, will never be able to gain title to stolen goods as a result of the expiry of the limitation period. A bona fide purchaser of such goods and any subsequent purchaser could gain title to them following the expiry of the long-stop limitation period. This seems to be the correct approach. Given that any claim by the original owner for the return of the goods (or for compensation for their loss) would be time-barred after the expiry of the long-stop limitation period, it would be anomalous to regard him (or her) as being the true owner after that time.

4.67 **In summary, we therefore recommend that:**

(1) **All claims for conversion should be subject to the primary limitation period of the core regime. For claims which are related to theft, that period will not start to run until the claimant knows, or ought to know, not only the facts giving rise to the cause of action, but also the whereabouts of the stolen property. (Draft Bill, Cl 14(2), (5)).**

(2) **In respect of claims for conversion which are not thefts or related to a theft, the long-stop limitation period should run from the date of the first conversion only. (Draft Bill, Cl 14(1)).**

(3) **In respect of claims for conversion which constitute thefts or are subsequent to a theft, the long-stop limitation period should not commence until the date on which the goods are purchased by a person acting in good faith. It will run from that date in favour of the good faith purchaser and anyone claiming through him. (Draft Bill, Cl 14(3), (5)).**

---

[73] It is only the expiry of the long-stop limitation period which extinguishes the claimant's right to bring a claim under the Consumer Protection Act 1987. See para 4.36 above.

(4) **The claimant's title to goods which have been converted shall be extinguished on the expiry of the long-stop limitation period.** (Draft Bill, Cl 14(4)).

10. CLAIMS BY A SUBSEQUENT OWNER OF DAMAGED PROPERTY

4.68 Property may change hands after a cause of action has accrued to the person owning the property at the time of the damage. We noted in the Consultation Paper that this raises two issues: first, whether the subsequent owner has a cause of action against the person responsible for the damage; and, secondly, whether the limitation period for a claim in respect of that cause of action starts running against the subsequent owner when the previous owner has or ought to have the necessary knowledge, or not until the subsequent owner has acquired an interest in the property.[74]

4.69 Under section 3 of the Latent Damage Act 1986, a fresh cause of action is treated as accruing to the subsequent owner on the date he or she acquires the property, if that precedes the date when the material facts became known, or ought to have become known, to a person with an interest in the property.[75] In other words, if the original owner of the property knew or could reasonably have been expected to acquire knowledge of the damage, the subsequent owner will not have a cause of action, unless it has been assigned to him. However, if the original owner did not know, nor could reasonably have known, of the relevant damage, a subsequent owner has a 'new' cause of action in respect of that damage. For limitation purposes, this 'new' cause of action is treated as having accrued on the date when the original cause of action accrued. The subsequent owner then has three years from the date he or she learns of the facts relevant to the cause of action, or six years from the date on which the cause of action accrued, to bring proceedings in relation to the cause of action.

4.70 We provisionally proposed in the Consultation Paper that (a) (contrary to the present law) a fresh cause of action should accrue to a subsequent owner of damaged property even where the previous owner had knowledge of the material facts; and (b) the core regime should apply subject to the minor modification that the primary limitation period should start on the date when the claimant acquires an interest in the property, where this is later than the date of knowledge.[76] These proposals were supported by over sixty per cent of consultees.

4.71 However, one issue caused particular concern to those consultees who disagreed. It was suggested that there is no justification for placing the purchaser of damaged property in a better position than the person who owned the property at the time when the cause of action accrued. More particularly, it was pointed out[77] that, if the primary limitation period were to start on the date when the claimant

---

[74] Limitation of Actions, Consultation Paper No 151 (1998), para 13.71 -13.72.

[75] See Limitation of Actions, Consultation Paper No 151 (1998), para 3.100.

[76] Limitation of Actions, Consultation Paper No 151 (1998), para 13.71 - 13.76.

[77] By, in particular, Professor Andrew Tettenborn, the Construction Industry Council, the Construction Confederation and the Royal Institute of Chartered Surveyors.

acquired an interest in the property (where this is later than the date of knowledge), one would be inviting transfers of property made to ensure that a relative or other party connected to the original owner would benefit from a new limitation period.

4.72 This is a serious problem. We have therefore looked again at the approach adopted under section 3 of the Latent Damage Act 1986. This limits the circumstances in which a new cause of action accrues to the subsequent owner to those cases where the previous owner has no knowledge (whether actual or constructive) of the defect in the property, or in other words, where the damage to the property remains wholly latent until it is discovered by the subsequent owner. This solution suffers from the weakness identified in the Consultation Paper, namely that it makes the cause of action of the subsequent owner dependent on the state of knowledge of the previous owner.[78]

4.73 However, the circumstances in which a cause of action accrues in negligence are part of the substantive law of tort, which does not (apart from section 3 of the Latent Damage Act 1986) afford a cause of action to the subsequent owner of defective property.[79] To create a fresh cause of action for the subsequent owner where the previous owner knew of the defect, and therefore had the opportunity to bring a claim against the defendant, would considerably extend the circumstances in which what is a pure economic loss[80] can be claimed in the tort of negligence. Arguably this should only be done as part of a review of tort law. Moreover, the present law on limitation periods has the merit that a new cause of action only accrues to the subsequent owner when the relevant damage is truly latent (so that no one with an interest in the property has had the opportunity to bring a claim against the defendant before the subsequent owner). We therefore intend to adopt the approach that is followed in section 3 of the Latent Damage Act 1986.

4.74 The claim by the subsequent owner will however still be subject to the core regime. The primary limitation period will run from the date on which the subsequent owner has (or ought to have) knowledge of the facts giving rise to the cause of action. The subsequent owner will have a cause of action in tort which does not accrue until he has suffered damage. The starting date, therefore, will be the date of the act or omission which gave rise to his claim, which (depending on the facts of the case), is likely to be the date on which the defective work was done to the property.

4.75 We therefore recommend that:

(1) **A cause of action shall accrue to the subsequent owner of damaged property as provided for in section 3 of the Latent Damage Act 1986, that is where**

---

[78] This aspect of the current law was criticised by N J Mullany, "Reform of the Law of Latent Damage" (1991) 54 MLR 349.

[79] See for example *Murphy v Brentwood District Council* [1991] 1 AC 398.

[80] *Murphy v Brentwood District Council* [1991] 1 AC 398.

(a)   a cause of action has accrued to any person in respect of any negligence to which damage to any property is attributable (in whole or in part); and

(b)   the subsequent owner acquires an interest in the property after the date on which that cause of action accrued, but before any person with an interest in the property has the knowledge relevant to the date of knowledge for a claim in respect of that cause of action.

(2)   **The claim by the subsequent owner shall be subject to the core regime.** (Draft Bill, Sch 3, para 23).

11.   CLAIMS FOR RESTITUTION

4.76   We provisionally proposed in the Consultation Paper that restitutionary claims should be subject to the core regime.[81] This was accepted by all consultees who responded to this question.[82]

4.77   Since the publication of the Consultation Paper, *Kleinwort Benson Ltd v Lincoln City Council*[83] has been decided by the House of Lords. This decision has recognised that money paid under a mistake of law should be recoverable, even where the 'mistake' in question results from a change in the law after the relevant payment has been made. The Law Lords held that section 32(1) of the Limitation Act 1980 applied, so that the period of limitation did not begin to run until the claimant could with reasonable diligence have discovered the mistake. Where the courts change an understanding of the law which has applied for several years (and under which the claimant made the relevant payment), the claimant will have six years from that date to bring his or her claim, however long ago the relevant payments were made. The following comments were made:

> I recognise that the effect of section 32(1)(c) is that the cause of action in a case such as the present may be extended for an indefinite period of time. I realise that this consequence may not have been fully appreciated at the time when this provision was enacted, and further that the recognition of the right at common law to recover money on the ground that it was paid under a mistake of law may call for legislative reform to provide for some time limit to the right of recovery in such cases. The Law Commission may think it desirable, as a result of the decision in the present case, to give consideration to

---

[81]   Limitation of Actions, Consultation Paper No 151 (1998), paras 13.77 - 13.83. For a summary of the current law, see paras 2.48 - 2.51 above.

[82]   Although Professor Birks preferred different terminology so as to make clearer the distinction between claims in (autonomous) unjust enrichment and restitution for wrongs. For this distinction and the meaning of autonomous unjust enrichment, see P Birks, *An Introduction to the Law of Restitution* (rev ed 1989) pp 22 - 25, 40 - 44, 346 - 355; A Burrows, *The Law of Restitution* (1993) pp 16 - 21, 376, 440. See also Limitation of Actions, Consultation Paper No 151 (1998), para 5.4.

[83]   [1999] 2 AC 349.

this question indeed they may think it wise to do so as a matter of urgency. (Lord Goff of Chieveley).[84]

The most obvious problem is the Limitation Act, which as presently drafted is inadequate to deal with the problem of retrospective changes in law by judicial decision. (Lord Hoffmann).[85]

4.78 The problems referred to will be considerably alleviated by the implementation of the core limitation regime which we propose. The primary limitation period of three years will run from the date on which the claimant discovers, or ought reasonably to discover, the facts which give rise to the cause of action (including the fact that his view of the law was mistaken), the identity of the defendant and the fact that the defendant has received a significant benefit. This provides a similar starting point to that set out under section 32(1)(c) of the Limitation Act 1980, namely the date of the decision changing the law. However, the long-stop limitation period, of ten years, will run from the date of the accrual of the cause of action. In a claim to recover money paid under mistake of law this will be the date on which the defendant is enriched. No enrichment received by the defendant over ten years before the date of the judgment could therefore be recovered.

4.79 **We recommend that the core regime should apply to restitutionary claims.**[86]

12. CLAIMS FOR A CONTRIBUTION OR AN INDEMNITY

(1) Contribution under section 1 of the Civil Liability (Contribution) Act 1978[87]

4.80 We provisionally proposed in the Consultation Paper that claims for a contribution under section 1 of the Civil Liability (Contribution) Act 1978 should be subject to the core regime, subject to the modification that, to avoid the problem of a chain of contribution claims, there should be a single long-stop limitation period running from the date of the judgment or settlement in the original proceedings to which the contribution claim relates.[88] Over sixty per cent of consultees responding on this issue approved this proposal. There was some opposition to the extension of the limitation period from the present two year period, on the grounds that three years was too long a period, and that there is no justification for the extension other than a desire for consistency.[89] There was also

---

[84]   [1999] 2 AC 349, 389.

[85]   [1999] 2 AC 349, 401.

[86]   That is, claims in autonomous unjust enrichment and, in so far as independent from a claim for a wrong, a claim for restitution for wrongful enrichment.

[87]   See para 2.77 above for a summary of the current law.

[88]   Limitation of Actions, Consultation Paper No 151 (1998), paras 13.84 - 13.92.

[89]   The view of the Royal Institute of Chartered Surveyors and Ernst & Young.

some concern that the suggested long-stop limitation period exposed the defendant to potential liability for too long.[90]

4.81 The benefits of ensuring that such claims are subject, as far as possible, to the same limitations regime as other causes of action appear to us to outweigh the suggested disadvantages. We appreciate that, if the long-stop is to start from the date of judgment or settlement the long-stop limitation period will be considerably extended from the date of the events giving rise to liability in the original proceedings. However, the relevant liability of the defendant to a contribution action is his or her liability to make contribution to his or her co-obligor and this is triggered not by the act or omission of the contributor vis-à-vis the claimant in the original proceedings but by the judgment or settlement giving rise to the contribution action (and for the avoidance of doubt we will retain the provisions of the 1980 Act in relation to the accrual of the cause of action under the Civil Liability (Contribution) Act 1978 to define the starting date for the long-stop limitation period). We believe that in practice the long-stop limitation period is unlikely to be relevant in many cases, because a person entitled to contribution will normally have the relevant knowledge to start the primary limitation period shortly after the judgment or settlement in the original proceedings.

4.82 We have however been persuaded to reconsider our original proposal that a *single* long-stop limitation period should apply to all claims for a contribution which arise out of the same facts, because of the significant problems that we discuss below in relation to claims for a contractual indemnity.[91] We do not believe that a sufficient distinction can be drawn between a claim for contribution under the Civil Liability (Contribution) Act 1978, and a claim for a contractual contribution or indemnity, to justify applying a different limitations regime to a claim in respect of each cause of action. We therefore propose that each claim for a contribution should be subject to a separate long-stop limitation period, which will run from the date of the judgment or settlement in the proceedings to which the claim relates. This leaves open the risk that there could be a chain of contribution claims, with a final trial of the claim several years after the events which gave rise to it. However, we have received no evidence to suggest that this is a significant problem under the current law (which can in theory also give rise to a chain of limitation periods, each starting from the date of the judgment or settlement giving rise to the cause of action).

4.83 **We recommend that the core regime should apply to claims for contribution under section 1 of the Civil Liability (Contribution) Act 1978, and that the provisions of the Limitation Act, section 10 (which define the date on which the cause of action for such claims accrues)**

[90] A concern expressed by Professor Andrew Tettenborn, Victor Joffe QC, John Grace QC, responding on behalf of the South Eastern Circuit, Munich Reinsurance Company, Holborn Law Society, the Construction Federation and Ernst & Young.

[91] See paras 4.88 - 4.93 below.

should be retained to define the starting date for the long-stop limitation period (Draft Bill, Cl 13).

(2) Contractual Indemnity

(a) Introduction

4.84 We provisionally proposed in the Consultation Paper that claims for a contractual indemnity should be subject to the core regime but with the modification that, to avoid the problem of a chain of indemnities, there should be a single long-stop limitation period running from the date of the judgment or settlement in the original proceedings to which the indemnity claim relates.[92] This proved to be controversial. A substantial proportion of consultees responding on this issue (over forty-five per cent) approved the proposal that claims for a contractual indemnity should be subject to the core regime. However considerable concern has been voiced by representatives of the insurance and reinsurance industries, both as to the application of the core regime, and more particularly, to the proposal that a single long-stop limitation period should apply to all claims for a contractual indemnity arising from the same facts. These concerns are discussed below.

(b) The primary limitation period

4.85 Although some consultees suggested that the reduction of the limitation period from six years to three years would impose considerable additional costs on reinsurers and lead to increased litigation,[93] others felt that the three year limitation period would be acceptable in the context of reinsurance contracts, and even one of those opposed to the primary limitation period noted that:

> there is an argument for saying that reinsureds need to be more efficient in pursuing their reinsurance recoveries. ... A reduced initial limitation period may have the advantage of encouraging that.[94]

4.86 A more significant concern was that the introduction of the three year limitation period without transitional provisions could have the effect of reducing the reinsurance assets of insurers and reinsurers. Excess Insurance noted that this could "wipe millions of pounds from balance sheets, potentially resulting in many insolvencies".[95] We discuss this point below.

4.87 The majority of consultees agree that the core regime should be applied to claims for a contractual indemnity. The use of the primary limitation period of three years generates little concern outside the reinsurance industry; and the concern of consultees from that industry would be considerably reduced if the new Act provides for a transitional period, which is sufficiently long to ensure that claimants are not deprived of an existing right to bring a claim. We accept that

---

[92] Limitation of Actions, Consultation Paper No 151 (1998), paras 13.93 - 13.98.

[93] A point made by Unionamerica Insurance Company Ltd, Excess Insurance and Lovells.

[94] Paisner & Co.

[95] See paras 5.33 - 5.40 below in which we discuss commencement provisions.

such a transitional period is needed. Our proposals for transitional provisions are discussed at paragraphs 5.33 to 5.40 below.

(c)   A single long-stop limitation period

4.88   Our provisional proposal that where there are chains of indemnity contracts in respect of the same liability there should be a single long-stop limitation period starting from the date of the judgment or settlement in the original proceedings to which the claim relates has caused the greatest concern. Consultees have universally expressed the view that this would be unworkable in the context of the reinsurance industry. As Paisner & Co have noted, "Chains of indemnity in the form of contracts of reinsurance is the mechanism by which the reinsurance industry operates". All reinsurance consultees responding have made the point that the chains involved may be very lengthy, and that it is not unusual for claims to be paid several decades after the events which gave rise to them.[96] If a single ten year long-stop limitation period is applied to reinsurance claims, the limitation period would be likely to expire before the claim reached the ultimate retrocessionaire. This will mean that the reinsurance purchased by reassureds further down the chain has no value, reducing the assets of such companies, and increasing the risk of insolvencies. Concern was also expressed that this proposal could damage the amount of international business transacted in the London market.

4.89   Thus although over forty-five per cent of consultees who responded on this issue favoured the suggestion that claims for a contractual indemnity should be subject to a single long-stop, it is clear from the unanimous submissions we have received from representatives of the insurance and reinsurance industry that subjecting all reinsurance claims in a chain of reinsurance contracts to a single long-stop would have a very adverse effect on the London reinsurance market, and would probably prove to be unworkable.

4.90   One option would be to retain the proposed single long-stop limitation period but only in respect of contracts other than insurance or reinsurance contracts. Adopting this option could create additional problems in defining those contracts for an indemnity which would be exempt from the modification.[97] It is also

---

[96]   We have been informed by the Institute of Actuaries, for example, that reinsurance claims in respect of Hurricane Alicia, which took place in 1983, are still being paid, and may continue to be paid for the next ten or fifteen years.

[97]   There does not appear to be a widely accepted statutory definition of 'insurance' or 'reinsurance'. Instead, varying definitions, often surprisingly circular, are adopted according to the context of the particular legislation. The Insurance Companies Act 1982 itself defines 'contract of insurance' in s 96 as including "any contract the effecting of which constitutes the carrying on of insurance business by virtue of s 95 above." Section 95 (also an inclusive definition) itemises the main forms of insurance business. No clearer definition is available from the authorities. Malcolm Clarke has remarked in *The Law of Insurance Contracts* (3rd ed, 1997) p 1, that "The English Courts know an elephant when they see one, so too a contract of insurance, and talk, for example, of 'those who are generally accepted as being insurers'". He also notes "Insurance contracts are best seen (and defined, if at all) according to the angle or line of approach, that is, the context or issue before the court" (*ibid*, p 2).

unclear whether it is necessary, or justifiable, to introduce a modification to the core regime which is limited to a small subset of contracts for an indemnity.

4.91   It seems better to subject all claims for a contractual indemnity to the core regime. Where a chain of indemnity claims is in question, therefore, the long-stop limitation period for a claim by one party in the chain of indemnity claims against the party next in the chain would be determined entirely by the date of the breach of contract of that party, irrespective of when the liability covered by the indemnity actually arose. With a reinsurance claim (or other form of liability insurance) the long-stop limitation period would run from the date on which the liability of the reinsured in respect of the risk reinsured has been settled, by judgment or agreement.[98] A new long-stop limitation period would arise for each claim in the chain.

4.92   We have little evidence from our consultees that chains of indemnity are felt to be a real problem even in the other area in which they occur, the construction field.[99] On the contrary, the responses we have received from consultees connected to the construction industry who dealt with this point suggest that it is not a real problem. We have therefore decided to follow the first option.

4.93   **We recommend that the core regime should apply to claims for a contractual indemnity. This will mean that where there is a chain of indemnity claims, a new long-stop limitation period will arise in respect of each new claim in the chain.**

13.   CLAIMS FOR BREACH OF TRUST AND RELATED CLAIMS

4.94   Generally, a claim by a beneficiary to recover trust property in respect of any breach of trust is subject to a limitation period of six years from the date on which the cause of action accrued. But in two cases no limitation period applies: first, where the beneficiary's claim is in respect of any fraud or fraudulent breach of trust to which the trustee was a party or privy; and secondly where the beneficiary's claim is to recover trust property, or its proceeds, from the trustee.[100]

4.95   In the Consultation Paper, we provisionally proposed that the core regime should apply to all claims for breach of trust and claims to recover trust property, and expressed the view that the core regime, and in particular our proposals for deliberate (or dishonest) concealment, obviated the need for separate provisions in

---

[98] In the case of other forms of insurance, such as property insurance, the long-stop limitation period will run from the date of the breach of contract, which, as under the present law, will be the date of the occurrence of the insured event.

[99] The Construction Industry Council noted that "In the great majority of instances all in an indemnity chain are aware of the likelihood of being required to meet their liability. Cascades of actions are rare." IN Duncan Wallace QC commented: "Certainly in the construction industry, any such chain is not likely to be very long, and protective writs or notices of arbitration can, as stated, be expected at an earlier stage given the practical realities of multipartite construction disputes."

[100] Limitation Act 1980, s 21. See paras 2.39 - 2.45 above.

respect of fraudulent breaches of trust.[101] We also provisionally proposed that the core regime should apply in the same way to claims for breach of fiduciary duty; for breach by a trustee of the 'self-dealing' and 'fair-dealing' rules; for dishonestly assisting or procuring a breach of fiduciary duty, in so far as these do not constitute a breach of trust;[102] and to claims in respect of the personal estate of a deceased person.[103]

4.96 These proposals have been widely supported by the majority of consultees. Over eighty-five per cent of consultees responding on this issue agreed with our provisional view that claims for breach of trust should be subject to the core regime. Over eighty per cent agreed with our provisional view with respect to fraud, and around seventy per cent with respect to 'fair-dealing' and 'self-dealing'. Over eighty-five per cent of consultees agreed that the core regime should apply to claims in respect of the personal estate of a deceased person. However, some opposition has been expressed to the proposal that claims for fraudulent breach of trust and claims to recover trust property should be subject to the core regime.

(1) Fraudulent Breach of Trust

4.97 It has been argued that, as a matter of public policy, trustees who have been guilty of a fraudulent breach of trust should never be able to claim the benefit of a limitation period.[104] Concern has also been expressed[105] that disapplying the long-stop limitation period only where the defendant has been guilty of dishonest concealment does not provide the claimant with adequate protection.

4.98 We have previously taken the view that the only conduct of the defendant which should have implications for the limitation regime is conduct which directly affects the operation of the regime. For this reason, we have recommended that where the defendant has dishonestly concealed facts relevant to the cause of action the long-stop limitation period should be suspended until the concealed fact was or could have been discovered, but that neither the primary nor the long-stop limitation period should be disapplied merely because the claim is for fraud. Equally, we consider that the arguments against applying the primary limitation period to a claim for fraudulent breach of trust are not persuasive. If the claimant is aware (or ought to have been aware) of the facts necessary to bring proceedings in respect of his or her cause of action, such proceedings should be commenced promptly, even against a fraudulent trustee. Indeed it has been suggested that where an allegation of fraud has been made, it is particularly important in the interests of justice (not least to the defendant) to ensure that the claim is brought before the courts to be tried as soon as possible after the alleged fraud has been discovered.[106]

---

[101] Limitation of Actions, Consultation Paper No 151 (1998), paras 13.99 - 13.102.

[102] Limitation of Actions, Consultation Paper No 151 (1998), paras 13.103 - 13.104.

[103] Limitation of Actions, Consultation Paper No 151 (1998), paras 13.105 - 13.108.

[104] By the Country Landowners Association.

[105] By the General Council of the Bar.

[106] Lynton Tucker, responding on behalf of the Chancery Bar Association.

4.99 The case for disapplying the long-stop limitation period for claims for fraudulent breach of trust is stronger, but ultimately unpersuasive. We have previously taken the view that a fraudulent breach of trust will in most cases necessarily imply that the trustee has also been guilty of dishonest concealment, and that the date of knowledge requirement in the primary limitation period on the one hand, and the suspension of the long-stop on the other, in all cases where there has been dishonest concealment provides sufficient protection.[107] In practice therefore, the long-stop limitation period will rarely apply in respect of claims against a fraudulent trustee.

4.100 We have considered whether the core regime should be modified to disapply the long-stop limitation period where the trust property has passed from the fraudulent trustee to a third person. There would be a claim against the third party if he or she was either a purchaser who was not acting in good faith, or a recipient of the goods who did not provide value for them. Under the present law, no limitation period would apply to such a claim.[108] Although, as in the case of theft (discussed in paragraphs 4.60 to 4.61 above) it is not clear that such a person could be said to have dishonestly concealed relevant facts from the beneficiary, he or she would be claiming through the trustee - who would in most cases have been guilty of dishonest concealment from the claimant. In addition, each time there is a transfer of the trust property in breach of trust (whether fraudulent or not) a fresh long-stop limitation period will start running. This will further limit the risk that the claimant will not have knowledge of the relevant facts before the long-stop limitation period has expired.[109] We do not therefore consider that it is necessary to disapply the long-stop limitation period.

4.101 **Accordingly, we recommend that (subject to our recommendations in paragraph 4.112 below) all claims for breach of trust should be subject to the core regime.**

(2) Claims to recover trust property

(a) Should there be a limitation period?

4.102 The justification for the exclusion under the present law of any limitation period in respect of claims to recover trust property from the trustee is that the trustee bears a special responsibility to the beneficiaries of his or her trust, and that it would be wrong to allow the trustee to benefit from the property which he or she holds for others. This is a variation of the argument that fraud and related civil claims should be given special treatment by the limitation regime to mark society's disapproval of the defendant's conduct. There is no suggestion that the fact that the defendant trustee has retained trust property makes it uniquely difficult for

---

[107] Limitation of Actions, Consultation Paper No 151 (1998), para 13.104.

[108] *G L Baker Ltd v Medway Building and Supplies Ltd* [1958] 1 WLR 1216. See Limitation of Actions, Consultation Paper No 151 (1998), para 4.16.

[109] The same problem is not as significant in relation to theft, as in the majority of cases the claimant merely has to show that there has been a theft, and does not have to identify the original thief.

the claimant to discover the facts relating to his or her cause of action, or otherwise to bring proceedings against the defendant. We do not therefore believe that the fact that the claimant is bringing a claim to recover property against his or her trustee is sufficient ground to give the claim special limitation treatment.

(b) Should the long-stop limitation period run from the date of the first breach of trust?

4.103 It has been suggested that claims against third parties to recover trust property could create difficulties where there have been multiple substitutions and transfers of the property which the claimant seeks to recover. This could indeed give rise to a chain of potential claims. Under the current law, a fresh cause of action - and in consequence a fresh limitation period - will accrue on each occasion trust property is received by a third party in breach of trust. In relation to claims for conversion we have recommended that, where there has been a chain of successive conversions, the long-stop limitation period should commence on the date of the first conversion only.[110] Since one might regard a claim to recover trust property as equity's equivalent to the common law claim in conversion, we therefore need to consider whether the same modification should be made where there is a potential chain of claims in relation to the equitable, rather than legal, title.

4.104 Although we have found this question difficult to answer, we do not believe that such a modification is necessary. This is for three principal reasons. First, no such protection is provided under the present limitation regime. Secondly, no consultee suggested that such a modification was required or that the present regime gave rise to any difficulty. Thirdly, unlike the position in relation to claims for conversion, a bona fide purchaser will have a defence to the claimant's claim for recovery of trust property. The recommencement of the long-stop limitation period is therefore far less likely to create risk of commercial insecurity over a long period of time in relation to claims for equitable, as opposed to legal, title.

(c) Bare trusts

4.105 In the case of a bare trust, it is arguable that a claim to recover the trust property will arise as soon as a declaration of trust is executed on terms that the trustee holds property on trust for the beneficiary absolutely. That is, the cause of action does not depend on the trustee acting inconsistently with the terms of that trust.[111] Clearly, it would be inappropriate for the primary limitation period to run from the date on which the beneficiary has knowledge of the relevant facts: namely the fact of the declaration of trust and the identity of the trustee. And it would also cause problems where there is a long term trust if the long-stop limitation period were to run from the date of the declaration of trust. If that were the case, the long-stop limitation period may well have expired before the beneficiary has any cause for complaint against the trustee. To avoid this result, we propose to provide that, in the case of a claim for the recovery of trust property held on a bare trust,

---

[110] See paras 4.52 - 4.53 above.

[111] We are grateful to Lynton Tucker, responding on behalf of the Chancery Bar Association, for drawing our attention to this point.

the cause of action shall not accrue unless and until the trustee acts in breach of trust (whether by failing to transfer the property to the beneficiary or in any other way). As a result, the primary limitation period will not commence until the claimant knows of that breach of trust in addition to the other the facts giving rise to the cause of action; and the long-stop limitation period will not commence until the date on which the breach of trust takes place.

4.106 **Accordingly, we recommend that:**

(1) **claims to recover trust property should be subject to the core regime; but**

(2) **in the case of a claim for the recovery of trust property held on a bare trust, the cause of action shall not accrue unless and until the trustee acts in breach of trust.** Draft Bill, Cl 22(2).

(d)   Miscellaneous

(i)   No benefiting from another beneficiary's claim

4.107 Section 21(4) of the Limitation Act 1980 incorporates the rule in equity that where a claim by one beneficiary has become time-barred, that beneficiary should not be permitted to benefit from a successful claim by another beneficiary which is not time-barred. Under the present limitation regime, this becomes relevant where the beneficiaries under a trust include both beneficiaries with an interest in possession and beneficiaries with a future interest. Time does not start to run against those with a future interest until their interest has fallen into possession.[112] The same applies under the core regime. We therefore recommend that this equitable provision is retained.

(ii)   Limiting the liability of the trustee?

4.108 Section 21(2) of the Limitation Act 1980 provides protection for a trustee who wrongly distributes trust property to beneficiaries including him or herself. Provided that the trustee acted honestly and reasonably, his or her liability in any claim for breach of trust commenced after the expiry of the limitation period relating to claims brought to recover trust property against persons other than trustees is limited to the amount which he or she retained in excess of the rightful entitlement. This protection is provided in recognition of the fact that it will be too late for the trustee to commence any claim against the other beneficiaries to recover their wrongful distributions.

4.109 In contrast to the position under the current law, under our recommendations, all claims for the recovery of trust property will be subject to a limitation period. Where the trustee has honestly and reasonably but wrongly distributed trust property, the limitation period in respect of his or her action to recover that property from the overpaid beneficiaries will not commence until the trustee knows, or ought to know, of the wrongful distribution. If the trustee only becomes

---

[112] Limitation Act 1980, s 21(3). See paras 4.116 - 4.118 below.

aware of the wrongful distribution when an action is brought for breach of trust against him or her, the trustee will therefore have sufficient time to commence proceedings against those other beneficiaries who have been overpaid. Though it is still possible that a beneficiary might bring a claim against the trustee just within the long-stop limitation period, so that the trustee only became aware of his potential liability after the period had ended, the same applies under the current law. We do not consider it necessary, therefore, to re-enact this provision.

(iii) Claims by persons other than beneficiaries

4.110   The present general six year limitation period applies only to claims by a beneficiary. A claim by the Attorney General against the trustees of a charitable trust is not therefore subject to any limitation period.[113] The same would seem to apply to a claim by the Charity Commission under section 32 of the Charities Act 1993 for breach of charitable trust. It has been suggested to us[114] that the application of the primary limitation period to such claims would cause major problems, because neither the Attorney General nor the Charity Commissioners have the resources to investigate each potential cause of action about which they receive information. Three years may well go by before either agency is able to commence proceedings. We are also informed that the priority of the Attorney General is often to ensure that the future administration of the charity will be satisfactory, to protect the interests of the beneficiaries. This aim, which requires the co-operation of the existing trustees, would be prejudiced by an immediate investigation of the facts made with a view to ascertaining liability for past breaches of trust. For these reasons, and to ensure that the effectiveness of the role of the Attorney General and the Charity Commissioners in the oversight of public and charitable trusts is not reduced, we consider that the primary limitation period should not apply claims brought by them.

4.111   The application of the long-stop limitation period of ten years would also cause difficulties. In the case of charitable trusts it may be some time before evidence of any breach of trust reaches the attention of anyone in a position to take action against the trustees. Registered charities with an annual income or expenditure of over £10,000 have to send a report and accounts every year, and an annual return of specific information. However, we are informed[115] that these charities are less than one-third of the total number of registered charities, and that a substantial further number of charities are either excepted from the requirement to register with the Charity Commission, or exempt from the supervisory jurisdiction of the Charity Commission. The application of the long-stop limitation period might therefore in many cases prevent any claim being brought against a charitable trustee who is in breach of trust. We therefore consider that the long-stop limitation period should not apply to claims for breach of trust which are brought by either the Attorney General or the Charity Commissioners.

[113] *Attorney-General v Cocke* [1988] Ch 414. See Limitation of Actions, Consultation Paper No 151 (1998), para 4.30.

[114] On behalf of the Attorney General.

[115] By the Charity Commission.

4.112   **Accordingly, we recommend that:**

(1)   **Legislation should provide that where a claim by one beneficiary has become time-barred, that beneficiary should not be permitted to benefit from a successful claim by another beneficiary whose claim is not time-barred.** (Draft Bill, Cl 22(4)).

(2)   **Pursuant to the application of the core regime, there is no need to provide a trustee with protection equivalent to that which is currently found in Limitation Act 1980, section 21(2).**

(3)   **Neither the primary limitation period nor the long-stop limitation period should apply to claims for breach of trust or to recover trust property which are brought by either the Attorney General or the Charity Commissioners.** (Draft Bill, Cl 22(3)).

(3)   Exclusions from the Core Regime

4.113   It has been suggested to us that the core regime should not apply to applications to the court relating to the appointment, retirement or removal of trustees, judicial trustees or a vesting order, applications to vary the terms of a trust, or for directions relating to the administration of a trust by the trustees. Such applications relate purely to the administration of the trust and are not claims in which one party is claiming relief against another. It is foreseeable that these questions in relation to the administration of the trust may arise over ten years after the founding of a trust. The determination of such an application may be necessary for the continuation of the trust and a limitation period should not prevent this. We agree. Such applications will not be 'claims' within the definition which we propose, in that the claimant does not seek a remedy for a wrong, restitution or the enforcement of a right. They will, therefore, not be subject to the limitation regime which we recommend.

(4)   Distinctions between Law and Equity

(a)   Introduction

4.114   In principle, we believe that, since both common law title and equitable title are forms of ownership, the limitation regime should aim to apply the same treatment to each.[116] Under the core regime, the differences between the limitation regime applicable to claims to recover property at common law and in equity will be minimal. We have, however, already noted one difference: we have recommended that the long-stop provisions of the core regime should be modified for claims for conversion, but not for claims to recover trust property. We have explained our reasons for this recommendation.[117]

---

[116]   We are grateful to Professor Andrew Tettenborn for drawing our attention to the importance of this point.

[117]   See paras 4.52 - 4.53 and 4.103 - 4.104 above.

4.115 The core regime, as applied to claims for breach of trust under our provisional proposals, would have given rise to a further distinction between the limitation regime applying to common law and equitable ownership, in the treatment of future or contingent interests. This is discussed below.

(b) Future or contingent interests

4.116 Under the current law, no right of action can accrue to any beneficiary who is entitled to a future interest in trust property until that interest has fallen into possession.[118] The rationale for this rule, as explained in *Armitage v Nurse*,[119] is that a beneficiary with a future interest should not be made to litigate (at considerable personal expense) in respect of an injury to an interest which he or she may never live to enjoy. In addition, in some cases a beneficiary with a future interest will not be in a position to bring proceedings to protect that interest. This applies where the beneficiaries are not of full age and capacity, or where the beneficiaries have not been ascertained.

4.117 Although we provisionally recommended that provision should be made for future interests in the context of claims to recover land[120] we did not suggest in the Consultation Paper that the same should apply to future interests in trust property. However, in principle we believe that it should. The need for such a provision may not arise frequently in respect of the primary limitation period since the time at which the beneficiary would be expected to discover the relevant facts will be affected by the fact that the beneficiary does not have an interest in possession. A beneficiary with a future or contingent interest would not be acting unreasonably if he or she did not scrutinise the affairs of the trust until the interest fell into possession. However, in the case of a family trust, the beneficiary with a future or contingent interest may well be aware that the trustee has acted in breach of trust, yet it would still not be reasonable to expect him or her to commence litigation until that interest has fallen into possession. We therefore recommend that the primary limitation period in respect of a claim by a beneficiary with a future or contingent interest in trust property will not start until that interest has fallen into possession.

4.118 The long-stop limitation period presents a further problem. It could expire before the beneficiary has an interest in possession. Our recommendations in respect of claimants under a disability will provide some protection where the beneficiary is a minor. But where the beneficiary is an adult it becomes considerably more likely that the long-stop limitation period will expire before there has been anything to put the beneficiary on notice of the existence of a breach of trust. It has been suggested to us by Lynton Tucker, responding on behalf of the Chancery Bar Association, that it would be excessively burdensome and wrong to require adult beneficiaries with future interests to scrutinise the affairs of the trust just in case there has been a breach of trust about which they should complain (particularly as

---

[118] See Limitation Act 1980, s 21(3). See also Sch I, para 4 to the Act (relating specifically to future interests in land).

[119] [1998] Ch 241, 261, per Millett LJ.

[120] Limitation of Actions, Consultation Paper No 151 (1998), paras 13.118 - 13.121.

the beneficiaries concerned may not appreciate that they are beneficiaries). The same applies to beneficiaries with a contingent interest. And there may be cases where no beneficiary is able to commence proceedings in respect of a breach of trust: most obviously where the beneficiary is unascertained. For this reason, and to ensure consistency with our recommendations for land-related claims, we propose that the long-stop limitation period for claims by a beneficiary with a future or contingent interest shall not start before the date on which the interest falls into possession.

4.119 **We recommend that neither the primary limitation period nor the long-stop limitation period in respect of a claim for breach of trust or to recover trust property by a beneficiary with a future or contingent interest will start until that interest has fallen into possession.** (Draft Bill, Cl 22(1)).

(5) Claims in respect of the personal estate of the deceased

4.120 The present limitation period in respect of any claim in respect of the personal estate of a deceased person is twelve years from the date on which the right to recover the share or interest accrues. The limitation period to recover arrears of interest in respect of any legacy is six years from the date on which the interest became due. However, no limitation period applies where the personal representative is acting as trustee and there is a fraud, or where the claim is to recover trust property or its proceeds from the personal representative.[121]

4.121 In the Consultation Paper we provisionally proposed that the core regime should apply to claims in respect of the personal estate of a deceased person (including any claims in respect of arrears of interest on legacies).[122] These proposals have been approved by around ninety per cent of consultees. However, the Country Landowners Association suggested that a limitation period of three years would not be sufficient in the context of the administration of complicated estates. This point has not been raised by any other consultee, and there do not appear to be any problems unique to claims in respect of the personal estate of a deceased person which would justify changing the length of the primary limitation period which would otherwise be applicable to them under the core regime.

4.122 Under the current law the limitation period commences on "the date on which the right to receive the share or interest accrued".[123] The courts have held that in the case of an immediate legacy, this is the date of death of the deceased, despite the fact that the personal representative is entitled to a year after the date of death ("the executor's year") before being obliged to distribute the assets.[124] The

---

[121] Limitation Act 1980, s 22 and s 21(3).

[122] Limitation of Actions, Consultation Paper No 151 (1998), para 13.108.

[123] Limitation Act 1980, s 22(a).

[124] Administration of Estates Act 1925, s 44 provides that "Subject to the foregoing provisions of this Act, a personal representative is not bound to distribute the estate of the deceased before the expiration of one year from the death." See Limitation of Actions, Consultation Paper No 151 (1998), para 4.36.

Chancery Bar Association suggested that it should be made clear that neither limitation period could start to run before the end of the executor's year, or if later, before the date of the grant of probate or letters of administration to the personal representative.

4.123 However, we have concluded that such modification is not necessary. It is not entirely clear when the cause of action will be treated as accruing for the purpose of the application of the core regime. That is, does the executor's year prevent the cause of action accruing until at the earliest the expiry of one year from the date of death, or can the cause of action accrue immediately, the executor's year merely representing a restriction on the claimant's right to sue? If the former is the correct interpretation, then the primary limitation period will not in any event commence until on or after this date. If the latter is correct, then although the claimant may have a right of action, his or her ability to commence proceedings is subject to a legal restriction. We recommend that special provision is made for such cases later in this paper.[125] On either interpretation, the primary limitation period will not start until the end of the year.

4.124 The long-stop limitation period for a claim to a share in the personal estate of the donor will start from the date on which the cause of action accrues, which is likely to be the last date on which the personal representative should have distributed the estate. Where the personal representative has simply been dilatory (so that the claimant is relying on an omission) it may well be unclear when the long-stop limitation period started. Providing that the long-stop for a claim against a personal representative shall always run from the last day of the executor's year would provide a definite and clearly ascertained starting point, but this may not be the appropriate date. Even in the case of an immediate legacy, the personal representatives do not necessarily become immediately liable to the beneficiaries under the will if they do not distribute the deceased's estate by the end of the executor's year. The consequence of the end of this period is that an onus falls on the personal representatives to show some valid reason for the delay.[126] As the cause of action may not, therefore, have accrued by the end of the executor's year, it is difficult to justify a general rule that the long-stop limitation period should start at that date.

4.125 **Accordingly we recommend that the core regime should apply to claims in respect of the personal estate of a deceased person (including any claims to arrears of interest on legacies).**

14. CLAIMS TO RECOVER LAND AND RELATED CLAIMS

(1) The General Position

4.126 Generally, claims to recover land are subject to a limitation period of twelve years, which runs from the date on which the claimant's right of action accrued, or, if

---

[125] See paras 5.24 - 5.28 below.

[126] See Williams, Mortimer and Sunnucks, *Executors, Administrators and Probate* (18th ed, 2000) p 116, citing *Grayburn v Clarkson* (1868) LR 3 Ch App 605.

the right first accrued to some other person through whom the claimant claims, then the date on which the right accrued to that person. This date will usually be when the land first came to be in adverse possession, but special provision is made in certain cases, in particular when the claimant has only a future interest in the land.[127]

4.127　In the Consultation Paper we provisionally recommended that the primary limitation period of three years running from the date of knowledge should not apply to claims to recover land.[128] We explained that in many cases the defendant's trespass will be discoverable immediately, or very soon after. Applying the core regime would therefore mean that the limitation period would have been reduced from twelve years to three, and we believed this to be unacceptably short. On the other hand, in cases where there was an issue as to whether the claimant had knowledge of the adverse possession, there could be enormous uncertainty. It would be necessary to ascertain not only when the adverse possession commenced, but also when the claimant knew (or ought to have known) that the defendant was in possession of the piece of land in question and had the necessary *animus possidendi*. Although we are generally content that the degree of uncertainty inherent in any test for the 'date of knowledge' is a price worth paying for the fairness of the result, we explained that in the case of ownership of land we believed that the need for certainty was of particular importance. Moreover, we explained that the date of knowledge test did not sit easily with the existing rule that time runs against an owner regardless of his or her knowledge of the adverse possession, and we were reluctant to put forward any reform that would alter the nature of adverse possession.

4.128　Instead, therefore, we provisionally recommended that a long-stop limitation period commencing on the date of adverse possession should be the sole limitation period applying to such claims. We asked consultees whether that limitation period should be ten years (as under the core regime) or twelve years (the period applying under the current law).[129]

4.129　The suggestion that a single limitation period running from the date of adverse possession (as defined under the current law) should apply to claims to recover land received substantial support from consultees: over seventy-five per cent agreed. There was less agreement as to the length of that period. The largest proportion of consultees (around twenty-five per cent) would accept a limitation period of ten years. A smaller proportion argued in favour of a period of twelve years. Periods of fifteen years or twenty years were also suggested.[130]

---

[127]　Limitation Act 1980, s 15 and Sch 1. See further paras 2.52 - 2.59 above and paras 4.133 - 4.134 below.

[128]　Limitation of Actions, Consultation Paper No 151 (1998), para 13.121.

[129]　Limitation of Actions, Consultation Paper No 151 (1998), para 13.121.

[130]　Three per cent favoured each of the following options: fifteen years, twenty years, and a period between ten and fifteen years (unspecified).

4.130   It has been suggested that, as land-related claims need to be given special treatment, the attempt to bring them partially within the core regime by applying the long-stop limitation period to them is misguided. We accept that the regime applying to claims to recover land is substantially different to other claims within the core regime, not least because the effect of the expiry of the limitation period is to extinguish the claimant's title to the land rather than to provide the defendant with a defence to any claim made by the claimant. We propose therefore, instead of legislating for a defence to a claim to recover land, to retain the existing statutory formula that no claim to recover land may be brought after the expiry of the limitation period. This is however a change in emphasis rather than in substance. The limitation period applying to claims to recover land will be ten years - the length of the long-stop limitation period. It will start on the day on which the claimant's cause of action accrues (as would be the case with the long-stop limitation period), and we propose to re-enact the current provisions in relation to the accrual of the cause of action for a claim to recover land. In addition, the provisions of the core regime in relation to the extension of limitation period (namely in relation to agreements, concealment, acknowledgments and part payments and disability) will apply.

4.131   It was suggested that the doctrine of adverse possession should be abolished. One of the original justifications for the doctrine of adverse possession (to prevent claims when all evidence is lost and to ensure certainty of title) no longer applies because of the existence of the Land Register. We noted in our Consultation Paper that any radical reform of the concept of adverse possession was beyond the remit of a project reviewing the law on limitation periods.[131] In fact the existence of the system of land registration seems to strengthen the case for a ten year period. Proposals for the reform of adverse possession of registered land have now been put forward by the Law Commission in Land Registration for the Twenty-First Century: A Consultative Document.[132] Under these proposals, a person in adverse possession of land which has a registered title would be able to apply for registration as proprietor of that land following ten years of adverse possession. Notice of the application would be given to anyone who appeared from the Land Register to have title to the land, who would thereupon have the opportunity to object to the application. Any such objection would lead to the dismissal of the application for registration, unless the adverse possessor could show: (i) that it would be unconscionable for registered proprietor to seek to dispossess the applicant, and that the adverse possessor ought to be registered as proprietor; (ii) that he had some independent right to the land that entitled him to be registered as proprietor; or (iii) that the land in adverse possession is adjacent to his own land and the exact line of the boundary between the two has never been determined, that he has been in adverse possession of the land in question in the reasonable belief that the land in question belonged to him, and that the estate he seeks was registered more than one year ago. The registered proprietor would then have two years within which to bring a claim to recover the land from the adverse

---

[131]   Limitation of Actions, Consultation Paper No 151 (1998), para 13.113.

[132]   Law Com No 254 (1998).

possessor.[133] If these proposals are accepted, it is likely that the recommendations made in this report will only apply to unregistered land, and claims in respect of interests in registered land which are not themselves capable of registration.[134]

4.132 The proposals contained in the Consultative Document on Land Registration give the landowner significantly greater protection against the squatter where title to the land is registered. If the owner of unregistered land wishes to benefit from the same protection, he or she can apply for registration of his or her land. This removes much (if not all) of the cause for concern expressed over our provisional proposal that the general limitation period for claims to recover land should be reduced to ten years.

4.133 The general rule we recommend in this Report, of ten years running from the date of adverse possession, would, however, require modification where the claimant has only a future interest in the land. Such an interest might include not only the reversionary interest expectant on the determination of a life interest, but also the reversion of a lease. Under the present law, time does not generally run in such cases until the interest falls into possession.[135] That is, the right of action is treated as arising when the interest falls into possession through the determination of the preceding interest, provided that the person entitled to the preceding interest was in possession of the land at that time, and that no-one had already taken possession by virtue of the future interest claimed.[136] Where the person entitled to the preceding interest in the land was not in possession at the date when that interest determined, the limitation period is the longer of (i) twelve years from the date the right of action accrued to the person entitled to the preceding interest or (ii) six years from the date on which the right of action accrued to the person entitled to the succeeding interest.[137]

4.134 As we explained in the Consultation Paper, we do not think it appropriate, in the course of this review, to change the law so as to accelerate the running of time against future interests. We therefore recommend that the general rule is subject to an exception so that where the claimant's interest is a future interest, the limitation period should not begin to run until that interest falls into possession, where this is later than the date of adverse possession. This exception would itself

---

[133] If the registered proprietor failed to do so within this time, the adverse possessor could apply to be registered as proprietor as of right.

[134] Such as a short lease, or a tenancy or licence at will of registered land.

[135] See further, Limitation of Actions, Consultation Paper No 151 (1998), para 13.118.

[136] Limitation Act 1980, Sch 1, para 4. The same general rule also applies to leases.

[137] Limitation Act 1980, s 15(2). But this provision does not apply in the case of any estate or interest which falls into possession on the determination of an entailed interest and which might have been barred by the person entitled to the entailed interest. Here, time will run against a person entailed in remainder, even though he or she may have no entitlement to possession of the land during the limitation period: Limitation Act 1980, s 15(3). In addition, where the claimant has both a present and a future interest in land, and his or her right to bring an action to recover the present interest has become time-barred, he or she may not bring an action to recover the future interest unless in the meantime someone has recovered possession of the land under an intermediate interest: Limitation Act 1980, s 15(5).

be subject to the exceptions which currently allow time to run against a claimant with a future interest,[138] though where the person entitled to the preceding interest was not in possession when that interest determined, we do not propose to impose a separate limitation period as in section 15(2) of the 1980 Act. Instead, the normal limitation period will apply.

4.135   **We therefore recommend that:**

(1)   **a long-stop limitation period of ten years commencing on the date that the claimant's right to recover the land accrued[139] (or, if later, the date on which the claimant's interest becomes an interest in possession) should apply to, and (subject to the recommendation in paragraph 4.147 below) be the sole limitation period for claims to recover land[140] (Draft Bill, Cl 16(1), (2));**

(2)   **that a claimant entitled to a future interest to land which was in adverse possession before that interest fell into possession should be subject to a limitation period of ten years from the date on which his or her interest fell into possession rather than a reduced period;**

(3)   **the expiry of the limitation period will extinguish the claimant's rights to the land in question, and after that period, no claim may be made. (Draft Bill, Cl 18(1)). But we would emphasise that, if the Law Commission's proposals on adverse possession in registered land are accepted, the recommendation will only be applicable to interest in unregistered land and unregistrable interests in registered land.**

4.136   Subject to the special rules in relation to claims by beneficiaries in respect of any fraud or fraudulent breach of trust to which the trustee was a party or privy and in respect of claims against trustees,[141] the provisions in relation to claims to recover land contained in the Limitation Act 1980 apply to claims to recover equitable interests in land in exactly the same way as they apply to recover legal interests in land.[142] Further provision is made in recognition of the special structure of holdings of settled land and land held on trust. In the case of settled land, where the limitation period relating to a tenant for life's or statutory owner's claim to

---

[138]   Limitation Act 1980, s 15(3) and (5). See para 4.133 n 137 above.

[139]   We do not intend to change the date of accrual of the cause of action from that provided for under the present law. This will generally be the date of the commencement of adverse possession as provided under Part I of Schedule I to the Limitation Act 1980 (Draft Bill, Schedule 1). We also recommend that provision should be made to retain the special rules in respect of the relation back of actions to recover land by an administrator of an estate (Limitation Act 1980, s 26) and the cure of defective disentailing assurances (Limitation Act 1980, s 27) (Draft Bill, Cl 17(4) and 21).

[140]   Subject to the exceptions presently set out in Limitation Act 1980, s 15(3) and (5).

[141]   See Limitation of Actions, Consultation Paper No 151 (1998) paras 4.14 - 4.16.

[142]   Limitation Act 1980, s 18.

recover land has expired, his or her legal estate is not extinguished if the right of action to recover the land of any person entitled to a beneficial interest in the land either has not yet accrued or has not yet become statute-barred. Only if and when every such right is barred is the title of the tenant for life or statutory owner extinguished.[143] Similar provisions apply in relation to land held on trust. Where the limitation period relating to the trustees' claim to recover land has expired, their title is not extinguished so long as the right of any beneficiary has not yet accrued or is not yet time-barred.[144] The statutory owner and the trustees are then expressly empowered to bring a claim on behalf of any person entitled to a beneficial interest to recover the land, even though their own claim to recover the land may be time-barred.[145]

4.137 We consider that the same general position should apply under our recommended regime. However, we have recommended that those special rules in relation to claims by beneficiaries in respect of fraudulent breaches or against their trustees should no longer apply. **We therefore recommend that the limitation period in relation to all claims to recover equitable interests in land should be the same as that which applies in relation to claims to recover legal interests in land.** (Draft Bill, Cl 17(2), (3)). **The further provisions presently contained in section 18(2) to 18(4) of the Limitation Act 1980 should be retained.** (Draft Bill, Cl 18(2), (3), (4)).

(2)   Special Protection: Claims by the Crown (other than in relation to foreshore)[146] and by a Spiritual or Eleemosynary Corporation Sole

4.138 Under the present law, the limitation period for claims to recover land is extended to thirty years in the case of a claim brought by the Crown or by a spiritual or eleemosynary corporation sole ('the Church').[147] In the Consultation Paper we provisionally proposed that the special protection applicable to claims by the Crown or by a spiritual or eleemosynary corporation sole should be abolished.[148] This would reduce the limitation period applicable to such claims from thirty years to ten years. We explained that we did not consider that the amount of land held by either the Crown or the Church gives sufficient reason to qualify either of them for special protection, given that there are other landowners in both the public and the private sector with extensive holdings which might justify similar treatment. Around fifty-five per cent of consultees who considered this issue

---

[143]   Limitation Act 1980, s 18(2).

[144]   Limitation Act 1980, s 18(3).

[145]   Limitation Act 1980, s 18(4).

[146]   See paras 4.145 - 4.147 below.

[147]   Part II of Schedule I to the Limitation Act 1980. A special limitation period of sixty years applies in the case of actions by the Crown to recover foreshore: see further paras 4.145 - 4.147 below.

[148]   Limitation of Actions, Consultation Paper No 151 (1998), para 13.126.

agreed with our provisional proposals. Three government departments[149] and the Ecclesiastical Law Association disagreed.

4.139   The responses that we received from government departments noted that our proposals would oblige the Crown (a) to reduce public access to much of its land, and (b) to incur disproportionate costs in policing that land. In addition, the Ministry of Agriculture, Fisheries and Food ('MAFF') argued that it held extensive parcels of land, the husbandry of which is left to independent contractors, scientific institutions and other third parties. MAFF officials would therefore not very often be in a position to ascertain the factual position in relation to that land, let alone the legal position.

4.140   While we recognise the force of these arguments, we believe that much of this concern would be allayed by the adoption of the proposals contained in Land Registration in the Twenty First Century, A Consultative Document.[150] Any government department that is concerned that it would not necessarily become aware of encroachments onto its land within the ten year limitation period would then be able to register its interest in the relevant land,[151] and rely on objecting to any application for registration made by a squatter. Accordingly we adhere to our original view that there is no need for a special limitation period in relation to claims by the Crown (subject to paragraphs 4.145 to 4.147 below) or the Church to recover land.

4.141   However, the Ecclesiastical Law Association noted in its submission to us that there are separate concerns affecting only the Church. The Association explained that our proposals would cause problems in respect of parsonage land, and churches and churchyards. Both categories of land are vested in the incumbent for the time being of the benefice, and thus in a spiritual corporation sole. However, there are often long periods during which a benefice is vacant (most often when presentation to the benefice has been suspended under the Pastoral Measure 1983).[152] During the periods when there is no incumbent, the freehold is 'in abeyance'. Therefore, although the land remains vested in the corporation sole, there is no means of animating the corporation. The Association was concerned that during this period encroachments might occur and time run in favour of an adverse possessor, despite the fact that no person would be in a position to commence proceedings to recover the land.[153]

---

[149]   The Ministry of Defence, the Ministry of Agriculture, Fisheries and Food and the Treasury Solicitor's Department.

[150]   Law Com No 254 (1998).

[151]   Although at present the Crown is unable to register its title to land it holds in demesne as paramount lord under the Land Registration Act 1925, this will change under the proposals made by the Law Commission in relation to Land Registration.

[152]   This may, we are informed, apply at any one time to over a quarter of the benefices in England.

[153]   Although it is possible that the sequestrators of the benefice could commence proceedings for trespass in respect of parsonage land: Church of England (Miscellaneous Provisions) Measure 1992.

4.142   We recognise this problem. However, we believe that it can, and should, be resolved without retaining the thirty year limitation period. A more satisfactory approach to extending the relevant limitation period would be to provide some mechanism to ensure that there is never a period during which no claim could in practice be commenced by the Church to recover the land. This could be achieved by providing that, in any case where the freehold is in abeyance because there is no incumbent, a claim may be brought in the name of, and on behalf of the spiritual corporation sole by

     (1)   the priest-in-charge of the benefice, or

     (2)   the sequestrators of the benefice.[154]

4.143   Analogous solutions have been adopted in other contexts. For example, the Land Compensation Act 1961 provides: "Where the fee simple of any ecclesiastical property, not being property in Wales or Monmouthshire, is in abeyance, it shall be treated for the purposes of this Act as being vested in the Church Commissioners".[155] Likewise, the Church Commissioners are deemed to hold, or are enabled to act in relation to, land belonging to a vacant benefice by, for example, the Commons Registration Act 1965,[156] the Town and Country Planning Act 1990,[157] and the Water Resources Act 1991.[158]

4.144   **Accordingly we recommend that**

     (1)   claims brought by, or by a person claiming through, the Crown (subject to paragraphs 4.145 to 4.147 below) or any spiritual or eleemosynary corporation sole to recover land should be subject to the same limitation period applying to a claim by any other party to recover land; and

     (2)   in any case where the land is vested in the incumbent from time to time of a benefice as a spiritual corporation sole but the benefice is vacant a claim to recover the land or any part of it may be made by

         (a)   the priest-in-charge of the benefice, or

         (b)   by the sequestrators of the benefice. (Draft Bill, Cl 17(5)).

---

[154]   As defined in section 1(1) of the Church of England (Miscellaneous Provisions) Measure 1992.

[155]   Land Compensation Act 1961, s 34.

[156]   Commons Registration Act 1965, s 19.

[157]   Town and Country Planning Act 1990, s 318.

[158]   Water Resources Act 1991, s 67.

(3) Special Protection: Claims by the Crown to Recover Foreshore

4.145 Special protection is given to claims by the Crown to recover foreshore.[159] The relevant limitation period is sixty years from the date of accrual of the cause of action, or thirty years from the date when the land ceased to be foreshore (whichever first expires). We asked consultees whether (as an alternative to abolishing all the protections offered to the Crown) retaining a special limitation period for claims relating to the foreshore could be justified.[160] We recognised that the nature of this land, not least the fact that the boundaries of foreshore are subject to constant change as the coast erodes, and that much of the sea bed is concealed, creates particular difficulties for monitoring the land.

4.146 The majority of consultees who considered this issue thought that special protection should be retained in relation to claims by the Crown to recover foreshore. They pointed to the difficulty of monitoring the boundaries of this land. The Crown faces particular difficulties as the Marine Department of the Crown Estate has to police almost all the foreshore in England and Wales. We have been persuaded by these arguments that special protection should be afforded to the Crown in respect of claims to recover foreshore. Accordingly we do not propose any reform to the general limitation period currently applying to claims to recover foreshore. Where the land has ceased to be foreshore, we believe that the ten year limitation period which we generally recommend in relation to claims to recover land (rather than the present thirty year period) should apply.

4.147 **We therefore recommend that the limitation period applicable to claims by the Crown to recover foreshore should be**

(1) sixty years from the date of accrual of the right of action or

(2) ten years from the date when the land ceased to be foreshore

whichever period first expires. (Draft Bill, Cl 16(4), (7)).

(4) Miscellaneous Provisions

(a) Squatters and the Crown

4.148 We discussed in the Consultation Paper whether any new Limitation Act should clarify the effect of successful adverse possession against the Crown of land which does not fall within the Crown's sovereign title but is owned by the Crown.[161] If section 17 of the Limitation Act 1980 is read literally, adverse possession against the Crown extinguishes the whole of the Crown's title so that the squatter would

---

[159] That is "the shore and bed of the sea and of any tidal water, below the line of the medium high tide between the spring tides and the neap tides." (Limitation Act 1980, Sch 1, para 11(3)).

[160] Limitation of Actions, Consultation Paper No 151 (1998), para 13.126.

[161] Land which falls within the Crown's sovereign title cannot be the subject of adverse possession.

acquire a title to land which is allodial.[162] However, there does not in practice appear to be any uncertainty as to the intention behind this section, and we do not now consider that it is necessary to include any provision on this matter.

(b)   The commencement of adverse possession

4.149   Subject to one point, we do not propose to change the present law as to the date on which the cause of action accrues in relation to a claim to recover land. As under the current law, this will depend on the date on which the defendant, or some person from whom he derived title, has taken adverse possession of the land in question, and the rules laid down in Schedule 1 to the Limitation Act 1980 will be re-enacted. The one change we wish to make relates to the position where there has been a series of adverse possessors of the land in question. Under the current law, a change in the identity of those in adverse possession of the land will not affect the running of the limitation period against the claimant. Even if a second squatter has dispossessed an earlier squatter, he or she is able to claim the benefit of the adverse possession by that squatter to allege that the limitation period has expired against the claimant.[163] This seems unreasonable. We therefore propose that a new cause of action should accrue to the claimant when there is a change in the identity of the people in adverse possession of the land. Where more than one person is in possession of the land, this will not apply unless all the existing squatters leave. There will be two other exceptions to this principle. If the second squatter claims through the first squatter because, for example, he 'bought' the land in dispute from the first squatter, no new cause of action will accrue to the claimant. The same will apply where a squatter who was himself dispossessed of the land in question returns to resume his adverse possession. In each case the squatter will continue to be able to claim the benefit of the earlier adverse possession by the squatter who has been replaced.

4.150   **We therefore recommend that**

(1)   **Where the identity of the person in adverse possession of the land changes, a new cause of action shall accrue to the claimant, unless anyone in adverse possession of the land before the change continues to be in adverse possession after that date. (Draft Bill, Sch 1, para 1(4), (5)(a))**

(2)   **However, no new cause of action will accrue to the claimant**

(a)   **where the second person in adverse possession claims possession through his or her predecessor (Draft Bill, Sch 1, para 1(5)(b)) and**

---

[162]   That is, held independently of any ultimate lordship. Similarly, the Land Registration Act 1925, s 75(1) can be construed so that the statutory trust in favour of the squatter is a trust of the whole of the Crown's registered interest.

[163]   See *Mount Carmel Investments Ltd v Peter Thurlow Ltd* [1988] 1 WLR 1078, CA.

(b) **where the squatter coming into possession is recovering possession of the land from a squatter who had previously dispossessed him or her** (Draft Bill, Sch 1, para 1(6)).

(5) Claims to recover the proceeds of the sale of land

4.151 Under the present law, no claim may be brought to recover the proceeds of the sale of land after the expiry of twelve years from the date on which the right to receive the money accrued.[164] A vendor of land possesses an equitable lien on the property for the amount of the purchase money. This lien, which is not dependent on possession, entitles the vendor to apply to the court for a sale of the property in satisfaction of his or her claim, or to rescind the contract and recover possession of the land. As with other claims to enforce a sum of money secured on property, we consider that such a claim is analogous to a claim to recover land, and that the same limitation regime should apply. **Accordingly, we recommend that claims to recover the proceeds of the sale of land should not be subject to the primary limitation period of three years from the date of knowledge but only to the long-stop limitation period of ten years running from the date when the vendor became entitled to recover the proceeds (by, for example, enforcing a lien over the land).** (Draft Bill, Cl 19).

(6) Provisions of the core regime which modify the long-stop limitation period

4.152 We have recommended that under our core regime the long-stop limitation period of ten years should be modified in two circumstances: first, where the claimant is a minor,[165] and secondly, where the defendant has dishonestly concealed relevant facts from the claimant.[166] Where the claimant is a minor, we have recommended that the long-stop limitation period should run, but not so as to bar a claim before the claimant has reached the age of twenty-one. This recommendation fits easily with our recommendations in relation to claims to recover land. Where, for example, the claimant is a beneficiary with an equitable interest in land, the limitation period applicable to his or her claim to recover that land may run, but will not expire before he or she is aged twenty-one. We should note that, in accordance with our recommendations that the long-stop limitation period should run where the claimant is under a disability other than minority, the limitation period applying to a claim to recover land will not be extended where an adult claimant is under a disability.

4.153 Our recommendations in relation to the long-stop limitation period and dishonest concealment also apply in this area. We have recommended that where the defendant dishonestly conceals relevant facts from the claimant, the long-stop

---

[164] Limitation Act 1980, s 20(1).

[165] See para 3.121 above.

[166] See para 3.145 above.

limitation period shall be suspended until the fact concealed by the defendant was or should have been discovered.[167]

(7)   Claims to recover rent

4.154   Under the present law, no claim may be brought (or distress made) to recover arrears of rent, or damages in respect of arrears of rent, more than six years from the date on which the arrears became due.[168] In the Consultation Paper we provisionally proposed that claims to recover arrears of rent should fall within our core regime (that is, a primary limitation period of three years from the date of knowledge with a long-stop of ten years from when the rent should have been paid).[169] As we noted in the Consultation Paper, there is less reason to depart from the core regime in respect of such claims as opposed to other land-related claims.

4.155   This proposal was accepted by over ninety per cent of the consultees who responded on this issue. The Country Landowners' Association argued against this reduction on the grounds that, particularly in family situations, there may be good reasons for a landlord to delay suing for rent:

> a landlord may hold back from suing for rent because a tenant has been making plans to give up the holding due to ill-health or age, in which case the outstanding rent could be offset against other claims, e.g. by compensation that will be due to the tenant. Similarly a landlord might refrain from demanding outstanding rent in times of financial hardship for the tenant, such as during the current economic climate.

4.156   We appreciate that in some cases a reduced limitation period may discourage the benevolence of landlords. However, even if the limitation period is reduced, there are alternative means by which a landlord who does not wish to sue a tenant may protect his or her entitlement to the outstanding rent. For example, a landlord could agree an extension of the limitation period with the tenant. Or, before the expiry of the limitation period, he or she could seek a written acknowledgment from the tenant of the amount of rent owed. Such acknowledgment would extend the limitation period. We therefore remain of the view that there are not sufficient grounds to afford special treatment to these claims.

4.157   **Accordingly, we recommend that the core regime should apply to claims to recover rent, claims to recover damages in respect of arrears of rent, and the levying of distress for unpaid rent.**

---

[167]   See para 3.145 above.

[168]   Limitation Act 1980, s 19.

[169]   Limitation of Actions, Consultation Paper No 151 (1998), para 13.136.

15. CLAIMS RELATING TO MORTGAGES AND OTHER CHARGES

(1) Introduction

4.158 We discuss below how we recommend that the core regime should apply to claims related to mortgages and other charges, that is a claim by the mortgagee or chargee to enforce the security, or to recover the debt secured, and claims by a mortgagor or chargor to redeem the security.

4.159 The provisions of the Limitation Act 1980 which relate to claims in respect of mortgages and charges under the current law only refer to claims to recover a principal sum of money or arrears of interest which are secured by a mortgage.[170] No express provision is made for claims whereby the claimant seeks to enforce an obligation other than the payment of money which is secured by a mortgage or charge. Thus, if a guarantor of a lease agrees to take an assignment of the lease if the tenant defaults, and secures that undertaking by a charge on his or her property, it is not clear whether a claim to enforce the charge falls within the limitation regime currently applying to claims relating to charges.[171] This is unsatisfactory. We do not consider that a valid distinction can be drawn between claims to enforce an obligation to pay money and claims to enforce any other obligation when each obligation is secured by a mortgage or charge. Our recommendations in relation to mortgages and charges will therefore apply to all such claims irrespective of the nature of the obligation secured by the mortgage or charge.

(2) Claims by a mortgagee or chargee

(a) Claims to enforce a mortgage or charge over land

4.160 Under the present law, no claim may be brought to recover any principal sum of money secured by a mortgage or charge over land after the expiry of twelve years from the date on which the right to receive the money accrues.[172] A claim to recover arrears of interest payable in respect of any sum of money secured by a mortgage or charge over land, or to recover damages in respect of such arrears, is subject to a limitation period of six years from the date on which the interest becomes due.[173] Foreclosure claims are treated as claims to recover land, and are subject to a limitation period of twelve years from the date on which the right of action accrues to the claimant, or a person through whom he claims.[174] Similarly, claims for possession of land are claims to recover land, and are subject to a

---

[170] Limitation Act 1980, s 20. See paras 2.62 - 2.66 above.

[171] See, generally, Land Registration for the Twenty-First Century: A Consultative Document, Law Com No 254 (1998), paras 9.1 - 9.3.

[172] Limitation Act 1980, s 20(1).

[173] Limitation Act 1980, s 20(5). Foreclosure actions in respect of land are specifically excluded from the operation of this provision: Limitation Act 1980, s 20(4). Thus, it would appear that no period of limitation applies to the recovery of interest where a mortgagee forecloses on a mortgage of land.

[174] Limitation Act 1980, ss 20(4) and 15(1). Generally, the mortgagee's right to foreclose accrues when the mortgagor is in default on the proviso for redemption and the mortgagee's estate is, at law, absolute.

limitation period of twelve years from the date on which the right of action accrues to the claimant, or a person through whom he claims.[175]

4.161 In the Consultation Paper we provisionally proposed that only the long-stop limitation period should apply to claims to enforce a mortgage or charge over land, and that the primary limitation period should not apply to such claims.[176] A majority of consultees, over sixty per cent of those responding on this issue, agreed with our provisional proposal. Around ten per cent more agreed that only a long-stop limitation period should apply, but argued that the relevant period should be twelve, rather than ten, years. A minority of consultees (around fifteen per cent), argued that the core regime should apply in its entirety.

4.162 The justification for excluding claims to enforce a mortgage or charge over land from the application of the primary limitation period is twofold. First, as a matter of principle, the underlying and primary remedy of a mortgagee or chargee is the realisation of security. Thus, a claim to enforce a mortgage or charge over land is a species of claim to recover land, and it would be anomalous if a different limitation regime were to apply from that which is generally applied to claims to recover land.[177] Secondly, as a matter of practice, the primary species of mortgage or charge over land is the mortgage or charge over dwelling houses. Reducing the limitation period applicable to claims to enforce a mortgage or charge over land from twelve to three years might lead the lender to resort more rapidly to enforcing the security, making the borrower homeless as a consequence. It would, of course, be possible to treat claims to enforce a mortgage or charge over a dwelling house differently from claims to enforce a mortgage or charge over other forms of land.[178] However, we consider that this would create unnecessary complexity.

4.163 A number of consultees argued that allowing mortgagees or chargees a longer limitation period than the three year primary limitation period for claims to enforce a mortgage or charge over land would have equally adverse practical consequences. It was suggested that mortgagees will delay commencing proceedings until the amount outstanding on the mortgage is so large that the borrower has no opportunity to pay it within a realistic time-frame, so that the mortgagee has no alternative but to take possession. This argument was rejected by other consultees, most notably the Land Registry, which argued that reducing the limitation period could increase the number of occasions on which a lender will enforce its security.

---

[175] Limitation Act 1980, ss 38(7) and 15(1). Generally, the mortgagee's right to possession accrues immediately the mortgage is executed: *Four Maids Ltd v Dudley Marshall* [1957] Ch 317, 320, *per* Harman J. However, where the mortgage provides for quiet enjoyment by the mortgagor until default, the mortgagee's right to possession accrues on the date of default: *Wilkinson v Hall* (1837) 3 Bing NC 508, 132 ER 506.

[176] Limitation of Actions, Consultation Paper No 151 (1998), para 13.131.

[177] Our recommendations in respect of actions to recover land are set out at para 4.135 above.

[178] As one consultee suggested.

4.164   Accordingly, notwithstanding the views of those consultees who argued that the core regime should apply to claims to enforce a mortgage or charge over land in its entirety, we adhere to our provisional proposal that these claims should be treated analogously to claims to recover land.

4.165   In the Consultation Paper we provisionally proposed that the long-stop limitation period should begin to run on the date when the principal sum of money repayable on a loan, or interest thereon, is due but not paid.[179] However this would not cover those situations where the obligation secured by the mortgage or charge is an obligation other than the payment of money. We therefore consider that the long-stop limitation period should begin to run on the date on which the mortgagee's or chargee's right to enforce the mortgage or charge accrues.

4.166   **Accordingly, we recommend that**

   (1)   the primary limitation period should not apply to claims to enforce a mortgage or charge over land; and

   (2)   the long-stop limitation period should apply to claims to enforce a mortgage or charge over land, running from the date on which the mortgagee's or chargee's right to enforce the mortgage or charge accrues (Draft Bill, Cl 15(2)).

   (b)   Claims to enforce a mortgage or charge over personal property

4.167   Under the current law, the limitation period applying to a claim to recover any principal sum of money secured by a mortgage or charge over personal property is twelve years from the date on which the right to receive the money accrues.[180] A claim to recover arrears of interest payable in respect of any sum of money secured by a mortgage or charge over personal property, or to recover damages in respect of such arrears, is subject to a limitation period of six years from the date on which the interest becomes due.[181] The limitation period applying to a foreclosure claim in respect of mortgaged personal property is twelve years from the date on which the right to foreclose accrues.[182]

4.168   We recommended at paragraph 4.166 above that the primary limitation period should not apply to claims to enforce a mortgage or charge over land. There were two justifications for this departure from the core regime. First, that claims to recover land, whether directly or by the enforcement of a security over land, should be treated similarly. Secondly, reducing the limitation period applicable to claims relating to mortgages of land (and thus of houses) might have an adverse impact on the housing market. Neither apply in the case of claims to enforce a mortgage or charge over personal property. Nor are there any other reasons not to

---

[179]   Limitation of Actions, Consultation Paper No 151 (1998), para 13.131.

[180]   Limitation Act 1980, s 20(1)(a). The 1980 Act does not define "personal property", other than providing that "personal property" does not include chattels real (s 38(1)).

[181]   Limitation Act 1980, s 20(5).

[182]   Limitation Act 1980, s 20(2).

apply the full core regime to such claims. The primary limitation period would commence on the date on which the claimant knows, or ought reasonably to know, the facts which establish that his or her right to enforce the mortgage or charge has accrued. The long-stop limitation period would start from the date on which the right of action accrues. Establishing the relevant dates should not give rise to undue difficulty.

4.169 **We recommend that claims to enforce a mortgage or charge over personal property should be subject to the core regime.**

(c)   Claims to enforce a mortgage or charge over both land and personal property

4.170 Applying different limitations regimes to mortgages or charges over land and over personal property raises the question which regime should apply when the security in question covers both land and personal property. Under the current law, as we have seen,[183] the same limitation periods are applied to claims to recover money both secured by mortgages or charges over land and over personal property. Limitation periods in respect of mortgages or charges over personal property were introduced on the recommendation of the Law Revision Committee, who criticised the lack of limitation periods for such claims:

> This position appears to us to be unsatisfactory and gives rise to such anomalous cases as *Re Jauncey* ([1926] Ch 471) where there was a mixed fund consisting of the proceeds of the sale of real and personal property and the mortgagee of the fund was held to be entitled to enforce his security against so much of the fund as consisted of the proceeds of the personalty, but to be statute-barred in respect of the proceeds of the realty.[184]

Accordingly, they recommended that the limitation periods applicable to claims for the recovery of money charged on real property should also apply where money is charged on personal property.

4.171 We do not consider that it is unacceptable to have separate limitation periods applying to claims in respect of mortgages or other charges over real property and over personal property (as illustrated by our recommendations above). However, where the charge concerned is over a mixed fund comprising both land and personal property, it would appear to be more desirable for a single limitations regime to apply to any claim to enforce the mortgage. This would avoid the potential anomaly identified by the Law Revision Committee.

4.172 If a single limitation period is to apply to claims to enforce mortgages or charges over mixed funds, the relevant limitation regime must be that applying to claims in relation to securities over land. Applying the full core regime, including the primary limitation period of three years from the date of knowledge, to mortgages

---

[183] See paras 4.160 and 4.167 above.

[184] Law Revision Committee, *Fifth Interim Report (Statutes of Limitation)* (1936) Cmd 5334, p 15.

over mixed funds would increase precipitate litigation which might otherwise have been avoided, and, where the land in question included a dwelling house, could increase the number of repossessions (so potentially increasing homelessness).[185]

4.173 **Accordingly, we recommend that**

(1) **the primary limitation period should not apply to claims to enforce a mortgage or charge over both land and personal property;[186] and**

(2) **the long-stop limitation period should apply to claims to enforce a mortgage or charge over land and personal property, running from the date on which the mortgagee's or chargee's right to enforce the mortgage or charge, *vis-à-vis* the land, accrues (Draft Bill, Cl 15(2), (9).**

(d) *Claims to enforce an obligation secured by a mortgage or charge by suing on the covenant to repay.*

4.174 In some cases, a mortgagee may bring a claim on a secured loan and seek a money judgment only, without relying in any way on the security. The position is not entirely clear, but it appears that the limitation period applying to such a claim under the current law is twelve years from the date on which the right to receive the money accrues.[187] Similarly, where the claimant seeks arrears of interest payable in respect of the secured loan (but without relying on the security) the limitation period is six years from the date on which the interest becomes due.[188]

4.175 This position can be contrasted with the treatment of claims on secured loans in other areas. It was held in *National Westminster Bank v Kitch plc,*[189] for example, that a claim by a bank for repayment of an overdraft secured by mortgage is not a 'mortgage action' for the purposes of Order 88 of the Rules of the Supreme Court,[190] unless the bank was seeking to rely on the mortgage.

---

[185]   As we note in para 4.162 above.

[186]   Where a floating charge is capable of applying to both real and personal property, the applicable limitation period will depend on the property which is subject to the charge at the moment of crystallisation.

[187]   Limitation Act 1980, s 20(1); *Sutton v Sutton* (1882) 22 Ch D 511; *Fearnside v Flint* (1883) 22 Ch D 579; *Re Powers* (1885) 30 Ch D 291, 297, *per* Bowen LJ: "An action against the mortgagor for the debt is an action to recover money which is charged on land." However, it has also been held that the expiry of the limitation period applying to a personal action to enforce an obligation secured by a mortgage or charge does not operate to bar an action to enforce the security: *Hugill v Wilkinson* (1888) 38 Ch D 480; *London & Midland Bank v Mitchell* [1899] 2 Ch 161.

[188]   Limitation Act 1980, s 20(5). A court may grant arrears of interest by way of damages where the instrument creating the mortgage or charge does not contain any provision for payment of interest after the legal date of repayment: *Re Roberts* (1880) 14 Ch D 49; *Mellersh v Brown* (1890) 45 Ch D 225, 228-229, *per* Kay J.

[189]   [1996] 1 WLR 1316.

[190]   Schedule 1 to the Civil Procedure Rules, which assigns 'mortgage actions' to the Chancery Division.

4.176   We have been asked by two consultees to clarify how our recommendations will apply to such claims.[191] We are of the view that, in accordance with the current law on limitation periods, any claim to recover money in relation to a loan which is secured by a mortgage should be treated as a 'mortgage' claim for limitation purposes, whether or not the claimant is invoking a remedy under the mortgage. We are concerned that, if claims by a mortgagee to enforce the borrower's personal covenant independently of the mortgage were to be time-barred after three years, the mortgagee would feel under pressure to pursue all his remedies within that time period if there was any question that the value of the security would not cover the amount outstanding on the loan.

4.177   **Accordingly, we recommend that only the long-stop limitation period should apply to claims to enforce an obligation secured by a mortgage or charge by suing on the covenant to repay. (Draft Bill, Cl 15(2)(b)).[192]**

(e)   Miscellaneous

4.178   In each of the claims discussed above, we have recommended that either the long-stop limitation period or the full core regime should apply. However, in the cases discussed below, we consider that further modifications are required to the core regime.

(i)   Mortgages and charges over future interests or life insurance policies

4.179   Under the current law, where a mortgage or charge comprises any future interest or any life insurance policy, the right to receive any principal sum of money secured by the mortgage or charge is not treated as accruing until the future interest determines or the life insurance policy matures.[193] Similarly, where a mortgage or charge comprises any future interest or life insurance policy, and it is a term of the mortgage or charge that arrears of interest shall be treated as part of the principal sum of money secured by the mortgage or charge, interest is not treated as becoming due before the right to recover the principal sum of money accrues or is treated as having accrued.[194] Where a mortgage of personal property comprises any future interest or any life insurance policy, the right to foreclose on the property subject to the mortgage is not treated as accruing until the future interest determines or the life insurance policy matures.[195] Similarly, where a mortgage of land comprises an estate or interest in reversion or remainder, or any other future estate or interest, and no person has taken possession of the land by virtue of the estate or interest claimed, the right to foreclose on the mortgage is

---

[191]   Michael Lerego QC and the Holborn Law Society.

[192]   Though once a debt is no longer secured (as where the amount realised by the mortgagee on sale of the property which secured the mortgage is insufficient to repay the full amount owed), the primary limitation period will apply to any claim to recover the remainder of the debt.

[193]   Limitation Act 1980, s 20(3).

[194]   Limitation Act 1980, s 20(7).

[195]   Limitation Act 1980, s 20(3).

not treated as accruing until the date on which the estate or interest falls into possession by the determination of the preceding estate or interest.[196]

4.180 In each case, these provisions delay the start of the limitation period until the date on which a future interest has fallen into possession. As the Law Revision Committee noted in relation to life insurance policies:

> It would be a hardship to the mortgagee, and outside the contemplation of the parties, that the mortgagee (if not in possession) should have to realise the security within the period of limitation or else lose his rights by default. In many cases he would prefer to keep the policy alive until it matures for payment.[197]

We agree, and we intend, therefore, to retain these provisions in any new Limitation Act.

4.181 **We therefore recommend that where a mortgage or charge comprises a future interest or a life insurance policy, the limitation period applying to claims to enforce the mortgage or charge should not begin to run until the future interest determines or the life insurance policy matures.** (Draft Bill, Cl 15(4)).

(ii)   Possession by a prior incumbrancer

4.182 Where a prior mortgagee or other incumbrancer has been in possession of mortgaged or charged property and a claim is brought within one year of the discontinuance of that possession by a subsequent incumbrancer, the subsequent incumbrancer may, under the current law, recover by that claim all the arrears of interest which fell due during the period of possession by the prior incumbrancer, or damages in respect of those arrears, notwithstanding that the period exceeds six years.[198]

4.183 The rationale underlying this provision, with which we agree, is that inasmuch as the possession of a prior incumbrancer prevents a subsequent mortgagee from entering into possession of the mortgaged property and obtaining the rents and profits therefrom, it would be unjust to limit the subsequent mortgagee to six years arrears of interest.[199] The subsequent mortgagee should be allowed a reasonable time within which to bring a claim for all interest arrears.

4.184 **We recommend that, where a prior mortgagee is in possession of the property which is subject to the mortgage, the limitation period**

---

[196] Limitation Act 1980, s 15 and Sch I, para 4. In fact, there is scope for argument as to whether foreclosure actions in respect of land fall within the terms of these provisions: see *Hugill v Wilkinson* (1888) 38 Ch D 480; *Wakefield and Barnsley Union Bank v Yates* [1916] 1 Ch 452; *Re Witham* [1922] 2 Ch 413.

[197] Law Revision Committee, *Fifth Interim Report (Statute of Limitation)* (1936) Cmd 5334, p 16.

[198] Limitation Act 1980, s 20(6).

[199] *Chinnery v Evans* (1864) 11 HLC 115, 136, 11 ER 1274, 1283, *per* Lord Westbury LC.

applicable to a claim by the subsequent mortgagee to recover arrears of interest (or damages in lieu) should (if necessary) be extended so that it does not end before the date one year after the prior mortgagee ceases to be in possession. (Draft Bill, Cl 15(3)).

(iii)   Possession by a mortgagee

4.185   Where a mortgagee is in possession of mortgaged property after the date on which the right to foreclose accrues, the right to foreclose on the property in his or her possession is not treated as accruing under the current law until the date on which his or her possession discontinues.[200] We do not intend to alter the effect of these provisions. **Accordingly, we recommend that the limitation period applying to foreclosure proceedings should be suspended during the period that the mortgagee is in possession of the mortgaged property.** (Draft Bill, Cl 15(5)).

(3)   Claims by a mortgagor to redeem mortgaged property

(a)   Claims to redeem mortgaged land

4.186   Under the current law, the limitation period applying to claims to redeem mortgaged land is twelve years from the date on which the mortgagee takes possession of the land.[201] In the Consultation Paper we provisionally proposed that only the long-stop limitation period should apply to claims to redeem mortgaged land, and that the primary limitation period should not apply to such claims.[202]

4.187   We have reconsidered our policy in this area. There are a number of objections to there being any limitation period on the mortgagor's right to redeem the mortgage. The limitation period in the Limitation Act 1980, section 16 was first enacted in the Real Property Limitation Act 1832, section 28, and then variously re-enacted in 1874[203] and 1939.[204] During that period mortgages have changed significantly in nature. Mortgages are no longer made by an outright transfer of the mortgagor's legal estate to the mortgagee, with a proviso for reconveyance on redemption.[205] Instead, the mortgagor remains the owner of the legal estate. The remedy of foreclosure is no longer the main remedy for the mortgagee - indeed it has become virtually obsolete.[206] A legal mortgagee has had a statutory power of sale since 1860,[207] and will invariably be able to realise his security, if the

---

[200]   Limitation Act 1980, ss 15 and 20(2) and Sch I, para 1.

[201]   Limitation Act 1980, s 16.

[202]   Limitation of Actions, Consultation Paper No 151 (1998), para 13.134.

[203]   Real Property Limitation Act 1874, s 7.

[204]   Limitation Act 1939, s 12.

[205]   See the Law of Property Act 1925, ss 85 - 86.

[206]   See *Palk v Mortgage Services Funding plc* [1993] Ch 330, 336.

[207]   Lord Cranworth's Act, 23 & 24 Vict c 145, s 32. The present provisions are found in the Law of Property Act 1925, ss 101(1) and 103.

mortgagor is in default under the mortgage.[208] Even in those rare cases when the power of sale is excluded, the mortgagee can still seek sale under the power for the court to order sale in lieu of foreclosure.[209] There is no need to allow the mortgagee, in addition, the opportunity to extinguish the mortgagor's rights by taking possession of the property for ten years.

4.188   In addition, it is possible to envisage situations where the Limitation Act 1980, section 16, could lead to hardship. A mortgagee might take possession of property where there is a "negative equity" due to the decline in the value of the property since its purchase, and lease it under his statutory powers.[210] He intends to sell the property when prices have risen and recoup his 'loss' from the proceeds. This state of affairs continues for 12 years, as the mortgagor is never in a position to redeem it.[211] The mortgagee will, as the law stands, be entitled to the property absolutely at the end of that period. This will be so even though the rental the mortgagee has earned is equal to, or even exceeds the interest due under the mortgage. Furthermore, unless the mortgagor is in a position to redeem, or the property has risen in value so as to exceed the sums due under the mortgage (taking into account the rent received by the mortgagee), the mortgagor is, as the authorities now stand, unlikely to be able to compel the mortgagee to sell.[212]

4.189   **Accordingly, we recommend that no limitation period should apply to a claim by the mortgagor to redeem a mortgage over land.** (Draft Bill, Cl 15(1)).

(b)   The rule in Edmunds v Waugh[213]

4.190   Where a mortgagor brings a claim for redemption, the mortgagee is entitled to retain out of the sale proceeds any arrears of interest, even if a claim by the mortgagee to that interest is statute-barred.[214] The mortgagee can recover the arrears of interest because redemption is a form of equitable relief, and equitable relief is only available where the mortgagor discharges all sums outstanding.

4.191   In the Consultation Paper we provisionally proposed that the rule in *Edmunds v Waugh* should be reviewed, if at all, as part of a review of mortgage law rather than

---

[208]   See Law of Property Act 1925, s 103.

[209]   Law of Property Act 1925, s 91(2); see *Twentieth Century Banking Corporation v Wilkinson* [1977] Ch 99.

[210]   See Law of Property Act 1925, s 99.

[211]   This is not wholly fanciful, given that the last recession in property prices lasted for 9 years.

[212]   It was held in *Palk v Mortgage Services Funding plc* [1993] Ch 330 that a sale could be ordered under the Law of Property Act 1925, s 91(2), even where the proceeds would not discharge the indebtedness. However, the facts of that case were exceptional and, for reasons connected with the county court's jurisdictional limits, there are considerable difficulties which lie in the path of a mortgagor who wishes to seek a sale under that subsection if proceedings are brought against him for possession in the county court: see *Cheltenham and Gloucester plc v Krausz* [1997] 1 WLR 1558.

[213]   (1866) LR 1 Eq 418, 421.

[214]   (1866) LR 1 Eq 418, 421, *per* Kindersley V-C.

the law on limitation periods.[215] A substantial majority of consultees (around eight-five per cent) agreed. We do not, therefore, make any recommendations in respect of this matter.

(c) Claims to redeem mortgaged personal property

4.192 Claims to redeem mortgaged personal property are not subject to any period of limitation. The Law Revision Committee, considering whether a limitation period should apply to such claims, said:

> This would in our opinion give rise to serious practical difficulties, e.g., in a case where a customer of a bank charges bonds or other securities in favour of the bank as security for an advance. The bonds would be deposited with the bank and an equitable mortgage created. They would, in many cases, remain so charged for an indefinite period, to cover a more or less permanent overdraft, and unless the bank acknowledged the title of the mortgagor, the effect of section 7 of the Real Property Limitation Act, 1874, would be to extinguish the equity of redemption and give the bank an absolute title.[216]

4.193 We recommend above that no limitation period should apply to a claim to redeem mortgaged land. We consider that the same should apply in relation to personalty. In contrast to the position in relation to mortgaged land, the mortgagee of personal property may well have possession of that property from the date of the original transaction: this possession does not imply any reduction of the mortgagor's rights under the transaction. To impose a limitation period on the mortgagor's right to redeem personal property would change the nature of the transaction between the parties, and in consequence limit the usefulness of mortgages of personal property. We therefore consider that claims to redeem mortgaged personal property should not be subject to a period of limitation.

4.194 **Accordingly, we recommend that claims to redeem mortgaged personal property should not be subject to a limitation period.** (Draft Bill, Cl 15(1)).

(3) Expiry of the limitation period

4.195 Under the current law, the expiry of the limitation period applying to claims to redeem a mortgage over land or to enforce a mortgage over land extinguishes the interest of the claimant in the land, in the same way as the expiry of the limitation period for a claim to recover land will extinguish the claimant's interest in the land.[217] We have recommended that this should continue to be the case in respect of claims to recover land.[218] We consider that the expiry of the limitation period applying to claims to enforce a mortgage over land should also extinguish the claimant's interest in the land. Furthermore, we consider that the expiry of the

---

[215] Limitation of Actions, Consultation Paper No 151 (1998), para 13.135.

[216] Law Revision Committee, *Fifth Interim Report (Statutes of Limitation)* (1936) Cmd 5334, p 15.

[217] Limitation Act 1980, s 17.

[218] See para 4.135 above.

limitation period applying to claims to enforce a mortgage over personal property should have the same effect.

4.196 **Accordingly, we recommend that the expiry of the limitation period applying to claims to enforce a mortgage should extinguish the claimant's interest in the mortgaged property.** (Draft Bill, Cl 15(6)).

16. CLAIMS ON A JUDGMENT OR ON AN ARBITRATION AWARD

4.197 We provisionally proposed that claims on a judgment,[219] and claims on an arbitration award,[220] should be subject to the core regime. Over eighty per cent of consultees responding on this issue agreed. Concern was however expressed by the Law Society about the interaction between the limitation period applicable to claims on a judgment and enforcement proceedings.[221] The Construction Industry Council, the Constructors' Liaison Group and the Construction Confederation each expressed the view (in connection with claims on a judgment or arbitration award) that three years was too long, as all the parties concerned would be well aware of the position.

4.198 The limitation period for a claim on a judgment has no direct effect on the periods within which enforcement proceedings may be brought. We have expressly excluded reform of the time limits set by Rules of Courts from our review.[222] Although the limitation period for a claim on a judgment is currently the same as the period within which, for example, a writ of execution can be entered in respect of a judgment or order, there is no reason why the two periods need to remain the same. The discrepancy between the two periods is not therefore a good reason to modify the core regime for claims on a judgment.

4.199 The Law Society also noted that claimants might justifiably delay in bringing a claim on a judgment or an arbitration award because the defendant does not have the resources necessary to satisfy the judgment. However, the impecuniosity of the defendant is not a factor which we consider justifies allowing the claimant an extended limitation period under the core regime, and there seems to be no reason to make an exception in the case of claims on a judgment.

4.200 **We therefore recommend that claims on a judgment and claims on an arbitration award should be subject to the core regime.**

17. CLAIMS ON A STATUTE

4.201 We provisionally proposed that claims on a statute should be subject to the core regime.[223] This proposal was accepted by all those consultees who responded on

---

[219] Limitation of Actions, Consultation Paper No 151 (1998), paras 13.137 - 138. See paras 2.67 - 2.68 above for a summary of the current law.

[220] Limitation of Actions, Consultation Paper No 151 (1998), para 13.139. See paras 2.69 - 2.70 for a summary of the current law.

[221] Such as the issue of a writ of execution under CPR, Sch 1, RSC, O 46, r 2.

[222] See Limitation of Actions, Consultation Paper No 151 (1998), para 1.40.

[223] Limitation of Actions, Consultation Paper No 151 (1998), paras 13.140 - 13.141.

this issue. This will considerably reduce the confusion which arises under the current law, under which claims on a statute are subject to at least two different regimes. Where the claim is for "any sum recoverable by virtue of any enactment" the limitation period is six years from the date the cause of action accrued.[224] Where the relief sought is something other than the payment of a sum of money, the limitation period is twelve years from the date the cause of action accrued, on the grounds that a statute is a form of specialty.[225] Further the present theoretical problem of distinguishing between claims on a statute as opposed to claims founded on simple contract or tort would no longer arise.[226]

4.202 **We therefore recommend that claims on a statute should be subject to the core regime.**

18.   CLAIMS AGAINST PUBLIC AUTHORITIES

4.203 In the Consultation Paper we expressed the provisional view that no special protection in limitations law should be given to public authorities. Where the core regime would apply to any other defendant, it should therefore apply in same way to claims against public authorities.[227] This view was universally approved by those consultees who responded on this point, on the grounds that the interests of fairness and certainty require that no special limitation period should be given to public authorities. It was also noted that any attempt to provide a more favourable limitation position for public bodies sued for breach of a community law wrong would potentially infringe European law: a shorter limitation period for public authorities would not be consistent with the principle that national law governing liability for community law damages must not be less favourable than it is for equivalent domestic claims. **We therefore recommend that no special protection should be given in limitations law to public authorities.**

19.   PROCEEDINGS UNDER THE COMPANIES ACT 1985

4.204 In the Consultation Paper we did not consider how the core regime would apply to applications under the Companies Acts, other than claims under section 459 of the Companies Act 1985. A number of consultees have raised a number of issues in respect of the application of the core regime to such claims.[228] In this section we address those issues and explain how we envisage that the core regime will apply in this area.

---

[224] Limitation Act 1980, s 9. See Limitation of Actions, Consultation Paper No 151 (1998), paras 7.10, and 7.12 - 7.14, and paras 2.71 - 2.76 above.

[225] Limitation Act 1980, s 8. See Limitation of Actions, Consultation Paper No 151 (1998) paras 3.1 and 7.10 - 7.11.

[226] Limitation of Actions, Consultation Paper No 151 (1998), paras 7.17 - 7.21.

[227] Limitation of Actions, Consultation Paper No 151 (1998), para 13.153.

[228] We received responses from consultees both directly in response to Limitation of Actions, Consultation Paper No 151 (1998), and in answer to the Department of Trade and Industry's consultation exercise on Shareholder Remedies (1998).

(1) Derivative claims

4.205 In *Estmanco Ltd v Greater London Council*,[229] Megarry V-C described a derivative claim as "an action by a member of a company who sues on behalf of the company to enforce rights derived from that company."[230] A derivative claim constitutes an exception to the general rule that A cannot bring a claim against B to recover damages or secure other relief on behalf of C for an injury done by B to C.[231]

4.206 The claimant in a derivative claim does not seek redress for a wrong done to him or her personally. Rather the claimant seeks redress for a wrong committed against the company of which he or she is a shareholder. The cause of action is vested not in the shareholder, but in the company. It follows that a minority shareholder cannot maintain a derivative claim where the expiry of the limitation period would prevent the company bringing proceedings in respect of the same cause of action on its own behalf: the derivative claim would seek to recover for the benefit of the company a remedy to which it is not entitled.

4.207 A derivative claim may potentially be brought by any of the shareholders of a company. This raises two issues for the application of the core regime:

(1) Whose knowledge is relevant for the purposes of the primary limitation period?

(2) How does the long-stop limitation period apply?

(a) The primary limitation period

4.208 Where a minority shareholder brings a derivative claim, he is acting on behalf of the company. It was noted in *Dominion Cotton Mills v Amyot*[232] that "it is obvious that in such an action the plaintiffs cannot have a larger right to relief than the company itself would have if it were plaintiff ...". Where therefore the primary limitation period has expired in respect of any claim by the company itself, this defence may be available to the derivative claim. This would however defeat the object of the derivative claim. The claimant in such a case is, in practice, a minority shareholder.[233] The shareholder is compelled to bring the claim because those with the requisite authority will not do so. If the only knowledge relevant to determine the start of the primary limitation period is to be that of the company, there will be a risk that the primary limitation period expires before any minority shareholder is in a position to bring a claim. To avoid this problem, we consider that, by way of exception to the general rule, the start of the primary limitation

---

[229] [1982] 1 WLR 2.

[230] [1982] 1 WLR 2, 10.

[231] *Prudential Assurance Co Ltd v Newman Industries Ltd (No. 2)* [1982] 1 Ch 204, 210.

[232] [1912] AC 546, PC.

[233] It is interesting to note that although the cause of action which a minority shareholder seeks to enforce is vested in the company, the company is, in fact, a defendant to the shareholder's action.

period in respect of a derivative claim should be determined by reference to the date of knowledge of the shareholder who is bringing the claim. And in line with our recommendations for joint and representative claims,[234] the expiry of the primary limitation period *vis-à-vis* minority shareholder A will not affect the ability of minority shareholder B, or the company,[235] to initiate legal proceedings in respect of the relevant claim.[236] In practice, the most relevant limitation period applicable to a derivative claim will be the long-stop limitation period.

(b) The long-stop limitation period

4.209 Under the core regime, the long-stop limitation period will start from the date on which the cause of action accrues to the claimant. As the minority shareholder is in practice acting as a representative of the company, this will be the date on which the cause of action accrued to the company. It will not be affected by the fact that the claim is brought by a minority shareholder.

4.210 **We therefore recommend that derivative claims should be subject to the core regime, but that the start of the primary limitation period should be decided by reference to the knowledge of the shareholder who is bringing the claim** (Draft Bill, Cl 24).

(2) Proceedings under section 459 of the Companies Act 1985

4.211 Section 459 of the Companies Act 1985 allows any member of a company to petition the court for relief on the grounds that the affairs of the company are being, have been or are about to be conducted in a manner which is unfairly prejudicial to the interests of some of its members (including at least the petitioner). Under the current law, such proceedings are not subject to any limitation period, though delay may bar relief.[237] We provisionally proposed that such claims should be subject to the core regime. There was general agreement from consultees that a limitation period should apply to applications under section 459 of the Companies Act 1985, on the grounds that it would increase transparency[238] and reduce uncertainty.[239] AG Bompas QC also noted that

> The growth in the number of applications for Part XVII relief, coupled with the opportunity for oppression of respondents which such applications offer, lends support for the view that a limitation

---

[234] See paras 3.81 - 3.91 above.

[235] An action by the company is not inconceivable. A liquidator, administrator or administrative receiver might be appointed; or a majority shareholder might sell his shares to a minority shareholder or an independent third party.

[236] This is analogous to the rule, relating to beneficiaries under a trust, that the expiry of the limitation period against one beneficiary does not bar an action by another beneficiary in respect of the same cause of action: see para 4.107 above.

[237] See *Re DR Chemicals Ltd* [1989] BCC 39, 53 *per* Peter Gibson J.

[238] Noted by the Institute of Credit Management.

[239] Argued by the Association of Investment Trusts Companies.

period should be introduced to prevent stale allegations being relied upon in support of such applications.

4.212　The major difficulty seen in applying the core regime to section 459 applications is that the right to make such an application will frequently arise not from a single act or omission by the defendant, but as a result of a course of conduct. In some cases, no particular act can be identified as having caused prejudice to the claimant - the prejudice arises because of the cumulative effect of a series of incidents. It may therefore be more difficult to identify the facts which give rise to the cause of action which the claimant must know before the primary limitation period is triggered.

4.213　A related argument is that, given that it is so often the cumulative effect of several incidents which gives rise to a claim under section 459, it would be unjust to debar the claimant from referring in his or her application to an event which may have happened more than a decade previously, but which is nevertheless important to understand the effect of later incidents.

4.214　We suggested in the Consultation Paper that where each of the incidents relied on would be sufficient of itself to found a claim under section 459, the primary limitation period should start from the date on which the claimant knows, or ought reasonably to know of the first such incident.[240] That is, the claimant will be unable to bring a claim for unfair prejudice which relies on that incident more than three years after he or she knew or ought reasonably to have known of the incident. This will not prevent the claimant from bringing a claim for unfair prejudice in relation to a later incident. An application under section 459 of the Companies Act 1985 is in this sense analogous to a continuing claim (such as nuisance) where a fresh cause of action arises with each subsequent act by the defendant.

4.215　Where it is only the cumulative effect of a whole series of incidents which gives rise to the claim for unfair prejudice, the primary limitation period will only start on the date on which the claimant knows (or should know) of the event which gives him or her grounds to bring a claim under section 459. This may be the last event in the series. Alternatively, there may have been a number of events which were each sufficiently prejudicial to the claimant's interests to ground an application under section 459. Providing that the claimant brings an application within three years of the date on which he should know of the latest such incident, the claimant will be within the primary limitation period. The claimant would not be able to rely on an earlier event as itself giving rise to unfair prejudice after the primary limitation period had expired. However, he or she will not be debarred from referring to earlier incidents to show why the later event has caused him or her unfair prejudice. There may, for example, be three events, one taking place in 1993, one in 1996 and one in 2000, none of which is sufficient on its own to support a petition under section 459 but whose cumulative effect does give rise to unfair prejudice against the claimant. The claimant knows of each event within days of its taking place. In this case the primary limitation period would not start

---

[240] Limitation of Actions, Consultation Paper No 151 (1998), para 13.157.

to run until 2000. If, in contrast, the claimant would have enough to show unfair prejudice on the happening of the first and second event, the primary limitation period would start to run in 1996. If he delays for more than three years he or she will not be able to bring a claim relying on these two events. The third event in 2000, though insufficient by itself to ground a claim, is sufficient to support a fresh petition for unfair prejudice in the light of the earlier events, and the claimant has a fresh right to make such a claim.

4.216   It has been suggested that a limitation period of three years is too short, because it may take many years for a course of unfairly prejudicial conduct to become apparent, and, particularly in the context of the small family company, a potential claimant may be prepared to tolerate apparently 'prejudicial' conduct for a number of years before being goaded into taking action. Similarly, a claimant may prefer to rely on negotiations before bringing proceedings in court. However the fact that the primary limitation period starts from the date of knowledge provides considerable protection for the claimant who has difficulties in obtaining information on the management of the company from the management. Once the claimant has, or ought to have, knowledge of the facts which would support a claim for unfair prejudice under section 459, it does not seem unreasonable to oblige that claimant to take action within three years. A shareholder with a potential section 459 claim may well wish to try to resolve the dispute by negotiation without precipitate reference to the courts. However, this is not a problem unique to claimants under section 459. The same position will occur, for example, where there is a long running contractual relationship which breaks down (as where there are disputes within a partnership). Regardless of the length of the limitation period, potential claimants would need at some time to decide whether or not to issue proceedings against the defendant.

4.217   The application of the long-stop limitation period to claims under section 459 poses no greater difficulty than the primary limitation period. The long-stop limitation period will start from the date on which the cause of action accrues. Where the claimant is relying on a series of acts or omissions rather than a single act or omission, the long-stop limitation period will therefore start from the date of the first incident which gives the claimant grounds to bring the claim. So, where there is a succession of events, none of which individually is sufficient to found a cause of action, the long-stop limitation period will not start running. Only when something has happened which has given the claimant grounds to claim that he or she has been unfairly prejudiced will time start to run.

4.218   We are not therefore convinced that there will be substantial problems in the application of the core regime to applications under section 459 (a view shared by the Company Law Review Working Party at the Department of Trade and Industry).[241] Over forty-five per cent of consultees responding on this issue agreed that the core regime should apply to these applications.[242] Around ten per cent of

---

[241]   As expressed in a letter dated 17 December 1999 from Jonathan Rickford, Project Director of the Company Law Review to Sir Robert Carnwath, Chairman of the Law Commission.

[242]   As noted above in relation to proceedings under the Companies Act 1985, we received responses from consultees both directly in response to Limitation of Actions, Consultation

consultees agreed that the core regime should apply, but argued that it should be modified (by, for example, the adoption of a longer primary limitation period, or a discretion for the court to disapply the limitation period in exceptional circumstances). Against this, over twenty-five per cent of consultees argued that no limitation period should be applied to section 459 applications, or that it should be left to the discretion of the court to decide whether an application should be heard. We tend to agree with the Association of International Accountants, who say "it would seem difficult to give examples of reasons why claims under section 459 should be subject to their own regime as far as limitation is concerned".[243] **Accordingly, we recommend that applications under section 459 of the Companies Act 1985 should be subject to the core regime.**

20. INSOLVENCY PROCEEDINGS

4.219 The Consultation Paper did not discuss the impact of the core regime on insolvency claims. We received a number of responses from consultees suggesting that the core regime would need to be modified in its application to claims made by or against companies, partnerships and individuals subject to insolvency proceedings. We consider the issues raised by insolvency proceedings in this section.

(1) Arrangements and Compromises

4.220 An individual, company or partnership unable to pay its debts may be able to make an arrangement or compromise with its creditors to satisfy its outstanding debts. Here we consider the effect of the core regime in relation to schemes of arrangement under section 425 of the Companies Act 1985, and voluntary arrangements under the Insolvency Act 1986. Though there are other methods by which arrangements and compromises can be made and enforced, such as a deed of arrangement, we are of the view that such arrangements made by a contract between the parties do not pose specific issues for the core regime, and we do not consider them here.

(a) Section 425 of the Companies Act 1985

4.221 Section 425 of the Companies Act 1985 allows a company or a creditor to approach the court to sanction a scheme approved by the requisite majority of creditors (at least seventy-five per cent). Once approved the scheme binds all creditors intended to be bound, and the company.[244] The schemes are generally self-administering and the Act does not provide for the replacement of the current controllers of the company. The provision does not prevent claims being made against the company, apart from actions challenging the scheme by bound creditors. A creditor could bring a different claim, though any judgment obtained

---

Paper No 151 (1998), and in answer to the Department of Trade and Industry's consultation exercise on Shareholder Remedies (1998).

[243] Letter of 24 February 1999 to Company Law Investigations Division, Department of Trade and Industry.

[244] Companies Act 1985, s 425(2).

would be unenforceable if it conflicted with the scheme which bound the creditor. A scheme approved under section 425 has no impact on the abilities of the company to issue proceedings. In consequence it does not appear to be necessary to make any modifications to the core regime either to protect claimants who may have a claim against a company subject to the arrangement, or to protect the company itself.

(b) Voluntary Arrangements

4.222 The individual voluntary arrangement exists to enable an insolvent debtor to arrange for a moratorium on his or her debts by entering into an arrangement with his or her creditors without becoming bankrupt. The company voluntary arrangement, and the voluntary arrangement for insolvent partnerships, serve the same purpose. The first stage in proceedings for an individual voluntary arrangement is the grant of an interim order, which acts as a moratorium preventing creditors from enforcing their rights against the individual, and lasts until a creditors' meeting has taken place which approves the proposal by the debtor, or the court revokes the order.[245] Under the Insolvency Act 2000 the directors of the company may apply for a moratorium which will prevent the creditors of the company from enforcing their rights against the company.[246] In both cases, the moratorium would act as a restriction on the right of the claimant creditor to issue proceedings, and in consequence will suspend both the initial and the long-stop limitation period under our recommendations in paragraph 5.28 below.

(i) Claims against a company, partnership or individual subject to a voluntary arrangement.

4.223 Once a voluntary arrangement has been made, any creditors who were given notice of the creditors' meeting to agree the arrangement and were entitled to vote at that meeting, are bound by it.[247] They cannot therefore attempt to enforce their claims against the company, partnership or individual in question otherwise than through the voluntary arrangement. To the extent that the existence of the voluntary arrangement therefore acts as a legal restriction preventing such creditors from issuing proceedings against the company, partnership or individual who is subject to the arrangement, as noted above, the primary limitation period and long-stop limitation period for their claims will be suspended.

4.224 The voluntary arrangement does not bind any creditors of the debtor who were not given notice of the arrangement, or whose claims post-date the arrangement.[248] If there is no moratorium, there is nothing to prevent such

---

[245] Insolvency Act 1986, ss 252 and 254.

[246] Insolvency Act 2000, s 1, and Sch 1, which insert the moratorium procedure into Part I of the Insolvency Act 1986. By virtue of the Insolvent Partnerships Order 1994, SI 1994 No 2421 ("the 1994 Order"), Art 4, this procedure also applies to insolvent partnerships.

[247] See Insolvency Act 1986, s 5(2)(b) and s 260(2)(b), and the 1994 Order, Art 4 and Sch 1.

[248] And the meeting agreeing the voluntary arrangement may have agreed that it should not include certain creditors.

creditors from issuing proceedings against the debtor though, where there are no assets which are not subject to the voluntary arrangement and are therefore available for enforcement proceedings, this may appear to be an unattractive option.[249] Equally, the voluntary arrangement may not prejudice the rights of a secured creditor to enforce his or her security without the agreement of the creditor concerned.[250] We have elsewhere taken the view that the limitation period should not be extended by the fact that the potential defendant has no financial resources to meet the claim.[251] We do not therefore propose to modify the core regime in its application to claims which are brought against an individual, company or partnership which is subject to a voluntary arrangement.

(ii) Claims by a company, partnership or individual during the existence of a voluntary arrangement.

4.225 Once a voluntary arrangement has been agreed, a supervisor will be appointed to oversee its implementation. Those assets which are subject to the arrangement are held by the supervisor for the benefit of the creditors who are participants in the arrangement.[252] The assets may, depending on the terms of the arrangement, include a cause of action which has accrued to the debtor. However, though the debtor must do everything necessary to put the supervisor in possession of the assets, they do not automatically vest in the supervisor as would happen were the debtor to be made bankrupt.[253] The claimant, for the purposes of calculating the date of knowledge for the start of the primary limitation period, would remain the debtor. The existence of the voluntary arrangement by itself does not impose a restriction on the issue of proceedings by the debtor.[254] **We recommend that claims brought by a debtor who is subject to a voluntary arrangement should be subject to the core regime.**

---

[249] It appears that, for example, where the debtor becomes bankrupt subsequent to the agreement of the voluntary arrangement, the voluntary arrangement remains in existence, and the assets of the debtor which are covered by the arrangement are impressed with a trust for the benefit of the creditors participating in the voluntary arrangement, and are not available to the trustee in bankruptcy, or the liquidator, though the point is not free from doubt. See *In re Bradley-Hole* [1995] 1 WLR 1097 and *Doorbar v AllTime Securities Ltd* [1996] 1 WLR 456.

[250] Insolvency Act 1986, ss 4(3) and 258(4), and the 1994 Order, Art 4 and Sch 1.

[251] See para 3.27 above.

[252] The debtor must do everything necessary to put the supervisor in possession of the assets covered by the arrangement: Insolvency Rules 1986, SI 1986 No 1925, r 1.23.

[253] The supervisor is effectively in the position of a trustee. See Insolvency Act 1986, s 1(2) and 253(2) and the 1994 Order, Art 4 and Sch 1, *Re Leisure Study Group Ltd* [1994] 2 BCLC 65; *In re Bradley-Hole* [1995] 1 WLR 1097. In *Re McKeen* [1995] BCC 412, though not finding that there was a trust in favour of the creditors, the court held that the assets covered by the arrangement were held subject to the rights of the creditors to have them applied in accordance with the agreement.

[254] Though the terms of the agreement may do so. Any such restriction would be a contractual restriction which would not, under our recommendations, operate to suspend the primary limitation period. See para 5.28 below.

(2)   Administrative Receivership and Administration Orders.

(a)   Claims by a company or partnership

4.226   Similar issues arise when a company or insolvent partnership is subject to an administration order or where an administrative receiver has been appointed. The court may appoint an administrator to realise one of four objectives, namely:

(1)   the survival of the company, and the whole or any part of its undertaking, as a going concern;[255]

(2)   the approval of a voluntary arrangement;

(3)   the sanctioning of a compromise or arrangement under section 425 of the Companies Act 1985;[256] or

(4)   a more advantageous realisation of the company's assets or of the partnership property than would be effected on a winding-up.[257]

An administrative receiver is appointed by the chargee under a floating charge, to manage the whole (or substantially the whole) of a company's property.[258]

4.227   In contrast to the position where a company or partnership is subject to a voluntary arrangement, in the case of both an administration and administrative receivership, the power to manage the company or partnership will have passed from the directors or partners to the administrator or the administrative receiver. An administrator is empowered to do all such things as may be necessary for the management of the affairs, business and property of the company or partnership,[259] including *inter alia* the initiation of legal proceedings in its name and on its behalf.[260] Moreover, section 14(4) of the 1986 Act provides that "Any power conferred on the company or its officers ... which could be exercised in such a way as to interfere with the exercise by the administrator of his powers is not exercisable except with the consent of the administrator...".[261]

---

[255] Or in the case of an insolvent partnership, "the survival of the whole or any part of the undertaking of the partnership as a going concern": the 1994 Order, Sch 2, para 2.

[256] An objective which does not apply to insolvent partnerships.

[257] Insolvency Act 1986, s 8(3), and the 1994 Order, Art 6 and Sch 2, para 2. An administration order can only be made where a debtor is unable to meet a judgment given against it and the amount of its total indebtedness is less than £5,000; County Courts Act 1984, s 112.

[258] Insolvency Act 1986, s 29. In practice this will affect very few partnerships. Only agricultural partnerships are able to grant floating charges over their property, and the 1994 does not extend the provisions relating to administrative receivers in the Insolvency Act 1986 to partnerships generally.

[259] Insolvency Act 1986, s 14(1)(a); the 1994 Order, Art 6, and Sch 2, para 8.

[260] Insolvency Act 1986, Sch 1, para 5; the 1994 Order, Art 6, and Sch 2, para 10.

[261] This is applied to insolvent partnerships by the 1994 Order, Art 6 and Sch 2, para 8.

4.228   An administrative receiver is empowered to "carry on the business of the company",[262] and exercises complete control over the assets subject to the charge under which he or she was appointed.[263] Moreover, immediately an administrative receiver is appointed, the directors and officers of the company are dispossessed of their authority to act on the company's behalf in relation to those assets which are covered by the charge.[264] A cause of action that has accrued to a company falls within the class of assets to which the floating charge may attach.[265] Accordingly, during the period that a company is in administrative receivership, only the administrative receiver can initiate legal proceedings in respect of a cause of action that has accrued to the company.[266] There is a single exception to this proposition: the directors and officers of a company in administrative receivership can initiate legal proceedings in the name and on behalf of the company against the administrative receiver.[267]

4.229   Under the current law, neither the making of an administration order nor the appointment of an administrative receiver affects the limitation period which applies to claims by the company. It will continue to run. Under the core regime the primary limitation period would in each case start on the date when either a person with actual (or apparent) authority to initiate legal proceedings on behalf of the company or partnership, or an employee of the company or partnership who could be expected to report the information to someone with that authority (or another employee), acquires knowledge of the relevant facts. Where the primary limitation period has started before the appointment of an administrator or an administrative receiver, it would, prima facie, continue to run. After the appointment, as each has authority to bring proceedings on behalf of the company or partnership, the primary limitation period will start when either the administrator (or administrative receiver) or an employee of the company or partnership who is under a duty to report to the administrator (or administrative receiver) or another employee has actual or constructive knowledge of the relevant facts. Once the period has started, it will continue to run after the company or partnership comes out of administration or the administrative receiver is discharged.

---

[262]   Insolvency Act 1986, s 42 and Sch 1, para 14.

[263]   Insolvency Act 1986, s 42(2)(b).

[264]   In most cases, the receiver will control all the company's property. In *Moss Steamship Ltd v Whinney* [1912] AC 254, 263, Lord Atkinson observed that the appointment of a receiver "entirely supersedes the company in the conduct of its business, deprives it of all power to enter into contracts in relation to that business, or to sell, pledge, or otherwise dispose of the property put into the possession, or under the control of the receiver and manager. Its power in these respects are entirely in abeyance." See further *Re Emmadart Ltd* [1979] Ch 540, 544, *per* Brightman J; *Gomba Holdings UK Ltd v Homan* [1986] 3 All ER 94, 98, *per* Hoffmann J.

[265]   *Tudor Grange Holdings Ltd v Citibank NA* [1992] Ch 53, 62, *per* Browne-Wilkinson V-C.

[266]   The decision in *Newhart Developments Ltd v Co-operative Commercial Bank Ltd* [1978] QB 814 casts some doubt on the validity of this proposition. However, the correctness of that decision was doubted by Browne-Wilkinson V-C in *Tudor Grange Holdings Ltd v Citibank NA* [1992] Ch 53, 62-63.

[267]   *Watts v Midland Bank plc* [1986] BCLC 15.

4.230 The operation of the primary limitation period applicable to claims brought by the company or partnership could therefore create problems both for companies and partnerships in administration, and for companies in administrative receivership. The manner in which an administrator may exercise his or her powers is limited. The administrator is subject to an overriding duty to realise one of the objectives specified in paragraph 4.226 above. The initiation of legal proceedings in respect of a claim would not materially contribute to the realisation of those objectives. Indeed, to the extent that the costs attending such proceedings would deplete the company's or partnership's available assets, the initiation of legal proceedings would frustrate the objectives mentioned at paragraph 4.226 above. Therefore, it is unlikely that the company or partnership will be able to rely on the administrator to bring a claim on its behalf.

4.231 The extent of the duties owed by an administrative receiver to the company are limited by an overriding duty to protect the interests of the holder of the floating charge by whom he or she is appointed, and to realise the charged assets for the benefit of the chargee. An administrative receiver is under a duty to the company to obtain a proper price on a sale of any of the charged assets.[268] However, the duties owed to the company do not extend very much further. In particular, an administrative receiver does not owe a duty to the company to initiate legal proceedings in respect of a cause of action that has, or may have, accrued to the company. Indeed, the existence of such a duty would derogate from his primary duty of protecting the interests of the charge holder, in that the costs attending legal proceedings would dissipate the charged assets. The administrative receiver is no more likely than the administrator (indeed is rather less likely) to bring proceedings on behalf of the company.

4.232 In each case, the directors of the company or the partners will at the same time have lost the ability to bring proceedings themselves. Thus, there is a clear risk that the primary limitation period applying to a cause of action that has accrued to a company or partnership in administration or administrative receivership could expire because the management of the company or partnership are powerless to institute legal proceedings. To protect against this, we consider (subject to the exception mentioned in the following paragraph) that the primary limitation period should be suspended during the period in which a company or partnership is in administration or administrative receivership.[269]

4.233 We have already seen that the directors of a company in administrative receivership can institute legal proceedings in the name and on behalf of the company against the administrative receiver.[270] It follows that the primary limitation period should not be suspended in respect of a claim against the administrative receiver.

---

[268] See for example *American Express International Banking Corporation v Hurley* [1985] 3 All ER 564.

[269] This will apply when a claim is brought within this jurisdiction by any company or partnership which is subject to an insolvency procedure which is equivalent to administration or administrative receivership, wherever the body in question is domiciled.

[270] See para 4.228 above.

4.234 **Accordingly, we recommend that the primary limitation period should be suspended in respect of claims by a company or partnership during any period in which the company or partnership is in either administration or administrative receivership, except where the administrative receiver is the defendant to the company's claim.** (Draft Bill, Sch 2, paras 1, 2).

(b) Claims against a company or partnership in administration

4.235 During the period beginning with the presentation of a petition for an administration order and ending with the making of such an order or the dismissal of the petition, no steps may be taken to enforce any security over the company's or partnership's property, or to repossess goods in the company's or partnership's possession under any hire-purchase agreement, except with leave of the court.[271] Similarly, no other proceedings and no execution or other legal process may be commenced or continued, and no distress may be levied, against the company or partnership or its property except with leave of the court.[272] The same restrictions apply during the period when an administrative order is in force (save that the consent of the administrator is required as an alternative to leave of the court).[273]

4.236 These requirements amount to a legal restriction on the claimant's ability to commence proceedings against the company or partnership. We recommend below that both the initial and long-stop limitation periods should be suspended during the period when there is a legal restriction on the claimant's ability to commence legal proceedings.[274] Accordingly, both the initial and long-stop limitation periods will be suspended during the period beginning with the presentation of a petition for an administration order and ending with the making of such an order or the dismissal of the petition, and during the period an administration order is in force. Time will start to run again when the restriction is lifted, or (if earlier) on the date when if the claimant had taken all reasonable steps open to him, the restriction would have been lifted.[275] In determining whether these steps have been taken, the court will consider the manner in which the discretion to grant leave to commence proceedings is normally exercised.[276]

4.237 Our recommendation that the limitation period should be suspended where there is a legal restriction on the claimant's ability to bring proceedings should provide adequate protection for claimants where the defendant has gone into administration. We do not consider that any other modifications of the core regime are necessary in this case. **We therefore recommend that claims against a company or partnership in administration should be subject to the core regime.**

---

[271] Insolvency Act 1986, s 10(1)(b); the 1994 Order, Art 6 and Sch 2, para 4.

[272] Insolvency Act 1986, s 10(1)(c); the 1994 Order, Art 6 and Sch 2, para 4.

[273] Insolvency Act 1986, s 11(3); the 1994 Order, Art 6 and Sch 2, para 5.

[274] See para 5.28 below.

[275] See para 5.28 below.

[276] See *Re Atlantic Computer Systems plc* [1992] Ch 505.

(c) Claims against a company in administrative receivership

4.238 The position is different where a company has gone into administrative receivership. There is no moratorium on claims against the company, so that the claimant can initiate legal proceedings and, if he substantiates his claim, obtain judgment. However, it has been suggested by Michael Crystal QC and Simon Mortimore QC that the limitation period should be suspended in respect of claims against a company which is in administrative receivership; and that the necessity for this suspension is well-illustrated by the decision in *Re Joshua Shaw & Sons Ltd.*[277] In that case receivers, who were appointed under various charges on 9 March 1976, indicated that there was unlikely to be any money available for distribution to the unsecured creditors. The unsecured creditors took no further steps, but waited for the receivership to proceed. The receivership took a very long time, but by 1985 it appeared that there would be a surplus of about £350,000 after payment of the secured and preferential creditors. The directors procured the passing of an order for the voluntary winding-up of the company on 4 June 1986. The liquidator examined the claims of the unsecured creditors and concluded that all of them, apart from Crown debts, were statute-barred. There being no other creditors who still had enforceable claims against the company, the liquidator proposed to distribute the remaining surplus to the shareholders. The creditors applied to the court to be admitted to proof. Hoffmann J rejected their application, but indicated that there might be a gap in the law. He said:

> It is true that they [the creditors] could have petitioned to wind up the company within the six-year period after their respective debts arose. But given the existence of the receivership, it is not totally surprising that they did not take that step. However, and it may be that there is a gap in the law, the appointment of a receiver does not stop time running for the purposes of limitation.[278]

4.239 The assets of the company which are subject to the floating charge (which will cover the whole or substantially the whole of the company's property) will not be available for the payment of unsecured debts. If an unsecured creditor issues proceedings against the company and is successful, there will be no assets available to satisfy the judgment debt unless there are assets not covered by the floating charge. It has been argued therefore that it is unreasonable to expect creditors to bring proceedings and that the limitation period applying to their claims should be suspended.

4.240 The difficulty with this argument is that its logical conclusion is that the limitation period should be suspended throughout the period that a defendant is unable to satisfy a judgment debt.[279] Suspending the limitation period throughout the period when the defendant lacks the funds to meet the claim would generate uncertainty: in each case it would be necessary to determine whether the defendant could have satisfied the judgment debt on any particular date. In contrast to the position

---

[277] [1989] BCLC 362.

[278] [1989] BCLC 362, 363.

[279] An argument we have rejected elsewhere. See para 3.27 above.

where a company goes into administration, there is no restriction on claimant's ability to bring legal proceedings against a company in order to safeguard their limitation position. In addition, potential creditors may be able to safeguard their position in relation to contractual claims in advance of a claim by making it a term of the contract that the limitation period shall be suspended during any period of administrative receivership.[280]

4.241   **Accordingly, we recommend that claims against a company in administrative receivership should be subject to the core regime.**

(3)   Winding-up Proceedings

(a)   *Claims by a company or partnership[281] during the course of the winding-up procedure*

4.242   Where a company is wound up, either voluntarily or by the court, the powers of its directors and officers are determined[282] and the liquidator is empowered to carry on the business of the company so far as may be necessary for its beneficial winding-up.[283] In particular, a liquidator is empowered to bring or defend any claim or other legal proceeding in the name and on behalf of the company.[284] The liquidator is also empowered to bring or defend in his or her official name any claim or legal proceeding for the purpose of effectively winding-up the company and recovering its property.[285] However, generally the liquidator institutes proceedings in the name and on behalf of the company.[286]

4.243   Under the current law, where a limitation period in respect of a claim by the company has started it will continue to run after a winding-up order has been made. Under the core regime, the primary limitation period will start on the date when either an officer of the body (or a person with authority to initiate legal proceedings on behalf of the company), or an employee of the company who is under a duty to report the information to someone with that authority (or a fellow employee), acquires the knowledge of the relevant facts. When the date of knowledge occurs before the date of the winding-up order, the primary limitation

---

[280]   See our recommendation at para 3.175 above.

[281]   Parts IV and V of the Insolvency Act 1986 (the winding up of registered and unregistered companies) apply, with certain modifications, to insolvent partnerships by virtue of Arts 7 - 10 of the 1994 Order. In paras 4.242 - 4.253 we refer only to companies in the text for reasons of clarity, but it should be remembered that these paragraphs apply equally to insolvent partnerships.

[282]   Insolvency Act 1986, ss 91(2) and 103; the 1994 Order, Arts 7 - 10. *Madrid Bank v Bayley* (1866) LR 2 QB 37.

[283]   Insolvency Act 1986, ss 165 - 167, and Sch 4, para 5; the 1994 Order, Arts 7 - 10 and Sch 3, para 10. In certain circumstances this power is subject to the approval of the court or the liquidation committee.

[284]   Insolvency Act 1986, ss 165 - 167, and Sch 4, para 4; the 1994 Order, Arts 7 - 10 and Sch 3, para 10. This power is also subject to the approval of the court or the liquidation committee.

[285]   Insolvency Act, s 145(2); the 1994 Order Arts 7 - 10.

[286]   L S Sealy, *Annotated Guide to the Insolvency Legislation* (5th ed 1999), p 185.

period will not, prima facie, be affected by the making of the order: time will continue to run. After the making of the winding-up order the primary limitation period will be triggered by the knowledge of the liquidator, or of an employee of the company who is under a duty to report to the liquidator, or a fellow employee.

4.244 We have recommended above that the primary limitation period should be suspended when an administrator or administrative receiver is appointed.[287] The position of a company which has been wound up is similar, for limitation purposes. However, there are important distinctions. A liquidator owes a duty to all the creditors of the company to maximise the assets of the company - he is not obliged to protect the interests of a particular creditor. The liquidator is therefore far less likely than either the administrator or the administrative receiver to be reluctant to commence proceedings when it is in the interest of the creditors to do so. Further, unlike administration, and administrative receivership, the liquidation is not a temporary state of affairs following which the company may continue as a going concern under its original management.

4.245 It has been suggested that there should at least be an extended limitation period when a company has gone into liquidation. As the liquidator will be responsible for instituting any proceedings brought by the company, Simon Mortimore QC and Michael Crystal QC argue that sufficient time should be allowed for the liquidator to investigate the claim and bring proceedings. Where the primary limitation period for a claim by the company has started before the making of a winding-up order (because for example the necessary information reached one of the directors of the company) there may in practice be very little time between the appointment of the liquidator and the expiry of the limitation period.[288] This may not be sufficient to enable the liquidator to bring proceedings. It has also been suggested that there may be an incentive for the directors of a company to delay the inception of the insolvency process in order to protect themselves from proceedings.

4.246 In addition, it should be considered that, where a company has gone into insolvent liquidation, the liquidator often has few funds with which to finance a claim against the directors. It takes time for the liquidator to arrange such funding by either realising the assets of the company or approaching the creditors for a contribution. In some cases a liquidator may consider that it is advisable to await the outcome of any disqualification proceedings before bringing such a claim. The net result is that, even when the liquidator acquires the relevant knowledge soon after the date of liquidation of the company, the primary limitation period may have expired before the liquidator is in a position to bring proceedings. We therefore consider that where the primary limitation period has started running against a company before that company went into insolvent liquidation but has not expired before that date it should be suspended for a year from the date of the liquidation. This will in practice allow the liquidator a further year within which to

---

[287] See para 4.234 above.

[288] The position is of course exacerbated by the fact that the majority of claims available to an insolvent company will be for breach of contract. In practice the limitation period for most claims for breach of contract will be reduced from six years to three years.

start proceedings. Where the primary limitation period in respect of a claim has not started before the date of liquidation, we consider that it should start on the later of the date of knowledge of the liquidator, or one year after the date on which the company went into liquidation. This will ensure that the liquidator has at least four years from the date of liquidation within which to start proceedings. In neither case will the long-stop limitation period be affected. Under our proposals, this protection will apply to all claims brought in this jurisdiction by a liquidator, or anyone who performs that function under the law of another jurisdiction, regardless of the domicile of the company in question.

4.247 **Accordingly we recommend that claims brought by a liquidator on behalf of a company or partnership in liquidation should be subject to the core regime, subject to the modification that**

(1) **where the primary limitation period in respect of a claim has started running against the company or partnership before it went into insolvent liquidation but has not expired by that date, it should be suspended for one year from the date of liquidation;**

(2) **where the primary limitation period in respect of a claim has not started running before the date of liquidation, it should start on the later of**

(a) **the date of knowledge of the liquidator; or**

(b) **the date one year after the date of the liquidation.** (Draft Bill, Sch 2, para 3).

4.248 In some cases, there may already be an administrative receiver in office on the date on which the liquidator is appointed. Under our recommendations in paragraph 4.234 above, the primary limitation period applying to claims made by the company will therefore already be suspended. This will not increase the length of the suspension of the limitation period applying to claims of the company as far as the liquidator is concerned. Where the appointment of the liquidator overlaps that of the administrative receiver, and the primary limitation period had started to run before the appointment of the administrative receiver (the date on which it would have been suspended), it will start running against the liquidator on the date one year after his appointment.

(b) *Claims against a company or partnership during the course of the winding-up procedure*

4.249 During the period beginning with the presentation of a petition for a winding-up order and ending with the making of such an order or the dismissal of the petition, a creditor can issue proceedings as of right in respect of any cause of action he or she has, or may have, against the company or partnership (even though the claim may thereafter be stayed).[289] Accordingly, during the period

---

[289] Insolvency Act 1986, s 126; the 1994 Order, Arts 7 - 10; *Re Cases of Taffs Well Ltd* [1992] Ch 179, 193, *per* Judge Baker QC, sitting as a judge of the High Court.

beginning with the presentation of a petition for a winding-up order and ending with the making of such an order or the dismissal of the petition, both the initial limitation and long-stop limitation periods will apply in the normal way.

4.250　The court may appoint a provisional liquidator during the period beginning with the presentation of a petition for a winding-up order and ending with the making of such an order or the dismissal of the petition.[290] Where a provisional liquidator is appointed, section 130(2) of the 1986 Act provides that "no action or proceeding shall be proceeded with or commenced against the company or its property, except by leave of the court and subject to such terms as the court may impose".[291] This constitutes a legal restriction on the claimant's ability to commence proceedings against the company, and will therefore suspend the running of the initial and long-stop limitation periods in accordance with our recommendations at paragraph 5.28 below once the claimant has taken all reasonable steps to obtain that leave. Time will start to run again from the date when the restriction is lifted. The claimant will therefore not be able to prolong the limitation period by failing to apply for leave to bring proceedings, and where the claimant seeks merely to protect himself from the expiry of the limitation period, an application for leave to issue proceedings under section 130(2) is generally given as a matter of course.[292]

4.251　Where a company is wound up, either voluntarily or by the court, claims against the company that fall within the winding-up procedure are converted into proprietary rights under a statutory trust.[293] Immediately the statutory trust comes into force, limitation issues relating to claims within the winding-up procedure fall away: "it is not simply that time has stopped running against the creditor; the cause of action itself is destroyed and replaced by other rights."[294] Thus, limitation is only relevant in determining whether or not the claimant's cause of action was statute-barred on the date that the shareholders resolved, or the court ordered, the company to be wound up.[295] Claims that are statute-barred on the date that the company is wound up are not admissible to proof in the winding-up even if it transpires that the company is solvent.[296] Conversely, claims that are not statute-barred on the date that the company is wound up are admissible to proof in the

[290]　Insolvency Act 1986, s 135; the 1994 Order, Arts 7 - 10.

[291]　This is applied to insolvent partnerships by virtue of the 1994 Order, Arts 7 - 10.

[292]　*Re Cases of Taffs Well Ltd* [1992] Ch 179, 193, *per* Judge Baker QC.

[293]　*Re Cases of Taffs Well Ltd* [1992] Ch 179, 191, *per* Judge Baker QC.

[294]　*Re Cases of Taffs Well Ltd* [1992] Ch 179, 189, *per* Judge Baker QC.

[295]　See *Ex parte Lancaster Banking Corporation; Re Westby* (1879) 10 Ch D 776, 784, *per* Bacon CJ.

[296]　*Re Art Reproduction Co Ltd* [1952] Ch 89, 93 - 94, *per* Wynn-Parry J; *Government of India, v Taylor* [1955] AC 491, 509, *per* Viscount Simonds; *Re Overmark Smith Warden Ltd* [1982] 1 WLR 1195, 1202, *per* Slade J; *Re Cases of Taffs Well Ltd* [1992] Ch 179, 190, *per* Judge Baker QC.

winding-up.[297] This position will not be changed by the adoption of the core regime.

4.252 A number of claims against a company fall outside the winding-up procedure. The paradigm case is a claim to enforce a proprietary right against property in the possession of the company.[298] Time continues to run in respect of proceedings to enforce these claims notwithstanding that the shareholders have resolved, or the court has ordered, the company to be wound up.[299]

4.253 Where a company is wound up by the court, section 130(2) of the 1986 Act provides that "no action or proceeding shall be proceeded with or commenced against the company or its property, except by leave of the court and subject to such terms as the court may impose".[300] The making of a winding-up order is therefore a legal restriction on the ability of the claimant to bring proceedings in the same way as the appointment of a provisional liquidator. It is equally unlikely to delay the running of time in the limitation periods: where the claimant seeks to enforce a claim falling outside the winding-up procedure, an application for leave to issue proceedings under section 130(2) is generally given as a matter of course.[301] We do not consider that the claimant requires any further protection. **We therefore recommend that claims brought against a company or partnership during the course of the winding-up procedure should be subject to the core regime.**

(4) Bankruptcy

(a) *Claims against an individual bankrupt during the course of the bankruptcy procedure*

4.254 There is no restriction on a creditor issuing proceedings against an individual bankrupt during any time when a petition for bankruptcy is being considered (providing that an interim receiver has not been appointed) although the proceedings may be stayed.[302] Accordingly, during the period beginning with the presentation of a petition for a bankruptcy order and ending with the making of

---

[297] *Re General Rolling Stock Company* (1872) LR 7 Ch App 646, 649 - 650, *per* Mellish LJ; *Re Cases of Taffs Well Ltd* [1992] Ch 179, 189, *per* Judge Baker QC.

[298] *Re Aro Co Ltd* [1980] Ch 196, 207, *per* Brightman LJ.

[299] *Re Benzon* [1914] 2 Ch 68, 75, *per* Channell J; *Cotterell v Price* [1960] 3 All ER 315, 320 - 321, *per* Buckley J.

[300] This is applied to insolvent partnerships by virtue of the 1994 Order, Arts 7 - 10. The 1986 Act does not make any provision in respect of a voluntary winding-up. However, it would appear that the same principles apply: "... if a winding-up order has been made, proceedings are automatically stayed but the court may on application by the creditor allow them to be continued; while in a voluntary winding-up, or where a petition has been presented but not adjudicated on, there is no automatic stay but the court may on application by an interested party restrain proceedings." (*Re Aro Co Ltd* [1980] Ch 196, 204, *per* Brightman LJ).

[301] *Re David Lloyd & Co* (1877) 6 Ch D 339, 344-345, *per* James LJ; *Re Aro Co Ltd* [1980] 1 Ch 196, 204, 207, *per* Brightman LJ; *Re Coregrange Ltd* [1984] BCLC 453, 456-457, *per* Vinelott J.

[302] Insolvency Act 1986, s 285(1) and (2).

such an order or the dismissal of the petition, both the initial limitation and long-stop limitation periods apply in the normal way.[303]

4.255 During the period beginning with the presentation of a petition for a bankruptcy order and ending with the making of such an order or the dismissal of the petition the court may appoint an interim receiver.[304] Where an interim receiver is appointed, section 285(3) of the Act, as applied by section 286(6), provides that "no person who is a creditor of the bankrupt in respect of the debt provable in bankruptcy shall... (b)... commence any action or other legal proceedings against the bankrupt except with the leave of the court and on such terms as the court may impose". This constitutes a legal restriction on the claimant's ability to commence proceedings against the individual bankrupt, which will suspend the running of the limitation period in accordance with our recommendations at paragraph 5.28 below. Time will start to run again from the date when the restriction is lifted, or, if earlier, the date when, if the claimant had taken all reasonable steps open to him or her, it would have been lifted (so that the claimant will not be able to prolong the limitation period by failing to apply for leave to bring proceedings).

4.256 Once an individual is declared bankrupt, just as when a winding-up order has been made against a company, time stops running as against claims in the bankruptcy.[305] Thus, limitation is only relevant in determining whether or not the claim was statute-barred on the date that the court declared the individual bankrupt. For claims not related to the bankruptcy time will not stop running as against the claimants.[306] This position will not be changed by the adoption of the core regime.

4.257 A number of claims against an individual bankrupt fall outside the bankruptcy procedure. For example, forfeiture of a lease for non-payment is not a "remedy against the property", but the determination of the lessee's right to remain in possession of the property following a breach of covenant. Accordingly a claim for possession relating to forfeiture of a lease does not require the leave of the court.[307]

4.258 Where an individual is declared bankrupt, section 285(3) of the 1986 Act provides that "no person who is a creditor of the bankrupt in respect of a debt provable in the bankruptcy shall (a) have any remedy against the property or person of the bankrupt in respect of that debt, or (b) before the discharge of the bankrupt, commence any action or other legal proceedings against the bankrupt except with the leave of the court and on such terms as the court may impose." The making of a bankruptcy order is therefore a legal restriction on the ability of the claimant to bring proceedings in the same way as the appointment of an interim receiver, and

---

[303] A bankruptcy petition can only be presented on debts which are enforceable. Debts which are time-barred will not support a petition.

[304] Insolvency Act 1986, s 286.

[305] *Re Benzon* [1914] 2 Ch 68.

[306] *Re Benzon* [1914] 2 Ch 68.

[307] *Ezekiel v Orakpo* [1977] QB 260.

we do not consider that any additional protection is required for claimants. **We therefore recommend that claims brought against an individual during the course of bankruptcy procedures should be subject to the core regime**.

(b) Claims brought by a trustee in bankruptcy on behalf of an individual during the course of the bankruptcy procedure

4.259 Where the estate of an individual who has been declared bankrupt is being administered the trustee is empowered to realise and distribute the estate.[308] Immediately on the trustee's appointment the estate, including rights of action, vests in him.[309] (The exception to this is rights of action in relation to claims in respect of personal injury to, or the personal inconvenience of, the bankrupt).[310] In particular, a trustee is empowered to bring, institute, or defend any claim relating to the property comprised in the bankrupt's estate, with the permission of the creditors' committee.[311] The trustee is also empowered to sue or be sued in his or her official name in connection with the exercise of any of his powers, without permission.[312]

4.260 Currently where a limitation period in respect of a claim by the bankrupt has started it will continue to run after a bankruptcy order has been made. Under the core regime, the primary limitation period will start on the date when the bankrupt acquired the knowledge of the relevant facts. Where the primary limitation period has expired before the right of action vested in the trustee, the defendant will be able to rely on that defence against a claim brought by the trustee. Where the period has started to run, but has not expired, time will continue to run against the trustee in bankruptcy. After the making of the bankruptcy order the knowledge of the trustee will trigger the primary limitation period.

4.261 The position of the trustee is similar to that of a liquidator in a winding-up claim relating to a company. We have recommended that for a winding-up an extended primary limitation period should be applied to allow the trustee time to investigate claims and bring proceedings. The same concerns arise over the rights of a trustee to pursue proceedings for the estate of a bankrupt (and, as in the case of companies, and partnerships, we consider that this protection should be available for all claims brought in this jurisdiction by a trustee in bankruptcy, or anyone performing that function under the laws of a different jurisdiction, regardless of the domicile of the bankrupt). This does not, however, apply to claims made by the bankrupt in respect of rights of action which do not vest in the trustee in bankruptcy, and our recommendation does not cover such claims.

---

[308] Insolvency Act 1986, s 305(2).

[309] Insolvency Act 1986, s 306.

[310] See *Beckham v Drake* (1849) 2 HL Cas 579; 9 ER 1213.

[311] Insolvency Act 1986, s 314 and Schedule 5, para 2.

[312] Insolvency Act 1986, Schedule 5, para 14.

4.262   Accordingly we recommend that claims brought by a trustee on behalf of a bankrupt should be subject to the core regime, subject to the modification that:

(1)   where the primary limitation period which would have applied to a claim brought by the bankrupt has expired before the date of the bankruptcy order, the defendant may rely on that defence against the trustee in bankruptcy (Draft Bill, Sch 2, para 6(2));

(2)   where the primary limitation period in respect of a claim has started running against the bankrupt but has not expired by that date, it should be suspended for one year from the date of the bankruptcy order (Draft Bill, Sch 2, para 6(3));

(3)   where the primary limitation period in respect of a claim has not started running before the date of bankruptcy, it should start on the later of

(a)   the date of knowledge of the trustee; or

(b)   the date one year after the date of the bankruptcy order. (Draft Bill, Sch 2, para 6(4)).

(5)   Clawback claims: Corporate Insolvency

4.263   The Insolvency Act 1986 provides a number of claims allowing assets to be clawed back on behalf of an insolvent company.[313] Section 212 of the Insolvency Act 1986 gives a convenient procedure for obtaining a summary remedy against, for example, delinquent directors.[314] Sections 213 and 214 allow the liquidator to seek a remedy for fraudulent or wrongful trading,[315] and sections 238 and 239 give a liquidator or an administrator the power to seek relief in relation to transactions

---

[313]   These claims are also available in the administration and winding up of insolvent partnerships by virtue of the 1994 Order, Arts 6 - 10.

[314]   It provides that if, during the course of a winding-up, it appears that an officer, liquidator, administrator, administrative receiver or any other person concerned in the company's management, misapplied, retained or became accountable for any money or other property of the company, or was guilty of any misfeasance or other breach of duty, the official receiver, liquidator or any creditor or contributory may apply to the court for relief.

[315]   Section 213 of the Insolvency Act 1986 provides that if it appears "in the course of the winding-up of a company ... that any business of the company has been carried on with intent to defraud creditors of the company or creditors of any other person, or for any fraudulent purpose", the court, on the application of the liquidator, may declare that any persons who were knowingly parties to the carrying on of the business in that manner are liable to make such contributions (if any) to the company's assets as the court thinks proper. Section 214 of the Insolvency Act 1986 provides that if it appears "in the course of the winding-up of a company" that a director, who knew or ought to have concluded that there was no reasonable prospect that the company would avoid going into insolvent liquidation, failed to take every step with a view to minimising the potential loss to the company's creditors as he or she ought to have taken, the court, on the application of the liquidator, may declare that that person is liable to make such contribution (if any) to the company's assets as the court thinks proper.

entered into at an undervalue, or in respect of any preference given by the company or partnership. Under section 423 the liquidator can apply for relief where the company has entered into a transaction in order to defraud its creditors. The liquidator or administrator bringing claims under these provisions is in the same position as the liquidator pursuing claims which are already vested in the company at the date of liquidation, and we consider that, similarly, each should be allowed a further year in addition to the three year limitation period within which to bring the claim.

4.264 **We recommend that applications under section 212 - 214, 238 - 239 and 423 of the Insolvency Act 1986 should be subject to the core regime, subject to the modification that:**

(1) **where the primary limitation period in respect of a claim under section 212 has started running against the company or partnership before it went into insolvent liquidation but has not expired by that date, it should be suspended for one year from the date of liquidation;**

(2) **where the primary limitation period in respect of any claim under these sections has not started running before the date on which the liquidator (or administrator) was appointed, it should start on the later of:**

(a) **the date of knowledge of the claimant; or**

(b) **the date one year after the date of the liquidation (or, where a claim is brought by the administrator, one year after the date of his or her appointment). (Draft Bill, Sch 2, para 4).**

(6) Clawback Claims: Personal Insolvency

4.265 The Insolvency Act 1986 contains similar 'claw-back' provisions in relation to personal insolvency. Under sections 339 and 340 the trustee in bankruptcy may apply to the court for the adjustment of prior transactions where the bankrupt has entered into transactions at an undervalue, or has given a preference to any person. The court may, on such an application, restore the position to what it should have been if the transaction had not taken place. The transactions covered by these sections include gifts for no consideration, transactions in consideration of marriage, transaction at a value less than money's worth, and excessive pension contributions. Section 343 allows the trustee in bankruptcy to apply to the court for a remedy when the bankrupt has entered into a transaction prior to the bankruptcy for the provision of credit on terms which are judged to be extortionate. Under section 423, the trustee in bankruptcy can apply for relief where the bankrupt has entered into a transaction in order to defraud his or her creditors.

4.266 Under the core regime the primary limitation period for an application would begin to run on the date that the trustee acquires actual or constructive knowledge of the relevant facts. We have recommended above that the core regime should be modified in its application to 'claw-back' applications made in respect of an insolvent company,[316] to ensure that the liquidator has at least four years from the date on the liquidation to make an application to the court. We consider that the same factors apply in relation to applications made by the trustee in bankruptcy, and that the start of the primary limitation period should be similarly modified. The long stop limitation period, starting from the date on which the cause of action accrues, will not create similar problems for the trustee in bankruptcy.

4.267 **We therefore recommend that applications under sections 339 - 343 and 423 of the Insolvency Act 1986 should be subject to the core regime, subject to the modification that the primary limitation period should start on the later of:**

    (1)   the date of knowledge of the trustee; or

    (2)   the date one year after the date of the bankruptcy order. (Draft Bill, Sch 2, para 7).

21.   EQUITABLE REMEDIES

(1)   Equitable Remedies and Limitation Periods[317]

4.268 We provisionally proposed that where the core regime applies to common law remedies for a cause of action, it should also apply to equitable remedies.[318] There was general agreement amongst consultees that the desirability of consistency, simplification and uniformity favours the general application of the core regime to equitable remedies for a cause of action as it applies to common law remedies for that cause of action. Our provisional proposal was accepted by over seventy-five per cent of those consultees who responded on this issue. As Michael Lerego QC noted

> There may be good reasons for having different limitation periods for different causes of action, but 125 years after the fusion of law and equity the historical origin of the remedy is not one of them.

4.269 However, we also provisionally proposed that no limitation period should apply to an application for specific performance where under the present law (as exemplified by *Williams v Greatrex*)[319] delay does not operate to bar specific performance of a contract.[320] This was intended to avoid our proposals affecting the long-established rule that a contract to transfer a legal interest is as good as a transfer of that interest.

---

[316] See paras 4.263 - 4.264 above.

[317] See paras 2.100 - 2.102 above for a statement of the current law.

[318] Limitation of Actions, Consultation Paper No 151 (1998), para 13.165.

[319] [1957] 1 WLR 31.

[320] Limitation of Actions, Consultation Paper No 151 (1998), para 13.167.

4.270   Over sixty-five per cent of consultees responding on this issue agreed with our provisional proposal that an exception should be made in the case of an application for specific performance where delay does not, under the present law, operate to bar the remedy. Some consultees saw no reason for any exception to be made.[321] They noted that making no exception would increase the consistency offered by the core regime, and suggested that there is no reason for the claimant to be excused unnecessary delay in cases such as *Williams v Greatrex*.

4.271   We appreciate that it would be more consistent to omit the exception which we provisionally proposed. However, we consider that the benefit of the exception would outweigh the minor inconsistency which it would require. The rationale for the position under the current law is that "equity treats as done that which ought to be done", so that the claimant is treated in equity, as having already obtained what was promised. In other words, the transfer of the legal title is treated as a technicality that should not be barred by delay. The most common situation where the exception would apply would be where the claimant has purchased either a leasehold interest or freehold interest in land, but the vendor has not completed the sale by executing a transfer. The exception would mean that no limitation period would apply. In addition, under the present law the equitable rule that delay bars the claimant's remedy does not apply as regards the enforcement of equitable mortgages, effected by the deposit of documents with the mortgagee. It would be unfortunate if this device was no longer available or was subject to a three year limitation period which would reduce its effectiveness. We therefore adhere to our provisional view that where delay does not operate to bar specific performance of a contract (as exemplified in *Williams v Greatrex*), then, as under the present law, no limitation period should apply to an application for specific performance.

4.272   We also asked consultees whether, if no limitation period applied to an application for specific performance in this situation, they would favour a limitation period being introduced for damages in lieu of specific performance.[322] Over thirty per cent of the consultees who responded on this issue argued that, even if no limitation period is to apply to such applications for specific performance, the court's ability to award damages in lieu of specific performance should be subject to the limitation period applying to other claims for damages. However, the majority (over sixty-five per cent) disagreed. They made the point that, whatever we decided with respect to the limitation period to be applied to applications for specific performance, the same limitation period would inevitably have to apply to the court's power to award damages in lieu of specific performance:

> Specific performance is a discretionary remedy and it would produce an unjust result if the court, having exercised its discretion not to order specific performance but was minded in the alternative to award

[321]   Victor Joffe QC, Henriques J (responding on behalf of the Northern Circuit), Dr Peter Handford, The London Solicitors Litigation Association and Lovells.

[322]   Limitation of Actions, Consultation Paper No 151 (1998), para 13.167.

damages in lieu thereof, could not do so because, whilst the former claim was not statute-barred, the latter was.[323]

We find this persuasive,[324] and we do not therefore propose to limit this exception to the claim for specific performance as opposed to a claim for specific performance or damages in lieu.

4.273 **We therefore recommend that:**

(1) **where the core regime applies to common law remedies available for a claim in respect of a particular cause of action, it should also apply to equitable remedies available for that cause of action** (Draft Bill, Cl 1);

(2) **but no limitation period should apply to applications for specific performance where under the present law (as exemplified by *Williams v Greatrex*) delay does not operate to bar such applications.** (Draft Bill, Cl 34(1)).

(2) **Limitation Periods and Delay in Claims in Equity**[325]

4.274 The remaining question we raised was whether the doctrine of laches (or delay) should continue to have any role under the core regime so as to bar an equitable remedy before the expiry of the limitation period. We expressed no provisional view on this point, but suggested the following three options to consultees:[326]

(1) Option 1: The equitable concept of delay should not apply to final equitable remedies where the relevant cause of action is governed by the core regime but should continue to be relevant to applications for interlocutory relief (for example, interlocutory injunctions).

(2) Option 2: The equitable concept of delay should not apply to (final) equitable monetary remedies where the relevant cause of action is governed by the core regime but should continue to apply to equitable specific remedies (for example, specific performance or injunctions) whether interlocutory or final.

(3) Option 3: The equitable concept of delay should continue to apply to all (interlocutory or final) equitable remedies (including specific performance, injunctions, an account of profits, equitable damages, equitable compensation, and rescission) as opposed to common law remedies.

---

[323] Lovells.

[324] Though it is unlikely that a court would reject an application for specific performance in this situation.

[325] See paras 2.97 - 2.99 above for a summary of the current law.

[326] Limitation of Actions, Consultation Paper No 151 (1998), para 13.176.

4.275   Professor Andrew Tettenborn suggested that the distinction between final and interlocutory orders is in many cases fictitious. The grant of an interlocutory injunction will decide the case. It may also add unnecessary complexity to the law.

4.276   Around forty per cent of consultees responding on this issue favoured option one; over ten per cent favoured option two and over thirty-five per cent favoured option three. In favour of option three, it was argued that the court should be able to retain its discretion whether or not to grant equitable relief. It was suggested that total abolition of the equitable rule that delay bars the claimant's remedy would either have no effect, because the court would simply find another way of arriving at the desired result,[327] or would serve to fetter the court's ability to take into account delay when exercising its discretion whether or not to grant equitable relief.[328] We accept that it is desirable not to fetter the court's exercise of its discretion. We therefore prefer option 3. We should also point out that what we say on equitable delay applies *a fortiori* to other equitable defences (in particular acquiescence) to which delay may also have some relevance.

4.277   The effect of our recommendations will be that claims for equitable relief will be subject not only to the core regime we propose (being 'civil claims' within the meaning of clause 1(4) of the Bill) but also to the court's equitable jurisdiction to deny the claimant relief because of his delay. The expiry of the limitation period applicable under the core regime will bar the claimant's claim. In addition, the claimant may bring a claim within the limitation period, but after delay which would lead to the claim being barred under the current law for *laches*. Under our recommendations the court with retain the power to deny the claim on the grounds of delay even though the relevant limitation period has not expired.

4.278   **We therefore recommend that nothing in the new Limitation Act should be taken to prejudice any equitable jurisdiction of the court to refuse an application for equitable relief (whether final or interlocutory) on the grounds of delay (or because of any other equitable defence such as acquiescence), even though the limitation period applicable to the claim in question has not expired.** (Draft Bill, Cl 34(2)).

22.   THE INTER-RELATIONSHIP BETWEEN OUR PROPOSED CORE REGIME AND STATUTORY LIMITATION PERIODS OUTSIDE THE 1980 ACT.

4.279   We provisionally proposed that, analogously to section 39 of the Limitation Act 1980, the core regime we are proposing should not apply where a limitation period is prescribed in another enactment.[329] We also proposed that, as an exception to this general principle, the limitation periods in the following statutes should be brought within the core regime: the Rent Act 1977, section 94; the Vaccine Damage Payments Act 1979, section 3; the Compulsory Purchase

---

[327]   As noted by Mrs EJ Cooke and Kim Lewison QC.

[328]   The Chancery Bar Association.

[329]   Limitation of Actions, Consultation Paper No 151 (1998), paras 13.177 - 13.184.

(Vesting Declarations) Act 1981, section 10; the Copyright, Designs and Patents Act 1988, sections 113 and 203.[330]

4.280 Over seventy-five per cent of consultees responding on this issue agreed that the core regime should not apply where a limitation period is prescribed in another enactment. There was also general agreement that the statutory limitation periods identified in the Consultation Paper (save for the limitation period in section 3 of the Vaccine Damage Payments Act 1979 and section 10 of the Compulsory Purchase (Vesting Declarations) Act 1981) should be subject to the core regime. It was also suggested that it should be made clear, for the avoidance of doubt, that claims under the Defective Premises Act 1972 should be brought within the core regime. We agree (though it should be noted that the starting date for the long-stop limitation period applying to claims under that Act will continue to be determined in accordance with section 1(5) of the Defective Premises Act 1972).

4.281 The majority of consultees agreed that claims under the Vaccine Damage Payments Act 1979 should be subject to the core regime. It has however been suggested by one consultee that the limitations regime applicable to such claims is an integral part of the scheme for payments under the Act, and that claims under the Act should be treated differently to other claims for compensation because of their nature (and in particular the fact that strict liability attaches to them). However, we do not consider that the distinctions between claims under the Vaccine Damage Payments Act 1979 and other claims are sufficient to justify excluding claims under the Act from the core regime. We are not, for example, excluding other strict liability torts from the core regime.

4.282 It was suggested that subjecting compulsory purchase claims to the core regime could create difficulties. It is noted that the claim under section 10 of the Compulsory Purchase (Vesting Declarations) Act 1981 only provides compensation for one method of compulsory acquisition. Where an interest in land is acquired by serving a notice to treat and notice of entry, the claim to compensation is governed by the Land Compensation Act 1961, the Compulsory Purchase Act 1965 and the Land Compensation Act 1973, which do not provide an individual limitation period. The Land Compensation Act 1973, sections 19(2A) and 32(7A) provide when the right to compensation is to be deemed to accrue for the purposes of the Limitation Act 1980, and it was held in *Hillingdon London Borough Council v ARC Ltd*[331] that a claim for compensation under the Compulsory Purchase Act 1965, section 11 is subject to a limitation period of six years under section 9 of the Limitation Act 1980.[332]

---

[330] Limitation of Actions, Consultation Paper No 151 (1998), para 13.183 - 13.184. We consider that the same applies to claims under Copyright, Patents and Designs Act 1988, s 23 and Trade Marks Act 1994, s 18.

[331] [1999] Ch 139.

[332] Notably the Court of Appeal also held in that case that making a reference to the Lands Tribunal to assess the compensation due would be sufficient to stop time running against the claimant. Claims on a statute are discussed at para 4.201 above. See also Limitation of Actions, Consultation Paper No 151 (1998), paras 7.10 - 7.21.

4.283   It was suggested (by the Royal Institute of Chartered Surveyors) that all such claims should be treated in the same way for limitation purposes, but that the relevant period should be six years, rather than three years:

> A three year claim 'window' would be unrealistically short and potentially prejudicial to claimants; in particular, it can often take longer than 3 years for the full physical effect of a scheme of public works to become known.

4.284   The Holborn Law Society went further, suggesting that such claims should be subject to the same limitation period as claims for land, or money secured on land:

> It is difficult to see how the acquiring authority could be prejudiced by a long limitation period. Section 9 of the Compulsory Purchase Act 1965 is there to provide for the problem of the inactive or untraceable owner. The section gives the authority power to vest the property in itself by deed poll and pay the compensation money into court. Thereupon the owner's rights against the authority cease, and there is no limitation at all on the time within which the owner may apply for payment out of court. We see no attraction in a limitation period whose effect is to allow an authority to choose not to pay into court in the hope of enjoying a windfall at the expense of the owner whose claim may soon become statute-barred.

They therefore suggested that the relevant limitation period should be extended from six years to ten years.

4.285   There is a case for treating all claims for compensation for compulsory purchase in the same way, as we suggested in the Consultation Paper. However, in the light of the comments made by consultees we agree, with some hesitation, that claims under the Compulsory Purchase (Vesting Declarations) Act 1981 should be excluded from the core regime.[333] We do not however consider that the limitation period needs to be any longer than six years.

4.286   There are a number of cases in which claims for statutory compensation are subjected to the Limitation Act 1980, but provision is made for the cause of action to accrue on the date on which the claimant has notice of particular facts. This applies to, for example, claims under the Law of Registration Act 1925 and the Law of Property Act 1969 for compensation or indemnity for loss suffered as a result of an error on the Land Register and claims under the Local Land Charges Act 1975 for the non-registration of a land charge or production of a defective official certificate. If these notice provisions are retained the claims will be subject to two conflicting 'knowledge' regimes. We believe this should be avoided. The concern which led to the provisions in question can be met by providing that the

---

[333]   The Law Commission has published a preliminary study on the simplification and consolidation of compulsory purchase and compensation legislation. It does not seem appropriate to make recommendations in relation to the law on compulsory purchase in advance of the completion of that review. We do however propose to bring claims under Land Compensation Act 1973, s 34 under the core regime.

long-stop limitation period (which would run from the date on which the error was made, and might end considerably before the claimant had any opportunity to discover it) shall not apply to these claims. They will be subject only to the primary limitation period of three years from the date of knowledge.

4.287   **We therefore recommend that the core regime should not apply where a limitation period has been prescribed in another enactment (Draft Bill, Cl 36), but that claims under:**

   (1)   **section 94 of the Rent Act 1977 (Draft Bill, Sch 3, para 18, 19);**

   (2)   **section 3 of the Vaccine Damage Payments Act 1979 (Draft Bill, Sch 3, para 20);**

   (3)   **sections 113(1), 203(2) and 230 of the Copyright, Designs and Patents Act 1988 and section 18 of the Trade Marks Act 1994; (Draft Bill, Sch 3, paras 25 - 29),**

   (4)   **section 34 of the Land Compensation Act 1973 (Draft Bill, Sch 3, para 14) and, for the avoidance of doubt**

   (5)   **section 1 of the Defective Premises Act 1972 (Draft Bill, Cl 3(4) and Sch 3, para 11)**

should be brought within the core regime.

4.288   **We also recommend that claims under section 83 of the Land Registration Act 1925, section 25 of the Law of Property Act 1969 and section 10 of the Local Land Charges Act 1975 should be subject to the primary limitation period running from the date of knowledge, but not the long-stop limitation period (Draft Bill, Cl 20; Sch 3, paras 3, 9, 16).**

23.   A 'SWEEPING-UP' OR 'DEFAULT' PROVISION

4.289   We provisionally proposed that a new Limitations Act should include a 'sweeping-up' or 'default' clause stating that the core regime applies to all claims unless excluded by another provision in the Act (or any other enactment).[334] This proposal received widespread support: over eighty-five per cent of consultees answering this question agreed, as against approximately five per cent who disagreed.[335] The Land Registry noted:

> In order to achieve the certainty desired as a result of the new regime, this sweeping up clause is important. If it were found that a provision not previously considered had been adversely and unfairly affected, then it is possible for this oversight to be remedied by Parliament. This would be preferable to establishing a regime which was not universal

---

[334]   Limitation of Actions, Consultation Paper No 151 (1998), paras 13.185 - 13.187.

[335]   Seven per cent of consultees responding on this issue did not express a final view.

and which gave rise to initial questions of whether the regime applied at all.

We therefore confirm as a final recommendation that the new Limitations Act will apply to all civil claims, namely claims in civil proceedings for a remedy for a wrong, restitution, or the enforcement of a right.[336]

4.290   We asked consultees the question whether, contrary to the present law, a limitation period (and if so what limitation regime) should apply to proceedings by the Crown for the recovery of any tax or duty or to forfeiture proceedings under the Customs & Excise Acts. The possibility that proceedings by the Crown to recover tax might be subject to a limitation period caused particular concern to the Inland Revenue. The Inland Revenue argue that imposing a limitation period on such claims would seriously damage the current system of tax collection, which makes considerable use of settlements with taxpayers, by obliging the Inland Revenue to issue proceedings unnecessarily. They predicted that the cost of tax collection would increase substantially, and at the same time the level of recoveries would fall sharply.

4.291   Though it would increase the consistency of the core regime if claims by the Inland Revenue and HM Commissioners for Customs & Excise to recover tax were subject to the core regime, we appreciate that there are good reasons to exempt them. Such claims are *sui generis*, and if a limitation period were imposed we have been informed by the Inland Revenue that the revenues collected through the tax system may fall significantly. Further, the usual justifications for a limitation period are not as strong. There are adequate limitation periods applying to the Inland Revenue's right to assess tax, and a full appeal system allowing the tax-payer to dispute any assessment made by the Inland Revenue. The only claims to which a limitation period does not apply under the current law, and which would be affected by imposing the core regime, are claims to recover tax which has already been assessed. The taxpayer has an opportunity to challenge the assessment when it is made. Once any such challenge has been resolved the tax payer will know precisely what his or her maximum liability is. There is therefore no need to impose a limitation period to ensure certainty,[337] or to protect the defendant by preventing stale claims, which the defendant cannot defend.

4.292   We do not however propose to exempt forfeiture proceedings (or "condemnation proceedings", as they should more correctly be called)[338] from the core regime. We are informed by HM Customs & Excise that there would not be any difficulty in applying a three year limitation period to the right of HM Customs & Excise to bring condemnation proceedings under the Customs and Excise Acts. They note

---

[336]   See further paras 3.2 - 3.4 above, for a discussion of what we mean by "civil claims" in this context.

[337]   If tax-payers wish to have the certainty that no further claim can be made against them, they need only pay the tax due.

[338]   Under sections 88 - 91 of the Customs and Excise Management Act 1979, HM Customs & Excise may bring proceedings for the forfeiture of a ship, aircraft or vehicle on the ground that, for example, a ship in United Kingdom waters has been adapted for the purpose of concealing goods.

that, in any event, it has been judicially observed that condemnation proceedings should be instituted with diligence and within a reasonable time, notwithstanding the open-ended limitation period allowed by Limitation Act 1980, section 37(2)(b).[339] Further, there is a six month time limit from the notice of claim for bringing condemnation proceedings under the Magistrates Court Act 1980 (subject "as otherwise expressly provided by any enactment"). However, HM Customs & Excise argue that the three year period should start from the date on which a notice of claim is given by the owner of the article seized, challenging the seizure, and not from the date of knowledge. It is suggested that, though HM Customs & Excise institute the proceedings, they are unable to take any action until the notice of claim has been given. Although this is the case, the notice of claim must be issued by the owner of the goods seized within one month of receipt of the notice of seizure. There will not therefore be a substantial lapse between the date of knowledge of HM Customs & Excise of facts giving rise to the condemnation proceedings, and receipt of the notice of claim. We do not therefore consider that it is necessary to modify the core regime in relation to condemnation proceedings under the Customs & Excise Acts. Nor does there appear to be any greater reason to exclude forfeiture proceedings otherwise than under the Customs and Excise Acts from the core regime.

4.293 **We therefore recommend that:**

(1) **A new Limitations Act should include a 'sweeping-up' or 'default' clause. This will provide that the standard limitation defences which we propose apply to all civil claims. For these purposes, a civil claim means a claim in civil proceedings in which the claimant seeks**

(a) **a remedy for a wrong,**

(b) **restitution, or**

(c) **the enforcement of a right (Draft Bill, Cl 1).**

(2) **There should be an exception to this general rule where other provision is made in the Bill itself, or in any other enactment (Draft Bill, Cl 36).**

(3) **As under the present law, no limitation period should apply to proceedings by the Crown for the recovery of any tax or duty. (Draft Bill, Cl 35(2)).**

---

[339] *Moylan v Commissioners of Customs & Excise* [1963] CLR 347.

PART V
ADDITIONAL ISSUES

1. WHAT THE CLAIMANT NEEDS TO DO TO PREVENT THE EXPIRY OF THE LIMITATION PERIOD: ISSUE OR SERVICE OF PROCEEDINGS?

5.1   In the Consultation Paper we provisionally recommended that no change should be made to the current law under which the limitation period stops running when proceedings are issued against the defendant.[1] This provisional recommendation was overwhelmingly supported by consultees: over ninety-five per cent of those who responded on this point agreed.

5.2   Consultees agreed with our provisional view that the principal advantage of the present rule is that the date of issue is certain, so that there can be no argument as to whether the relevant step has been taken, and that it is simple, so that the claimant is able to act quickly in order to preserve his or her rights. Any change to a rule whereby the limitation period expired only on the date of service of the claim form on the defendant would result in uncertainty, and would require special provision to deal with cases where the defendant deliberately tried to evade service.

5.3   The Practice Direction supplementing Part 7 of the Civil Procedure Rules[2] clarifies that proceedings are started when the court issues a claim form at the request of the claimant, but where the claim form as issued was received in the court office on a date earlier than the date on which it was issued by the court, the claim is 'brought' for the purposes of the Limitation Act 1980 and any other statute on that earlier date.[3]

5.4   **We therefore recommend that no change is needed to the present position that the limitation period should stop running when proceedings are issued (or, if earlier, the date on which the claim form was received in the court office).**

2. ADDING NEW CLAIMS IN EXISTING PROCEEDINGS

5.5   The addition of new claims to existing proceedings[4] is governed by section 35 of the Limitation Act 1980 as supplemented by the Civil Procedure Rules.[5] The addition of a new claim may seem a matter of procedure, and therefore outside the scope of this Report. However, since the end result can be to allow a claim to be brought which would otherwise have been time-barred, substantive limitation issues arise. Since this area is governed by the Limitation Act 1980, it cannot be

---

[1]   Limitation of Actions, Consultation Paper No 151 (1998), para 14.10.

[2]   The Civil Procedure Rules 1998, SI 1998/3132.

[3]   CPR Part 7, PD 5.1.

[4]   Limitation of Actions, Consultation Paper No 151 (1998), paras 9.28 - 9.33.

[5]   See paras 2.105 - 2.113 above.

reformed without primary legislation. And the provisions of the current law have proved difficult to apply. We have therefore felt it appropriate and necessary to consider whether reform is needed in this area.

5.6   Where a party seeks to add a new claim[6] to existing proceedings[7] the new claim is treated as having been commenced on the same date as the original proceedings (that is, the claim is 'related back' to the date on which the original proceedings were commenced).[8] Where any fresh proceedings to commence such a claim would have been time-barred, the effect of this provision is to deny the defendant to the new claim an opportunity to raise a limitation defence.[9] For this reason special restrictions are imposed on the ability to add such new claims.[10]

(1)   New claims involving new causes of action after the expiry of the relevant limitation period

5.7   A new claim involving a new cause of action may not be added to existing proceedings after the expiry of any limitation period under the Limitation Act which would affect new proceedings to enforce the claim unless (i) "the new cause of action arises out of the same facts or substantially the same facts as are already in issue on any claim previously made in the original action"; and (ii) any relevant rules of court are satisfied.[11] The relevant rules of court are contained in Part 17 of the Civil Procedure Rules 1998 and provide that the new claim is only allowed if it "arises out of the same facts or substantially the same facts as a claim in respect of which the party applying for permission has already claimed a remedy in the proceedings".[12]

---

[6]   A new claim is defined as being "any claim by way of set-off or counterclaim, and any claim involving either (a) the addition or substitution of a new cause of action; or (b) the addition or substitution of a new party": Limitation Act 1980, s 35(2).

[7]   Third party proceedings are defined as being "any proceedings brought in the course of any action by any party to the action against a person not previously a party to the action, other than proceedings brought by joining any such person as defendant to any claim already made in the original action by the party bringing the proceedings": Limitation Act 1980, s 35(2).

[8]   For detailed discussion, see Limitation of Actions, Consultation Paper No 151 (1998), paras 9.28 - 9.33.

[9]   *Welsh Development Agency v Redpath Dorman Long* [1994] 1 WLR 1409.

[10]   Two exceptions are made to the imposition of these special restrictions: Limitation Act 1980, s 35(3). First, no restrictions are imposed where the court exercises its discretion under Limitation Act 1980, s 33 to exclude the relevant time limits for actions in respect of personal injuries or death. Secondly, no restrictions are imposed where the new claim is brought by way of an original set-off or counterclaim. An original set-off or an original counterclaim is a claim made by way of set-off or (as the case may be) counterclaim by a party who has not previously made any claim in the action. The purpose of this second exception is to protect the defendant's position where the claimant commences proceedings very close to the expiry of the limitation period. We do not intend to make any recommendations for reform in relation to these provisions. See Draft Bill, Cl 25(1).

[11]   Limitation Act 1980, s 35(3), (4) and (5).

[12]   CPR, r 17.4(2).

5.8   In the Consultation Paper we explained that the object of the restrictions in section 35 was to prevent a party from being able to circumvent the provisions of the Limitation Act by instituting proceedings in respect of a time-barred claim in the guise of an amendment to an existing claim. But we explained that there is also a conflicting principle, that when proceedings have been brought in respect of a claim, it should be possible for all matters relating to that claim to be resolved in the same proceedings. We suggested that section 35 failed to strike an appropriate balance by its narrow definition of the situations in which a new claim can be made. This restricted the ability of the court to deal adequately with new situations as they arose. We therefore provisionally proposed that "new claims should be permitted provided that they are sufficiently related to the original cause of action, even where the limitation period has expired since the proceedings were started".[13]

5.9   Around eighty per cent of consultees who considered this question agreed with our provisional proposal. However, several consultees suggested that a test based on whether the new claim is 'sufficiently related' to the existing cause of action was vague, and asked whether it would be possible to provide additional clarification. The aim of a provision such as section 35 must be to ensure that where the court is in any event examining material for the purpose of deciding the claim brought on the original cause of action, new claims arising out of that same material can be added, so that the 'real issues in the case' can be decided. The defendant should not be unduly prejudiced, since he or she will know of the conduct or events described in the original pleading and so should not destroy any evidence relating thereto.[14] We therefore recommend that the new test should be phrased in such a way as to ensure that the new claim is linked to 'the conduct, transaction or events' on which the existing claim is based. The Alberta Law Reform Institute recommended a similar test: "the added claims are related to the conduct, transaction or events described in the original pleading".[15] The New Zealand Law Commission also recommended that a new claim may be added where it is "properly related to the subject matter of the original claims".[16] However, we prefer to say that the new claim should "arise out of" the conduct, transactions or events already in issue, rather than being "related to" them, as this seems to be a clearer test.

5.10   An advantage of this test, by comparison with the current law, is that it does not depend as heavily on the facts which were pleaded by the claimant to the original claim. Under the present law, the claimant can only be certain that a new claim will be allowed if he or she does not need to plead any new facts to substantiate the claim. Thus, where the claimant has brought a claim for nuisance against the

---

[13]   Limitation of Actions, Consultation Paper No 151 (1998), paras 14.11 - 14.14.

[14]   Institute of Law Research and Reform, Alberta *Limitations,* Report for Discussion No 4 (1986) para 5.22.

[15]   See Alberta Law Reform Institute *Limitations,* Report No 55 (1989) pp 41 - 42 and s 6 of the Limitations Act 1996 c L-15.1.

[16]   New Zealand Law Commission, Report No 6, Limitation Defences in Civil Proceedings, NZLC R6 (1988) paras 430 - 433.

defendant because his excavations in land adjoining the claimant's land have undermined the claimant's land, the claimant will not be able to add a claim for breach of a restrictive covenant after the expiry of the limitation period. Although the claim arises out of the same conduct as the claim for nuisance (namely the excavations made by the defendant) so that it would be within our test, the claimant needs to prove a new fact - the existence of a restrictive covenant. The claim does not therefore arise out of the same facts as the claim already pleaded.[17] *Paragon Finance v DB Thakerar* is another example where the test we propose may lead to a different result. The claimant, a mortgage lender brought a negligence claim against the solicitors who had acted for it in relation to mortgage loans made to five borrowers. In each case the borrowers immediately defaulted. The Court of Appeal refused to allow the claimant to amend his claim to include claims for fraud, conspiracy to defraud and fraudulent breach of trust after the expiry of the limitation period. The claimants needed to make allegations of fraud and dishonesty which had not been included in the original pleadings. Under our test, however, it would be open to the claimants to show that such a claim arose out of the same transaction as the claim already in issue. We believe that such a reform would result in the court being able to decide the 'real issues' between the parties, but without unduly prejudicing the defendant. And the claimant should no longer suffer as a result of sparsely worded original pleadings.

5.11 **Accordingly, we recommend that the addition of new claims made between parties to existing proceedings after the expiry of the limitation period relevant to the new claim should be permitted where**

   (1) the new claim arises out of the conduct, transaction or events on which a claim in the existing proceedings is based; and

   (2) the existing proceedings were commenced within the relevant limitation period.

We also recommend that the Rules Committee amend Rule 17.4(2) of the Civil Procedure Rules, which currently repeats the wording of the test laid down in Limitation Act 1980, section 35. (Draft Bill, Cl 25(2)).

(2) New claims involving the addition or substitution of a party after the expiry of the relevant limitation period

5.12 A new claim involving the addition or substitution of a party may not be added to an existing claim after the expiry of any limitation period under the Limitation Act which would affect new proceedings to enforce the claim unless (i) "the addition or substitution of the new party is necessary for the determination of the original action"; and (ii) any relevant rules of court are satisfied.[18] The addition or substitution shall not be regarded as necessary unless either (a) the new party is substituted for a party whose name was given in any claim made in the original proceedings in mistake for the new party's name; or (b) any claim made in the

---

[17] See, for example, *Benzie v Happy Eater Limited*, 18 May 1990 (unreported).

[18] Limitation Act 1980, s 35(3), (4) and (5).

original proceedings cannot be maintained by or against an existing party unless the new party is joined or substituted as claimant or defendant to those proceedings.[19]

5.13   The relevant rules of court are Rules 19.5(2) and (3). Rule 19.5(2) states that the court may only add or substitute a party if (a) the relevant limitation period was current when the proceedings were started; and (b) the addition or substitution is necessary. Rule 19.5(3) states that the addition or substitution is necessary only if the court is satisfied that:

(a)   the new party is to be substituted for a party who was named in the claim form in mistake for the new party;

(b)   the claim cannot properly be carried on by or against the original party unless the new party is added or substituted as claimant or defendant; or

(c)   the original party has died or had a bankruptcy order made against him and his interest or liability has passed to the new party.

5.14   Also relevant is Rule 17.4(3). This states that the court may allow an amendment to correct a mistake as to the name of a party, but only where the mistake was a genuine one and not one which would cause reasonable doubt as to the identity of the party in question.[20]

5.15   Several consultees were concerned that our provisional recommendation (that new claims should be permitted provided that they are sufficiently related to the original cause of action) should not apply to the addition or substitution of new parties, and felt that justice required additional restrictions in these cases. We agree.

5.16   First, it may be unfair to add claimants. For example, say that two passengers are injured in a car accident. C1 brings timely proceedings, but C2 delays beyond the expiry of the relevant limitation period. C2 subsequently seeks to add him or herself as a claimant to C1's claim. His or her cause of action is undoubtedly related to the same events as the cause of action in respect of which the existing proceedings have been brought, but there would seem to be no good reason to deny the defendant a limitation defence against C2.

5.17   Secondly, it may be unfair to add defendants. It would be possible to add a new defendant to existing proceedings even though he or she was unaware that his or her liability may be questioned, and, since the limitation period has expired, the defendant might quite reasonably have disposed of relevant documents and let any insurance cover lapse. In recognition of this potential injustice, the Alberta Law

---

[19]   Limitation Act 1980, ss 35(5)(b) and 35(6).

[20]   Limitation Act 1980, s 35(7) permits rules of court to provide for a party to an action to be allowed to claim relief in a new capacity even though he had no title to make that claim at the date on which the action was commenced. We propose to preserve this power (see Draft Bill, Cl 25(5) and (6)).

Reform Institute recommended that the defendant must have had sufficient notice of the original proceedings before the end of the relevant limitation period such that he or she will not be prejudiced by being joined.[21] However, the Institute conceded that even with this additional protection the policy reasons for a limitations system based on 'peace and repose' will not be satisfied.

> Until the termination of the proceeding previously commenced, a potential defendant will be vulnerable to being drawn into it, he will enjoy neither peace nor repose, his economic mobility will be threatened by a potential liability of uncertain magnitude, he will have to continue protective insurance and he will have to retain his defensive evidence.[22]

5.18 Is it necessary to relax the restrictions imposed on the addition of new parties? Any such reform must be viewed in the light of our overall recommendations for reform of the limitations regime. If the person seeking to add or substitute a new party has only just identified the correct claimant or defendant, then the relevant limitation period will not have expired (unless either the claimant *ought* to have identified the correct claimant or defendant at an earlier date, or the long-stop limitation period has expired). Section 35 of the Limitation Act 1980 will therefore most frequently be needed to correct mistakes, and these are permitted under the present provision.[23] To some extent the position has been relaxed by the introduction of the Civil Procedure Rules. Unlike the Rules of the Supreme Court which they replaced,[24] these no longer list the only five circumstances in which an addition is necessary to determine a claim, but simply repeat the wording of section 35.

5.19 **Accordingly we recommend that there should be no reform in relation to the addition of new claims to existing proceedings where the new claim involves the addition or substitution of new parties.** (Draft Bill, Cl 25(3), (4)).[25]

---

[21] See Alberta Law Reform Institute, *Limitations*, Report No 55 (1989) pp 41 - 42, 81 - 82 and s 6 of the Limitations Act 1996 c L-15.1. The Law Reform Institute's proposals were based on a model suggested by G D Watson in "Amendment of Proceedings after Limitation Periods" (1975) 53 Can Bar Rev 237.

[22] Alberta Law Reform Institute, *Limitations*, Report No 55 (1989) p 89.

[23] The Rules of the Supreme Court previously only included one provision (Ord 20 r 5(3)) in relation to the addition or substitution of new parties to rectify a mistake, in wording similar to that now in Rule 17.4(3). This had been construed narrowly, so that a distinction was drawn between a mistake as to the identity of the person intending to sue and a mistake as to the name of the party. An amendment was only allowed in the latter case: *IBSSL v Minerals and Metals Trading Corporation* [1996] 1 All ER 1017. However, new Rule 19.5(3)(a) also deals with the rectification of mistakes in broader terms, and has not had such a narrow interpretation: *Gregson Channel Four Television Corporation*, CA, *The Times*, 11 July 2000 and *Re HHR Litigation*, QBD, unreported, 26 February 2001.

[24] RSC, Ord 15, r 6(6).

[25] Although we recommend that the Rules Committee reconsider Rule 17.4(3), with a view to its repeal to the extent that it overlaps with Rule 19.5(3)(a).

3. THE EFFECT OF THE EXPIRY OF THE LIMITATION PERIOD

5.20 We have seen that as a general rule the expiry of the limitation period under the 1980 Act operates to bar the claimant's remedy, rather than extinguish his or her rights.[26] The present exceptions to this general rule are land-related claims,[27] claims for conversion,[28] and claims barred by the long-stop under the Consumer Protection Act 1987.[29]

5.21 In the Consultation Paper we provisionally proposed that no change should be made to the general rule that the expiry of the limitation period should merely bar the remedy. We explained that we could see no advantages in changing the present position, and that making 'extinction' the general rule could create difficulties, most notably in contribution cases.[30] Nor did we think that it would be practicable to change the position in relation to the exceptional cases where the limitation period extinguishes the right, so that a uniform rule of barring the remedy could be applied. In land-related claims and conversion, such a reform would undermine the claimant's title acquired on the expiry of the relevant limitation period. The position relating to the expiry of the 'long-stop' period under the Consumer Protection Act 1987 is governed by European law and is consequently outside the remit of this Paper.

5.22 Our provisional proposals were overwhelmingly supported by consultees. Over ninety-five per cent of those who responded on this point agreed with the views expressed in the Consultation Paper that no change should be made to the present law on the effect of the expiry of a limitation period.

5.23 **Accordingly we recommend that no change should be made to the present law on the effect of the expiry of a limitation period.**

4. RESTRICTIONS ON THE CLAIMANT'S RIGHT TO SUE

5.24 Although rare, situations exist where a cause of action has accrued and the limitation period commenced, but there is some procedural bar which prevents the claimant from commencing proceedings. The classic case illustrating this problem is *Sevcon Ltd v Lucas CAV Ltd.*[31] The claimant argued that his patent had been infringed by the defendant at some point between the date on which the specification of the patent was published by the Patent Office and the date on which the patent was granted to the claimant. Under section 13(4) of the Patents

---

[26] See para 2.93 above.

[27] Limitation Act 1980, s 17.

[28] Limitation Act 1980, s 3.

[29] Limitation Act 1980, s 11A(3). In addition, there are cases outside the ambit of the Limitation Act 1980, where the expiry of the limitation period extinguishes the right. For example, the expiry of the one-year limitation period imposed under article 3(6) of the Hague-Visby Rules also serves to extinguish the right, rather than merely bar the remedy.

[30] Limitation of Actions, Consultation Paper No 151 (1998), para 14.21.

[31] [1986] 1 WLR 462, HL.

Act 1949[32] no proceedings could be commenced for infringement of a patent before the date of grant. But the House of Lords held that the cause of action for infringement accrued to the claimant on the date of the infringement, so that the limitation period started running at that point. As a result, the limitation period expired before the claimant was able to bring proceedings.

5.25 Although the position in relation to patent infringement has been much improved by the implementation of the Patents Act 1977, which restricts the period of time which may pass between the publication of a patent and its grant, a similar problem arises in miscellaneous other cases.[33] In the Consultation Paper we therefore provisionally proposed the introduction of a general rule that, where the claimant's right to bring the claim is subject to a restriction, the running of time, for the purposes of the primary limitation period and long-stop limitation period, should be suspended from the date the claimant has done all that he or she could do to lift that restriction.[34] Although this proposal in relation to the long-stop limitation period cuts across our general proposition that the defendant should not have to defend claims that relate to events which occur more than ten years before the claim is commenced,[35] we believe that such is the unfairness to the claimant where a restriction prevents his or her ability to bring a claim within the long-stop limitation period, that the usual rule should be disapplied.

5.26 Our provisional proposal was greatly supported by consultees. Over ninety per cent of those who expressed a view agreed. Three consultees pointed out that it would be helpful if any new legislation further defined what was meant by a 'restriction'. First, it should be made clear that only legal restrictions, and not, for example factual restrictions such as a disability, were in contemplation. Secondly, the provision should exclude contractual restrictions. In particular, nothing should suggest that time does not run where the parties have agreed that obtaining an arbitration award is a restriction on their right to bring legal proceedings. We agree with both these suggestions and have included them in our recommendation. We will also make it clear that the fact that the cause of action has not yet accrued will not be considered a restriction suspending the long-stop limitation period.

5.27 In the Consultation Paper we proposed that time should stop running when the claimant has done all that he or she could do to lift the restriction. This is most relevant where the only restriction on the claimant is a requirement to obtain leave to make the claim. If the limitation period is only to be suspended when the

---

[32] Now replaced by the Patents Act 1977, s 69(2).

[33] For example, a solicitor is forbidden to bring an action on a bill of costs until the expiry of one month from the delivery of the bill to his or her client. The cause of action for recovery of costs, however, accrues on completion of the work: *Coburn v Colledge* [1897] 1 QB 702. And a cause of action for false imprisonment against justices for exceeding their jurisdiction accrues on the date of the false imprisonment, even though the plaintiff is unable to bring proceedings until the order on which the imprisonment was based is formally quashed: *O'Connor v Isaacs* [1956] 2 QB 288.

[34] Limitation of Actions, Consultation Paper No 151 (1998), para 14.27.

[35] See paras 3.99 - 3.101 above.

claimant has done everything within his or her ability to remove any other restriction might not provide sufficient protection. For example, it may be that the restriction is imposed in year 1, and it is year 5 before the claimant could act to lift the restriction. Yet the primary limitation period, assuming that the cause of action is immediately discoverable, will have expired by this date. We therefore recommend that the suspension of the primary limitation period and the long-stop limitation period should commence as soon as the restriction is imposed, but that the claimant should not be considered to be under a restriction where leave is required to make the claim until he or she has taken all reasonable steps to obtain that leave.

5.28 **Accordingly we recommend that**

(1) **the primary limitation period and the long-stop limitation period will be suspended during any period after the accrual of the cause of action in which the claimant is prevented from making a claim by any enactment or other rule of law** (Draft Bill, Cl 30(1));

(2) **the claimant will not be considered to be under a restriction if**

(a) **the claim could have been made by a litigation friend,**

(b) **the claimant is prevented from making the claim only because of the terms of a contract or**

(c) **if leave is required to make the claim, unless and until the claimant has taken all reasonable steps to obtain that leave** (Draft Bill, Cl 30(2)).[36]

5. THE BURDEN OF PROOF

5.29 We explained in the Consultation Paper that under the current law it is not entirely clear who has the burden of proof on limitation.[37] However, it seems to be the case that the burden of proof is on the claimant: that is, the claimant has the burden of disproving a limitation defence where the defendant has pleaded one.[38] We provisionally proposed that, in general, the burden of proof should continue to rest on the claimant, but asked consultees whether they would favour placing the burden of proving the expiry of the long-stop limitation period on the defendant.[39]

5.30 Over eighty per cent of the consultees who considered this issue agreed with our provisional proposal that, in general, the burden of proof on limitation should remain with the claimant. They endorsed the provisional view expressed in the

[36] We are grateful to Professor Andrew Tettenborn who suggested that we should adopt wording similar to this.

[37] Limitation of Actions, Consultation Paper No 151 (1998), paras 9.23 - 9.25.

[38] CPR, Part 16, PD 14.1 provides that in his or her defence, the defendant must give details of the expiry of any relevant limitation period relied on.

[39] Limitation of Actions, Consultation Paper No 151 (1998), paras 14.31 - 14.32.

Consultation Paper that it would be easier and less expensive for the claimant to provide evidence of his or her knowledge at any given time for the purpose of establishing the date of knowledge, than it would be for the defendant to provide such evidence. We agree. The same applies in the case of defences which are dependant not on the knowledge of the claimant, but on the knowledge, for example, of any person through whom the claimant claims, such as a previous assignor.[40] Some concern was expressed as to how the proposal would work where the defendant alleges that the claimant had constructive as opposed to actual knowledge of the relevant facts. We suggest that where the claimant proves that he or she (or any person in whom the claim was previously vested) took all steps (if any) that a person in his or her circumstances and with his or her knowledge would reasonably have taken to acquire actual knowledge of the relevant facts, he or she would successfully discharge the burden of proof.

5.31 A substantial majority of consultees who expressed a view were of the opinion that, as an exception to the general rule, the burden of proving that the claim is barred by the long-stop should be placed on the defendant. Two principal reasons were given. First, the defendant is likely to be best placed to know when the cause of action accrues (or the date of the relevant act or omission which starts the long-stop limitation period running). Secondly, such a rule would be consistent with the general principle that a defendant must prove any 'defence' on which he or she intends to rely, and the objections to this which apply in the case of the primary limitation period do not apply to the long-stop limitation period.

5.32 **Accordingly we recommend that:**

(1) **the burden of proof in relation to the primary limitation period and the date of knowledge of any person should be on the claimant (Draft Bill, Cl 37(1));**

(2) **the burden of proof in relation to any other defence under the Bill should be placed on the defendant. (Draft Bill, Cl 37(2)).**

6. COMMENCEMENT

5.33 In the Consultation Paper we provisionally proposed that the new Act should apply to all causes of action accruing before it commences, except where the cause of action has been barred by the expiry of a limitation period under the provisions of a previous Act or proceedings have been instituted in respect of a cause of action before the commencement of the Act. Where there is a discretion under the present law for the court to disapply the limitation period (as in personal injury, death and defamation cases) the claim would not be treated as time-barred unless that discretion had already been exercised in favour of the defendant.

5.34 We suggested that this limited form of retrospective application would have two advantages over a general rule of prospective application. First, it would allow for a more rapid implementation of the new Act's provisions. This is particularly

---

[40] See paras 3.92 - 3.94 above.

important in those cases, such as sexual abuse claims, where the shortcomings of the present law are very evident. Secondly, it would prevent the present regime running in tandem with the new regime for an indefinite period of time into the future.[41] At the same time the proposal would not act to deprive a defendant of an accrued limitation defence. We did, however, point out that where the relevant limitation period would be reduced under our proposals, the effect would be to deprive claimants of an existing right to bring a claim.[42]

5.35 Consultees expressed considerable opposition to our provisional proposals (over thirty-five per cent disagreed with the proposals altogether). The most marked criticism of the provisional proposals came from insurance companies. They were concerned that the retrospective reduction in the limitation period applicable to claims for breach of contract from six to three years would have particularly harsh consequences for the insurance industry, since reinsurance receivables form a very important part of an insurance company's assets. It was suggested to us that the risk that an insurance company would be deprived of the right to bring a claim in respect of an existing cause of action under a reinsurance contract would result in a substantial reduction in the value of its assets and could ultimately lead in some cases to insolvency.

5.36 A similar problem applies in relation to claims on a specialty. In some cases, the parties will have entered into a contract in the form of a deed in order to take advantage of the present twelve year limitation period that applies to specialties. That is, the parties effectively agreed that the relevant limitation period for breach of their agreement should be twelve years, but rather than including this as an express term, they simply executed the contract as a deed. To apply the core regime to a claim in respect of the breach of such an agreement would risk upsetting the bargaining position between the parties, by effectively altering this one term of the contract. Accordingly, we recommend that where a specialty has been entered into prior to the commencement of the new Act, the present limitation regime only should apply to a claim on that contract, regardless of the date on which that cause of action arises.

5.37 Concern was also expressed on behalf of the Crown. The present limitation period in respect of such claims is thirty years, but we recommend that this should be reduced to ten.[43] Without further provision, the Crown (and the Church of England) would be given only the length of the 'lead-in' time to the Act (together with any prior notice they may have of the proposed provisions as the Bill passes through Parliament) in which to survey all their land and, if necessary, commence proceedings against squatters. Some government departments with extensive holdings of land have told us that this would not be feasible.

---

[41] As would be the case if the new Act were only to apply prospectively, for example, in defamation claims, in theft claims, claims by a beneficiary in respect of a fraudulent breach of trust or against the trustee, claims where the defendant has deliberately concealed relevant facts or has been fraudulent, and claims based on the claimant's mistake.

[42] Limitation of Actions, Consultation Paper No 151 (1998), paras 14.33 - 14.36.

[43] See paras 4.138 - 4.144 above.

5.38   In the light of these concerns, we have reconsidered our proposals, with a view to limiting their retrospective effect. In principle, the new Act will still apply to all claims accruing before its commencement except where the claim has been barred by the expiry of a limitation period under the provisions of a previous Act or proceedings have been issued in respect of the claim before the commencement of the Act and there will be a year's delay after the Act is passed before any provisions come into force. However, we propose to provide that, in addition, where the cause of action accrued before the commencement of the new Act, the limitation period should expire on the later of the following two dates:

(1)   the date on which time would have expired under the previous law or

(2)   the date on which time would expire under the new Act.

5.39   This will ensure that, in most cases, the claimant whose cause of action accrued before commencement will not be prejudiced by the implementation of the new Act. Where the old law would allow the claimant the benefit of a longer limitation period, that limitation period will continue to apply. This will be subject to the following exceptions. Where no limitation period at all applies to a claim under the current law, following this rule would mean that the limitation regimes under the old law would continue to co-exist with the new regime we propose for an indefinite period. We do not think that this is acceptable. We therefore propose that in this case, the claimant should be allowed at least six years from the date of commencement of the new Act, but no longer (unless the claimant would have the benefit of a longer period under the current law, because he or she does not have the relevant knowledge to trigger the limitation period). Similarly, we propose that the limitation period applying under the previous law in the case of a claim founded on fraud or mistake should not continue to apply for more than six years after the commencement of the new Act. We consider that it would be unfortunate if, for example, if the claimant who made a payment in reliance on a mistake of law shortly before the new Act came into force but only discovered the mistake twenty or more years later was still able to rely on the old law. In addition, in considering what date the limitation period would have expired under the previous we propose that no account should be taken of the effect of 'deliberate concealment' under the previous law. This is necessary to ensure that our provisions on deliberate concealment apply immediately the new Act comes into force.

5.40   **Accordingly, we recommend that:**

(1)   **The new Act should come into force one year after the day on which it is passed (Draft Bill, Cl 40(1)).**

(2)   **The proposed new Act should apply to causes of action accruing before it commences, except where the claim has been barred by the expiry of a limitation period under the provisions of a previous Act or proceedings have been instituted in respect of a claim before the commencement of the Act. (Draft Bill, Cl 40(2), (3)(a), (b))**

(3)   Any claim arising under a contract entered into under seal before the commencement of the new Act shall be subject to a limitation period of twelve years from the date of accrual of the cause of action. (Draft Bill, Cl 40(3)(c)).

(4)   Where the cause of action accrued before commencement, and no limitation period applied to that claim under the previous law, the limitation period will expire on the later of

(a)   the date six years from commencement or

(b)   on the expiry of the limitation period applying under the new Act. (Draft Bill, Cl 40(4)).

(5)   In any other case, where the cause of action accrued before commencement, the limitation period will expire on the later of

(a)   the date on which time would have expired under the previous law or

(b)   the date on which time would expire under the new Act. (Draft Bill, Cl 40(5))

(6)   In determining when the limitation period applicable under the previous law would have expired,

(a)   no account shall be taken of the effect of deliberate concealment under section 32(1)(b) of the 1980 Act (Draft Bill, Cl 40(6)(a));

(b)   section 32(1)(a) and (c) of the 1980 Act shall be considered to extend the limitation period for no more than six years from the date on which the Act comes into force (Draft Bill, Cl 40(6)(b)).

7.   THE DECISION IN ARNOLD V CENTRAL ELECTRICITY GENERATING BOARD[44]

5.41   In the Consultation Paper[45] we drew attention to the decision of the House of Lords in *Arnold v Central Electricity Generating Board*.[46] A claim was brought under the Law Reform (Miscellaneous Provisions) Act 1934 and the Fatal Accidents Act 1976 by the widow of a man who died in 1982 from mesothelioma caused by exposure to asbestos during his employment with the defendant's predecessor, a public authority. It was agreed that his cause of action accrued at the latest by April 1943, although the deceased only discovered his injury in 1981. The defendant pleaded a limitation defence under section 21 of the Limitation Act

---

[44]   [1988] AC 228.

[45]   Limitation of Actions, Consultation Paper No 151 (1998), para 9.38.

[46]   [1988] AC 228.

1939, which applied a limitation period of one year from the date the cause of action accrued to claims against public authorities. This provision was repealed by the Law Reform (Limitation of Actions, etc.) Act 1954, which was itself followed by the Limitation Act 1963, the Limitation Act 1975 and the Limitation Act 1980. The question at issue was therefore whether any of these successive Limitation Acts had had the effect of reviving a previously time-barred cause of action.

5.42   It was not in dispute that the 1963 Act operated retrospectively, when certain conditions were satisfied, to deprive a defendant of an accrued time bar in respect of a claim for damage for personal injuries in which the cause of action had accrued since 4 June 1954 (the date of implementation of the 1954 Act). It was the 1963 Act that first introduced the concept of discoverability for personal injury claims in order to prevent injustice where the claimant suffered a latent disease. And it was quite clear that it was intended to have some retrospective effect. However, after detailed consideration of the relevant provisions of the Act, the House of Lords held that it did not operate retrospectively to remove an accrued time-bar in any personal injury case where the cause of action accrued before 4 June 1954, whether the claim was brought against a public authority or other defendant. This decision represented a considerable curtailment of the retrospective effect of the Limitation Act 1963.

5.43   In the Consultation Paper[47] we noted that the decision clearly had potential to cause injustice and the Law Reform Advisory Committee for Northern Ireland had recommended that it should be reversed by legislation.[48] However, since we believed that its likely future impact would be very limited, we did not recommend overruling it by way of legislation. These comments were made in the light of our provisional proposal that a thirty year long-stop limitation period should apply in personal injury claims. Under these provisional proposals, a claim in respect of a cause of action that accrued before 1954 would, therefore, have been in any event time-barred, so that a reversal of the *Arnold* decision would have no practical effect. However, we now recommend that no long-stop should apply in personal injury claims.[49] We have reconsidered whether the new Act should overrule the effect of the *Arnold* decision in the light of this change to our recommendations. Clearly, therefore, without further provision, the *Arnold* decision could still, in some cases, operate to time-bar causes of action in respect of personal injuries. However, we remain concerned that the result of any such legislation would be to allow claims dating before 1954 to be brought fifty years or more after the events giving rise to the claims. After so long, it would be very difficult to give a fair trial to the matters concerned. Any such legislation would also deprive the defendants (after several decades) of an accrued limitation defence. We are not convinced that such a provision would be of sufficient benefit to justify this. Accordingly we do not recommend legislating to overrule the decision in *Arnold v Central Electricity Generating Board.*

[47]   Limitation of Actions, Consultation Paper No 151 (1998), para 9.38 n 107.

[48]   Law Reform Advisory Committee for Northern Ireland, Fourth Annual Report (1992-93) p 10 - 11 and Discussion Paper No 2 on Actions Arising out of Insidious Diseases (July 1992).

[49]   See paras 3.102 - 3.107 above.

PART VI
SUMMARY OF RECOMMENDATIONS

We recommend that:-

When should time start to run?

(1)   The primary limitation period should start to run from the 'date of knowledge' rather than, for example, the date the cause of action accrues (Paragraph 3.7, Draft Bill, Cl 1(1)).

(2)   The date of knowledge (which is when the primary limitation period should start to run) should be the date when the claimant has (actual or constructive) knowledge of the following facts:-

    (a)   the facts which give rise to the cause of action;

    (b)   the identity of the defendant; and

    (c)   where injury, loss or damage has occurred or a benefit has been received, that the injury, loss, damage or benefit are significant. (Paragraph 3.32, Draft Bill, Cl 2(1)).

(3)   For the purposes of the definition of the date of knowledge, a claimant will be deemed to know that the injury, loss, damage or benefit is significant if

    (a)   the claimant knows the full extent of the injury, loss, damage suffered by the claimant (or any other relevant person), or (in relation to a claim for restitution) of any benefit obtained by the defendant (or any other relevant person); or

    a reasonable person would think that, on the assumption that the defendant does not dispute liability and is able to satisfy a judgment, a civil claim was worth making in respect of the injury, loss, damage or benefit concerned. (Paragraph 3.33, Draft Bill, Cl 2(5)).

(4)   For the purposes of the test for the 'date of knowledge', the claimant is presumed to know the law, so that the claimant's lack of knowledge that the facts would or would not, as a matter of law, give rise to a cause of action shall be irrelevant. (Draft Bill, Cl 2(2)). This will not apply to

    (a)   a cause of action in respect of breach of duty where the breach of duty concerned is a failure to give correct advice as to the law, and the fact that correct advice had not (or may not) have been given shall be treated as one of the facts giving rise to the cause of action (Draft Bill, Cl 2(3)); or

(b) a cause of action in respect of restitution based on a mistake of law, and the fact that a mistake of law has been, or may have been, made, shall be treated as one of the facts giving rise to the cause of action. (Paragraph 3.39, Draft Bill, Cl 2(4)).

(5) "Actual knowledge' should not be defined in the proposed legislation and should be treated as a straightforward issue of fact which does not require elaboration. (Paragraph 3.44).

(6) The claimant should be considered to have constructive knowledge of the relevant facts when the claimant in his or her circumstances and with his or her abilities ought reasonably to have known of the relevant facts. (Paragraph 3.50, Draft Bill, Cl 4(1)(a), 4(2)).

(7) Unless the claimant has acted unreasonably in not seeking advice from an expert, the claimant should not be treated as having constructive knowledge of any fact which an expert might have acquired. Where an expert has been consulted, the claimant will not be deemed to have constructive knowledge of any information which the expert either acquired, but failed to communicate to the claimant, or failed to acquire. (Paragraph 3.60, Draft Bill, Cl 4(1)(b)).

(8) A claimant is to be treated as knowing any fact of which his or her agent has actual knowledge if, the agent in question

(a) is under a duty to communicate that fact to the principal, or

(b) has authority to act in relation to the cause of action.

but if this does not apply, no person shall be treated as having knowledge of a fact merely because an agent of his has knowledge of a fact (Paragraph 3.62, Draft Bill, Cl 4(3)).

(9) Our provisions in respect of 'corporate knowledge' should apply to the following 'relevant bodies': all corporations (whether bodies corporate or corporations sole), and all other bodies which have a right to sue or be sued in their own names, including Government departments which are 'authorised departments' in accordance with section 17 of the Crown Proceedings Act 1947 and partnerships. (Paragraph 3.66, Draft Bill, Cl 5(2)).

(10) A relevant body should be considered to have actual or constructive knowledge when that knowledge is imputed to the body under our recommendations in relation to agency, or when

(a) an officer of the body (including a partner in the case of a partnership), or a person with authority to take the relevant decisions on its behalf; or

(b)   an employee of the relevant body who is under a duty to disclose that information to someone with that authority or to any other employee

has that knowledge. For these purposes, decisions in relation to the claim are (a) a decision to seek legal advice in relation to the claim and (b) a decision whether or not to issue proceedings in relation to the claim. (Paragraph 3.78, Draft Bill, Cl 5(1), (3) and (5)).

(11)   Where an officer of the body, or a person with authority to act on the information on behalf of the relevant body, or any employee of the relevant body who is under a duty to communicate that information to a person with that authority or another employee

   (a)   is a defendant to the claim of the relevant body; or

   (b)   has dishonestly concealed information relevant to that claim from someone whose knowledge would be attributed to the relevant body under the rule set out in paragraph (10) above

that person's knowledge shall not be regarded as the knowledge of the relevant body. (Paragraph 3.80, Draft Bill, Cl 5(4), (5)).

(12)   Where a claim is brought by two or more claimants who are jointly entitled to the remedy sought, the start of the primary limitation period shall be calculated separately for each claimant, by reference to the knowledge of that claimant. A defence may only be raised against those claimants against whom the primary limitation period has expired. (Paragraph 3.87, Draft Bill, Cl 6(1), (2)).

(13)   Where a claim must be brought by two or more claimants acting as trustees or personal representatives, the primary limitation period in respect of that claim should start from the earliest date on which one of the trustees or personal representatives has actual or constructive knowledge of the relevant facts. (Paragraph 3.91, Draft Bill, Cl 6(3), (4)).

(14)   Where a cause of action has been assigned to the claimant:

   (a)   the expiry of the primary limitation period in relation to a claim by any person in whom the cause of action was vested before the claimant will give rise to a defence (Draft Bill, Cl 7(2));

   (b)   where the primary limitation period had started to run in relation to a claim by any person in whom the cause of action was vested before it was assigned to the claimant because that person acquired the relevant knowledge at the time when he or she had the right to bring a claim, it will continue to run against the claimant (Draft Bill, Cl 7(3), (6));

(c) where the primary limitation period has not started to run before the date of the assignment it will run from the later of

(i) the date of the assignment and

(ii) the date of knowledge of the claimant (Paragraph 3.94), Draft Bill, Cl 7(4)).

How long should the primary limitation period be?

(15) **The primary limitation period applying under the core regime should be three years.** (Paragraph 3.98, Draft Bill, Cl 1(1)).

The long-stop limitation period

(16) **A claim, other than in respect of a personal injury, should be subject to a long-stop limitation period of ten years.** (Paragraph 3.101, Draft Bill, Cl 1(2)).

(17) **No long-stop limitation period should be applied to claims in respect of personal injuries to the claimant (or, in the case of an action brought under the Law Reform (Miscellaneous Provisions) Act 1934 or the Fatal Accidents Act 1976, to the deceased).** (Paragraph 3.107, Draft Bill, Cl 9).

(18) **The long-stop limitation period should, as a general rule, start to run from the date on which the cause of action accrues, but that there should be an exception for those claims in tort where injury, loss or damage is an essential element of the cause of action and for claims for breach of statutory duty. In these cases, the long-stop limitation period will start to run from the date of the act or omission that gives rise to the cause of action.** (Paragraph 3.113, Draft Bill, Cl 3).

Factors extending or excluding the limitation periods

(19) **During the period when the claimant lacks capacity because he or she is under the age of eighteen**

(a) **the primary limitation period shall not run;**

(b) **any long-stop limitation period shall run but will end on the later of the following dates:**

(i) **the date on which the claimant reaches the age of twenty-one; or**

> (ii) the date ten years after the starting date for the long-stop limitation period. (Paragraph 3.121, Draft Bill, Cl 28).

(20) There should be no specific provision for the psychological incapacity suffered by victims of sexual abuse. (Paragraph 3.125).

(21) During the period when a claimant over eighteen lacks capacity because he or she is unable by reason of mental disability to make a decision for him or herself on the matters in question, or he or she is unable to communicate his or her decision on that matter because of mental disability or physical impairment (Draft Bill, Cl 29(6)):

> (a) subject to sub-paragraph (c) below, the primary limitation period should not run. (Draft Bill, Cl 29(2))
>
> This will apply whether the lack of capacity exists on the date when the cause of action accrues (so that the primary limitation period does not start running), or develops after that date (suspending the primary limitation period after it has begun to run). When the claimant regains capacity, the primary limitation period will continue to run from the point at which it was suspended, so that the claimant has the benefit of the unexpired part of the limitation period;
>
> (b) in claims which are not related to personal injuries, a long-stop limitation period should run;
>
> (c) in personal injury cases, after a period of ten years from the accrual of the cause of action or, if later, from the onset of the lack of capacity, the primary limitation period should run but with the knowledge of the claimant's Representative Adult regarded as the knowledge of the claimant, except where the cause of action is against the Representative Adult. Where the claimant was a minor at the end of the ten year period, the primary limitation period shall not run by reference to the knowledge of the Representative Adult until the claimant's majority. (Paragraph 3.133, Draft Bill, Cl 29(3), (4) and (5)).

(22) 'Mental disability' for the purposes of this definition is defined as 'a disability or disorder of the mind or brain, whether permanent or temporary, which results in an impairment or disturbance of mental functioning'. (Paragraph 3.133, Draft Bill, Cl 29(7)).

(23) A person is a Representative Adult if he or she is the member of the claimant's family who is responsible for the day to day care of the claimant, or a person who is authorised under Part VII of the

Mental Health Act 1983 to conduct proceedings in the name of the claimant. (Paragraph 3.133, Draft Bill, Cl 29(8)).

(24) Where:

(a) the defendant or any person through whom the defendant claims (or any of their agents) has concealed any of the relevant facts from the claimant or any person through whom he claims (or any of their agents) (whether before or after the cause of action has accrued) and

(b) the concealment was dishonest

the long-stop limitation period or any limitation period agreed between the parties should be suspended from the date on which the fact was concealed until the date on which it was discovered (or should have been discovered) by the claimant (or any person through whom he or she claims) (Paragraph 3.145, Draft Bill, Cl 26(1), (2), (4)).

(25) The defendant will be regarded as concealing a fact from the claimant

(a) if the defendant takes any action, or is a party to any action the effect of which is to prevent the claimant discovering that fact for some time, or

(b) if the defendant fails to disclose that fact to the claimant in breach of a duty to do so (Paragraph 3.145, Draft Bill, Cl 26(6)).

(26) The long-stop limitation period applying to a claim by the purchaser of defective property will be extended where the defendant has dishonestly concealed the relevant facts from the seller of that property. (Paragraph 3.145, Draft Bill, Cl 26(3)).

(27) The long-stop limitation period applying to a claim against a bona fide purchaser of property to recover that property (or its value) or to enforce a charge (or set aside a transaction) affecting it will not be extended by dishonest concealment if

(a) the purchase took place after the concealment and

(b) the purchaser was not party to the concealment and had no reason to suppose that it had taken place. (Paragraph 3.145, Draft Bill, Cl 26(5)).

(28) A written acknowledgment or a part payment, by the defendant (or someone previously liable to the claim), and irrespective of the nature of the claim, should restart the running of time for both the primary and long-stop limitation periods applying to the claim. This applies whether the acknowledgment or payment was made

before or after the cause of action accrued (Paragraph 3.155, Draft Bill, Cl 27(1), (7), (8)).

(29) A written acknowledgment or a part payment should not be effective to revive a cause of action once the primary or long-stop limitation period has expired (Paragraph 3.155, Draft Bill, Cl 27(1)(c)).

(30) Subject to special rules applying to mortgages and for the possession of land (and in the case of trustees and personal representatives), only the acknowledgor, the person making the part payment or the principal of the agent giving the acknowledgment or making the part payment, and his or her successors, should be bound by the acknowledgment or part payment (Paragraph 3.155, Draft Bill, Cl 27(2), (4), (5), (9)).

(31) Similarly, where an acknowledgment or part payment is made to one or more of a number of joint (or joint and several) claimants (who are not trustees or personal representatives), only the person (or persons) to whom it is made may rely on it to extend the limitation period (Paragraph 3.155, Draft Bill, Cl 27(3), (4)).

(32) Where the purchaser of defective property has a cause of action under section 3 of the Latent Damage Act 1986, an acknowledgment made by the defendant to the previous owner of that property in relation to the original cause of action will also extend the limitation period apply to a claim brought by the purchaser against the defendant (Paragraph 3.155, Draft Bill, Cl 27(6)).

(33) As under the present law, the acknowledgment shall be valid only if made to the person, or to the agent of the person, whose title or claim is being acknowledged or in respect of whose claim the payment is being made. (Paragraph 3.155, Draft Bill, Cl 27(1), (9)).

A judicial discretion?

(34) In respect of a personal injury claim, the court may direct that the limitation period which would otherwise bar the claimant's claim shall be disapplied if, but only if, it is satisfied that it would be unjust not to give such a direction having regard to

(a) any hardship which would be caused to the defendant if the direction were given; and

(b) any hardship which would be caused to the claimant if the direction were not given (Paragraph 3.169, Draft Bill, Cl 12(1), (2)).

(35) The court shall take into account the following factors in the exercise of its discretion:

(a) the length of, and the reasons for, the delay on the part of the claimant;

(b) the effect of the passage of time on the ability of the defendant to defend the claim;

(c) the effect of the passage of time on the cogency of any evidence which might be called by the claimant or the defendant;

(d) the conduct of the defendant after the cause of action arose, including the extent (if any) to which he or she responded to requests reasonably made by the claimant for information or inspection for the purpose of ascertaining facts which were or might be relevant to the claim;

(e) the extent to which the claimant acted promptly and reasonably once he or she knew that the facts gave rise to a claim;

(f) the steps, if any, taken by the claimant to obtain medical, legal or other expert advice and the nature of any such advice he or she may have received;

(g) any alternative remedy or compensation available to the claimant; and

(h) the strength of the claimant's case.

In addition the court should be empowered to consider any other relevant circumstances. (Paragraph 3.169, Draft Bill, Cl 12(3)).

Agreements to change the limitation period

(36) Subject to (37) and (38) below, nothing in the new Act shall prevent the making of an agreement which modifies or disapplies any of its provisions or makes alternative provision (Paragraph 3.175, Draft Bill, Cl 31(1)).

(37) Any clause in such an agreement which affects the limitation period will be valid only if it is shown by the party seeking to rely on it to be fair and reasonable within the meaning of section 11 of the Unfair Contract Terms Act 1977 (Paragraph 3.175, Draft Bill, Cl 31(3)).

(38) An agreement will be unenforceable to the extent that its terms modify or disapply, or make provision in place of the Act's provision in relation to disability, dishonest concealment or the ten year limitation period applying to claims under the Consumer Protection Act 1987. (Paragraph 3.175, Draft Bill, Cl 31(2)).

(39) The cause of action in relation to a claim for repayment of a 'qualifying loan' should not accrue until a written demand for repayment has been made. "Qualifying loan" for the purposes of this recommendation will have the same meaning as in section 6 of the Limitation Act 1980. (Paragraph 4.6, Draft Bill, Cl 32).

(40) Specialties should be subject to the core regime (Paragraph 4.9).

(41) Claims under the Law Reform (Miscellaneous Provisions) Act 1934 should be subject to the core regime, save that (as under the present law in relation to the survival of personal injury claims) the primary limitation period should start from the later of the date the cause of action was discoverable by the claimant (that is, the personal representative) or the date of death of the deceased. (Draft Bill, Cl 10). As regards the survival of personal injury claims, where, as we have seen, we recommend no long-stop limitation period and a judicial discretion to disapply the primary limitation period, the court in exercising that discretion shall take into account the deceased's delay as well as that of the personal representative. (Paragraph 4.15, Draft Bill, Cl 12(4), (8)(b)).

(42) Claims under the Fatal Accidents Act 1976 should be treated as analogous to personal injury claims under our core regime (so that proceedings in respect of such claims should not be subject to a long-stop limitation period and there should be a judicial discretion to disapply the primary limitation period) save that the date of knowledge should refer to the knowledge of the dependants for whom the claim is brought. (Paragraph 4.22, Draft Bill, Cl 11, Cl 12(5), (6)).

(43) Claims by child abuse victims should be subject to the core regime as modified in relation to other personal injury claims. (Paragraph 4.32).

(44) The core regime should apply to claims under the Consumer Protection Act 1987, subject to the following modifications:

    (a) The starting date for the long-stop limitation period will be the date on which the defective product is supplied by the producer of the product, or by the person who imported the product into a Member State of the European Union. (Draft Bill, Cl 8(1), (2)).

    (b) The long-stop limitation period will apply to all claims under the Consumer Protection Act 1987, including personal injury claims. (Draft Bill, Cl 8(2), (4)).

(c) The expiry of the long-stop limitation period will extinguish the claimant's right of action. (Draft Bill, Cl 8(3)).

(d) The court's discretion to disapply the limitation period in respect of personal injury claims will only apply to the primary limitation period. (Draft Bill, Cl 8(4)).

(e) The parties may agree to extend the primary limitation period applicable to a claim under the Consumer Protection Act 1987. Otherwise, the starting date of the initial and long-stop limitation period and the length of those periods so far as they apply to a claim under that Act may not be changed by agreement between the parties. (Paragraph 4.37, Draft Bill, Cl 31(2)).

(45) Claims for defamation and for malicious falsehood should be subject to the core regime. (Paragraph 4.46).

(46) All claims for conversion should be subject to the primary limitation period of the core regime. For claims which are related to theft, that period will not start to run until the claimant knows, or ought to know, not only the facts giving rise to the cause of action, but also the whereabouts of the stolen property. (Paragraph 4.67, Draft Bill, Cl 14(2), (5)).

(47) In respect of claims for conversion which are not thefts or related to a theft, the long-stop limitation period should run from the date of the first conversion only. (Paragraph 4.67, Draft Bill, Cl 14(1)).

(48) In respect of claims for conversion which constitute thefts or are subsequent to a theft, the long-stop limitation period should not commence until the date on which the goods are purchased by a person acting in good faith. It will run from that date in favour of the good faith purchaser and anyone claiming through him. (Paragraph 4.67, Draft Bill, Cl 14(3), (5)).

(49) The claimant's title to goods which have been converted shall be extinguished on the expiry of the long-stop limitation period. (Paragraph 4.67, Draft Bill, Cl 14(4)).

(50) A cause of action shall accrue to the subsequent owner of damaged property as provided for in section 3 of the Latent Damage Act 1986; that is where

(a) a cause of action has accrued to any person in respect of any negligence to which damage to any property is attributable (in whole or in part); and

(b) the subsequent owner acquires an interest in the property after the date on which that cause of action accrued, but before any person with an interest in the property has the knowledge relevant to the date of knowledge for a claim in respect of that cause of action.

The claim by the subsequent owner shall be subject to the core regime. (Paragraph 4.75, Draft Bill, Sch 3, para 23).

(51) **The core regime should apply to restitutionary actions** (Paragraph 4.79).

(52) **The core regime should apply to claims for contribution under section 1 of the Civil Liability (Contribution) Act 1978, and that the provisions of the Limitation Act, section 10 (which define the date on which the cause of action for such claims accrues) should be retained to define the starting date for the long-stop limitation period** (Paragraph 4.83, Draft Bill, Cl 13).

(53) **The core regime should apply to claims for a contractual indemnity. This will mean that where there is a chain of indemnity claims, a new long-stop limitation period will arise in respect of each new claim in the chain.** (Paragraph 4.93).

(54) **Subject to our recommendations in paragraph 56 below all claims for breach of trust should be subject to the core regime** (Paragraph 4.101).

(55) **Claims to recover trust property should be subject to the core regime; but**

in the case of a claim for the recovery of trust property held on a bare trust, the cause of action shall not accrue unless and until the trustee acts in breach of trust. (Paragraph 4.106, Draft Bill, Cl 22(2)).

(56) **Legislation should provide that where a claim by one beneficiary has become time-barred, that beneficiary should not be permitted to benefit from a successful claim by another beneficiary whose claim is not time-barred** (Draft Bill, Cl 22(4)).

Pursuant to the application of the core regime, there is no need to provide a trustee with protection equivalent to that which is currently found in Limitation Act 1980, section 21(2).

Neither the primary limitation period nor the long-stop limitation period should apply to claims for breach of trust or to recover trust property which are brought by either the Attorney General or the Charity Commissioners. (Paragraph 4.112, Draft Bill, Cl 22(3)).

(57) **Neither the primary limitation period nor the long-stop limitation period in respect of a claim for breach of trust or to recover trust property by a beneficiary with a future or contingent interest will**

start until that interest has fallen into possession. (Paragraph 4.119, Draft Bill, Cl 22(1)).

(58) The core regime should apply to claims in respect of the personal estate of a deceased person (including any claims in respect of a claim to arrears of interest on legacies). (Paragraph 4.125).

(59) A long-stop limitation period of ten years commencing on the date that the claimant's right to recover the land accrued (or, if later, the date on which the claimant's interest becomes an interest in possession) should apply to, and (subject to the recommendation in paragraph 65 below) be the sole limitation period for claims to recover land[1] (Paragraph 4.135, Draft Bill, Cl 16(1), (2)).

(60) A claimant entitled to a future interest to land which was in adverse possession before that interest fell into possession should be subject to a limitation period of ten years from the date on which his or her interest fell into possession rather than a reduced period (Paragraph 4.135).

(61) The expiry of the limitation period will extinguish the claimant's rights to the land in question, and after that period, no claim may be made. (Paragraph 4.135, Draft Bill, Cl 18(1)).

(62) The limitation period in relation to all claims to recover equitable interests in land should be the same as that which applies in relation to claims to recover legal interests in land. (Draft Bill, Cl 17(2), (3)). The further provisions presently contained in section 18(2) to 18(4) of the Limitation Act 1980 should be retained. (Paragraph 4.137, Draft Bill, Cl 18(2), (3), (4)).

(63) Claims brought by, or by a person claiming through, the Crown (subject to paragraph 65 below) or any spiritual or eleemosynary corporation sole to recover land should be subject to the same limitation period applying to a claim by any other party to recover land (Paragraph 4.144).

(64) In any case where the land is vested in the incumbent from time to time of a benefice as a spiritual corporation sole but the benefice is vacant a claim to recover the land or any part of it may be made by

   (a) the priest-in-charge of the benefice, or

   (b) by the sequestrators of the benefice. (Paragraph 4.144, Draft Bill, Cl 17(5)).

(65) The limitation period applicable to claims by the Crown to recover foreshore should be

---

[1] Subject to the exceptions presently set out in Limitation Act 1980, s 15(3) and (5).

(a)   sixty years from the date of accrual of the right of action or

(b)   ten years from the date when the land ceased to be foreshore

whichever period first expires. (Paragraph 4.147, Draft Bill, Cl 16(4), (7)).

(66)   **Where the identity of the person in adverse possession of the land changes, a new cause of action shall accrue to the claimant, unless anyone in adverse possession of the land before the change continues to be in adverse possession after that date.** (Draft Bill, Sch 1, para 1(4), (5)(a))

However, no new cause of action will accrue to the claimant

(a)   **where the second person in adverse possession claims possession through his or her predecessor** (Draft Bill, Sch 1, para 1(5)(b)) **and**

(b)   **where the squatter coming into possession is recovering possession of the land from a squatter who had previously dispossessed him or her** (Paragraph 4.150, Draft Bill, Sch 1, para 1(6)).

(67)   **Claims to recover the proceeds of the sale of land should not be subject to the primary limitation period of three years from the date of knowledge but only to the long-stop limitation period of ten years running from the date when the vendor became entitled to recover the proceeds (by, for example, enforcing a lien over the land).** (Paragraph 4.151, Draft Bill, Cl 19).

(68)   **The core regime should apply to claims to recover rent, claims to recover damages in respect of arrears of rent, and the levying of distress for unpaid rent.** (Paragraph 4.157).

(69)   **The primary limitation period should not apply to claims to enforce a mortgage or charge over land; and**

the long-stop limitation period should apply to claims to enforce a mortgage or charge over land, running from the date on which the mortgagee's or chargee's right to enforce the mortgage or charge accrues (Paragraph 4.166, Draft Bill, Cl 15(2)).

(70)   **Claims to enforce a mortgage or charge over personal property should be subject to the core regime** (Paragraph 4.169).

(71)   **The primary limitation period should not apply to claims to enforce a mortgage or charge over both land and personal property; and**

the long-stop limitation period should apply to claims to enforce a mortgage or charge over land and personal property, running from

the date on which the mortgagee's or chargee's right to enforce the mortgage or charge, *vis-à-vis* the land, accrues (Paragraph 4.173, Draft Bill, Cl 15(2), (9)).

(72) Only the long-stop limitation period should apply to claims to enforce an obligation secured by a mortgage or charge by suing on the covenant to repay. (Paragraph 4.177, Draft Bill, Cl 15(2)(b)).

(73) Where a mortgage or charge comprises a future interest or a life insurance policy, the limitation period applying to claims to enforce the mortgage or charge should not begin to run until the future interest determines or the life insurance policy matures. (Paragraph 4.181, Draft Bill, Cl 15(4)).

(74) Where a prior mortgagee is in possession of the property which is subject to the mortgage, the limitation period applicable to a claim by the subsequent mortgagee to recover arrears of interest (or damages in lieu) should (if necessary) be extended so that it does not end before the date one year after the prior mortgagee ceases to be in possession. (Paragraph 4.184, Draft Bill, Cl 15(3)).

(75) The limitation period applying to foreclosure proceedings should be suspended during the period that the mortgagee is in possession of the mortgaged property. (Paragraph 4.185, Draft Bill, Cl 15(5)).

(76) No limitation period should apply to claims by the mortgagor to redeem a mortgage over land. (Paragraph 4.189, Draft Bill, Cl 15(1)).

(77) Claims to redeem mortgaged personal property should not be subject to a limitation period. (Paragraph 4.194, Draft Bill, Cl 15(1)).

(78) The expiry of the limitation period applying to claims to enforce a mortgage should extinguish the claimant's interest in the mortgaged property. (Paragraph 4.196, Draft Bill, Cl 15(6)).

(79) Claims on a judgment and claims on an arbitration award should be subject to the core regime. (Paragraph 4.200).

(80) Claims on a statute should be subject to the core regime. (Paragraph 4.202).

(81) No special protection should be given in limitations law to public authorities. (Paragraph 4.203).

(82) Derivative claims should be subject to the core regime, but the start of the primary limitation period should be decided by reference to the knowledge of the shareholder who is bringing the claim. (Paragraph 4.210, Draft Bill, Cl 24).

(83) Applications under section 459 of the Companies Act 1985 should be subject to the core regime. (Paragraph 4.218).

(84) Claims brought by a debtor who is subject to a voluntary arrangement should be subject to the core regime. (Paragraph 4.225).

(85) The primary limitation period should be suspended in respect of claims by a company or partnership during any period in which the company or partnership is in either administration or administrative receivership, except where the administrative receiver is the defendant to the company's claim. (Paragraph 4.234, Draft Bill, Sch 2, paras 1, 2).

(86) Claims against a company or partnership in administration should be subject to the core regime. (Paragraph 4.237).

(87) Claims against a company in administrative receivership should be subject to the core regime. (Paragraph 4.241).

(88) Claims brought by a liquidator on behalf of a company or partnership in liquidation should be subject to the core regime, subject to the modification that

    (a) where the primary limitation period in respect of a claim has started running against the company or partnership before it went into insolvent liquidation but has not expired by that date, it should be suspended for one year from the date of liquidation;

    (b) where the primary limitation period in respect of a claim has not started running before the date of liquidation, it should start on the later of

        (i) the date of knowledge of the liquidator; or

        (ii) the date one year after the date of the liquidation. (Paragraph 4.247, Draft Bill, Sch 2, para 3).

(89) Claims brought against a company or partnership during the course of the winding-up procedure should be subject to the core regime. (Paragraph 4.253).

(90) Claim brought against an individual during the course of bankruptcy procedures should be subject to the core regime. (Paragraph 4.258).

(91) Claims brought by a trustee on behalf of a bankrupt should be subject to the core regime, subject to the modification that:

(a) where the primary limitation period which would have applied to a claim brought by the bankrupt has expired before the date of the bankruptcy order, the defendant may rely on that defence against the trustee in bankruptcy (Draft Bill, Sch 2, para 6(2));

(b) where the primary limitation period in respect of a claim has started running against the bankrupt but has not expired by that date, it should be suspended for one year from the date of the bankruptcy order (Draft Bill, Sch 2, para 6(3));

(c) where the primary limitation period in respect of a claim has not started running before the date of bankruptcy, it should start on the later of

(i) the date of knowledge of the trustee; or

(ii) the date one year after the date of the bankruptcy order. (Paragraph 4.262, Draft Bill, Sch 2, para 6(4)).

(92) Applications under section 212 - 214, 238 - 239 and 423 of the Insolvency Act 1986 should be subject to the core regime, subject to the modification that:

(a) where the primary limitation period in respect of a claim under section 212 has started running against the company or partnership before it went into insolvent liquidation but has not expired by that date, it should be suspended for one year from the date of liquidation;

(b) where the primary limitation period in respect of any claim under these sections has not started running before the date on which the liquidator (or administrator) was appointed, it should start on the later of:

(i) the date of knowledge of the claimant; or

(ii) the date one year after the date of the liquidation (or, where a claim is brought by the administrator, one year after the date of his or her appointment). (Paragraph 4.264, Draft Bill, Sch 2, para 4).

(93) Applications under sections 339 - 343 and 423 of the Insolvency Act 1986 should be subject to the core regime, subject to the modification that the primary limitation period should start on the later of:

(a) the date of knowledge of the trustee; or

(b)   the date one year after the date of the bankruptcy order. (Paragraph 4.267, Draft Bill, Sch 2, para 7).

(94)   Where the core regime applies to common law remedies available for a claim in respect of a particular cause of action, it should also apply to equitable remedies available for that cause of action (Draft Bill, Cl 1);

but no limitation period should apply to applications for specific performance where under the present law (as exemplified by *Williams v Greatrex*) delay does not operate to bar such applications. (Paragraph 4.273, Draft Bill, Cl 34(1)).

(95)   Nothing in the new Limitation Act should be taken to prejudice any equitable jurisdiction of the court to refuse an application for equitable relief (whether final or interlocutory) on the grounds of delay (or because of any other equitable defence such as acquiescence), even though the limitation period applicable to the claim in question has not expired. (Paragraph 4.278, Draft Bill, Cl 34(2)).

(96)   The core regime should not apply where a limitation period has been prescribed in another enactment (Draft Bill, Cl 36), **but that claims under:**

(a)   section 94 of the Rent Act 1977 (Draft Bill, Sch 3, paras 18, 19);

(b)   section 3 of the Vaccine Damage Payments Act 1979 (Draft Bill, Sch 3, para 20);

(c)   sections 113(1), 203(2) and 230 of the Copyright, Designs and Patents Act 1988 and section 18 of the Trade Marks Act 1994; (Draft Bill, Sch 3, paras 25 - 29),

(d)   section 34 of the Land Compensation Act 1973 (Draft Bill, Sch 3, para 14) **and, for the avoidance of doubt**

(e)   section 1 of the Defective Premises Act 1972 (Draft Bill, Cl 3(4) and Sch 3, para 11)

should be brought within the core regime. (Paragraph 4.287).

(97)   Claims under section 83 of the Land Registration Act 1925, section 25 of the Law of Property Act 1969 and section 10 of the Local Land Charges Act 1975 should be subject to the primary limitation period running from the date of knowledge, but not the long-stop limitation period (Paragraph 4.288, Draft Bill, Cl 20; Sch 3, paras 3, 9, 16).

(98)   A new Limitations Act should include a 'sweeping-up' or 'default' clause. This will provide that the standard limitation defences

which we propose apply to all civil claims. For these purposes, a civil claim means a claim in civil proceedings in which the claimant seeks

(a) a remedy for a wrong,

(b) restitution, or

(c) the enforcement of a right (Draft Bill, Cl 1).

There should be an exception to this general rule where other provision is made in the Bill itself, or in any other enactment (Paragraph 4.293, Draft Bill, Cl 36).

(99) As under the present law, no limitation period should apply to proceedings by the Crown for the recovery of any tax or duty. (Paragraph 4.293, Draft Bill, Cl 35(2)).

Additional Issues

(100) No change is needed to the present position that the limitation period should stop running when proceedings are issued (or, if earlier, the date on which the claim form was received in the court office). (Paragraph 5.4).

(101) The addition of new claims made between parties to existing proceedings after the expiry of the limitation period relevant to the new claim should be permitted where

(a) the new claim arises out of the conduct, transaction or events on which a claim in the existing proceedings is based; and

(b) the existing proceedings were commenced within the relevant limitation period.

We also recommend that the Rules Committee amend Rule 17.4(2) of the Civil Procedure Rules, which currently repeats the wording of the test laid down in Limitation Act 1980, section 35. (Paragraph 5.11, Draft Bill, Cl 25(2)).

(102) There should be no reform in relation to the addition of new claims to existing proceedings where the new claim involves the addition or substitution of new parties. (Paragraph 5.19, Draft Bill, Cl 25(3), (4)).

(103) No change should be made to the present law on the effect of the expiry of a limitation period. (Paragraph 5.23).

(104) The primary limitation period and the long-stop limitation period will be suspended during any period after the accrual of the cause

of action in which the claimant is prevented from making a claim by any enactment or other rule of law (Draft Bill, Cl 30(1));

the claimant will not be considered to be under a restriction if

(a)   the claim could have been made by a litigation friend,

(b)   the claimant is prevented from making the claim only because of the terms of a contract or

if leave is required to make the claim, unless and until the claimant has taken all reasonable steps to obtain that leave (Paragraph 5.28, Draft Bill, Cl 30(2)).

(105)   **The burden of proof in relation to the primary limitation period and the date of knowledge of any person should be on the claimant** (Draft Bill, Cl 37(1));

the burden of proof in relation to any other defence under the Bill should be placed on the defendant. (Paragraph 5.32, Draft Bill, Cl 37(2)).

(106)   **The new Act should come into force one year after the day on which it is passed** (Draft Bill, Cl 40(1)).

The proposed new Act should apply to causes of action accruing before it commences, except where the claim has been barred by the expiry of a limitation period under the provisions of a previous Act or proceedings have been instituted in respect of a claim before the commencement of the Act. (Draft Bill, Cl 40(2), (3)(a), (b)).

Any claim arising under a contract entered into under seal before the commencement of the new Act shall be subject to a limitation period of twelve years from the date of accrual of the cause of action. (Paragraph 5.40, Draft Bill, Cl 40(3)(c)).

(107)   **Where the cause of action accrued before commencement, and no limitation period applied to that claim under the previous law, the limitation period will expire on the later of**

(a)   **the date six years from commencement or**

(b)   **on the expiry of the limitation period applying under the new Act.** (Draft Bill, Cl 40(4)).

In any other case, where the cause of action accrued before commencement, the limitation period will expire on the later of

(a)   **the date on which time would have expired under the previous law or**

(b)   the date on which time would expire under the new Act.
       (Paragraph 5.40, Draft Bill, Cl 40(5))

(108) In determining when the limitation period applicable under the
       previous law would have expired,

    (a)   no account shall be taken of the effect of deliberate
           concealment under section 32(1)(b) of the 1980 Act (Draft
           Bill, Cl 40(6)(a));

    (b)   section 32(1)(a) and (c) of the 1980 Act shall be considered to
           extend the limitation period for no more than six years from
           the date on which the Act comes into force (Paragraph 5.40
           Draft Bill, Cl 40(6)(b)).

                          (*Signed*) ROBERT CARNWATH, *Chairman*
                          HUGH BEALE
                          CHARLES HARPUM
                          MARTIN PARTINGTON
                          ALAN WILKIE

MICHAEL SAYERS, *Secretary*
3 April 2001

APPENDIX A

Draft
Limitation Bill

The draft Limitation Bill together with an arrangement of clauses and explanatory notes are on the following pages.

Limitation Bill

ARRANGEMENT OF CLAUSES

Limitation

PART III

GENERAL MODIFICATIONS OF THE STANDARD LIMITATION PROVISIONS ETC

Concealment

Limitation

DRAFT

OF A

B I L L

TO

Make provision about time limits on the making of civil claims; and for connected purposes.

A.D. 2001.

BE IT ENACTED by the Queen's most Excellent Majesty, by and with the advice and consent of the Lords Spiritual and Temporal, and Commons, in this present Parliament assembled, and by the authority of the same, as follows:—

PART I

THE STANDARD LIMITATION PROVISIONS

The standard limitation defences

1.—(1) It is a defence to a civil claim that the claim was not made before the end of the period of three years from the date of knowledge of the claimant.

(2) It is also a defence to a civil claim that the claim was not made before the end of the period of ten years from the starting date in relation to the cause of action on which the claim is founded.

(3) Subsections (1) and (2) are subject to the following provisions of this Act.

(4) In this Act "civil claim" means a claim made in civil proceedings in which the claimant seeks—

    (a) a remedy for a wrong,

    (b) restitution, or

    (c) the enforcement of a right.

(5) The reference in subsection (4) to a claim made in civil proceedings includes a reference to—

    (a) a claim made in the course of such proceedings by way of set-off or counterclaim,

    (b) a claim so made involving the addition or substitution of a new cause of action, and

The standard limitation defences.

226

EXPLANATORY NOTES

This Bill introduces a new limitation regime in place of that enacted in the Limitation Act 1980. Under the new regime, claims will be subject to two limitation periods, a primary limitation period, of three years, running from the date on which the claimant knows, or ought to know of the relevant facts, and a long-stop limitation period, of ten years, running from either the accrual of the cause of action or the date of the act or omission which gives rise to the claim. A claim may be barred by the expiry of the long-stop limitation period even where the primary limitation period has not started running.

Clause 1
This clause provides for the two limitation defences which are at the heart of the core limitation regime we recommend.

Subsection (1) implements the primary limitation period: it is a defence that the claimant failed to issue proceedings within three years of the date of his or her knowledge. The 'date of knowledge' is defined in clause 2.

Subsection (2) implements the long-stop limitation period: it is a defence that the claimant failed to issue proceedings within ten years of the starting date of the claim. This applies whether or not the primary limitation period has begun to run. The 'starting date' is defined in clause 3.

Subsection (3) provides that both the primary limitation period and the long stop limitation period are subject to the modifications made in the rest of the Bill.

Subsections (4) and (5) define the claims which will be subject to the provisions of the Bill. Purely administrative claims, such as an application for the appointment of a new trustee, or an application by a trustee for directions as to the exercise of his functions under the Settled Land Act, for example, will be excluded.

(c) a claim so made involving the addition or substitution of a party.

(6) Where a civil claim is founded on more than one cause of action, this Act shall apply as if a separate civil claim were made in respect of each cause of action.

(7) In this Act—

"civil proceedings" includes any proceedings in a court of law, including an ecclesiastical court,

"claimant" includes a person who makes a claim by way of set-off or counterclaim,

"defendant" includes a person against whom a claim by way of set-off or counterclaim is made.

The date of knowledge

The date of knowledge.

2.—(1) Subject to the following provisions of this section and this Act, any reference in this Act to a person's date of knowledge is a reference to the date on which he first had knowledge of—

(a) the facts which give rise to the cause of action,

(b) the identity of the defendant, and

(c) where injury, loss or damage has occurred or a benefit has been obtained, the fact that the injury, loss, damage or benefit is significant.

(2) Subject to subsections (3) and (4), in determining the date on which a person first had knowledge of the facts which give rise to a cause of action, there shall be disregarded the extent (if any) of his knowledge on any date of whether those facts would or would not, as a matter of law, give rise to a cause of action.

(3) In the case of a cause of action in respect of a breach of duty (whether in tort, in contract or otherwise) which involves a failure to give correct advice as to the law, subsection (1) shall have effect as if it also required knowledge to be had of the fact that correct advice had not been, or may not have been, given.

(4) In the case of a cause of action in respect of restitution based on a mistake of law, subsection (1) shall have effect as if it also required knowledge to be had of the fact that a mistake of law had been, or may have been, made.

(5) For the purposes of this section, a person ("A") shall be regarded as having knowledge of the fact that any injury, loss, damage or benefit is significant—

(a) if he has knowledge of the full extent of the injury, loss, damage or benefit, or

(b) if a reasonable person with A's knowledge of the extent of the injury, loss, damage or benefit would think, on the assumption that the defendant did not dispute liability and was able to satisfy a judgment, that a civil claim was worth making in respect of the injury, loss, damage or benefit.

EXPLANATORY NOTES

Subsection (6) ensures that where the claimant relies on more than one cause of action in bringing a claim, a separate limitation period will apply to each cause of action. It may therefore be the case that the defendant has a defence in respect of only one of the claims brought by the claimant.

Clause 2

This clause defines the date of knowledge, the point at which the primary limitation period starts to run under clause 1(1). (See paragraphs 3.5 - 3.44 of the Report).

Subsection (1) sets out the facts which the claimant needs to know in relation to the claim. Where the claimant (or any other relevant person) has suffered loss, damage or injury, or the defendant (or any other relevant person) has received a benefit, these facts include the fact that the injury, loss, damage or benefit is "significant".

Subsection (2) ensures that whether the claimant knows that the facts give rise to a legal claim is irrelevant. This will prevent the claimant who knows all the facts pleading ignorance of the law to extend the primary limitation period. This does not apply to claims which come within subsections (3) and (4).

Subsection (3) applies where the claim arises from the defendant's failure to give correct advice as to the law. It ensures, for the avoidance of doubt, that the fact that the advice in question was incorrect is considered to be one of the facts which give rise to the cause of action which the claimant needs to know under subsection (1) before the primary limitation period starts to run against him or her.

Subsection (4) applies where the claimant claims restitution based on a mistake of law. It ensures (again for the avoidance of doubt) that the fact that a mistake of law has been made is treated as one of the facts giving rise to the cause of action which the claimant needs to know under subsection (1) before the primary limitation period starts to run against him or her.

Subsection (5) defines what is meant by "significant", for the purpose of subsection (1), using a similar formula to that employed in section 11A(7) of the Limitation Act 1980 ("the 1980 Act") in relation to claims for negligence not involving personal injuries. To ensure that the start of the primary limitation period is not delayed where the loss suffered by the claimant is trivial (so that it can never be considered to be 'significant' under this test) the claimant is also considered to know that the loss, injury, damage or benefit is significant if he or she knows the full extent of his or her loss, or the benefit to the defendant.

Limitation

The starting date

3.—(1) Subject to the following provisions of this section and this Act, any reference in this Act to the starting date is a reference to the date on which the cause of action accrued.

5 (2) Subject to the following provisions of this section and this Act, any reference in this Act to the starting date—

(a) in the case of a cause of action in tort which does not accrue unless injury, loss or damage occurs, or

(b) in the case of a cause of action in respect of breach of statutory
10 duty,

is a reference to the date of occurrence of the act or omission which gives rise to the cause of action (whether the cause of action accrues on that date or on a later date).

(3) Where two or more acts or omissions give rise to a single cause of
15 action falling within subsection (2)(a) or (b), the starting date shall be determined by reference to the last of those acts or omissions.

(4) Subsections (2) and (3) do not apply to a cause of action in respect of a breach of the duty imposed by section 1 of the Defective Premises Act 1972.

20 ### Constructive knowledge etc

4.—(1) For the purposes of this Act, a person's knowledge includes knowledge which he might reasonably have been expected to acquire—

(a) from facts observable or ascertainable by him, or

(b) where he has acted unreasonably in not seeking appropriate
25 expert advice, from facts ascertainable by him with the help of such advice.

(2) In determining for the purposes of this section—

(a) the knowledge which a person might reasonably have been expected to acquire, or

30 (b) whether a person has acted unreasonably in not seeking appropriate expert advice,

his circumstances and abilities (so far as relevant) shall be taken into account.

(3) For the purposes of this Act, a person shall be treated as having
35 knowledge of a fact if an agent of his—

(a) who is under a duty to communicate that fact to him, or

(b) who has authority to take decisions about the cause of action concerned,

has actual knowledge of that fact; but except as so provided a person
40 shall not treated as having knowledge of a fact merely because an agent of his has knowledge of the fact.

(4) For the purposes of this section, a person has authority to take decisions about a cause of action if he has authority—

(a) to seek legal advice in connection with the making of a civil
45 claim in respect of the cause of action, or

EXPLANATORY NOTES

Clause 3

This clause defines the starting date, the point at which the long-stop limitation period under clause 1(2) starts to run. See paragraphs 3.108 to 3.113 of the Report.

Subsection (1) sets out the general rule that the long-stop limitation period starts to run on the date on which the cause of action accrues.

Subsection (2) provides for an exception to this general rule for claims in tort where the claimant must prove loss or damage for the claim to succeed, and for claims for breach of statutory duty. In these cases the starting date will be the date on which the act or omission giving rise to the claim takes place, not the date on which the claimant suffers loss.

Subsection (3) clarifies the operation of subsection (2) where the claimant has a single cause of action which is founded on more than one act or omission. In this case, the starting date is the date of the last such act or omission. For example, the claimant may seek relief under section 459 of the Companies Act 1985 on the grounds that he has been unfairly prejudiced by the conduct of the defendants. The conduct relied on in support of the claim may be a series of actions none of which are sufficient, considered individually, to amount to unfair prejudice, but which collectively do give the claimant grounds on which to base a petition. If it is only the happening of the last event which gives the claimant sufficient grounds to make a claim, it is the date of that event which decides the starting date.

Subsection (4) preserves the effect of section 1 of the Defective Premises Act 1972, which determines when a cause of action under that Act accrues, and therefore what the starting date will be for claims under that Act.

Clause 4

This clause defines the circumstances in which the claimant will be deemed to have constructive knowledge of the facts so that the primary limitation period will start running against him or her. See paragraphs 3.45 to 3.62 of the Report.

Subsection (1) provides that the claimant's constructive knowledge will depend first on those facts which the claimant can reasonably be expected to observe or ascertain for himself or herself. No account will be taken of any facts that the claimant could have discovered only with the assistance of an appropriate expert unless the claimant (a) has failed to consult any expert, and (b) was acting unreasonably in not consulting an expert. Where the claimant has consulted an expert, the claimant will not be fixed with knowledge of any facts which the expert either failed to find out, or failed to communicate to the claimant (unless the expert was also an agent of the claimant in which case facts which the expert knew but failed to communicate may be imputed to the claimant under subsection (3)).

Subsection (2) ensures that the circumstances and abilities of the claimant will be taken into account in determining what he or she could reasonably be expected to do.

Subsection (3) describes the circumstances in which the claimant will be considered to have knowledge of any facts known to his or her agent.

Subsection (4) defines the circumstances in which an agent will be considered to have the necessary authority for knowledge to be imputed to the claimant for the purposes of subsection (3).

(b) to take decisions about whether to make such a claim.

5.—(1) For the purposes of this Act, a relevant body shall be treated as having knowledge of a fact—

(a) if a qualifying individual has knowledge of that fact, or

(b) if the relevant body is treated as having knowledge of that fact by 5 virtue of section 4(3).

(2) In this section "relevant body" means—

(a) a body corporate,

(b) a corporation sole,

(c) a partnership, or 10

(d) a body of persons which does not fall within paragraph (a) or (c) but which is capable of suing and being sued in its own name.

(3) In this section "qualifying individual", in relation to a relevant body, means an individual—

(a) who is an officer of the body or has authority on behalf of the 15 body to take decisions about the cause of action concerned (or is one of a number of individuals who together have such authority), or

(b) who is an employee of the body and is under a duty to communicate any fact relevant to the cause of action concerned 20 to any other employee of the body or to an individual falling within paragraph (a),

but does not include an individual falling within subsection (4).

(4) An individual falls within this subsection if he is an individual—

(a) against whom the cause of action concerned subsists, or 25

(b) who has dishonestly concealed any fact relevant to the cause of action concerned from any other individual falling within subsection (3)(a) or (b).

(5) Sections 4(4) and 26(6) shall apply for the purposes of this section as they apply for the purposes of those sections. 30

(6) In this section "officer" includes a partner.

Application of s. 1(1) to particular cases

6.—(1) Subject to the following provisions of this section, where a cause of action is vested in two or more persons jointly or jointly and severally, section 1(1) shall apply separately in relation to each of them. 35

(2) Where, by virtue of subsection (1), the defence under section 1(1) is available against one or more, but not all, of the persons mentioned in that subsection, it may not be raised against the other or others.

(3) Subsection (1) does not apply to—

(a) a cause of action vested in a partnership, or 40

(b) a cause of action vested in trustees or personal representatives.

(4) Where a cause of action is vested in trustees or personal representatives, the date of knowledge of the trustees or personal

EXPLANATORY NOTES

Clause 5

This clause defines the circumstances in which an organisation such as a company will be considered to have knowledge for the purposes of the 'date of knowledge'. See paragraphs 3.63 to 3.80 of the Report.

Subsection (1) provides two ways in which an organisation will be treated as having the relevant knowledge. The knowledge (both actual and constructive) of 'qualifying individuals' will be treated as the knowledge of the organisation. In addition, the actual knowledge of its agents will be relevant under subsection 4(3).

Subsection (2) lists the organisations which are subject to the rules in this clause.

Subsections (3) and (6) identify those individuals whose knowledge is to be taken into account in determining the date of knowledge for an organisation which is subject to this clause.

Subsection (4) ensures that the organisation will not be fixed with knowledge which is possessed only by an individual who is a defendant to the claim, or who has dishonestly concealed information from the organisation.

Subsection (5) applies the test in clause 4(4) for "authority" to subsection (3) and the general test for 'dishonest concealment', set out in clause 26(6) of the Bill to subsection (4).

Clause 6

This clause explains how the primary limitation period will apply where there are two or more claimants who are jointly, or jointly and severally, entitled to the remedy sought (see paragraphs 3.81 to 3.91 of the Report). Under subsection (1), each claimant is to be considered individually. Thus, there may be a defence against one of the claimants, but not against the others.

Subsection (2) clarifies the fact that if the defendant can show that one claimant is time-barred this will not prevent the other claimants from succeeding in their claim against the defendant, and from recovering the full amount of the claim from the defendant. Only when the primary limitation period as expired as against all of the joint claimants will the defendant have a complete defence.

Subsection (3) provides for an exception to this rule where the claimants are partners (where the date of knowledge is to be determined in accordance with clause 5, as described above), or trustees or personal representatives.

Subsection (4) provides that the primary limitation period will start running against all the trustees (or personal representatives) from the earliest date on which any one of them has the relevant knowledge.

representatives shall be treated as falling on the same date as the earliest date of knowledge of any person who was a trustee or personal representative on that date.

PART I

7.—(1) This section applies where a civil claim in respect of a cause of action is made by a person to whom the cause of action has been assigned ("the assignee").

Assignment.

(2) It is a defence to a civil claim in respect of the cause of action made by the assignee that the assignment was made after the end of the limitation period under section 1(1) which would have applied to a civil claim in respect of the cause of action made by any person in whom the cause of action was vested before him.

(3) If the assignment was made after the limitation period mentioned in subsection (2) has begun to run but before it has ended, that limitation period shall apply to a civil claim in respect of the cause of action made by the assignee.

(4) If the assignment was made before the limitation period mentioned in subsection (2) has begun to run, the limitation period under section 1(1) which is to apply to a civil claim in respect of the cause of action made by the assignee shall be treated as running from the later of—

(a) the date of the assignment, and

(b) the date of knowledge of the assignee.

(5) For the purposes of this section, a cause of action is assigned by a person if he enters into any transaction the effect of which is to assign his right to make a civil claim in respect of the cause of action.

(6) In determining for the purposes of subsection (2) whether the limitation period under section 1(1) would have applied to a civil claim made by a person, his date of knowledge shall be disregarded if it falls after the cause of action ceased to be vested in him.

PART II

MODIFICATIONS OF THE STANDARD LIMITATION PROVISIONS FOR PARTICULAR CLAIMS ETC

Consumer protection

8.—(1) Section 1(2) does not apply to a civil claim under any provision of Part I of the Consumer Protection Act 1987 ("the 1987 Act").

Claims under Part
I of the Consumer
Protection Act
1987.

(2) A civil claim under any provision of Part I of the 1987 Act may not be made after the end of the period of ten years from the relevant time, within the meaning of section 4 of that Act.

1976 c. 30.

(3) Subsection (2) operates to extinguish any right to make the civil claim and does so—

(a) whether or not that right has accrued, and

(b) whether or not time under any other limitation period under this Act applicable to the claim has begun to run at the end of that ten year period.

EXPLANATORY NOTES

Clause 7

This clause explains how the primary limitation period will apply where the cause of action on which the claim is founded has been assigned to the claimant, ensuring that time starts running against the claimant from the first date on which someone had both the right to make a claim, and the knowledge of the relevant facts. See paragraphs 3.92 to 3.94 of the Report.

Subsection (1) sets out the circumstances in which the clause applies.

Subsection (2) applies where the primary limitation period in respect of a claim by a person in whom the cause of action was vested before the assignment has ended before the date of the assignment. It ensures that the defendant does not lose that defence because the cause of action has been assigned to a new claimant.

Subsection (3) applies where the primary limitation period has started to run in relation to a claim by a person in whom the cause of action was vested before the assignment, but has not ended before the date of the assignment. That limitation period will also apply to a claim by the claimant to whom the cause of action has been assigned. This ensures that the assignment will not extend the primary limitation period for the benefit of the new claimant.

Subsection (4) applies where the primary limitation period has not started to run in relation to any claim by a person in whom the cause of action was previously vested before the assignment of the cause of action. It ensures that where the new claimant knew the relevant facts before the cause of action was assigned to him that knowledge will not be taken into account to start the primary limitation period until the date of the assignment.

Subsection (5) explains what is meant by "assigns a cause of action".

Subsection (6) ensures that where anyone in whom the cause of action was previously vested acquired the knowledge of the relevant facts required for the "date of knowledge" only after he or she had assigned the cause of action to another person, no primary limitation period is to be treated as running from that date for the purposes of subsection (2). The defence under subsection (2) will therefore only arise if a prior assignor of the cause of action had both the relevant knowledge and the right to bring the claim at the same time. Equally the limitation period can only be considered to have begun to run for the purposes of subsection (3) if someone in whom the cause of action was vested before the assignee had both the relevant knowledge and the right to bring an action at the same time.

Clause 8

This clause modifies the core limitation regime in relation to claims brought under the Consumer Protection Act 1987, to ensure that the Bill complies with the terms of the Product Liability Directive 85/374 of 25 July 1985. See paragraphs 4.34 to 4.37 of the Report.

Subsection (1) provides that the long-stop limitation period does not apply to such a claim.

Subsection (2) provides that no claim may be brought more than ten years after the relevant time. This is defined in the Consumer Protection Act section 4 as the date on which the defective product is supplied by the producer of the product (or anyone holding himself out as the producer of the product), or by the person who imported the product into a Member State of the European Union. This ten year period replaces the long-stop limitation period provided for in subsection 1(2).

Subsection (3) provides that once this ten year period has expired, the rights of the claimant are extinguished.

PART II

(4) Nothing in the following provisions of this Act—

(a) shall operate to override or extend the limitation period under subsection (2), or

(b) shall affect the operation of subsection (3).

Personal injury claims, claims for the benefit of an estate and claims 5
under the Fatal Accidents Act 1976

Disapplication of section 1(2).

9. Section 1(2) does not apply to—

(a) a civil claim if and to the extent that the remedy sought by the claimant is damages in respect of personal injury to him,

1934 c.41.

(b) a civil claim made by virtue of section 1 of the Law Reform 10 (Miscellaneous Provisions) Act 1934 if and to the extent that the remedy sought by the claimant is damages in respect of personal injury to the deceased, or

1976 c. 30.

(c) a civil claim under the Fatal Accidents Act 1976.

Application of section 1(1) to claims for the benefit of an estate.

10.—(1) This section applies where a civil claim in respect of a cause of 15 action is made by virtue of section 1 of the Law Reform (Miscellaneous Provisions) Act 1934 ("the 1934 Act claim").

(2) It is a defence to the 1934 Act claim that the deceased died after the end of the limitation period under section 1(1) which would have applied to a civil claim in respect of the cause of action made by him. 20

(3) If the deceased died before the end of the limitation period mentioned in subsection (2), the limitation period under section 1(1) which is to apply to the 1934 Act claim shall be treated as running from the later of—

(a) the date of the deceased's death, and 25

(b) the date of knowledge of the deceased's personal representatives.

Claims under the Fatal Accidents Act 1976: further provision.

11.—(1) It is a defence to a civil claim under the Fatal Accidents Act 1976 ("the 1976 Act") that the person injured died when he could no longer maintain a civil claim for damages in respect of the injury.

(2) In relation to a civil claim under the 1976 Act— 30

(a) the limitation period under section 1(1) shall be treated as running from the date of knowledge of the person for whose benefit the claim is made, and

(b) where there are two or more persons for whose benefit the claim is made, section 1(1) shall apply separately in relation to each of 35 them.

(3) Where, by virtue of subsection (2)(b), the defence under section 1(1) is available against one or more, but not all, of the persons mentioned in subsection (2)(b), it may not be raised against the other or others. 40

(4) For the purposes of this section, the person injured shall be treated as having died when he could no longer maintain a civil claim for damages in respect of the injury if at the time of his death—

(a) a defence under this Act, or under any other enactment limiting the time within which proceedings may be taken, could have 45 been raised in respect of such a claim, or

EXPLANATORY NOTES

Subsection (4) ensures that neither the ten year period or its effect on the claimant's rights can be modified whether under another provision of the Act or otherwise.

Clause 9
This clause ensures that the long-stop limitation period does not apply to any personal injuries claim, including claims brought under the Law Reform (Miscellaneous Provisions) Act 1934 in respect of personal injuries to the deceased, and claims under the Fatal Accidents Act 1976. This exception only applies to claims for damages for personal injuries. Where the claimant brings a claim for another remedy (such as damages for property damage), the long-stop limitation period will apply to that claim. See paragraphs 3.102 to 3.107.

Clause 10
This clause modifies the core limitation regime in its application to claims brought by virtue of the Law Reform (Miscellaneous Provisions) Act 1934. See paragraphs 4.10 to 4.15 of the Report.

Subsection (2) ensures that the defendant will not lose the benefit of a limitations defence which would have been available if a claim had been brought by the deceased before his or her death.

Subsection (3) ensures that the primary limitation period will not start to run against the personal representatives before the death of the deceased, even if they had the relevant knowledge before that date. It starts from the later of the date of the death and the date on which the personal representatives themselves had the relevant knowledge.

Clause 11
This clause modifies the core limitation regime in its application to claims under the Fatal Accidents Act 1976. See paragraphs 4.16 to 4.22 of the Report.

Subsection (1) provides a defence where the deceased would not have been able to bring a claim at his or her death.

Subsection (2) provides that the start of the primary limitation period is determined by reference to the knowledge of the dependant for whose benefit the claim is made. Where there is more than one dependant, each will be treated as though he or she has a separate claim.

Subsection (3) provides, in consequence, that the primary limitation period may have expired against one dependant, but not the others. As a result, that dependant will not be able to recover anything in respect of his or her claim, but this will not prevent the other dependants receiving their full entitlement.

Subsection (4) defines the circumstances in which the deceased would be considered to be unable to bring a claim at his death (as, for example, where the deceased had entered into a compromise with the defendants in "full and final settlement" of his claims). Under subsection (5) the deceased will not be considered to have been capable of bringing a claim if the primary limitation period had expired, even though a defence to that claim might be disapplied under clause 12 of this Act.

(b) he could no longer maintain such a claim for any other reason.

(5) In determining for the purposes of this section whether the person injured died when he could no longer maintain a civil claim for damages in respect of the injury, no account shall be taken of the possibility of any defence under this Act which could have been raised in respect of such a claim being disapplied under section 12.

Court's discretionary power

12.—(1) This section applies where a defence under this Act is raised in respect of—

(a) a personal injury claim, or

(b) a civil claim under the Fatal Accidents Act 1976 ("the 1976 Act").

(2) The court may direct that the defence shall not apply in relation to the claim if it is satisfied, having regard to—

(a) any hardship which would be caused to the defendant (or any person whom he represents) if such a direction were given, and

(b) any hardship which would be caused to the claimant (or any person whom he represents) if such a direction were not given,

that it would unjust not to give such a direction.

(3) In acting under this section the court must take into account—

(a) the length of, and reasons for, the delay on the part of the claimant,

(b) the effect of the passage of time on the ability of the defendant to defend the claim,

(c) the effect of the passage of time on the cogency of any evidence adduced or likely to be adduced by the claimant or defendant,

(d) the conduct of the defendant after the cause of action arose, including the extent (if any) to which he responded to requests reasonably made by the claimant for information or inspection for the purpose of discovering facts which were or might be relevant to the claim,

(e) the extent to which the claimant acted promptly and reasonably once he knew that he might be entitled to make the claim,

(f) the steps, if any, taken by the claimant to obtain medical, legal or other expert advice and the nature of any expert advice he may have received,

(g) any alternative remedy or compensation available to the claimant,

(h) the strength of the claimant's case, and

(i) any other relevant circumstances.

(4) In relation to a personal injury claim falling within subsection (8)(b), any reference in subsection (3)(a) or (d) to (f) to the claimant includes a reference to the deceased.

(5) In relation to a civil claim under the 1976 Act, any reference in subsection (3)(a) or (d) to (f) to the claimant includes a reference to the deceased; and subsection (3) shall have effect with such modifications as may be appropriate in consequence of this subsection.

Court's discretionary power in certain cases.

1976 c. 30.

EXPLANATORY NOTES

Clause 12

This clause gives the court a discretion to disapply the three year primary limitation period applying to claims in respect of personal injuries claims and claims under the Fatal Accidents Act 1976 (under clause 9, no long-stop limitation period applies to these claims). See paragraphs 3.160 to 3.169 of the Report.

Subsection (2) sets out the test for the exercise of the discretion. The court may not exercise its discretion in favour of the claimant unless it is satisfied that it would be unjust not to allow the claim to proceed, and this will in practice only apply if the hardship which would be suffered by the claimant (if the claim were rejected) would exceed the hardship suffered by the defendant (if the claim were to be allowed to proceed).

Subsection (3) sets out the factors which the court must take into account in exercising its discretion.

These factors are modified by subsections (4) to (6) in respect of claims under the Law Reform (Miscellaneous Provisions) Act 1934 and the Fatal Accidents Act 1976 to take account not only of the actions and knowledge of the claimant, but of the deceased and (in the case of a Fatal Accidents Act claim) any person for whose benefit the claim is made.

(6) Where a civil claim under the 1976 Act is made by personal representatives, any reference in subsection (3) to the claimant includes a reference to the person for whose benefit the claim is made.

(7) Where the court gives a direction under this section disapplying the defence under 11(1), the person injured shall be treated for the purposes   5
of section 1(1) of the 1976 Act as if he had died when he could have maintained an action for damages in respect of the injury.

(8) In this section "personal injury claim" means—

(a) a civil claim if and to the extent that the remedy sought by the claimant is damages in respect of personal injury to him,   10

1934 c.41.

(b) a civil claim made by virtue of section 1 of the Law Reform (Miscellaneous Provisions) Act 1934 if and to the extent that the remedy sought by the claimant is damages in respect of personal injury to the deceased.

Claims for a contribution   15

Claims for a
contribution.
1978 c. 47.

13.—(1) The starting date in relation to a cause of action under section 1 of the Civil Liability (Contribution) Act 1978 to recover contribution in respect of any damage from any person shall be determined in accordance with this section.

(2) If the person concerned is held liable in respect of the damage—   20

(a) by a judgment given in any civil proceedings, or

(b) by an award made on any arbitration,

the starting date shall be the date on which the judgment is given or, as the case may be, the date of the award.

(3) For the purposes of subsection (2) no account shall be taken of any   25
judgment or award given or made on appeal in so far as it varies the amount of damages awarded against the person concerned.

(4) If, in a case not falling within subsection (2), the person concerned makes or agrees to make any payment to a person in compensation for that damage (whether he admits any liability in respect of the damage or   30
not), the starting date shall be the earliest date on which the amount paid or to be paid by him is agreed between him (or his representative) and that person.

Conversion

Conversion.

14.—(1) Where—   35

(a) a cause of action has accrued to a person in respect of a conversion of goods which was not a theft from that person, and

(b) before that person recovers possession of the goods, a further conversion takes place,

the starting date in relation to the further conversion shall be treated as   40
falling on the date on which the original conversion took place.

(2) Where a cause of action has accrued to a person in respect of a conversion of goods which was a theft from that person—

(a) section 2(1) shall have effect in relation to the theft, and any conversion related to the theft, as if it also required knowledge   45
to be had of the location of the goods, and

EXPLANATORY NOTES

No claim exists under the Fatal Accidents Act 1976 where the deceased is not able to maintain a claim at the date of death. Subsection (7) preserves the Fatal Accidents Act claim where, though a defence would have existed against a claim by the deceased, the court has exercised its discretion under this clause in favour of the claimant.

Subsection (8) defines 'personal injury claim' for the purpose of this clause.

Clause 13

This clause defines the starting date for the long-stop limitation period in relation to claims for a contribution under section 1 of the Civil Liability (Contribution) Act 1978. (See paragraphs 4.80 to 4.83 of the Report). It re-enacts the provisions of section 10(2) to (4) of the 1980 Act.

Under subsection (2), where there has been a judgment or arbitration award against the claimant the long-stop limitation period will start on the date of that judgement or award.

Subsection (3) ensures that a judgment on appeal which merely raises or lowers the amount of the damages awarded will be irrelevant to the starting date.

Subsection (4) defines the starting date where the claimant claims a contribution in relation to a claim which has been settled by reference to the date on which the claimant agreed the amount to be paid under the settlement.

Clause 14

This clause modifies the core limitation regime in relation to claims for conversion. See paragraphs 4.47 to 4.67 of the Report.

Subsection (1) only applies where there has not been a theft from the claimant. It provides that where there has been any further conversion of the same goods, the starting date for the long-stop limitation period shall be the date of the first conversion - the long-stop limitation period will not start to run again each time there is a fresh conversion. This preserves the rule in section 3(1) of the Limitation Act 1980.

Subsection (2) applies where the goods which are the subject of the claim have been stolen from the claimant. It modifies the definition of the date of knowledge by providing that the primary limitation period will not start to run until the claimant knows (or ought to know) of the location of the goods, in addition to the other relevant facts. It also provides that the long-stop limitation period under clause 1(2) will not apply.

(b) subject to subsection (3), section 1(2) shall not apply to the theft or any conversion related to the theft.

(3) Section 1(2) shall apply to—

(a) the first conversion related to the theft which involves a person purchasing the goods in good faith, and

(b) any subsequent conversion related to the theft;

and the starting date in relation to any conversion falling within paragraph (a) or (b) shall be treated as falling on the date on which the goods are purchased by the person mentioned in paragraph (a).

(4) Where—

(a) a cause of action in respect of the conversion of goods has accrued to a person,

(b) the limitation period under section 1(2) (if any) which applies to that or any further conversion has ended before a civil claim is made in respect of that or any further conversion, and

(c) that person has not recovered possession of the goods before the end of that period,

the title of that person to the goods shall be extinguished.

(5) A conversion of goods shall be treated for the purposes of this section as related to a theft of those goods if it occurs after the theft but before the person from whom they were stolen recovers possession of the goods.

(6) In this section—

"goods" includes all chattels personal other than things in action and money,

"theft" includes—

(a) any conduct outside England and Wales which would be theft if committed in England and Wales, and

(b) obtaining any goods (in England and Wales or elsewhere) in the circumstances described in section 15(1) of the Theft Act 1968 (obtaining by deception) or by blackmail within the meaning of section 21 of that Act. 1968 c. 60.

Mortgages

15.—(1) This Act does not apply to a civil claim to redeem a mortgage. Mortgages.

(2) Section 1(1) does not apply to—

(a) a civil claim for a remedy under a mortgage of land, or

(b) a civil claim which does not fall within paragraph (a) but which is a claim to enforce an obligation secured by a mortgage of land.

(3) Where any limitation period under this Act which applies to a civil claim by a mortgagee in respect of a mortgage would, apart from this subsection, end—

(a) during any period in which a prior mortgagee is in possession of the property subject to the mortgage, or

EXPLANATORY NOTES

However, subsection (3) provides for an exception where stolen goods have been purchased for value by a purchaser acting in good faith. In this case, the long-stop limitation period will run from the date on which the goods were purchased in good faith.

Subsection (4) provides that the claimant's title to the goods which are the subject of the claim will be extinguished if the long-stop limitation period under clause 1(2) expires before he or she has either brought a claim or recovered possession of the goods. This prevents the anomaly of the claimant being regarded as the owner of the goods in question even though he or she is unable to bring any claim to recover them, and ensures that the claimant cannot, for example, exercise any self-help remedies.

Subsection (5) defines the circumstances in which a conversion will be considered to be 'related to a theft' for the purposes of this clause.

Clause 15
This clause provides for the application of the core limitation regime to claims related to mortgages. It also provides mortgagees with protection equivalent to that given by the Limitation Act 1980. See paragraphs 4.158 to 4.196 of the Report.

Subsection (1) provides that the Act does not apply to a civil claim to redeem a mortgage. No limitation period will apply to such a claim (in contrast to section 16 of the Limitation Act 1980 which subjects claims to redeem land to a limitation period of 12 years).

Subsection (2) provides that the primary limitation period will not apply to mortgage related claims where the mortgaged property is land (just as claims to recover land are not subject to the primary limitation period, but only to an equivalent of the long-stop limitation period). 'Mortgage related claims' for this purpose means claims for a remedy under the mortgage or secured by the mortgage (that is, claims for payment of moneys secured by the mortgage, including claims on the mortgagor's covenant to repay the mortgagee, claims for sale of the mortgaged property, foreclosure, possession of the property or its reconveyance). The only limitation period applying to such claims will be the long-stop limitation period of ten years.

Subsection (3) provides a mortgagee who holds a second (or subsequent) mortgage with protection equivalent to that now given under section 20(6) of the Limitation Act 1980. Where the prior mortgagee is in possession of the mortgaged property at the date on which the limitation period applying to a claim by the second mortgagee expires (or at any time during the year before the expiry of the limitation period), that limitation period will be extended so that it cannot end earlier than the date one year after the prior mortgagee ceased to be in possession of the property.

(b) during the period of one year beginning with the date on which the prior mortgagee ceases to be in possession of the property,

it shall instead be treated as ending at the end of the period mentioned in paragraph (b).

(4) No limitation period under this Act which applies to a civil claim 5 by a mortgagee in respect of a mortgage shall run during any period in which the property subject to the mortgage consists of or includes any future interest or any life policy which has not matured or been determined.

(5) No limitation period under this Act which applies to a civil claim 10 to foreclose a mortgage shall run during any period in which the mortgagee is in possession of the property subject to the mortgage.

(6) Where the limitation period under section 1(2) which would apply to a civil claim by a mortgagee in respect of a mortgage has ended before any such claim is made, the interest of the mortgagee in the property 15 which is subject to the mortgage shall be extinguished.

(7) Any reference in this section to a civil claim by a mortgagee in respect of a mortgage is a reference to—

(a) a civil claim by a mortgagee for a remedy under the mortgage, or

(b) a civil claim by a mortgagee which does not fall within paragraph 20 (a) but which is a claim to enforce an obligation secured by the mortgage.

(8) Any reference in this section to a mortgage includes a reference to a charge, and any reference to a mortgagee shall be construed accordingly.

(9) Any reference in this section to a mortgage of land includes a 25 reference to a mortgage of land and other property.

Land

Recovery of land.

16.—(1) Subsections (1) and (2) of section 1 do not apply to a civil claim to recover land.

(2) Subject to the following provisions of this section, a civil claim to 30 recover land may not be made by a person after the end of the period of ten years from the earlier of—

(a) the date on which the right of action to recover the land first accrued to him, and

(b) if it first accrued to some person through whom he claims, the 35 date on which it first accrued to that person.

(3) In its application to a civil claim by the Crown to recover foreshore, subsection (2) shall have effect as if the period referred to in it were sixty years not ten years.

(4) Where any right of action to recover land which has ceased to be 40 foreshore accrued to the Crown when the land was foreshore, a civil claim by the Crown to recover the land may not be made after the end of the period of—

(a) sixty years from the date of accrual of the right of action, or

EXPLANATORY NOTES

Subsection (4) ensures that the limitation period will not run against the mortgagee where the property which has been mortgaged is not a present interest. It re-enacts section 20(3) of the Limitation Act 1980.

Subsection (5) suspends the limitation period for foreclosure claims where the mortgagee is in possession of the property concerned, providing equivalent protection to section 20(2) of the 1980 Act.

Subsection (6) extinguishes the rights of the mortgagee in the property once the long-stop limitation period applying to his claim has ended.

Clause 16

This clause, with clauses 17 and 18, makes provision for claims to recover land (see paragraphs 4.126 to 4.150 of the Report). In practice, if the recommendations in Land Registration for the Twenty-First Century: A Consultative Document, Law Com No 254 (1998) are enacted this provision will only apply to claims to recover unregistered land, and in respect of unregistrable interests in registered land.

Subsection (1) provides that the primary and long-stop limitation periods do not apply to claims to recover land.

Subsection (2) subjects claims to recover land to a limitation period of ten years, and defines the date on which that limitation period will start to run. In contrast to other claims, where, under clause 1, a defence will arise after the end of the limitation period, subsection (2) provides that no claim shall be brought after the end of the limitation period. This reflects the fact that the expiry of the limitation period will extinguish the claimant's title to the land.

Subsection (3) extends the limitation period applying by the Crown to claims to recover foreshore to sixty years. Subsection (4) ensures that the Crown benefits from this protection for claims to recover land which was once, but is no longer, foreshore for ten years from the date on which the land ceased to be foreshore.

(b) ten years from the date on which the land ceased to be foreshore, whichever period ends first.

(5) No civil claim may be made to recover any estate or interest in land under an assurance taking effect after the right of action to recover the land had accrued to—

    (a) the person by whom the assurance was made,

    (b) some person through whom he claimed, or

    (c) some person entitled to a preceding estate or interest,

unless the claim is made within the period in which the person by whom the assurance was made could have made such a claim.

(6) Where—

    (a) any person is entitled to any estate or interest in land in possession and, while so entitled, is also entitled to any future estate or interest in that land, and

    (b) his right of action to recover the estate or interest in possession is barred by this Act,

no civil claim may be made by that person, or by any person claiming through him, in respect of the future estate or interest, unless in the meantime possession of the land has been recovered by a person entitled to an intermediate estate or interest in the land.

(7) In this section "foreshore" means the shore and bed of the sea and of any tidal water, below the line of the medium high tide between the spring tides and the neap tides.

17.—(1) Schedule 1 (which contains provisions for determining the date of accrual of rights of action to recover land) has effect.

Recovery of land; supplementary.

(2) The provisions of this Act relating to civil claims to recover land shall apply to equitable interests in land as they apply to legal estates in land.

(3) Accordingly a right of action to recover land shall be treated for the purposes of this Act as accruing to a person entitled in possession to an equitable interest in the land in the like manner and circumstances, and on the same date, as it would accrue if his interest were a legal estate in the land (and any relevant provision of Schedule 1 shall apply in any such case accordingly).

(4) For the purposes of the provisions of this Act relating to civil claims to recover land, an administrator of the estate of a deceased person shall be treated as claiming as if there had been no interval of time between the death of the deceased person and the grant of the letters of administration.

(5) Where land is vested in the incumbent from time to time of a benefice as a spiritual corporation sole but the benefice is vacant, a civil claim to recover the land (or any part of it) may be made in the name of and on behalf of the corporation sole by the priest in charge of the benefice or the sequestrators of the benefice.

18.—(1) Subject to section 75 of the Land Registration Act 1925 and the following provisions of this section, where a civil claim to recover land is not made by a person before the end of the limitation period under

Extinction of title to land
1925 c. 21.

EXPLANATORY NOTES

Subsection (5) re-enacts section 15(4) of the 1980 Act, ensuring that a transfer of the land which is made after a cause of action to recover the land has accrued to the transferor (or anyone previously entitled to the land) will not extend the limitation period applying to a claim to that land by the person to whom it is transferred.

Subsection (6) re-enacts section 15(5) of the 1980 Act. It ensures that the claimant entitled to both a present and a future interest in land who has allowed the limitation period to expire without bringing a claim cannot benefit from the extended protection given to future interests unless someone else holds an intermediate estate in the land before the claimant's future interest falls into possession.

Clause 17

This clause contains a number of supplementary provisions relating to claims to recover land.

Subsection (2) re-enacts the first part of subsection 18(1) of the 1980 Act. It provides that claims in relation to equitable interests in land should be treated in the same way as claims to a legal estate in land.

Subsection (3) re-enacts the second part of subsection 18(1). It provides that the rules which determine when the cause of action accrues in relation to a legal estate in land should therefore apply similarly to equitable estates in land.

Subsection (4) re-enacts section 26 of the 1980 Act. It ensures that where a claim to recover land which forms part of a deceased's estate accrues on or after the date of death, the limitation period will start to run against the administrator from the date of accrual, whether or not letters of administration have been granted at that date.

Subsection (5) is a new provision. It ensures that the priest in charge or sequestrators of a benefice have the capacity to bring a claim to recover land on behalf of a spiritual corporation sole when no-one else is able to act because the freehold is in abeyance.

Clause 18

This clause provides for the consequences of the expiry of the limitation period in relation to a claim to recover land.

Subsection (1) provides for the extinction of the claimant's title to the land after the expiry of the limitation period.

section 16 which would apply to the claim, the title of that person to the land shall be extinguished.

(2) Where the limitation period under section 16 has expired for the making of a civil claim to recover land by a tenant for life or a statutory owner of settled land— 5

  (a) his legal estate shall not be extinguished if and so long as the right of action to recover the land of any person entitled to a beneficial interest in the land either has not accrued or has not been barred by this Act, and

  (b) the legal estate shall accordingly remain vested in the tenant for 10 life or statutory owner and shall devolve in accordance with the Settled Land Act 1925;

1925 c. 18.

but if and when every such right of action has been barred by this Act, his legal estate shall be extinguished.

(3) Where any land is held upon trust and the limitation period under 15 section 16 has expired for the making of a civil claim to recover the land by the trustees, the estate of the trustees shall not be extinguished if and so long as the right of action to recover the land of any person entitled to a beneficial interest in the land either has not accrued or has not been barred by this Act; but if and when every such right has been so barred 20 the estate of the trustees shall be extinguished.

(4) Where—

  (a) any settled land is vested in a statutory owner, or

  (b) any land is held upon trust,

a civil claim to recover the land may be made by the statutory owner or 25 trustees on behalf of any person entitled to a beneficial interest in possession in the land whose right of action to recover the land has not been barred by this Act, notwithstanding that the right of action to recover the land of the statutory owner or trustees would apart from this subsection have been barred by this Act. 30

Recovery of proceeds of the sale of land.

19. Section 1(1) does not apply to a civil claim to recover proceeds of the sale of land.

Certain claims for compensation or indemnity.
1925 c. 21.
1969 c. 59.

20.—(1) Section 1(2) does not apply to—

  (a) a civil claim for indemnity under the Land Registration Act 1925,

  (b) a civil claim to recover compensation under section 25 of the Law 35 of Property Act 1969, or

1975 c. 76.

  (c) a civil claim to recover compensation under section 10 of the Local Land Charges Act 1975.

(2) For the purposes of this Act, a person's date of knowledge in the case of a cause of action to recover compensation under section 10 of the 40 Local Land Charges Act 1975 shall be determined without regard to the

1925 c. 20.

provisions of section 198 of the Law of Property Act 1925 (under which registration under certain enactments is deemed to constitute actual notice).

EXPLANATORY NOTES

Subsections (2) and (3) re-enact section 18(2) and (3) of the 1980 Act. They ensure that the estate of a tenant for life or statutory owner of settled land (in subsection (2)) or of trustees (in subsection (3)) will not be extinguished until there is no-one entitled to a beneficial interest in that land with a right of action which has not accrued or has not been barred by the expiry of the limitation period, even if the limitation period for a claim by the tenant for life or statutory owner or trustees themselves has expired.

Subsection (4) re-enacts section 18(4) of the 1980 Act. It ensures that, even if the limitation period applying to a claim made by a trustee or statutory owner of land on their own behalf has expired, the trustee or statutory owner may bring a claim to recover land on behalf of anyone entitled to a beneficial interest in the land where the limitation period applying to a claim by that person has not expired.

Clause 19

This clause provides that the primary limitation period will not apply to a claim to recover the proceeds of a sale of land (see paragraph 4.151 of the Report). Such claims are treated as being equivalent to a claim to recover the land in question, and in consequence, only the long-stop limitation period will apply.

Clause 20

The Acts listed in subsection (1) apply a separate limitation period to claims under the appropriate provisions, running in each case from the date on which claimants should have had notice of certain facts (see paragraph 4.286 of the Report). To ensure that these claims are brought under the core limitation regime (and in particular the 'knowledge' provisions of that regime, which are set out in Part I of the Bill) these limitation provisions are repealed in Schedule 3 to this Bill (see paragraphs 3, 9, and 16). Subsection (1) ensures that the long-stop limitation period does not apply to any of the claims.

Subsection (2) ensures that the claimant seeking compensation under section 10 of the Local Land Charges Act will not be regarded as having sufficient knowledge to trigger the primary limitation period only because he or she would be regarded as having notice of any of the facts relevant to the date of knowledge under section 198 of the Law of Property Act 1925.

21.—(1) Subsection (2) applies where—

    (a) a person entitled in remainder to an entailed interest in any land makes an assurance of his interest which fails to bar the issue in tail or the estates and interests taking effect on the determination of the entailed interest, or fails to bar those estates and interests only, and

    (b) any person takes possession of the land by virtue of the assurance.

(2) If the person taking possession of the land by virtue of the assurance, or any other person whatsoever (other than a person entitled to possession by virtue of the settlement), is in possession of the land for a period of ten years from the commencement of the time when the assurance could have operated as an effective bar, the assurance shall thereupon operate, and be treated as having always operated, to bar the issue in tail and the estates and interests taking effect on the determination of the entailed interest.

(3) The reference in subsection (2) to the time when the assurance could have operated as an effective bar is a reference to the time at which the assurance, if it had then been executed by the person entitled to the entailed interest, would have operated, without the consent of any other person, to bar the issue in tail and the estates and interests taking effect on the determination of the entailed interest.

(4) Where—

    (a) a right of action to recover land has accrued to a person entitled to an estate or interest taking effect on the determination of an entailed interest,

    (b) time is running against that person under subsection (2), and

    (c) the person in possession of the land acknowledges the title of that person,

subsection (2) shall cease to apply to the land on the date of the acknowledgment.

Trusts and charities

22.—(1) No limitation period under this Act which applies to a civil claim by a beneficiary to recover trust property or the proceeds of trust property shall run against him during any period in which he is entitled to a future interest in the trust property.

(2) A cause of action to recover property held on a bare trust shall not accrue unless and until the trustee acts in breach of trust.

(3) This Act does not apply to a civil claim made by the Attorney General or the Charity Commissioners for England and Wales with respect to a charity or the property or affairs of a charity.

(4) A beneficiary under a trust as against whom a defence under this Act could have been raised may not derive any greater or other benefit from a judgment or order obtained by any other beneficiary under the trust than he could have obtained if he had made the civil claim and a defence under this Act had been raised.

EXPLANATORY NOTES

Clause 21

This clause provides for the consequences of making a defective disentailing assurance - that is, an assurance which attempts, but fails, to bar an entailed interest. It re-enacts section 27 and 29(2)(b) of the 1980 Act.

Clause 22

This clause modifies the core limitation regime in its application to certain trusts and charities-related claims. See paragraphs 4.94 to 4.119 of the Report.

Subsection (1) protects the beneficiary who only has a future interest in trust property by ensuring that no limitation period can run until his or her interest becomes an interest in possession.

Subsection (2) protects the beneficiary under a bare trust. In the absence of this provision, the cause of action for a claim to recover the trust property would accrue once the trustee holds the property on trust for the beneficiary absolutely, which may be when the trust was set up, since the beneficiary may claim the property as from that date. This sub-clause postpones the accrual of the cause of action until there has been a breach of trust (where for example the trustee refuses the transfer the property to the beneficiary on request).

Subsection (3) ensures that no limitation period will apply to a claim made by the Attorney General or the Charity Commissioners of England and Wales in relation to a charity.

Subsection (4) ensures that where the limitation period for a claim by one beneficiary has expired, he or she will not be able to benefit from a successful claim made by another beneficiary of the trust.

(5) In this section "charity" has the same meaning as in the Charities Act 1993.

Insolvency and bankruptcy

Insolvency and bankruptcy.

23. Schedule 2 (which makes provision as to the application of section 1(1) in the case of insolvency and bankruptcy) has effect.

Derivative claims

Derivative claims.

24.—(1) Where—

(a) a cause of action is vested in a body corporate or trade union, and

(b) a civil claim in respect of the cause of action is made on behalf of the body corporate or trade union by a member of it,

the limitation period under section 1(1) which is to apply to the claim shall be treated as running from the date of knowledge of the member.

(2) Where a civil claim falling within subsection (1) is made by two or more members, section 1(1) shall apply separately in relation to each of them.

(3) Where, by virtue of subsection (2), the defence under section 1(1) is available against one or more, but not all, of the persons mentioned in that subsection, it may not be raised against the other or others.

Certain new claims

Certain new claims.

25.—(1) Where—

(a) a civil claim is made in the course of any civil proceedings,

(b) the claim is by way of set-off or counterclaim by a party who has not previously made any claim in the proceedings, and

(c) if the claim had been made when the proceedings were commenced, it would not have been made after the end of any applicable limitation period under this Act,

no defence under this Act may be raised in respect of the claim.

(2) Where—

(a) a civil claim ("the new claim") is made in the course of any civil proceedings,

(b) the new claim involves the addition or substitution of a new cause of action,

(c) the new claim arises out of the same conduct, transaction or events as are already in issue in a civil claim previously made in the proceedings ("the existing claim"), and

(d) the existing claim was not made after the end of any applicable limitation period under this Act or any other enactment,

no defence under this Act may be raised in respect of the new claim.

(3) Where—

(a) a civil claim ("the new claim") is made in the course of any civil proceedings,

(b) the new claim involves the addition or substitution of a new party,

EXPLANATORY NOTES

Clause 24

This clause modifies the core regime in its application to derivative claims where a member of a company, for example, claims a remedy on behalf of the company. See paragraphs 4.205 to 4.210 of the Report.

Subsection (1) ensures that only the knowledge of the member bringing the claim is considered in order to determine when the primary limitation period started to run in respect of that claim. No account will be taken of the date on which the company itself or any other member acquired knowledge of the relevant facts.

Subsection (2) and (3) ensure that where two or more members bring a claim together on behalf of the company or trade union, each is to considered to have a separate claim for the purpose of the limitations Bill. Therefore, if the primary limitation period has expired, but only against one, no defence may be raised against the other member.

Clause 25

This clause modifies the core limitation regime in its application to some 'new claims': that is claims made after the start of proceedings by one of the parties to those proceedings. It also preserves the court's power to make rules in relation to those claims. See paragraphs 5.5 to 5.19 of the Report.

Subsection (1) applies to the first claim made by the defendant (or a third party) to the original proceedings (whether the claim is made by counter claim or by set off). It ensures that if the claim would have been made in time if it had been made at the start of the proceedings, no limitation defence may be raised against it even if either the primary limitation period or the long-stop limitation period has since expired.

Subsection (2) applies to new claims which seek to change the cause of action in issue in existing proceedings. Provided that the existing claim was made in time (that is before the end of any relevant limitation period), and that the new claim arises out of the same conduct, transaction or events as the existing claim, no limitation defence may be raised against the new claim.

Subsection (3) applies to new claims which add or substitute a party to the existing proceedings. Provided that the existing claim was made in time and the change to the existing parties is necessary to decide the existing claim, no limitation defence may be raised against the new claim.

(c) the addition or substitution is necessary for the determination of a civil claim previously made in the proceedings ("the existing claim"), and

(d) the existing claim was not made after the end of any applicable
5 limitation period under this Act or any other enactment,

no defence under this Act may be raised in respect of the new claim.

(4) The addition or substitution of a new party is not necessary for the determination of a civil claim previously made in civil proceedings unless—

10 (a) the new party is substituted for a party whose name was given in that claim in mistake for the new party's name, or

(b) that claim cannot be maintained by or against an existing party unless the new party is joined or substituted as a party to that claim.

15 (5) Rules of court may make provision which allows a party to a civil claim to claim relief in a new capacity in respect of a new cause of action notwithstanding that he had no title to make that claim at the time when the claim was made.

(6) Subsection (5) shall not affect the power of rules of court to make
20 provision which allows a party to a civil claim to claim relief in a new capacity without adding or substituting a new cause of action.

PART III

GENERAL MODIFICATIONS OF THE STANDARD LIMITATION PROVISIONS ETC

Concealment

25 **26.**—(1) This section applies where a person ("A") against whom a cause of action subsists (or an agent of his) has dishonestly concealed from a person ("B") in whom the cause of action is vested (or an agent of his) any fact relevant to the cause of action.

Concealment.

(2) In its application to a civil claim in respect of the cause of action
30 made by B, or any person claiming through him, against A, or any person claiming through him, the limitation period under section 1(2) or 16 shall not run during the period beginning with the date on which the fact was first dishonestly concealed and ending with the earliest date on which B, or any person claiming through him, first had knowledge of the fact.

35 (3) In the case of the fresh cause of action which accrues by virtue of section 3(1) of the Latent Damage Act 1986 (accrual of cause of action to successive owners in respect of latent damage to property), a fact dishonestly concealed from the person in whom the original cause of action mentioned in that section was vested (or an agent of his) shall be
40 treated for the purposes of subsection (1) as dishonestly concealed from the person in whom the fresh cause of action is vested.

1986 c. 37.

(4) Where the starting date in relation to a cause of action falling within section 3(2)(a) or (b) falls before the date of accrual of the cause of action, the cause of action shall be treated for the purposes of subsection
45 (1) as subsisting against A, and vested in B, from the starting date.

EXPLANATORY NOTES

Subsection (4) explains when such a change to the existing parties is necessary to decide the existing claim.

Subsections (5) and (6) re-enact section 35(7) of the 1980 Act. Subsection (5) gives the court the power to provide that a party may claim relief in a new capacity in a new cause of action even though that party had no title to make that claim at the start of the proceedings.

Subsection (6) preserves the power of the court to allow a party to claim relief in a new capacity in other circumstances.

Clause 26

This clause extends the limitation period where facts relevant to the cause of action have been dishonestly concealed from the person with a right to bring a claim founded on that cause of action. See paragraphs 3.134 to 3.145 of the Report.

Subsection (1) defines the circumstances in which the clause applies: the facts must be concealed from a person who at the time of the concealment had the right to bring the claim (whether the claimant or a predecessor in title of the claimant) or from their agent. Similarly, the facts must be concealed by a person who was liable to the claim at the time of the concealment. The clause will not apply unless the concealment was dishonest. This is a far more stringent test than applies under section 32 of the 1980 Act. It is intended to overturn the interpretation of 'deliberate concealment' given in *Brocklesby v Armitage & Guest.*[1]

Subsection (2) provides that dishonest concealment will suspend the long-stop limitation period and the limitation period applying to claims to recover land from the date on which the fact was concealed until the date on which it comes to the notice of the claimant. This suspension will apply to any claim made by the person from whom the facts were concealed, or by any person whose right to make a claim against the defendant derives from him. This clarifies the position which applied under section 32 of the Limitation Act 1980, which did not expressly extend this protection to any claimant claiming through the person from whom the facts were originally concealed. In contrast, section 32 of the 1980 Act did provide that concealment by any person through whom the defendant claims is sufficient to extend time as against the defendant. Subclause (2) retains this provision. This may be relevant where the defendant asserts a competing claim to property claimed by the claimant, and the person from whom the defendant derived the claim has been guilty of dishonest concealment from the claimant or his predecessor (as in *Eddis v Chicester Constable*).[2]

The primary limitation period will not be affected, since this will only run from the date of knowledge.

Subsection (3) ensures that a purchaser of property which has a latent defect can rely on any concealment by the defendant from the seller of that property to extend the long-stop limitation period which would apply to the purchaser's own claim against that defendant.

Subsection (4) ensures that our provisions on dishonest concealment are effective to suspend the long-stop limitation period where the concealment takes place between the starting date and the accrual of the cause of action if the starting date occurs before the accrual of the cause of action.

---

[1]   [2001] 1 All ER 172.
[2]   [1969] 2 Ch 345.

PART III

(5) Nothing in this section enables a civil claim—

(a) to recover, or recover the value of, any property, or

(b) to enforce any charge against, or set aside any transaction affecting, property,

to be made against the purchaser (or any person claiming through him) in any case where the property has been purchased for valuable consideration by an innocent third party since the concealment took place.

(6) A person shall not be treated for the purposes of this section as concealing a fact from another person unless—

(a) he is a party to, or is privy to, any action the effect of which is to prevent that other person from discovering the fact for some time, or

(b) he fails to disclose the fact to that other person in breach of a duty to do so.

(7) The provisions of Part I of this Act which apply for determining the date on which a person first had knowledge of a fact shall also apply for the purposes of subsection (2).

(8) For the purposes of subsection (2), knowledge acquired by a person after a cause of action ceased to be vested in him shall be disregarded.

(9) A purchaser is an innocent third party for the purposes of this section if he was not a party to the concealment and did not at the time of the purchase have reason to believe that the concealment had taken place.

Acknowledgments and part payments

Acknowledgments and part payments.

27.—(1) Subject to the following provisions of this section, where—

(a) a person ("A") against whom a cause of action subsists has acknowledged the cause of action or made a payment in respect of it,

(b) the acknowledgment or payment was made to a person ("B") in whom the cause of action is vested, and

(c) the acknowledgment or payment was made before any limitation period under this Act which would apply to a civil claim in respect of the cause of action made by B (or any successor of his) against A (or any successor of his) has ended,

any such limitation period which has begun to run before the date on which the acknowledgment or payment was made shall instead be treated as running from that date.

(2) Subject to subsections (4) and (5), where—

(a) a cause of action subsists against two or more persons jointly or jointly and severally, and

(b) an acknowledgment or payment under this section is made by one or more, but not all, of those persons,

this section shall not operate to extend any limitation period under this Act which applies to any such person who does not make the acknowledgment or payment (or any successor of his).

EXPLANATORY NOTES

Subsection (5) re-enacts subsection 32(3) of the 1980 Act, ensuring that the long-stop limitation period applying to a claim against an innocent purchaser (that is, one who has not therefore contributed to the concealment of the facts in any way, or been aware that any facts have been concealed) will not be extended by virtue of clause 26.

Subsection (6) defines 'concealment' for the purpose of this clause.

Subsection (7) provides that the date on which the claimant discovers the concealed fact is to be determined by the same rules which apply to the 'date of knowledge' which starts the primary limitation period.

Subsection (8) ensures that the suspension of the limitation period will only end if a person has the right to bring a claim at the same time as he or she acquires the relevant knowledge. If someone only acquires the relevant knowledge after the cause of action ceased to be vested in him or her, that person's knowledge will not be sufficient to start time running again in respect of the claim.

Clause 27
This clause extends the limitation period where a defendant to the claim has acknowledged the claimant's rights by a written acknowledgment or a part payment. See paragraphs 3.146 to 3.155 of the Report.

Subsection (1) sets out the conditions which must be satisfied if an acknowledgment is to be effective to extend the limitation period. First the acknowledgment or payment must be made by a person liable to the claim at the time the acknowledgment or payment is made. Secondly, it must be made to a person with a right to bring the claim. Thirdly, it must be made when a limitation period is running against the potential claimant. If these conditions are met, the limitation period concerned (which may be either the primary limitation period or the long-stop limitation period or both) will start again from the date on which the acknowledgment or part payment is made.

Subsection (2) applies where there are two or more joint, or joint and several, defendants to the claim. It provides that an acknowledgment or part-payment made by one of them will only extend the limitation period against the acknowledgor and his or her successors, and not the other defendants. However, although the other defendants will be able to raise a defence against a claim by the claimant, if the claimant succeeds against the defendant acknowledging the claim, that defendant may claim a contribution from his or her co-defendants.

(3) Subject to subsection (4), where—

(a) a cause of action is vested in two or more persons jointly or jointly and severally, and

5 (b) an acknowledgment or payment under this section is made to one or more, but not all, of those persons,

this section shall not operate to extend any limitation period under this Act which applies to any such person to whom the acknowledgment or payment is not made (or any successor of his).

(4) Where—

10 (a) a cause of action subsists against or is vested in, trustees or personal representatives, and

(b) an acknowledgment or payment under this section is made by or (as the case may be) to one or more, but not all, of the trustees or personal representatives,

15 the acknowledgment or payment shall bind or (as the case may be) be treated as made to all of the trustees or personal representatives.

(5) An acknowledgment or payment under this section in respect of the title to any land, benefice or mortgaged personal property by any person in possession of it shall bind all of the persons in possession of it during 20 the ensuing limitation period.

(6) Where this section extends the limitation period under section 1(2) which applies to a civil claim in respect of the original cause of action mentioned in section 3 of the Latent Damage Act 1986 (accrual of cause of action to successive owners in respect of latent damage to property)), it 25 shall also extend the limitation period under section 1(2) which applies to a civil claim in respect of the fresh cause of action which accrues by virtue of that section.

1986 c. 37.

(7) Where the starting date in relation to a cause of action falling within section 3(2)(a) or (b) falls before the date of accrual of the cause of 30 action, the cause of action shall be treated for the purposes of subsection (1) as subsisting against A, and vested in B, from the starting date; and subsection (2) to (4) and (11) and (12) shall be construed accordingly.

(8) To be effective for the purposes of this section an acknowledgment must be in writing.

35 (9) For the purposes of this section an acknowledgment or payment made by or to an agent of a person shall be treated as made by or to that person.

(10) A limitation period which has been extended under this section may be further extended under this section by further acknowledgments 40 or payments.

(11) For the purposes of this section, a person acknowledges a cause of action if—

(a) he acknowledges liability in respect of the cause of action, or

(b) he acknowledges any right or title upon which the cause of action is 45 based.

(12) For the purposes of this section, a person makes a payment in

EXPLANATORY NOTES

Subsection (3) applies where there are two or more joint, or joint and several, claimants. It provides that where an acknowledgment or part-payment is made to one (but not all) of them, the limitation period is only extended as regards the person to whom the acknowledgment or payment is made and his or her successors, rather than the other claimants. However, should the claimant to whom an acknowledgment is made be successful as against the defendants, his or her co-claimants may be able to recover their share from that claimant by a claim in restitution.

Subsection (4) provides for an exception to the rule set out in subsections (2) and (3) where the joint claimants (or defendants) are trustees or personal representatives. In this case, an acknowledgment or part payment made by (or to) one will extend the limitation period against (or for the benefit of, as the case may be) all the trustees or personal representatives.

Subsection (5) provides for a further exception to the rule set out in subsection (2) where an acknowledgment or payment is made by one of a number of people in possession of land or mortgaged property. This will serve to extend the limitation period against everyone who is in possession of the property during the ensuing limitation period.

Subsection (6) ensures that a purchaser of defective property who has a new cause of action under section 3 of the Latent Damage Act 1986 may rely on any acknowledgment or part-payment given by the defendant to the previous owner of that property to extend the long-stop limitation period applying to his or her own claim against the defendant.

Subsection (7) ensures that if an acknowledgment or part payment is given after the starting date of the long-stop limitation period but before the cause of action has accrued (in relation to a claim where the starting date for the long-stop limitation period is the date of the act or omission giving rise to the cause of action rather than the date of accrual), that acknowledgment or part-payment will be effective to restart the long-stop limitation period.

Subsection (8) imposes a requirement that the acknowledgment be made in writing, to minimise the uncertainty as to whether an acknowledgment has been given. The requirement in the 1980 Act, that any acknowledgment should be signed by the person giving it, is not being re-enacted, as this unnecessarily limits those documents which may serve as acknowledgments.

Subsection (9) ensures that an acknowledgment made by or to an agent is treated as made by or to the principal.

Subsection (10) provides that a limitation period may be extended more than once under this clause.

Subsection (11) defines an 'acknowledgment' for the purposes of the clause.

Subsection (12) defines a 'payment in respect of a cause of action' for the purposes of the clause.

PART III

respect of a cause of action if he makes a payment the effect of which is to—

    (a) acknowledge liability in respect of the cause of action, or

    (b) acknowledge any right or title upon which the cause of action is based.   5

(13) Where there is a payment of a part of the rent or interest due at any time, this section shall not operate to extend any limitation period under this Act which applies to a civil claim to recover the remainder then due.

(14) Any payment of interest shall be treated for the purposes of this 10 section as a payment in respect of a cause of action to recover the principal debt.

Special parties

Children.

28. Where a cause of action is vested in a person who was under the age of 18 on the starting date in relation to the cause of action, any 15 limitation period under this Act which would apply to a civil claim in respect of the cause of action made by him shall be treated as ending—

    (a) at the end of the period of three years from the date on which he attains the age of 18, or

    (b) at the end of the period when the limitation period would 20 otherwise end,

whichever is the later.

Persons under a disability.

29.—(1) This section applies where a cause of action has accrued to a person ("the relevant person") who is under a disability at any time after the date of accrual of the cause of action.   25

(2) Subject to the following provisions of this section, the limitation period under section 1(1), so far as applicable to a civil claim in respect of the cause of action made by the relevant person, shall not run during any period in which he is under a disability.

(3) Subsections (4) and (5) apply where—   30

    (a) the remedy sought by the relevant person in the civil claim mentioned in subsection (2) is damages in respect of personal injury to him,

    (b) the relevant person is under a disability at the end of the period of ten years from the later of the date of accrual of the cause of 35 action and the date of the onset of disability ("the ten year period"),

    (c) there is a person ("the responsible person") who has responsibility for the relevant person at the end of the ten year period,   40

    (d) the responsible person is not the defendant to the claim, and

    (e) whether by virtue of subsection (2) or otherwise, the limitation period under section 1(1) has not ended by the end of the ten year period.

EXPLANATORY NOTES

Subsections (13) and (14) explain the effect of a payment of rent or interest due on the limitation period. They re-enact section 29(6) of the 1980 Act.

Clause 28

This clause extends any limitation period which applies to a claim by a child, by ensuring that the limitation period cannot end before the date on which the claimant reaches the age of 21. See paragraphs 3.115 to 3.121 of the Report.

Clause 29

This clause extends the limitation period when the claimant is under a disability. See paragraphs 3.122 to 3.133 of the Report.

Subsection (1) ensures that the protection given to the disabled claimant applies not only when the disability existed on the date of accrual of the cause of action, but also (in contrast to the current law), where the disability only develops after that date.

Subsection (2) suspends the primary limitation period while the claimant is under a disability. The long-stop limitation period is not affected.

Subsections (3) defines the circumstances in which the protection given to the claimant in a personal injury claim (which is not subject to a long stop limitation period) will come to an end. This will be ten years after the later of the accrual of the cause of action or the onset of the disability if three conditions are satisfied on that date. First, the claimant must still be under a disability; secondly, the primary limitation period must not have expired at that date, and thirdly, there must be an adult who is responsible for the claimant at that date, who is not the defendant to the claim. If these conditions are not met, the protection given to the claimant will continue.

(4) Subsection (2) shall not apply after the end of the ten year period.

(5) The limitation period under section 1(1) shall instead be treated as running from the earlier of the following dates—

(a) the date of knowledge of the responsible person,

5 (b) the date of knowledge of any person who subsequently has responsibility for the relevant person, and

(c) if the relevant person ceases to be under a disability after the end of the ten year period, the date of knowledge of the relevant person;

10 but if any such date of knowledge falls before the end of the ten year period, it shall be treated for the purposes of this subsection as falling on the date immediately following the end of the ten year period.

(6) A person is under a disability for the purposes of this section if—

(a) he is unable by reason of mental disability to make decisions on
15 matters relating to the cause of action concerned, or

(b) he is unable to communicate such decisions because of mental disability or physical impairment.

(7) In subsection (6) "mental disability" means a disability or disorder of the mind or brain, whether permanent or temporary, which results in an
20 impairment or disturbance of mental functioning.

(8) For the purposes of this section a person has responsibility for the relevant person if—

(a) he is a member of the relevant person's family who has attained the age of 18 and is responsible for the day to day care of the
25 relevant person, or

(b) he is a person who is authorised under Part VII of the Mental Health Act 1983 to conduct proceedings in the name of the relevant person.

1981 c. 20.

Restrictions on making claims

30 **30.**—(1) No limitation period under this Act which applies to a civil claim made by a person shall run against that person during any period after the accrual of the cause of action in which he is prevented by any enactment (other than this Act) or any rule of law from making the claim.

Restrictions on making claims.

(2) A person shall not be regarded for the purposes of this section as
35 prevented from making a claim—

(a) where the claim could have been made on his behalf by a litigation friend,

(b) where he is prevented from making the claim by reason only of a contractual term, or

40 (c) if leave is required to make the claim, unless and until he has taken all reasonable steps to obtain that leave.

EXPLANATORY NOTES

Subsection (4) ensures that the protection given to the claimant under subsection (2) will come to an end after ten years if the conditions in subsection (3) are satisfied.

Subsection (5) defines the time at which the primary limitation period will start running against the claimant under a disability when the conditions in subsection (3) are satisfied. It provides that the knowledge of the responsible adult may be taken into account to decide whether the primary limitation period has started running.

Subsection (6) defines 'disability' for the purpose of this clause. The test is whether the claimant's ability to make decisions is impaired by mental disability, or his or her ability to communicate is impaired by mental disability or physical impairment. It is intended to include both those cases where the claimant lacks the capacity to know or understand the relevant facts, and where the claimant is unable to act on his or her knowledge of the facts.

Subsection (7) defines 'mental disability' for the purpose of this clause.

Subsection (8) defines the circumstances in which a person will be considered to be a 'responsible adult' for the purposes of this clause.

Clause 30
This clause protects the claimant where he or she is unable to bring proceedings in respect of the claim. See paragraphs 5.24 to 5.28 of the Report.

Subsection (1) suspends all limitation periods under the Bill where, after the cause of action has accrued, the claimant is subject to a legal restriction which means that he or she cannot bring a claim (such as the requirement that a solicitor may not bring a claim on a bill of costs until the expiry of one month after the delivery of the bill, although the cause of action accrues on completion of the work).

Subsection (2) defines three situations where the claimant will not be considered to be under such a restriction, so that subsection (1) will not apply. These are where the claimant is under a disability (whether minority or adult disability) so that he or she has to act through a litigation friend; where the claimant would be in breach of contract if he or she issued proceedings; and where the claimant requires the leave of the court to issue proceedings (unless, in this last case, the claimant has taken all reasonable measures to obtain the leave required).

PART IV

MISCELLANEOUS AND SUPPLEMENTAL

Miscellaneous

Agreements.

31.—(1) Subject to the following provisions of this section, nothing in this Act prevents the making of an agreement the terms of which— 5

    (a) modify or disapply any of the provisions of this Act, or

    (b) make provision in place of any of the provisions of this Act.

(2) An agreement is unenforceable if and to the extent that its terms—

    (a) modify or disapply, or make provision in place of, section 8 or this section, 10

    (b) in the case of the limitation period under section 1(2) or an agreed limitation period to which subsection (5) applies, reduces the protection given to a claimant by section 26,

    (c) reduces the protection given to a claimant by section 28, or

    (d) in the case of the limitation period under section 1(1) or an 15 agreed limitation period to which subsection (4) applies, reduces the protection given to a claimant by section 29.

1977 c. 50.
S.I. 1999/2083.

(3) Where neither the Unfair Contract Terms Act 1977 nor the Unfair Terms in Consumer Contracts Regulations 1999 apply to any terms of an agreement falling within subsection (1)(a) or (b), those terms shall be of 20 no effect except in so far as they satisfy the requirement of reasonableness as stated in section 11(1) of the Unfair Contract Terms Act 1977; but this subsection shall not apply to an agreement to compromise or settle litigation.

(4) Subject to subsection (7) and the terms of any agreement, the 25 provisions of this Act shall apply to an agreed limitation period which runs from a date determined by reference to a person's actual or constructive knowledge as they apply to the limitation period under section 1(1); and any reference in any provision of this Act (other than this section) to a limitation period or defence— 30

    (a) under section 1(1), or

    (b) under this Act,

shall be construed accordingly.

(5) Subject to the terms of any agreement, the provisions of this Act shall apply to an agreed limitation period which runs from a date 35 determined otherwise than by reference to a person's actual or constructive knowledge as they apply to the limitation period under section 1(2); and any reference in any provision of this Act (other than this section) to a limitation period or defence—

    (a) under section 1(2), or 40

    (b) under this Act,

shall be construed accordingly.

(6) Subject to subsection (7), section 29(1) and (2) shall apply to an agreed limitation period to which subsection (5) applies as if the reference in section 29(2) to the limitation period under section 1(1) were a 45 reference to the agreed limitation period.

EXPLANATORY NOTES

Clause 31

This clause gives parties the power to contract out of the core limitation regime by disapplying any of the provisions of the Act (with certain limited exceptions) and to agree that an alternative limitation period should govern their disputes. See paragraphs 3.170 to 3.175 of the Report.

Subsection (1) allows parties to make agreements which disapply or change provisions of the Bill in relation to limitation periods.

Subsection (2) ensures that, as an exception to this general rule, no change may be made to the provisions of the Bill in relation to claims under the Consumer Protection Act (clause 8), dishonest concealment (clause 26), minority (clause 28) or other disability (clause 29).

Subsection (3) provides that no agreement within subsection (1) will be valid unless it is 'reasonable' as defined by section 11 of the Unfair Contract Terms Act 1978. Agreements which are made in settlement of litigation between the parties do not have to satisfy this requirement.

Subsections (4), (5), (6) and (7) explain how the provisions of the Bill apply to limitation periods which have been modified between the parties. Subsection (4) ensures that all the provisions of the Bill which apply to the primary limitation period under clause 1(1) will apply to any agreed limitation period which runs from a date dependant on someone's knowledge. So if the parties have agreed that a limitation period of five years running from the date on which the claimant knows the relevant facts should apply to any disputes between them, all the provisions of the Bill relating to knowledge (including for example constructive knowledge, organisational knowledge, agency and disability) will apply to that limitation period unless they have been specifically excluded by the parties.

Similarly, subsection (5) ensures that where the parties have agreed that their disputes should be subject to a limitation period running from a date determined in any other way (for example, by reference to a set date or the happening of a particular event such as accrual) that limitation period will be subject to all of the provisions of the Bill which apply to the long-stop limitation period. The agreed limitation period will, for example, be subject to the provisions on acknowledgments and part payments, restrictions on making claims and burden of proof, unless those provisions are expressly excluded by the parties.

Subsection (6) and (7) explain how the provisions of the Bill in relation to disability are to apply to an agreed limitation period. Subsection (6) ensures that (subject to subsection (7)), even an agreed limitation period which runs from some date other than the date of knowledge (such as the accrual of the cause of action) will also be suspended while the claimant is under a disability. The equivalent effect is achieved in relation to agreed limitation periods which run from the date of a person's knowledge by subsection (4).

(7) Section 29 (whether it applies by virtue of subsection (4) or subsection (6)) shall not operate to extend an agreed limitation period beyond the period of ten years from the starting date in relation to the cause of action.

5   (8) Any reference in this section to an agreed limitation period is a reference to a limitation period for which provision is made by the terms of any agreement (whether those terms modify any limitation period under this Act or provide for a limitation period in place of any limitation period under this Act).

10   **32.**—(1) A cause of action to recover the debt under a qualifying loan shall not accrue unless and until a demand in writing for repayment of the debt is made by or on behalf of the creditor (or, where there are joint creditors, by or on behalf of any one or more of them).

Claims in respect of certain loans.

(2) In this section "qualifying loan" means a contract of loan which—

15   (a) does not provide for repayment of the debt on or before a fixed or determinable date, and

(b) does not effectively (whether or not it purports to do so) make the obligation to repay the debt conditional on a demand for repayment made by or on behalf of the creditor or on any other
20   matter,

but a contract of loan is not a qualifying loan if, in connection with taking the loan, the debtor enters into a collateral obligation to pay the amount of the debt or any part of it (as, for example, by delivering a promissory note as security for the debt) on terms which do not satisfy both of the
25 conditions in paragraphs (a) and (b).

33.—(1) This Act does not apply to civil proceedings which are business of a description which in the High Court is for the time being assigned to the Family Division and to no other Division by or under section 61 of, and Schedule 1 to, the Supreme Court Act 1981.

Family proceedings.

1981 c. 54.

30   (2) Subsection (1) applies whether or not the civil proceedings there mentioned are commenced in the High Court.

34.—(1) This Act does not apply to a civil claim for the specific performance of a contract to grant or transfer an interest in property if the claimant—

Equitable jurisdiction and remedies.

35   (a) has acquired an interest in the property by virtue of the contract, and

(b) is in possession of the property.

(2) Nothing in this Act affects any equitable jurisdiction to refuse relief on the ground of delay, acquiescence or otherwise.

40   **35.**—(1) This Act binds the Crown.

Crown application.

(2) This Act does not apply to any civil claim by the Crown for the recovery of any tax or duty or interest on any tax or duty.

EXPLANATORY NOTES

Subsection (7) ensures that this suspension does not extend the agreed limitation period more than ten years after the starting date. Under the standard limitation provisions of the Bill, the long-stop limitation period overrides the protection given to the claimant under a disability. An agreed limitation period is treated analogously, so that the claimant under a disability is assured ten years, but no more than ten years, of protection.

Clause 32

This clause changes the date on which the cause of action accrues in respect of a claim to recover a debt in relation to certain loans. It adopts the same policy as section 6 of the 1980 Act (See paragraphs 4.4 to 4.6 of the Report) .

Subsection (1) provides that the cause of action shall accrue on the date on which a demand is made for repayment of the loan.

Subsection (2) defines the loans to which this applies. It is limited to those cases where the debtor is not under an obligation to repay the loan on a fixed or determinable date, or on demand.

Clause 33

This clause ensures that the primary and long-stop limitation periods do not apply to any family-related proceedings. This includes, for example, any matrimonial proceedings, non-contentious probate applications or proceedings under the Children Act 1989 (among others).

Clause 34

Subsection (1) ensures that no limitation period will apply to a claim for specific performance of a contract to grant or transfer an interest in property, so that the Bill does not interfere with the rule that a contract to transfer a legal interest in property is as good as a transfer of that interest when a party has taken possession of the property in reliance on that interest (See paragraphs 4.269 to 4.273 of the Report). In consequence the court will remain free to make an award of damages in lieu of specific performance in the event that the claimant's application for specific performance is rejected however long after the events giving rise to the claim the claimant's application is made.

Subsection (2) preserves the court's equitable jurisdiction to deny the claimant the relief claimed because of his or her delay, even if the limitation period applicable to the claim under this Bill has not expired.

Clause 35

Subsection (1) provides for the application of the Bill to the Crown.

Subsection (2) ensures that claims by the Crown to recover tax or duty (or interest on either) are not subject to any limitation period. This exemption is limited to claims to recover tax which has been assessed. The Crown remains bound by the limitation periods in, for example the Taxes Management Act 1970, with regard to the assessment of tax.

PART IV

(3) For the purposes of this Act, a civil claim by petition of right shall be treated as made on the date on which the petition is presented.

Saving for other limitation enactments.

36. Except as provided by Schedules 3 and 4, this Act does not apply—

    (a) to any civil claim for which a limitation period is provided by any 5 other enactment (whenever passed or made), or

    (b) to any civil claim to which the Crown is a party and for which, if it were between subjects, a limitation period would be provided by any such other enactment.

Burden of proof.

37.—(1) Where a defence to a civil claim is raised under section 1(1), 10 7(2) or 10(2) or paragraph 6(2) of Schedule 2, it is for the claimant to prove that the claim was made before the end of the limitation period applicable to that defence.

(2) Where a defence to a civil claim is raised under any other provision of this Act, it is for the defendant to prove that the claim was not made 15 before the end of the limitation period applicable to that defence.

Supplemental

Interpretation.

38.—(1) In this Act—

"civil claim" shall be construed in accordance with section 1(4) to (6), 20

"civil proceedings" shall be construed in accordance with section 1(7),

"claimant" shall be construed in accordance with section 1(7),

"date of knowledge" shall be construed in accordance with sections 2, 6(4) and 14(2), 25

"defendant" shall be construed in accordance with section 1(7),

"enactment" includes an enactment comprised in subordinate

1978 c. 30.

    legislation (within the meaning of the Interpretation Act 1978),

"land" includes corporeal hereditaments, tithes and rentcharges and any legal or equitable estate or interest therein, but except as so 30 provided does not include any incorporeal hereditament,

"personal injury" includes any disease and any impairment of a person's physical or mental condition,

"personal representative" includes an executor who has not proved the will (whether or not he has renounced probate), but not 35 anyone appointed only as a special personal representative in relation to settled land,

"rent" includes a rentcharge and a rent service,

"rentcharge" means any annuity or periodical sum of money charged upon or payable out of land, except a rent service or interest on a 40 mortgage on land,

"settled land", "statutory owner" and "tenant for life" have the same

1925. c. 18.

    meaning as in the Settled Land Act 1925,

EXPLANATORY NOTES

Subsection (3) defines the point at which proceedings are commenced when a claim is made by petition of right.

Clause 36
This clause ensures that the provisions of the Bill do not affect any claim which is subject to a limitation period under any other Act or statutory instrument. See paragraphs 4.279 to 4.293 of the Report.

Clause 37
This clause lays down the burden of proof applying to a claim that a limitation period under the Bill has expired. See paragraphs 5.29 to 5.32 of the Report.

Subsection (1) provides that the burden of proof in relation to the primary limitation period lies on the claimant. The same applies both where the primary limitation period applies directly to a claimant, and in those cases where it is applied indirectly.

Subsection (2) provides that the burden of proof in relation to the long-stop limitation period lies on the defendant.

"starting date" shall be construed in accordance with sections 3, 13 and 14,

"successor", in relation to a person in whom a cause of action is vested or against whom a cause of action subsists, means his personal representatives or any other person on whom his rights or, as the case may be, liabilities in relation to the cause of action devolve (whether on death or bankruptcy or the disposition of property or the determination of a limited estate or interest in settled property or otherwise),

"trust" and "trustee" have the same meaning as in the Trustee Act 1925.

(2) Subject to subsection (3)—

(a) a person shall be treated for the purposes of this Act as claiming through another person if he became entitled by, through, under or by the act of that other person to the right claimed, and

(b) any person whose estate or interest might have been barred by a person entitled to an entailed interest in possession shall be treated for the purposes of this Act as claiming through the person so entitled.

(3) A person becoming entitled to any estate or interest by virtue of a special power of appointment shall not be treated for the purposes of this Act as claiming through the appointor.

(4) Any reference in this Act to a right of action to recover land shall include a reference to a right to enter into possession of the land or, in the case of rentcharges and tithes, to distrain for arrears of rent or tithe; and any reference in this Act to the making of a civil claim to recover land shall include a reference to the making of such an entry or distress.

(5) Any reference in this Act to the possession of land shall, in the case of tithes and rentcharges, be construed as a reference to the receipt of the tithe or rent; and any reference in this Act to the date of dispossession or discontinuance of possession of land shall, in the case of rentcharges, be construed as a reference to the date of the last receipt of rent.

(6) In the provisions of this Act relating to civil claims to recover land, any reference to the Crown includes a reference to the Duke of Cornwall.

(7) For the purposes of this Act a cause of action upon a judgment shall be treated as accruing on the date on which the judgment became enforceable.

39.—(1) Schedule 3 (minor and consequential amendments) has effect.

(2) Subject to subsection (3), the repeals set out in Schedule 4 have effect.

(3) Notwithstanding the repeal by this Act of the Limitation Act 1980, section 38(2) to (6) of that Act shall continue to have effect for the purposes of section 3(4) of the Charitable Trusts (Validation) Act 1954.

40.—(1) This Act comes into force at the end of the period of one year beginning with the day on which it is passed.

Marginal notes:

PART IV

1925 c. 19.

Amendments and repeals.

1980 c. 58.

1954 c. 58.

Commencement.

EXPLANATORY NOTES

Clause 40

This clause provides for the commencement of the Bill. See paragraphs 5.33 to 5.40 of the Report.

Subsection (1) provides that all provisions of the Bill will come into force twelve months after it receives Royal Assent.

(2) Subject to the following provisions of this section, this Act has effect in relation to causes of action accruing and things taking place before, as well as in relation to causes of action accruing and things taking place after, the commencement of this Act.

(3) Nothing in this Act—

5

1980 c. 58.

(a) enables any civil claim to be made which was barred by the Limitation Act 1980 or any other enactment before the commencement of this Act,

(b) applies to any civil claim made in civil proceedings which were commenced before the commencement of this Act or the title to 10 any property which is the subject of any such claim, or

(c) applies to any cause of action in respect of a contract under seal or executed as a deed where the contract was made before the commencement of this Act.

(4) Where—

15

(a) a cause of action has accrued before the commencement of this Act, and

(b) no provision was made by any enactment passed or made before the passing of this Act, or by any rule of equity, for a limitation period to apply to a civil claim in respect of the cause of action, 20

any limitation period under this Act which applies to a civil claim in respect of the cause of action shall, if it would otherwise end earlier, be treated as ending at the end of the period of six years beginning with the day on which this Act comes into force.

(5) Where—

25

(a) the starting date in relation to a cause of action falls before the commencement of this Act, and

(b) provision was made by any enactment passed or made before the passing of this Act, or by any rule of equity, for a limitation period to apply to a civil claim in respect of the cause of action, 30

any limitation period under this Act which applies to a civil claim in respect of the cause of action shall, if it would otherwise end earlier, be treated as ending at the end of the limitation period which would have applied to the claim if this Act had not been passed.

(6) In determining for the purposes of subsection (5) the limitation 35 period which would have applied if this Act had not been passed—

(a) section 32(1)(b) of the Limitation Act 1980 (concealment) shall be disregarded, and

(b) section 32(1)(a) or (c) of that Act (fraud and mistake) shall not operate to extend the end of any limitation period under that Act 40 beyond the end of the period of six years beginning with the day on which this Act comes into force.

(7) In determining for the purposes of this section whether a civil claim is barred by the Limitation Act 1980 or any other enactment, section 32A or 33 of that Act or any other enactment enabling a 45 limitation period to be overridden shall be disregarded.

1979 c. 17.

(8) For the purposes of this section, a right to a payment under section 1(1) of the Vaccine Damage Payments Act 1979 shall be treated as a

EXPLANATORY NOTES

Subsection (2) provides that the provisions of the Bill apply to all causes of action whether or not they have already accrued on the date on which the Bill comes into force.

Subsection (3) ensures that the Bill will not enable a claim which has become barred under the provisions of an earlier enactment to be revived, and that it will not apply to claims where the claimant has issued proceedings before the Bill came into force.

It also provides that the Bill will not apply to a claim on a contract made before it comes into force which is treated as a 'specialty' under section 8 of the 1980 Act. The claimant will in such a case therefore continue to benefit from a limitation period of twelve years running from the date on which the cause of action accrued.

Subsection (4) ensures that a claimant whose claim was not subject to any limitation period (whether under statute or in equity) before the Bill comes into force will have at least six years from that date within which to issue proceedings.

Subsection (5) ensures that a claimant whose claim accrued before the Bill comes into force will not be subject to a shorter limitation period in those cases where the Bill reduces the limitation period applying to his or her claim, but where the limitation period under the Bill is longer than that applying under the previous law, the claimant will have the benefit of the longer period.

Subsection (6) ensures that, in deciding whether the claimant's claim would be subject to a longer limitation period under the previous law, no account is to be taken of the provisions in section 32(1)(b) of the 1980 Act which extend the limitation period where the defendant is considered to have deliberately concealed any relevant facts from the claimant. Such a limitation period would only be extended by concealment which satisfies the definition of dishonest concealment under clause 26 of the Bill.

In addition subsection (6) ensures that in deciding whether the claimant's claim would be subject to a longer limitation period under the previous law, section 32(1)(a) and (c) of the 1980 Act shall be treated as extending the limitation period for no longer than six years from the date on which the Bill comes into force.

Subsection (7) ensures that a civil claim may be considered to be barred for the purposes of subsection (3) even if court has a discretion under any enactment to disapply the limitation period applying to the claim in question.

Subsection (8) ensures that the commencement provisions work properly for the amendments to the Vaccine Damage Payments Act 1979 made in Schedule 3 of the Bill.

cause of action and a claim for such a payment shall be treated as a civil claim in respect of the cause of action.

41.—(1) This Act may be cited as the Limitation Act 2001.

(2) This Act extends to England and Wales only.

Citation and extent.

SCHEDULES

Section 17.

SCHEDULE 1

ACCRUAL OF RIGHTS OF ACTION TO RECOVER LAND

Right not to accrue or continue unless there is adverse possession

1.—(1) No right of action to recover land shall be treated as accruing unless the land is in the possession of some person in whose favour a limitation period under section 16 can run (referred to in this paragraph as "adverse possession").

(2) Where under the following provisions of this Schedule—

    (a) a right of action to recover land is treated as accruing on a certain date, and

    (b) no person is in adverse possession on that date,

the right of action shall not be treated as accruing unless and until adverse possession is taken of the land.

(3) Where—

    (a) a right of action to recover land has accrued, and

    (b) after its accrual, but before the right of action is barred, the land ceases to be in adverse possession,

the right of action shall no longer be treated as having accrued and no fresh right of action shall be treated as accruing unless and until the land is again taken into adverse possession.

(4) Where—

    (a) a right of action to recover land has accrued, and

    (b) after its accrual, but before the right of action is barred, there is a change of person in adverse possession of the land,

the right of action shall no longer be treated as having accrued and a fresh right of action shall be treated as having accrued on the date of the change.

(5) Sub-paragraph (4) does not apply—

    (a) if any person in adverse possession of the land before the change continues to be in adverse possession of the land after the change, or

    (b) where a person's period of adverse possession of the land is followed by, and is continuous with, a period of adverse possession of the land by a person who claims through him.

(6) Where a person's period of adverse possession of land is interrupted by a period of adverse possession of the land by another person which comes between, and is continuous with, his own periods of adverse possession, sub-paragraph (4) shall not apply—

    (a) when his period of adverse possession of the land is interrupted, or

    (b) when his period of adverse possession of the land is resumed.

(7) For the purposes of this paragraph—

    (a) possession of any land subject to a rentcharge by a person (other than the person entitled to the rentcharge) who does not pay the rent shall be treated as adverse possession of the rentcharge, and

    (b) receipt of rent under a lease by a person wrongfully claiming to be entitled to the land in reversion immediately expectant on the determination of the lease shall be treated as adverse possession of the land.

(8) For the purpose of determining whether a person occupying any land is in adverse possession of the land it shall not be assumed by implication of law that his occupation is by permission of the person entitled to the land merely by virtue of the

EXPLANATORY NOTES

SCHEDULE 1

This Schedule lays down the rules which determine when a right of action to recover land accrues to the claimant, and thus the date on which the limitation period under clause 16 starts to run against the claimant. It re-enacts the provisions contained in Part I of Schedule 1 to the 1980 Act.

Paragraphs 1(1) and (2) re-enact paragraph 8(1) of Schedule 1 to the 1980 Act.

Paragraph 1(3) re-enacts paragraph 8(2) of the Schedule to the 1980 Act.

Paragraph 1(4),(5) and (6) are new provisions, which explain the consequences of a change in the identity of the person (or persons) in adverse possession. The general rule, given in paragraph 1(4), is that if the person in adverse possession changes, the adverse possession of the land is considered to have ended. The claimant is considered to have a new cause of action, and a new limitation period will therefore start running against him or her from the date on which the next person took adverse possession of the land.

Paragraph 1(5) provides for an exception to this rule in two situations: first, where more than one person was in adverse possession of the land and not all of them leave, so that, though there could be said to have been a 'change of person in adverse possession', at least one person remains in adverse possession before and after the 'change'; secondly, where the second adverse possessor claims possession in succession to the first adverse possession (because, for example, he has 'bought' the land from the first adverse possessor)

Paragraph 1(6) provides another exception to the rule where an adverse possessor who has himself been displaced returns to resume adverse possession of the land in question.

Paragraph 1(7) re-enacts paragraph 8(3) of Schedule 1 to the 1980 Act.

Paragraphs 1(8) and 1(9) re-enact paragraph 8(4) of Schedule 1 to the 1980 Act.

fact that his occupation is not inconsistent with that person's present or future enjoyment of the land.

(9) Sub-paragraph (8) shall not be taken as prejudicing a finding to the effect that a person's occupation of any land is by implied permission of the person
5 entitled to the land in any case where such a finding is justified on the actual facts of the case.

Accrual of right in case of present interests in land

2. Where the person making a civil claim to recover land, or some person through whom he claims—
10   (a) has been in possession of the land, and

    (b) has while entitled to the land been dispossessed or discontinued his possession,

the right of action to recover the land shall be treated as having accrued on the date of the dispossession or discontinuance.

15 3. Where—

    (a) a person makes a civil claim to recover any land of a deceased person (whether under a will or on intestacy),

    (b) the deceased person was on the date of his death in possession of the land or, in the case of a rentcharge created by will or taking effect
20   upon his death, in possession of the land charged, and

    (c) the deceased person was the last person entitled to the land to be in possession of it,

the right of action to recover the land shall be treated as having accrued on the date of his death.

25 4. Where—

    (a) a person makes a civil claim to recover an estate or interest in land in possession which was assured otherwise than by will to him, or to some person through whom he claims,

    (b) the person making the assurance was on the date on which the
30   assurance took effect in possession of the land or, in the case of a rentcharge created by the assurance, in possession of the land charged, and

    (c) no person has been in possession of the land by virtue of the assurance,

the right of action to recover the land shall be treated as having accrued on the date
35 on which the assurance took effect.

Accrual of right in case of future interests

5. Where—

    (a) the estate or interest claimed was an estate or interest in reversion or remainder or any other future estate or interest, and
40   (b) no person has taken possession of the land by virtue of the estate or interest claimed,

the right of action to recover the land shall be treated as having accrued on the date on which the estate or interest fell into possession by the determination of the preceding estate or interest.

45 6.—(1) Subject to sub-paragraph (2), a tenancy from year to year or other period, without a lease in writing, shall for the purposes of this Act be treated as being determined at the end of the first year or other period; and accordingly the right of action of the person entitled to the land subject to the tenancy shall be treated as having accrued on the date on which in accordance with this sub-
50 paragraph the tenancy is determined.

EXPLANATORY NOTES

Paragraph 2 re-enacts paragraph 1 of Schedule 1 to the 1980 Act.

Paragraph 3 re-enacts paragraph 2 of Schedule 1 to the 1980 Act.

Paragraph 4 re-enacts paragraph 3 of Schedule 1 to the 1980 Act.

Paragraph 5 re-enacts paragraph 4 of Schedule 1 to the 1980 Act.

Paragraph 6 re-enacts paragraph 5 of Schedule 1 to the 1980 Act.

(2) Where any rent has subsequently been received in respect of the tenancy, the right of action shall be treated as having accrued on the date of the last receipt of rent.

7.—(1) Where—

(a) a person is in possession of land by virtue of a lease in writing by   5 which a rent of not less than ten pounds a year is reserved,

(b) the rent is received by some person wrongfully claiming to be entitled to the land in reversion immediately expectant on the determination of the lease, and

(c) no rent is subsequently received by the person rightfully so entitled,   10

the right of action to recover the land of the person rightfully so entitled shall be treated as having accrued on the date on which the rent was first received by the person wrongfully claiming to be so entitled and not on the date of the determination of the lease.

(2) Sub-paragraph (1) does not apply to any lease granted by the Crown.   15

Accrual of right in case of forfeiture or breach of condition

8.—(1) Subject to sub-paragraph (2), a right of action to recover land by virtue of a forfeiture or breach of condition shall be treated as having accrued on the date on which the forfeiture was incurred or the condition broken.

(2) If—   20

(a) a right of action to recover land by virtue of a forfeiture or breach of condition has accrued to a person entitled to an estate or interest in reversion or remainder, and

(b) the land was not recovered by virtue of that right,

the right of action to recover the land shall not be treated as having accrued to that   25 person until his estate or interest fell into possession.

Possession of beneficiary not adverse to others interested in settled land or land held subject to a trust of land

9. Where any settled land or land subject to a trust of land is in the possession of a person—   30

(a) who is entitled to a beneficial interest in the land, and

(b) who is not solely or absolutely entitled to the land,

no right of action to recover the land shall be treated for the purposes of this Act as accruing during that possession to any person in whom the land is vested as tenant for life, statutory owner or trustee or to any other person entitled to a   35 beneficial interest in the land.

SCHEDULE 2

APPLICATION OF SECTION 1(1) IN CASE OF INSOLVENCY AND BANKRUPTCY

PART I

COMPANIES AND INSOLVENT PARTNERSHIPS   40

Administrator

1.—(1) The limitation period under section 1(1) shall not run against a company or insolvent partnership in which a cause of action is vested during any period in which there is an administrator of the company or partnership.

(2) An administrator of a company or insolvent partnership shall not be   45 regarded as a qualifying individual for the purposes of section 5.

EXPLANATORY NOTES

Paragraph 7 re-enacts paragraph 6 of Schedule 1 to the 1980 Act.

Paragraph 8 re-enacts paragraph 7 of Schedule 1 to the 1980 Act.

Paragraph 9 re-enacts paragraph 9 of Schedule 1 to the 1980 Act.

SCHEDULE 2
This Schedule modifies the application of the primary limitation period where the claimant is subject to insolvency or bankruptcy proceedings.

Part I of the Schedule applies to corporate insolvency proceedings. Paragraph 1 applies to a company or an insolvent partnership in administration. It suspends the running of the primary limitation period against a company or partnership whilst it is in administration, and ensures that the primary limitation period is not started by the administrator attaining the relevant knowledge about the claim.

(3) The reference in sub-paragraph (1) to a period in which there is an administrator includes a reference to a period in which there is a temporary vacancy in the office of administrator.

(4) Any reference in this paragraph to an administrator includes a reference to a person performing functions under the laws of a country outside Great Britain equivalent to those of an administrator.

Administrative receiver

2.—(1) Subject to sub-paragraph (2), the limitation period under section 1(1) shall not run against a company or insolvent partnership in which a cause of action is vested during any period in which there is an administrative receiver of the company or partnership.

(2) Sub-paragraph (1) does not apply to a cause of action which subsists against an administrative receiver.

(3) An administrative receiver of a company or insolvent partnership shall not be regarded as a qualifying individual for the purposes of section 5.

(4) The reference in sub-paragraph (1) to a period in which there is an administrative receiver includes a reference to a period in which there is a temporary vacancy in the office of administrative receiver.

(5) Any reference in this paragraph to an administrative receiver includes a reference to a person performing functions under the laws of a country outside Great Britain equivalent to those of an administrative receiver.

Winding up

3.—(1) This paragraph applies in the case of a cause of action vested in a company or insolvent partnership which is being wound up.

(2) Where the limitation period under section 1(1) has begun to run, but has not ended, before the date on which a liquidator of the company or partnership is first appointed, it shall be suspended for the period of one year beginning with the date of that appointment.

(3) Where the limitation period under section 1(1) has not begun to run before the date on which a liquidator of the company or partnership is first appointed, it shall be treated as running from the later of—

    (a) the first anniversary of the date of that appointment, and

    (b) the date of knowledge of the liquidator (or, where there are two or more liquidators, the earliest date of knowledge of any of them).

(4) Any reference in this paragraph to a company includes a reference to an unregistered company.

(5) Any reference in this paragraph to a liquidator includes a reference to a person performing functions under the laws of a country outside Great Britain equivalent to those of a liquidator.

Civil claims under section 213, 214, 238, 239 or 423 of 1986 Act

4.—(1) In its application to a civil claim by a liquidator under section 213 or 214 of the 1986 Act (fraudulent trading and wrongful trading), the limitation period under section 1(1) of this Act shall be treated as running from the later of—

    (a) the first anniversary of the date on which a liquidator is first appointed, and

    (b) the date of knowledge of the liquidator (or, where there are two or more liquidators, the earliest date of knowledge of any of them).

(2) In its application to a civil claim by an administrator or liquidator under section 238, 239 or 423 of the 1986 Act (transactions at an undervalue,

EXPLANATORY NOTES

Paragraph 1(4) ensures that the same protection applies to a foreign company or partnership or an English company or partnership which is subject to foreign insolvency proceedings equivalent to administration if it seeks to bring a claim in this jurisdiction.

Paragraph 2 applies to a company or insolvent partnership in administrative receivership. It suspends the running of the primary limitation period while the administrative receiver is in office and ensures that the primary limitation period is not started by the administrative receiver attaining the relevant knowledge about the claim. Paragraph 2(2) provides that this rule does not apply where the claim is one by the company or partnership against the administrative receiver. Paragraph 2(5) ensures that this also applies to a foreign company or partnership or an English company or partnership which is subject to foreign insolvency proceedings equivalent to administrative receivership.

Paragraph 3 applies when a company or insolvent partnership is being wound up. Paragraph 3(2) suspends the primary limitation period for one year after the appointment of a liquidator if the primary limitation period is already running when the liquidator is appointed. Paragraph 3(3) ensures that, if the primary limitation period has yet not started when the liquidator is appointed, it will not start for at least one year after that date. The same protection applies, under paragraph 3(5) to a foreign company or partnership or an English company or partnership which is subject to foreign insolvency proceedings equivalent to liquidation.

Paragraph 4 ensures that the primary limitation period for claims by liquidators under sections 213 and 214, and claims by administrators or liquidators under sections 238, 239 and 423 of the Insolvency Act 1986, will not start for at least one year after an administrator or liquidator is appointed.

SCH. 2

preferences and transactions defrauding creditors), the limitation period under section 1(1) of this Act shall be treated as running from the later of—

(a) the first anniversary of the date on which an administrator or (as the case may be) liquidator is first appointed, and

(b) the date of knowledge of the administrator or (as the case may be) 5 liquidator (or, where there are two or more administrators or liquidators, the earliest date of knowledge of any of them).

Interpretation of Part I

5.—(1) In this Part—

"administrator" means a person appointed as administrator, special 10 administrator or special railway administrator under any provision of the 1986 Act,

"administrative receiver" has the meaning given by section 251 of the 1986 Act,

1985 c. 6.

"company" means a company as defined in section 735 of the Companies 15 Act 1985 or a foreign company,

"foreign company" means a company incorporated outside Great Britain,

"insolvent partnership" includes an insolvent partnership under the laws of a country outside England and Wales,

"liquidator" means a persons appointed as liquidator or provisional 20 liquidator under any provision of the 1986 Act,

1986 c. 45.

"the 1986 Act" means the Insolvency Act 1986,

"unregistered company" means an unregistered company as defined in section 220 of the 1986 Act.

(2) Any reference in this Part to a person being appointed as a liquidator 25 includes a reference—

(a) to a person becoming liquidator by virtue of a nomination, and

(b) to the official receiver becoming liquidator by virtue of section 136 of the 1986 Act.

PART II   30

INDIVIDUALS

Bankruptcy

6.—(1) This paragraph applies where a cause of action has become vested in the trustee of a bankrupt's estate.

(2) It is a defence to a civil claim in respect of the cause of action made by the 35 trustee that the bankruptcy order was made after the end of the limitation period under section 1(1) which would have applied to a civil claim in respect of the cause of action made by the bankrupt.

(3) If the bankruptcy order was made after the limitation period mentioned in sub-paragraph (2) has begun to run but before it has ended, that limitation 40 period shall apply to a civil claim in respect of the cause of action made by the trustee but it shall be suspended for the period of one year beginning with the date of the bankruptcy order.

(4) If the bankruptcy order was made before the limitation period mentioned in sub-paragraph (2) has begun to run, the limitation period under section 1(1) 45 which is to apply to a civil claim in respect of the cause of action made by the trustee shall be treated as running from the later of—

(a) the first anniversary of that date, and

EXPLANATORY NOTES

Part II of the Schedule applies to bankruptcy proceedings. Paragraph 6 explains how the limitations regime will apply to claims which have become vested in a trustee in bankruptcy as a consequence of the individual's bankruptcy.

Paragraph 6(2) protects defendants from claims which were already time-barred at the date of bankruptcy being revived at a later date by the trustee in bankruptcy.

Paragraphs 6(3) suspends the primary limitation period for one year from the date on which the bankruptcy order is made if it is running at that date. Paragraph 6(4) ensures that, if the primary limitation period has yet not started on the date of the bankruptcy order, it will not start for at least one year after that date.

(b) the date of knowledge of the trustee (or, where there are two or more trustees, the earliest date of knowledge of any of them).

(5) This paragraph shall apply in relation to an individual who is subject to the insolvency laws of a country outside than England and Wales as it applies in relation to a bankrupt.

(6) In relation to such an individual—

(a) any reference in this paragraph to the trustee of a bankrupt's estate is a reference to a person performing functions under those laws which are equivalent to those of a trustee of a bankrupt's estate, and

(b) any reference in this paragraph to the making of bankruptcy order is a reference to the occurrence of any event under those laws which is equivalent to the making of a bankruptcy order.

Civil claims under section 339, 340, 342A, 343 or 423 of 1986 Act

7.—(1) The provisions to which this paragraph applies are—

(a) section 339 of the 1986 Act (transactions at an undervalue),

(b) section 340 of that Act (preferences),

(c) section 342A of that Act (recovery of excessive pension contributions),

(d) section 343 of that Act (extortionate credit transactions), and

(e) section 423 of that Act (transactions defrauding creditors).

(2) In its application to a civil claim by the trustee of a bankrupt's estate under a provision to which this paragraph applies, the limitation period under section 1(1) of this Act shall be treated as running from the later of—

(a) the first anniversary of the date of the bankruptcy order, and

(b) the date of knowledge of the trustee of the bankrupt's estate (or, where there are two or more trustees, the earliest date of knowledge of any of them).

Interpretation of Part II

8.—(1) In this Part "the 1986 Act" means the Insolvency Act 1986.

(2) Expressions which are used in this Part and the 1986 Act shall have the same meaning in this Part as they have in the 1986 Act.

SCHEDULE 3

MINOR AND CONSEQUENTIAL AMENDMENTS

Law of Property Act 1925 (c. 20)

1. In section 205 of the Law of Property Act 1925 (general definitions), in subsection (1)(xii) for "the Real Property Limitation Acts 1833, 1837 and 1874" substitute "the Limitation Act 2001 and any other enactments (whenever passed) limiting the time within which proceedings may be taken".

Land Registration Act 1925 (c. 21)

2. In section 3 of the Land Registration Act 1925 (interpretation), in paragraph (xii) for "the Real Property Limitation Acts 1833, 1837 and 1874, and any Acts amending those Acts" substitute "the Limitation Act 2001 and any other enactments (whenever passed) limiting the time within which proceedings may be taken".

3. In section 83 of that Act (indemnity for errors or omissions in the register), omit subsection (12).

EXPLANATORY NOTES

Paragraph 6(5) ensures that the same protection applies for an individual subject to foreign insolvency laws in relation to a claim in this jurisdiction.

Paragraph 7 ensures that the primary limitation period for claims by the trustee in bankruptcy under sections 339, 340, 342A, 343 and 423 of the Insolvency Act 1986 to recover assets for distribution to the bankrupt's creditors will not start for at least one year after the bankruptcy order is made.

SCHEDULE 3

Schedule 3 makes minor amendments to previous statutes to ensure that references to past Limitation Acts are read as references to the Bill, and to ensure that references which have become obsolete are deleted. In addition:

Paragraph 3 deletes section 83(12) of the Land Registration Act 1925. This subsection provided that a claim under section 83 of the 1925 Act for an indemnity for loss resulting from an error or omission on the Land Register was to be treated, for limitation purposes, as a simple contract debt (and subject therefore to a limitation period of six years), and that the cause of action was to be treated as accruing on the date on which the claimant should know of the claim. Instead, such claims will be subject to the primary limitation period of three years.

Administration of Estates Act 1925 (c. 23)

4. In section 21A of the Administration of Estates Act 1925 (debtor who becomes creditor's executor by representation or administrator to account for debt to estate), in subsection (2) for "the Limitation Act 1939" substitute "the Limitation Act 2001, or any other enactment (whenever passed) limiting the 5 time within which proceedings may be taken,".

Limitation (Enemies and War Prisoners) Act 1945 (c. 16)

5.—(1) In section 2 of the Limitation (Enemies and War Prisoners) Act 1945 (interpretation), in subsection (1), in the definition of "statute of limitation", for "the Limitation Act 1980" substitute "the Limitation Act 2001".   10

(2) After that subsection insert—

"(1A) The reference in section 1(1) of this Act to the period prescribed by any statute of limitation includes a reference to an agreed limitation period under section 31 of the Limitation Act 2001."

Law Reform (Contributory Negligence) Act 1945 (c. 28)   15

6.—(1) In section 1 of the Law Reform (Contributory Negligence) Act 1945 (apportionment of liability in case of contributory negligence), in subsection (5) for "the Limitation Act 1939" substitute "the Limitation Act 2001".

(2) After that subsection insert—

"(5A) The reference in subsection (5) of this section to a person 20 pleading the Limitation Act 2001 includes a reference to a person pleading the expiry of an agreed limitation period under section 31 of that Act."

Agriculture Act 1967 (c. 22)

7. In Schedule 3 to the Agriculture Act 1967 (conditions applying to 25 amalgamated agricultural units), in paragraph 7(6) for "the Limitation Act 1980" substitute "the Limitation Act 2001".

Mines and Quarries (Tips) Act 1969 (c. 10)

8. In Schedule 3 to the Mines and Quarries (Tips) Act 1969 (claims for compensation by owners and contributories), for paragraph 6(2) substitute—   30

"(2) In relation to England and Wales, Part III of the Limitation Act 2001 shall apply to the limitation period under sub-paragraph (1) above as it applies to the limitation period under section 1(2) of that Act."

Law of Property Act 1969 (c. 59)

9. In section 25 of the Law of Property Act 1969 (compensation in certain 35 cases for loss due to undisclosed land charges), omit subsection (5).

Animals Act 1971 (c. 22)

10. In section 10 of the Animals Act 1971 (application of certain enactments to liability under sections 2 to 4), for "the Law Reform (Contributory Negligence) Act 1945 and the Limitation Act 1980" substitute "and the Law Reform 40 (Contributory Negligence) Act 1945".

EXPLANATORY NOTES

Paragraph 5 ensures that the protection given to claimants by section 1 of the Limitation (Enemies and War Prisoners) Act 1945 applies not only to limitation periods set down in statute but also to limitation periods which have been agreed between the parties.

Paragraph 6 ensures that section 1(5) of the Law Reform (Contributory Negligence) Act 1945 applies both to defendants relying on the expiry of a limitation period set down in statute and defendants who rely on the expiry of a limitation period agreed between the parties.

Paragraph 9 deletes section 25(5) of the Law of Property Act 1969. This subsection provided that a claim by a purchaser under section 25 of the 1969 Act for compensation for loss caused by undisclosed land charges, was to be treated, for limitation purposes, as accruing when the charge came to the notice of the purchaser. Instead these claims will be subject to the primary limitation period.

Defective Premises Act 1972 (c. 35)

11. In section 1 of the Defective Premises Act 1972 (duty to build dwellings properly), in subsection (5) for the words from "for the purposes" to "accrued" (in the first place where it occurs) substitute "for the purposes of the Limitation Act
5 2001 to have accrued".

Land Compensation Act 1973 (c. 26)

12. In section 19 of the Land Compensation Act 1973 (interpretation of Part I), in subsection (2A) for "the Limitation Act 1939, a person's right" substitute "the Limitation Act 2001, a cause".

10 13. In section 32 of that Act (supplementary provisions about home loss payments), in subsection (7A) for "the Limitation Act 1939 a person's right" substitute "the Limitation Act 2001 a cause".

14.—(1) Section 36 of that Act (supplementary provisions about farm loss payments) is amended as follows.

15 (2) In subsection (1) for the words from "Subject to subsection (7)" to "complied with" substitute "No farm loss payment shall be made except on a claim in that behalf made by the person entitled thereto".

(3) For subsection (3) substitute—

"(3) Where a person entitled to a farm loss payment dies without
20 having claimed it, a claim to that payment may be made by his personal representatives.

(3A) For the purposes of the Limitation Act 2001, a cause of action to recover a farm loss payment shall be deemed to have accrued on the date on which the requirement in section 34(1)(b) above is complied with."

25 (4) In subsection (6) for "mentioned in subsection (1) above" substitute "on which the requirement in section 34(1)(b) above is complied with".

(5) Subsection (7) is omitted.

Control of Pollution Act 1974 (c. 40)

15. In section 88 of the Control of Pollution Act 1974 (civil liability for
30 contravention of section 3(3)), omit subsection (4)(c).

Local Land Charges Act 1975 (c. 76)

16. In section 10 of the Local Land Charges Act 1975 (compensation for non-registration or defective official search certificate), omit subsection (7).

Fatal Accidents Act 1976 (c. 30)

35 17. In section 1 of the Fatal Accidents Act 1976 (right of action for wrongful act causing death), in subsection (1) for "and recover" substitute "for".

Rent Act 1977 (c. 42)

18. In section 57 of the Rent Act 1977 (recovery from landlord of sums paid in excess of recoverable rent etc), in subsection (3) for paragraphs (a) and (b)
40 substitute "any limitation period under the Limitation Act 2001 which would apply to a civil claim to recover that amount".

19. In section 94 of that Act (recovery from landlord of sums paid in excess of recoverable rent etc), in subsection (3) for "2 years from the date of payment" substitute "any limitation period under the Limitation Act 2001 which would
45 apply to a civil claim to recover that amount".

EXPLANATORY NOTES

Paragraph 11 amends section 1(5) of the Defective Premises Act 1972 so that reference is made to the Bill. The amended provision preserves the date of accrual provided for in that section for the purposes of determining the start of the long-stop limitation period under the Bill.

Paragraph 14 deletes section 36(7) of the Land Compensation Act 1973, a transitional provision relating to farm loss payments, and makes amendments consequent upon that deletion. This paragraph also clarifies that the cause of action to recover such a payment is deemed for the purposes of the Bill to accrue on the date on which the right to receive the payment arises. Such claims will be subject to the core limitations regime.

Paragraph 16 deletes section 10(7) of the Local Land Charges Act 1975. This section provided that a claim for compensation for non-registration of a land charge (or the production of a defective official certificate) should be subject to a limitation period of 6 years running from the date on which the claimant should have notice of the facts. Instead the claim will be subject to the primary limitation period under the core limitations regime.

Paragraphs 18 and 19 replace the time limits laid down in sections 57 and 94 of the Rent Act 1977, with the limitation periods provides for under the Bill, to ensure that the core limitations regime applies to claims under these sections.

SCH. 3

Vaccine Damage Payments Act 1979 (c. 17)

20.—(1) Section 3 of the Vaccine Damage Payments Act 1979 (determination of claims) is amended as follows.

(2) In subsection (1) omit paragraph (c).

(3) After that subsection insert—   5

"(1A) A claim may not be made after the time limit which would apply to the claim if it were a civil claim under the Limitation Act 2001 for damages in respect of personal injury which was made by the disabled person or, as the case may be, his personal representatives against the Secretary of State.   10

(1B) In its application for the purposes of subsection (1A), the Limitation Act 2001 shall have effect—

(a) as if section 12 were omitted,

(b) as if the reference in section 28 to the starting date were a reference to the date of the vaccination to which the claim 15 relates,

(c) as if the references in section 29(1) and (3) to the date of accrual of the cause of action were references to the date of the vaccination to which the claim relates, and

(d) with such other modifications as may be appropriate."   20

Merchant Shipping (Liner Conferences) Act 1982 (c. 37)

21. In section 8 of the Merchant Shipping (Liner Conferences) Act 1982 (time for bringing legal proceedings), for subsection (2) substitute—

"(2) In England and Wales the following provisions of the Limitation Act 2001 apply to the limitation period prescribed by subsection (1) as 25 they apply to any limitation period under that Act—

(a) section 25 (certain new claims),

(b) section 26 (concealment),

(c) section 28 (children), and

(d) section 29 (disability)."   30

Foreign Limitation Periods Act 1984 (c. 16)

22. In section 1 of the Foreign Limitation Periods Act 1984 (application of foreign limitation law), in subsection (3) omit the words "and, accordingly" onwards.

Latent Damage Act 1986 (c. 37)   35

23.—(1) Section 3 of the Latent Damage Act 1986 (accrual of cause of action to successive owners in respect of latent damage to property) is amended as follows.

(2) For paragraph (b) of subsection (1) substitute—

"(b) another person acquires an interest in that property after the date on 40 which the original cause of action accrued but before the earliest date of knowledge (within the meaning of the Limitation Act 2001) in relation to that cause of action of any person who has any interest in the property on that date of knowledge;".   45

(3) For subsection (2) substitute—

"(2) A cause of action accruing to any person by virtue of subsection (1) above shall be treated as if based on breach of a duty of care at common law owed to the person to whom it accrues.

EXPLANATORY NOTES

Paragraph 20 applies the core regime, with some modifications, to claims under the Vaccine Damage Payments Act 1979. A claim under the 1979 Act will be treated as a personal injury claim and therefore subject to the primary limitation period (but not the long-stop limitation period).

Paragraph 23 re-enacts the present provisions of the Latent Damage Act 1986 in relation to the accrual of a cause of action to a successive owner of property with latent damage. This will ensure that a new cause of action accrues to the owner of property which has latent damage which occurred before he or she acquired the property, but only became known after that date. The claim by the successive owner is then subject to the core regime, although the 'starting date' for the long-stop limitation period remains the same as in the original owner's action. This paragraph also deletes the provisions relating to knowledge in sections 3(5) and (6) of the Latent Damage Act so that the general rules as to knowledge in the Bill apply.

(2A) For the purposes of the Limitation Act 2001, the starting date in relation to a cause of action accruing to any person by virtue of subsection (1) above shall be treated as falling on the same date as the starting date in relation to the original cause of action."

5   (4) Subsections (3), (5) and (6) are omitted.

Consumer Protection Act 1987 (c. 43)

24. In section 5 of the Consumer Protection Act 1987 (damage giving rise to liability) for subsections (5) to (7) substitute—

"(5) In determining for the purposes of this Part who has suffered any
10   loss or damage to property and when any such loss or damage occurred, the loss or damage shall be regarded as having occurred on the earliest time at which a person with an interest in the property had knowledge that the loss or damage was significant.

(6) For the purposes of subsection (5) above, a person has knowledge
15   that the loss or damage is significant—

(a) if he has knowledge of the full extent of the loss or damage, or

(b) if a reasonable person with his knowledge of the extent of the loss or damage would think that a civil claim was worth making in respect of the loss or damage against a defendant who did not
20   dispute liability and was able to satisfy a judgment.

(7) Sections 4 and 5 of the Limitation Act 2001 shall apply for the purposes of subsections (5) and (6) above as they apply for the purposes of that Act."

Copyright, Designs and Patents Act 1988 (c. 48)

25   25. In section 99 of the Copyright, Designs and Patents Act 1988 (order for delivery up), in subsection (2) for the words from "An application" to "no order" substitute "No order under this section."

26.—(1) Section 113 of that Act (period after which remedy of delivery up not available) is amended as follows.

30   (2) For subsection (1) substitute—

"(1) For the purposes of the Limitation Act 2001, the right to apply for an order under section 99 (order for delivery up in civil proceedings) shall be treated as accruing on the date on which the infringing copy or article in question was made."

35   (3) Subsections (2) and (3) are omitted.

27. In section 195 of that Act (order for delivery up), in subsection (2) for the words from "An application" to "no order" substitute "No order under this section."

28.—(1) Section 203 of that Act (period after which remedy of delivery up not
40 available) is amended as follows.

(2) For subsection (1) substitute—

"(1) For the purposes of the Limitation Act 2001, the right to apply for an order under section 195 (order for delivery up in civil proceedings) shall be treated as accruing on the date on which the illicit recording in question
45   was made."

(3) Subsections (2) and (3) are omitted.

EXPLANATORY NOTES

Paragraph 24 amends subsections 5(5) to 5(7) of the Consumer Protection Act 1987 so that the time when loss or damage to property giving rise to liability under the Act occurred is determined in accordance with the time the person with an interest in that property would be considered to know that the loss or damage is significant in accordance with the tests laid down in the Bill. It also ensures that the provisions of the Bill in relation to constructive and corporate knowledge apply in such a case.

Paragraphs 25 to 29 remove the six year time limits imposed in sections 113, 203 and 230 of the Copyright, Designs and Patents Act 1988 to claims for delivery up under the 1988 Act, so bringing these claims within the core regime. In addition, paragraphs 26, 28 and 29 also ensure that the date on which the cause of action is deemed to accrue for these claims is the same as the date on which the old time limits started to run.

29.—(1) Section 230 of that Act (order for delivery up) is amended as follows.

(2) In subsection (2), for the words from "An application" to "no order" substitute "No order under this section".

(3) For subsection (3) substitute—   5

"(3) For the purposes of the Limitation Act 2001, the right to apply for an order under this section shall be treated as accruing on the date on which the article or thing was made."

(4) Subsections (4) and (5) are omitted.

Environmental Protection Act 1990 (c. 43)   10

30. In section 73 of the Environmental Protection Act 1990 (appeals and other provisions relating to legal proceedings and civil liability), omit subsection (9)(c).

Water Industry Act 1991 (c. 56)

31. In section 209 of the Water Industry Act 1991 (civil liability of   15 undertakers for escapes of water etc), in subsection (4) for "the Fatal Accidents Act 1976 and the Limitation Act 1980" substitute "and the Fatal Accidents Act 1976".

Water Resources Act 1991 (c. 57)

32. In section 208 of the Water Resources Act 1991 (civil liability of the   20 Agency for escapes of water etc), in subsection (4) for "the Fatal Accidents Act 1976 and the Limitation Act 1980" substitute "and the Fatal Accidents Act 1976".

Coal Industry Act 1994 (c. 21)

33. In section 10 of the Coal Industry Act 1994 (protection for certain   25 interests in coal and coal mines), for subsection (2)(a) substitute—

"(a) under sections 15 or 17 of the Limitation Act 1980 or sections 16 to 18 of the Limitation Act 2001 (time limits on proceedings to recover land and extinction of titles); or".

Trade Marks Act 1994 (c. 26)   30

34. In section 16 of the Trade Marks Act 1994 (order for delivery up of infringing goods, materials or articles), in subsection (2) for the words from "An application" to "no order" substitute "No order under this section".

35.—(1) Section 18 of that Act (period after which remedy of delivery up not available) is amended as follows.   35

(2) For subsection (1) substitute—

"(1) For the purposes of the Limitation Act 2001, the right to apply for an order under section 16 (order for delivery up of infringing goods, material or articles) shall be treated as accruing—

(a) in the case of infringing goods, on the date on which the trade   40 mark was applied to the goods or their packaging,

(b) in the case of infringing material, on the date on which the trade mark was applied to the material, or

(c) in the case of infringing articles, on the date on which they were made."   45

EXPLANATORY NOTES

Paragraph 35 removes the six year time limit in section 18 of the Trade Marks Act 1994, so bringing claims for the delivery up under section 16 of the 1994 Act within the core regime, and ensures that the date on which the cause of action is deemed to accrue for these claims is the same as the date on which the old time limits started to run.

(3) Subsections (2) and (3) are omitted.

Arbitration Act 1996 (c. 23)

36. In section 13 of the Arbitration Act 1996 (application of Limitation Acts), in subsection (4)(a) for "the Limitation Act 1980" substitute "the Limitation Act 2001".

SCHEDULE 4

Section 39.

REPEALS

Chapter	Short title	Extent of repeal
1925 c. 21.	The Land Registration Act 1925.	Section 83(12).
1969 c. 59.	The Law of Property Act 1969.	Section 25(5).
1973 c. 26.	The Land Compensation Act 1973.	Section 36(7).
1974 c. 40.	The Control of Pollution Act 1974.	In section 88(4), paragraph (c) and the word "and" immediately preceding it.
1975 c. 76.	The Local Land Charges Act 1975.	Section 10(7).
1979 c. 17.	The Vaccine Damage Payments Act 1979.	In section 3(1), paragraph (c) and the word "and" immediately preceding it.
1980 c. 58.	The Limitation Act 1980.	The whole Act, except for sections 40(1) and 41(1) and (4) and paragraph 2 of Schedule 2.
1981 c. 66.	The Compulsory Purchase (Vesting Declarations) Act 1981.	Section 10(3).
1983 c. 20.	The Mental Health Act 1983.	In Schedule 4, paragraph 55.
1984 c. 16.	The Foreign Limitation Periods Act 1984.	In section 1(3), the words "and, accordingly" onwards.
1986 c. 37.	The Latent Damage Act 1986.	Sections 1 and 2. Section 3(3), (5) and (6). Section 4(1) and (2).
1987 c. 43.	The Consumer Protection Act 1987	In section 6(6), the words "the Limitation Act 1980 and". In Schedule 1, Part I.
1988 c. 48.	The Copyright, Designs and Patents Act 1988.	Section 113(2) and (3). Section 203(2) and (3). Section 230(4) and (5).
1990 c. 43.	The Environmental Protection Act 1990.	In section 73(9), paragraph (c) and the word "and" immediately preceding it.
1994 c. 26.	The Trade Marks Act 1994.	Section 18(2) and (3).

Chapter	Short title	Extent of repeal
1996 c. 31.	The Defamation Act 1996.	Section 5.
1997 c. 40.	The Protection from Harassment Act 1997.	Section 6.
1999 c. 31.	The Contracts (Rights of Third Parties) Act 1999.	Section 7(3).
2000 c. 14.	The Care Standards Act 2000.	In Schedule 4, paragraph 8.

5

APPENDIX B

LIST OF PEOPLE AND ORGANISATIONS WHO COMMENTED ON CONSULTATION PAPER NO 151

Consultation took place in 1998. The descriptions of consultees may have altered since then.

JUDICIARY

His Hon Judge John Altman
The Hon Mr Justice Bell
The Rt Hon Lord Justice Brooke
The Council of Her Majesty's Circuit Judges
The Rt Hon Lord Davidson
The Hon Mr Justice Holland
The Rt Hon Sir Michael Kerr
The Hon Mr Justice Longmore
The Hon Mr Justice Sedley
The Rt Hon The Lord Woolf

ACADEMIC LAWYERS

Neil Andrews, Clare College, Oxford
Professor Peter Birks, All Souls College, Oxford
Professor Richard Buckley, University of Reading
Mrs EJ Cooke, University of Reading
JW Davis, Brasenose College, Oxford
Rod Edmunds, University of Sussex
Dr Peter Handford, University of Western Australia
Richard James, University of Wales
John Lowry, Brunel University
Elizabeth Palmer, University of Essex
Professor Terence Prime, University of East Anglia
Professor Andrew Tettenborn, University of Exeter
Katherine Reece Thomas, City University
Professor Nick Wikely, University of Southampton

PRACTITIONERS: BARRISTERS

David Allan QC
Jalil Asif
Marc Beaumont
Dr Aisha Bijlani
AG Bompas QC
Andrew Buchan
Michael Brindle QC
Stuart C Brown QC (responding on behalf of the North Eastern Circuit)
Stanley Burnton QC
David Chivers
IN Duncan Wallace QC
John Grace QC and Edward Bailey (responding on behalf of the South Eastern Circuit)
RQ Henriques QC (responding on behalf of the Northern Circuit)

Victor Joffe
Michael Lerego QC
Kim Lewison QC
Colin Mackay QC
Simon Mortimore QC and Michael Crystal QC
Andrew Smith QC
Stephen Stewart QC
Caroline Swift QC
Nicholas Underhill QC
John Griffith Williams QC (responding on behalf of the Wales and Chester Circuit)

PRACTITIONERS: SOLICITORS

Trevor Aldridge QC
Barlow Lyde & Gilbert
Cameron McKenna
Farrer & Co
Field Fisher Waterhouse
Freshfields
Herbert Smith
Hugh James
John Pickering & Partners
Leigh Day & Co
Lovell White Durrant (Lovells)
Norton Rose
Paisner & Co
Pannone & Partners
Peter Carter-Ruck & Partners
Pinsent Curtis
Rowley Ashworth
Russell Jones & Walker
T G Baynes
Thompsons

GOVERNMENT DEPARTMENTS

The Charity Commission
The Crown Estate
HM Customs & Excise
The Department of the Environment, Transport and the Regions
The Department of Social Security
The Insolvency Service
The Inland Revenue
HM Land Registry
The Legal Secretariat to the Law Officers
The Lord Chancellor's Department
The Ministry of Agriculture, Fisheries and Food
The Ministry of Defence (Defence Estate Organisation)
The Treasury Solicitor's Department

DOCTORS

Dr GFA Benfield
Dr HW Clague
Dr CK Connolly

Dr DC Currie
Dr AG Davison
Dr AJ Dorward
Dr James P Finnerty
Dr MA Greenstone
Dr Simon Hanley
Dr BG Higgins
Dr N Horsfield
Dr AM Hunter
Dr CE Johnson
Dr Clive McGavin
Dr MF Muers
Dr LP Ormerod
Dr Richard Page
Dr MG Pearson
Prof CAC Pickering
Dr RM Rudd
Dr D Seaton
Dr CJ Warburton
Dr JG Williams
Dr MD Winson
Dr JH Winter
Dr RJ Wolstenholme

INDIVIDUALS

Duncan Alexander
Irvin Banks, Nicola Grant and Philippa McFarlane
Hugh Bayley MP
Michael Clapham MP
Teresa Cooper
Mike Hall MP
Dr Julian Lewis MP
Mr S J Mabey
Lee Teresa Moore
Malcolm Rodgers
Deborah Stevens
Kevan Stafford
Derek Twigg MP
Robert Woolley

INSURERS

The Association of British Insurers
Company Market Coordination Group Ltd
Equitas Ltd
Excess Insurance
Lloyd's
The London International Insurance and Reinsurance Market Association
   (International Underwriting Association)
Munich Reinsurance Company
NRG Victory Management Services Ltd
St Paul International Insurance Company Ltd
Unionamerica Insurance Company Ltd

OTHER ORGANISATIONS

The AB Welfare & Wildlife Trust
Action for Victims of Medical Accidents
The Amalgamated Engineering and Electrical Union
Associated Newspapers Ltd
The Association of Parents of Vaccine Damaged Children
The Association of Personal Injury Lawyers
The British False Memory Society
The British Broadcasting Corporation
The British Medical Association
The British Museum
The British Property Federation
The Chancery Bar Association
Christie's International plc
The Church Commissioners, Legal Department
The City of London Law Society, Insurance Law Sub-Committee
The City of London Law Society, Litigation Sub-Committee
The Commercial Bar Association
The Confederation of British Industry
The Construction Confederation
The Construction Industry Council
The Constructors' Liaison Group
The Country Landowners Association
The Duchy of Cornwall
The Duchy of Lancaster
The Ecclesiastical Law Association
Ernst & Young
The General Council of the Bar, Law Reform Committee
The Healthcare Lawyers Association
The Holborn Law Society
The Institute of Actuaries
The Institute of Legal Executives
The Law Reform Advisory Committee for Northern Ireland
The Law Society
The Liverpool & District Victims of Asbestos Support Group
The London Common Law and Commercial Bar Association
The London Solicitors Litigation Association
The Medical Defence Union
The Metropolitan Police Service
The Newspaper Publishers Association Ltd
The Newspaper Society
The Publishers Association
Redress
The SPTL Contract and Commercial Law Panel
The Royal Institution of Chartered Surveyors
TL Holden & Co
The Trades Union Congress
The Transport and General Workers Union, York 413 Branch
The Trust Law Committee

Printed in the UK for The Stationery Office Limited
On behalf of the Controller of Her Majesty's Stationery Office
Dd 5070072, 07/01, 636601, 019585, Ord TJ004774